"For fans of literature (from classics to contemporary) this series is worth a read…
*The Unwritten* is a roller-coaster ride through a library, weaving famous authors and characters

into a tale of mystery that is, at once, oddly familiar yet highly original."

**– USA TODAY**

"*The Unwritten* makes a leap from being just a promising new Vertigo title to being on track to

become the best ongoing Vertigo book since *Sandman*. And given that Vertigo has delivered the

likes of *100 Bullets*, *Y: The Last Man* and *Fables* since *Sandman* ended, that's saying something… A-"

**–THE A.V. CLUB**

ORPHEUS IN THE UNDERWORLD

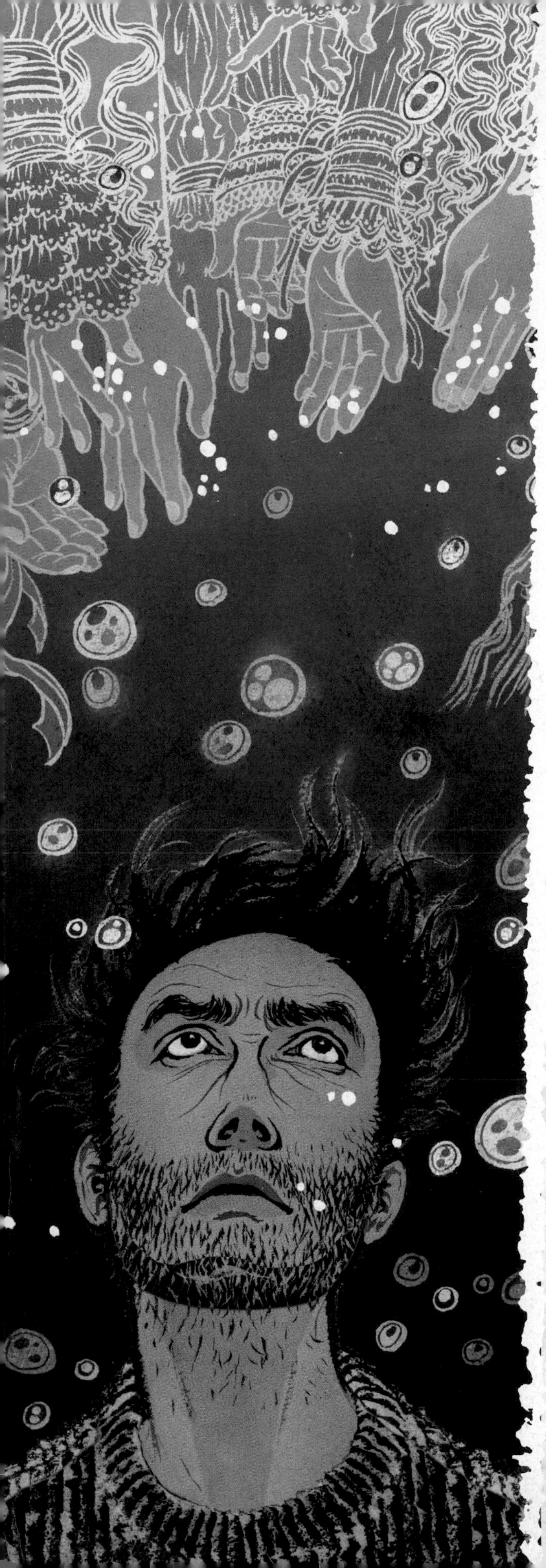

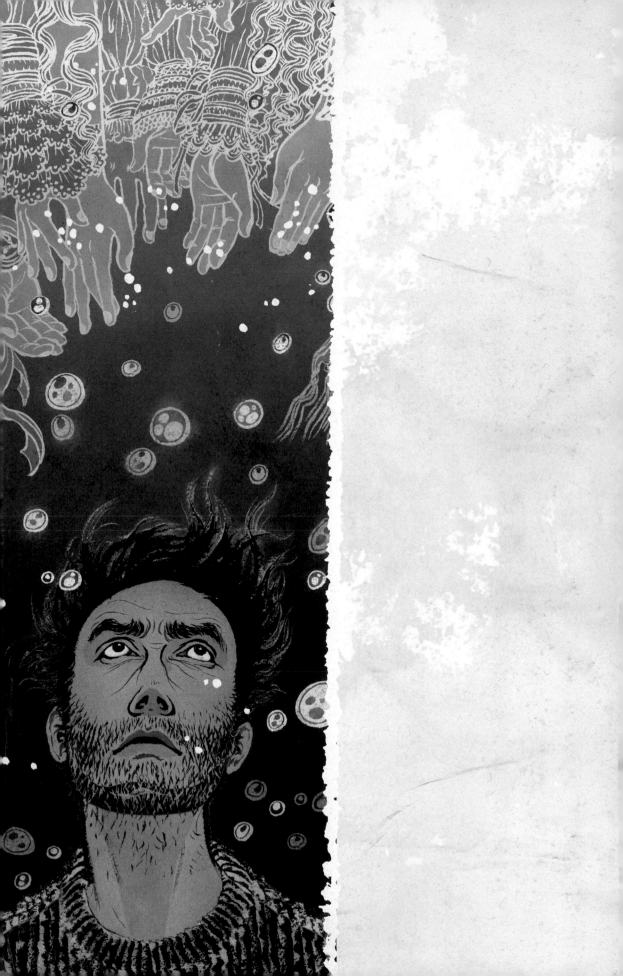

# the Unwritten

## ORPHEUS IN THE UNDERWORLD

Mike Carey & Peter Gross   Script - Story - Art

Dean Ormston "The Corpse Harvest Reiteration" Parts 1 & 2 Finishes

Chris Chuckry Colorist

Todd Klein Letterer   Yuko Shimizu Cover Artist

THE UNWRITTEN created by Peter Gross and Mike Carey

Special thanks to Barb Guttman & Britt Sabo

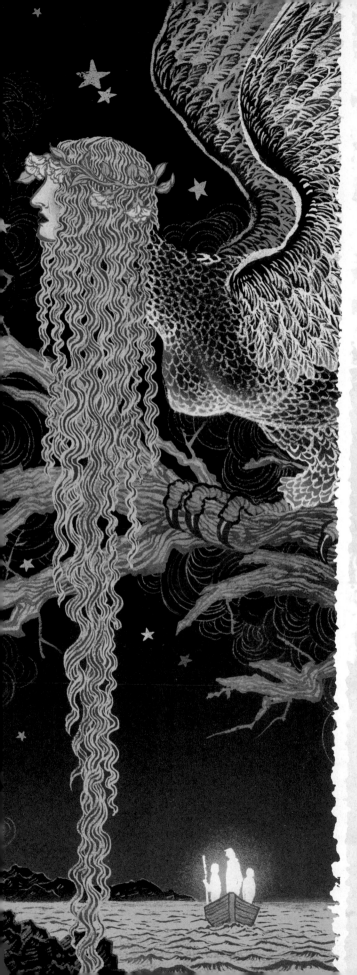

Shelly Bond  Gregory Lockard Editors – Original Series
Rowena Yow Editor
Robbin Brosterman Design Director – Books
Louis Prandi Publication Design

Shelly Bond Executive Editor - Vertigo
Hank Kanalz Senior VP – Vertigo & Integrated Publishing

Diane Nelson President
Dan DiDio and Jim Lee Co-Publishers
Geoff Johns Chief Creative Officer
John Rood Executive VP – Sales, Marketing & Business Development
Amy Genkins Senior VP – Business & Legal Affairs
Nairi Gardiner Senior VP – Finance
Jeff Boison VP – Publishing Planning
Mark Chiarello  VP – Art Direction & Design
John Cunningham  VP – Marketing
Terri Cunningham VP – Editorial Administration
Alison Gill Senior VP – Manufacturing & Operations
Jay Kogan VP – Business & Legal Affairs, Publishing
Jack Mahan VP – Business Affairs, Talent
Nick Napolitano  VP – Manufacturing Administration
Sue Pohja  VP – Book Sales
Courtney Simmons Senior VP – Publicity
Bob Wayne Senior VP – Sales

THE UNWRITTEN VOLUME 8:
ORPHEUS IN THE UNDERWORLD

Published by DC Comics. Copyright © 2014 Mike Carey
and Peter Gross. All Rights Reserved.

Originally published in single magazine form in THE
UNWRITTEN 42-49 © 2012, 2013 Mike Carey and Peter
Gross. All Rights Reserved. VERTIGO and all characters,
their distinctive likenesses and related elements featured in
this publication are trademarks of DC Comics. The stories,
characters and incidents featured in this publication are entirely
fictional. DC Comics does not read or accept unsolicited ideas,
stories or artwork.

DC Comics, 1700 Broadway, New York, NY 10019
A Warner Bros. Entertainment Company.
Printed in the USA. First Printing.
ISBN: 978-1-4012-4301-2

Library of Congress Cataloging-in-Publication Data

Carey, Mike, 1959- author.
 The Unwritten. Vol. 8, Orpheus in the Underworlds / Mike
Carey ; [illustrated by] Peter Gross.
     pages cm
  Summary: "In this eighth volume of the critically-acclaimed
new series from the Eisner-nominated creative team, Mike
Carey and Peter Gross, Tommy ventures into the land of the
dead to find and rescue Lizzie. But the journey through Hades
pits Tommy against all kinds of enemies of undead. But none of
these encounters prepare him for his meeting with the king -- or
for the responsibilities he has to take on for some very familiar
damned souls.  Collects #42-49 of The Unwritten"-- Provided
by publisher.
  ISBN 978-1-4012-4301-2 (pbk.)
 1.  Graphic novels.  I. Gross, Peter, 1958- illustrator. II. Title. III.
Title: Orpheus in the Underworlds.
 PN6727.C377U587 2014
 741.5'973—dc23
                                      2013040735

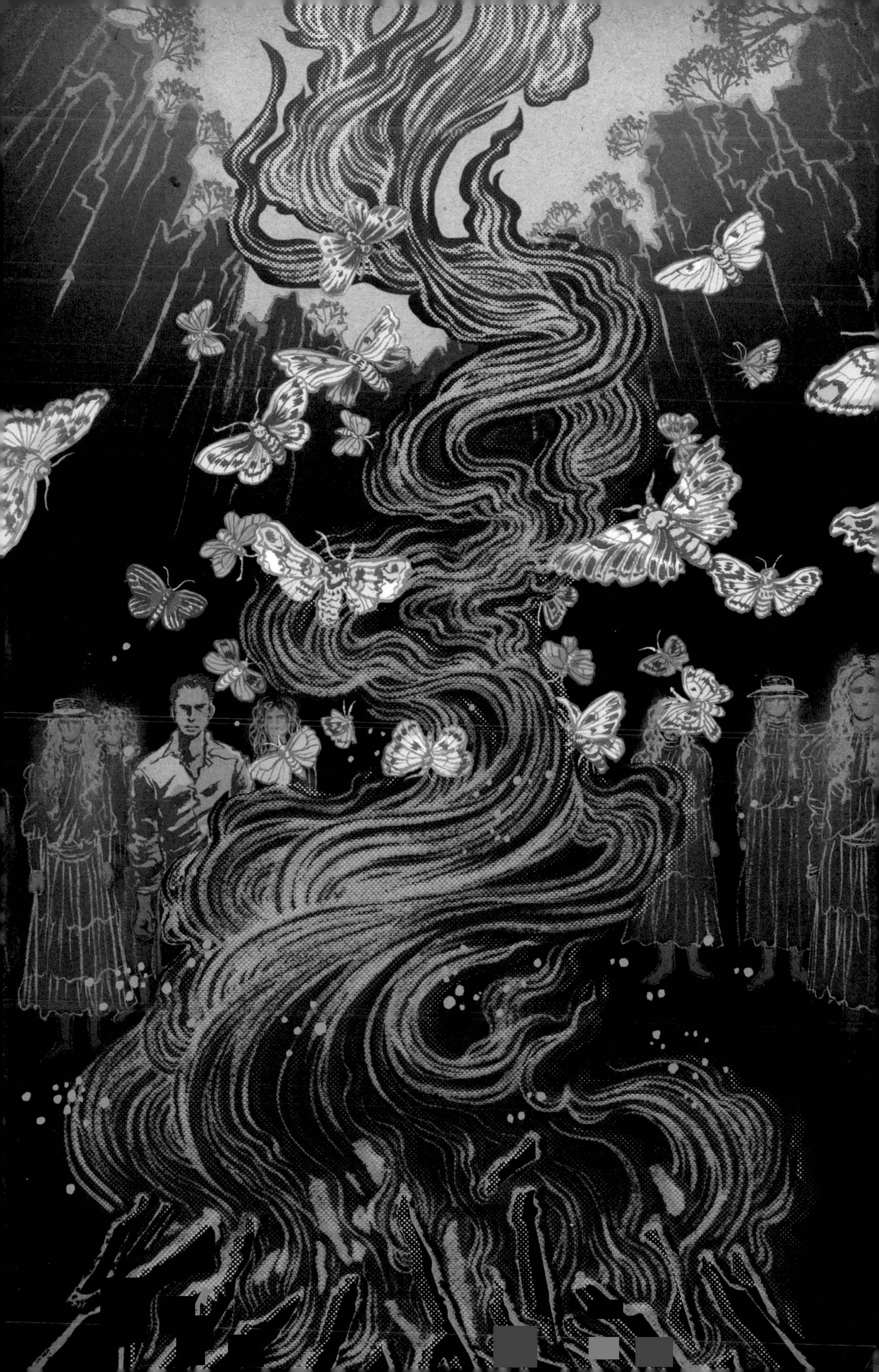

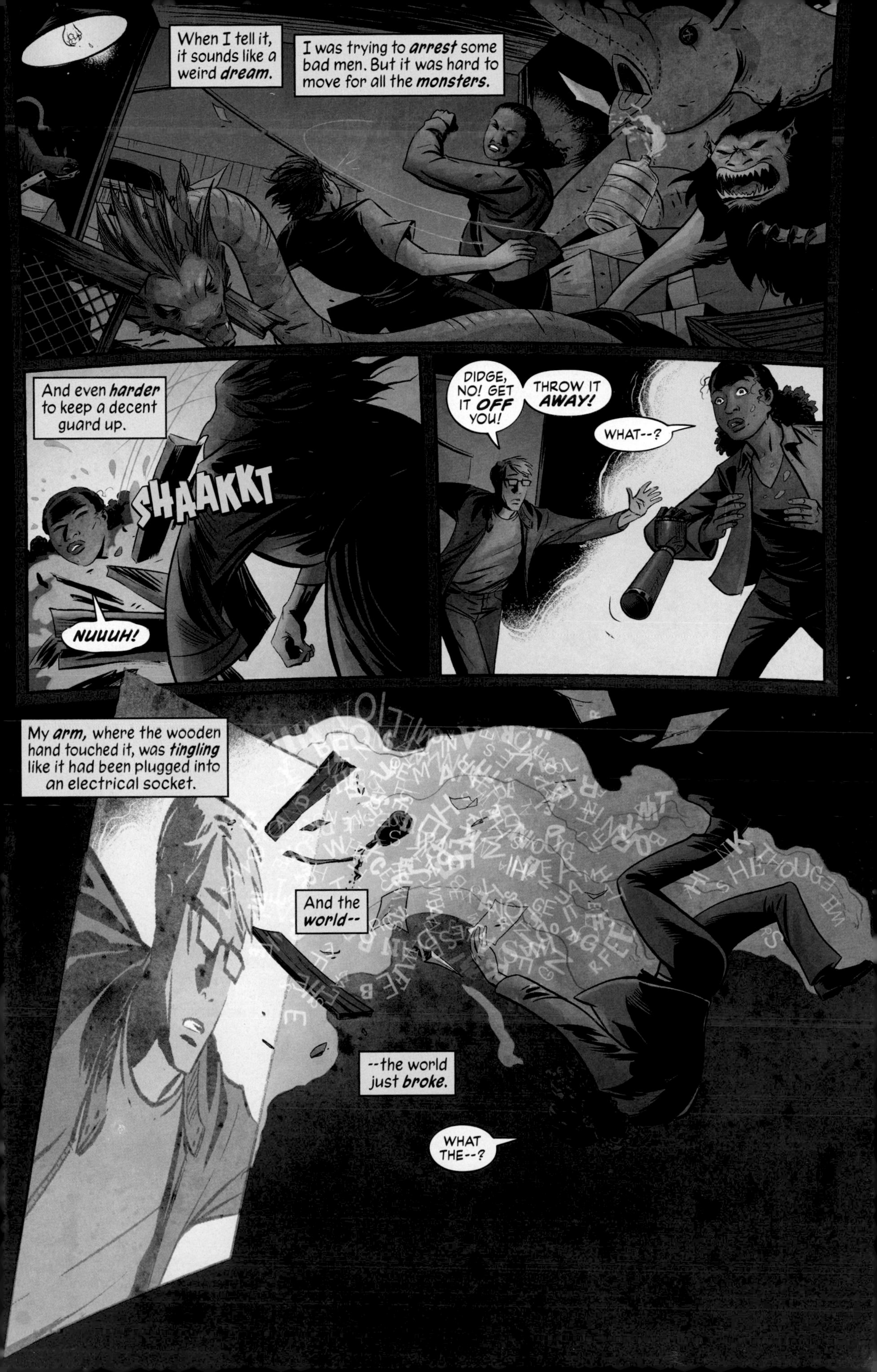
When I tell it, it sounds like a weird dream.
I was trying to arrest some bad men. But it was hard to move for all the monsters.
And even harder to keep a decent guard up.
SHAAKKT
NUUUH!
DIDGE, NO! GET IT OFF YOU!
THROW IT AWAY!
WHAT--?
My arm, where the wooden hand touched it, was tingling like it had been plugged into an electrical socket.
And the world--
--the world just broke.
WHAT THE--?

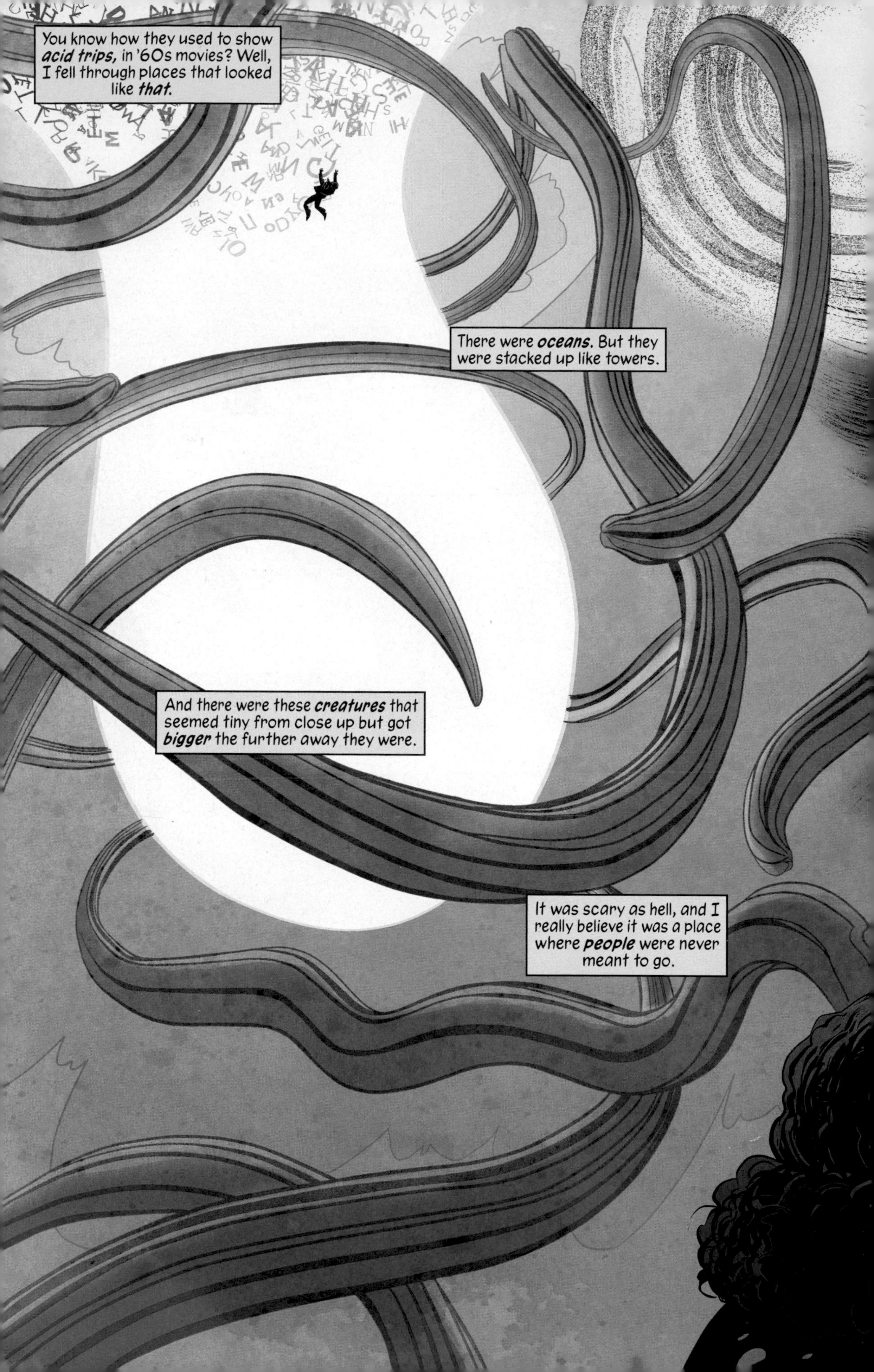
You know how they used to show *acid trips,* in '60s movies? Well, I fell through places that looked like *that.*
There were *oceans.* But they were stacked up like towers.
And there were these *creatures* that seemed tiny from close up but got *bigger* the further away they were.
It was scary as hell, and I really believe it was a place where *people* were never meant to go.

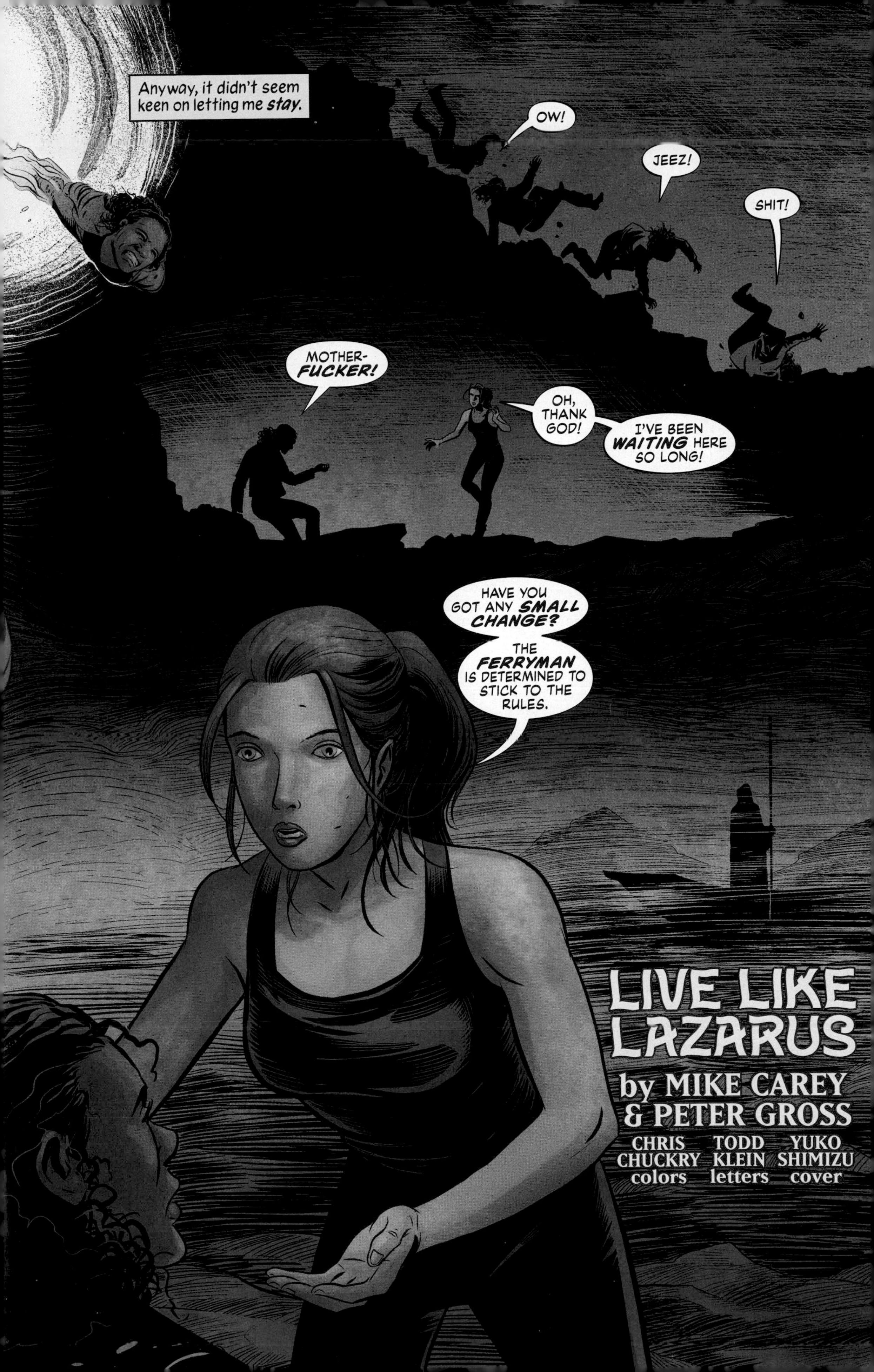
Anyway, it didn't seem keen on letting me stay.
OW!
JEEZ!
SHIT!
MOTHER-FUCKER!
OH, THANK GOD!
I'VE BEEN WAITING HERE SO LONG!
HAVE YOU GOT ANY SMALL CHANGE?
THE FERRYMAN IS DETERMINED TO STICK TO THE RULES.
LIVE LIKE LAZARUS
by MIKE CAREY & PETER GROSS
CHRIS CHUCKRY colors
TODD KLEIN letters
YUKO SHIMIZU cover

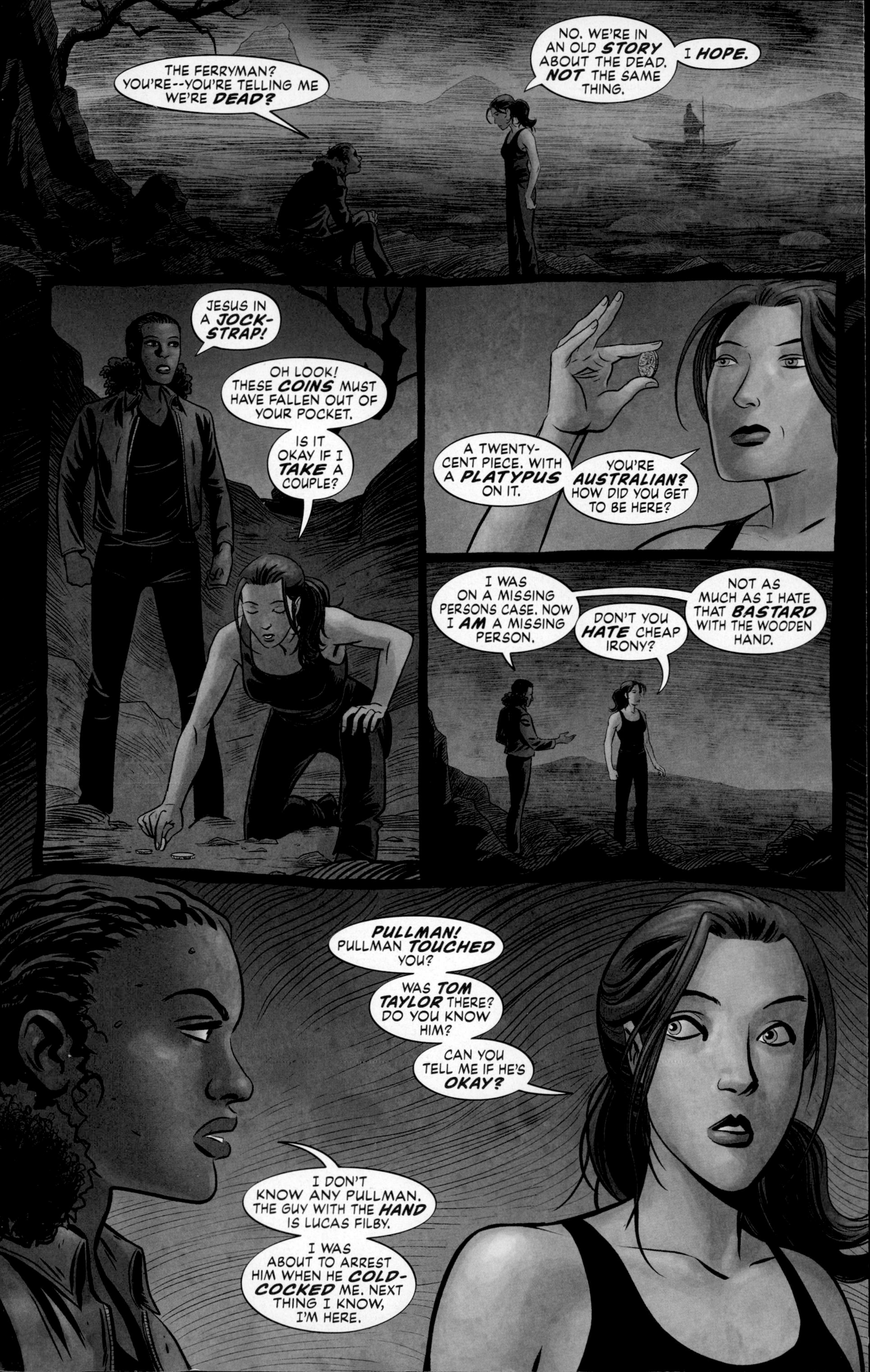

THE FERRYMAN? YOU'RE--YOU'RE TELLING ME WE'RE DEAD?
NO. WE'RE IN AN OLD STORY ABOUT THE DEAD. NOT THE SAME THING.
I HOPE.
JESUS IN A JOCK-STRAP!
OH LOOK! THESE COINS MUST HAVE FALLEN OUT OF YOUR POCKET.
IS IT OKAY IF I TAKE A COUPLE?
A TWENTY-CENT PIECE. WITH A PLATYPUS ON IT.
YOU'RE AUSTRALIAN? HOW DID YOU GET TO BE HERE?
I WAS ON A MISSING PERSONS CASE. NOW I AM A MISSING PERSON.
DON'T YOU HATE CHEAP IRONY?
NOT AS MUCH AS I HATE THAT BASTARD WITH THE WOODEN HAND.
PULLMAN! PULLMAN TOUCHED YOU?
WAS TOM TAYLOR THERE? DO YOU KNOW HIM?
CAN YOU TELL ME IF HE'S OKAY?
I DON'T KNOW ANY PULLMAN. THE GUY WITH THE HAND IS LUCAS FILBY.
I WAS ABOUT TO ARREST HIM WHEN HE COLD-COCKED ME. NEXT THING I KNOW, I'M HERE.

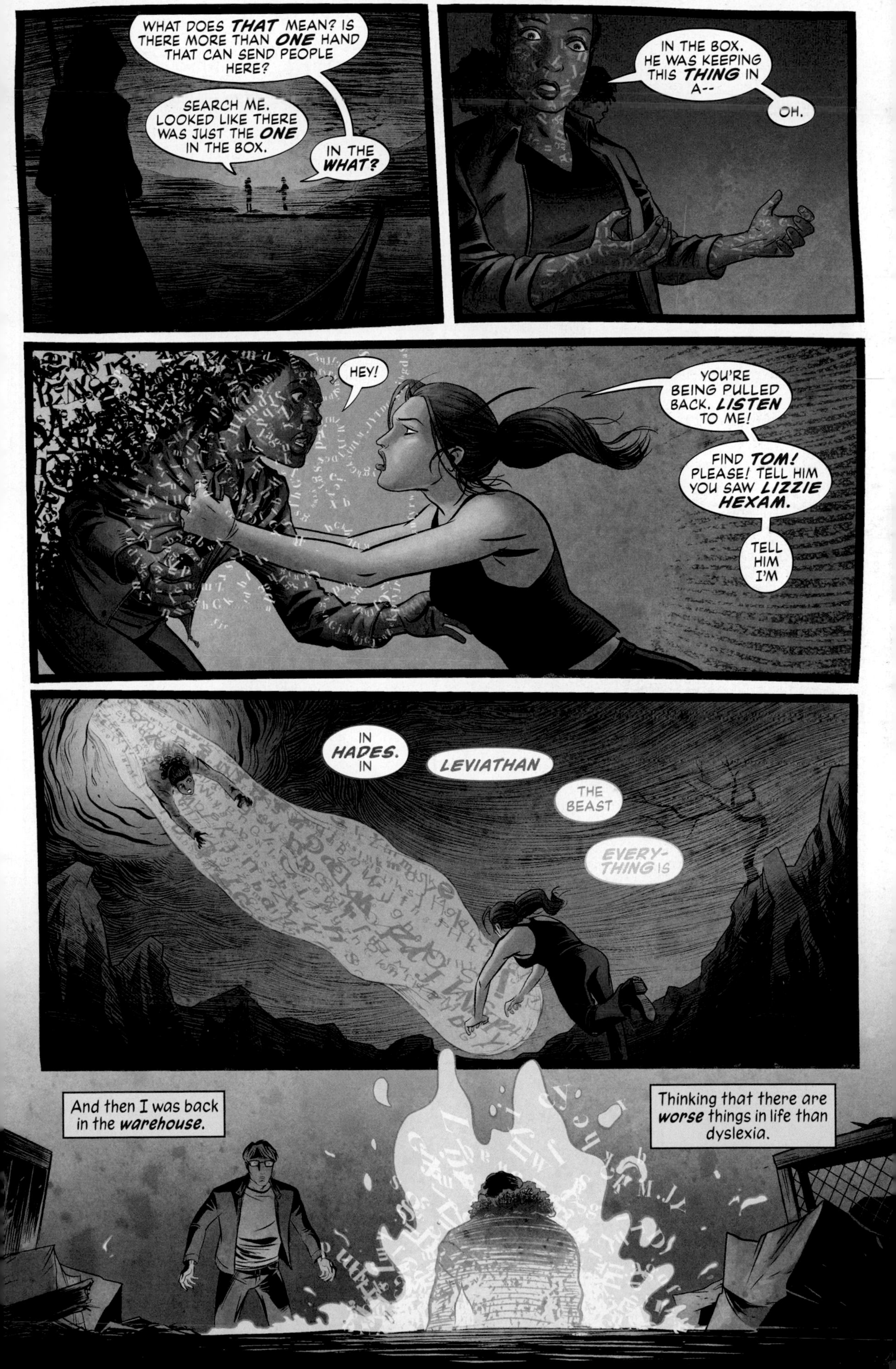
WHAT DOES THAT MEAN? IS THERE MORE THAN ONE HAND THAT CAN SEND PEOPLE HERE?
SEARCH ME. LOOKED LIKE THERE WAS JUST THE ONE IN THE BOX.
IN THE WHAT?
IN THE BOX. HE WAS KEEPING THIS THING IN A--
OH.
HEY!
YOU'RE BEING PULLED BACK. LISTEN TO ME!
FIND TOM! PLEASE! TELL HIM YOU SAW LIZZIE HEXAM.
TELL HIM I'M
IN HADES. IN
LEVIATHAN
THE BEAST
EVERY-THING IS
And then I was back in the warehouse.
Thinking that there are worse things in life than dyslexia.

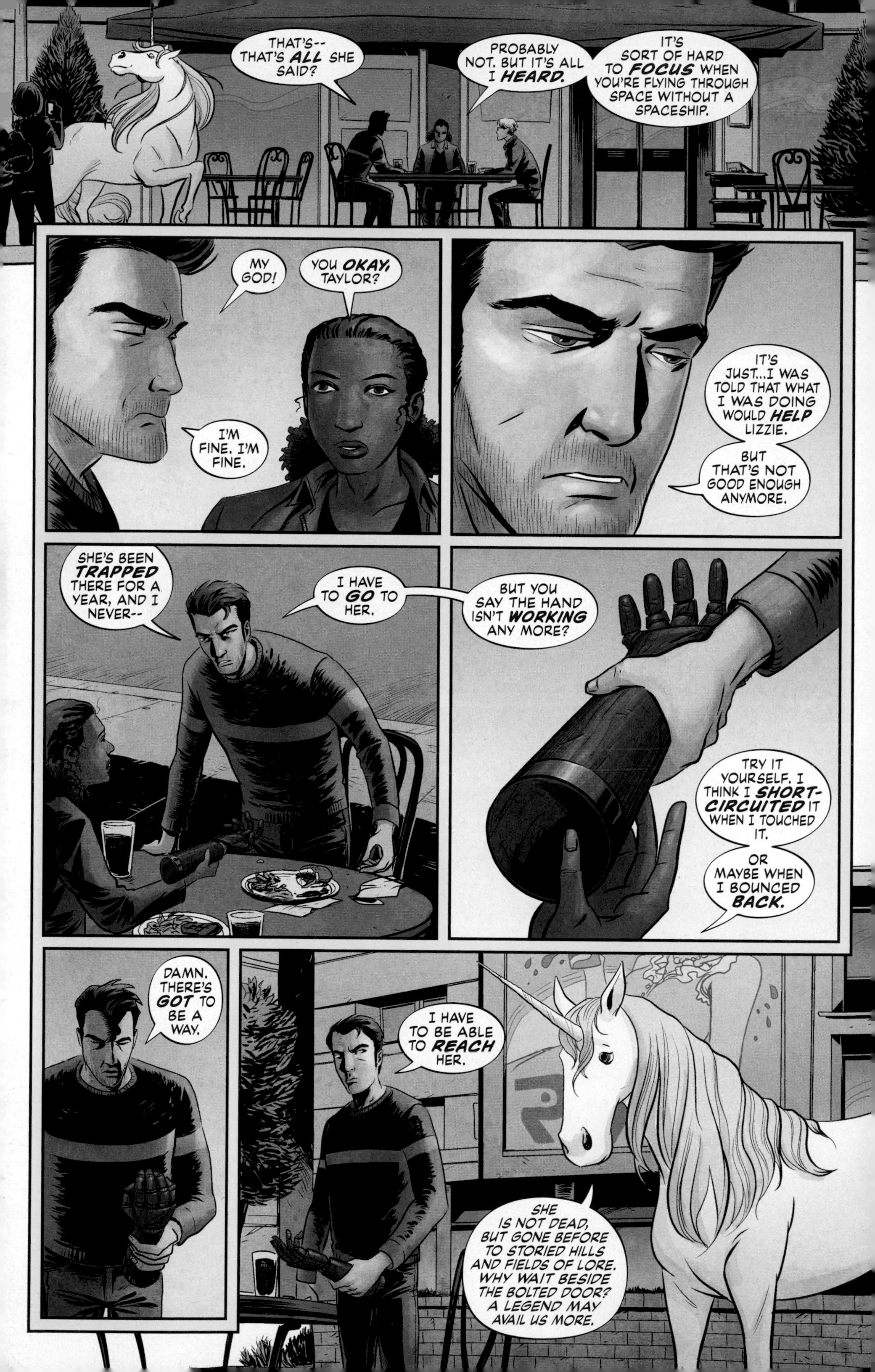
THAT'S-- THAT'S ALL SHE SAID?
PROBABLY NOT. BUT IT'S ALL I HEARD.
IT'S SORT OF HARD TO FOCUS WHEN YOU'RE FLYING THROUGH SPACE WITHOUT A SPACESHIP.
MY GOD!
YOU OKAY, TAYLOR?
I'M FINE. I'M FINE.
IT'S JUST...I WAS TOLD THAT WHAT I WAS DOING WOULD HELP LIZZIE.
BUT THAT'S NOT GOOD ENOUGH ANYMORE.
SHE'S BEEN TRAPPED THERE FOR A YEAR, AND I NEVER--
I HAVE TO GO TO HER.
BUT YOU SAY THE HAND ISN'T WORKING ANY MORE?
TRY IT YOURSELF. I THINK I SHORT-CIRCUITED IT WHEN I TOUCHED IT.
OR MAYBE WHEN I BOUNCED BACK.
DAMN. THERE'S GOT TO BE A WAY.
I HAVE TO BE ABLE TO REACH HER.
SHE IS NOT DEAD, BUT GONE BEFORE TO STORIED HILLS AND FIELDS OF LORE. WHY WAIT BESIDE THE BOLTED DOOR? A LEGEND MAY AVAIL US MORE.

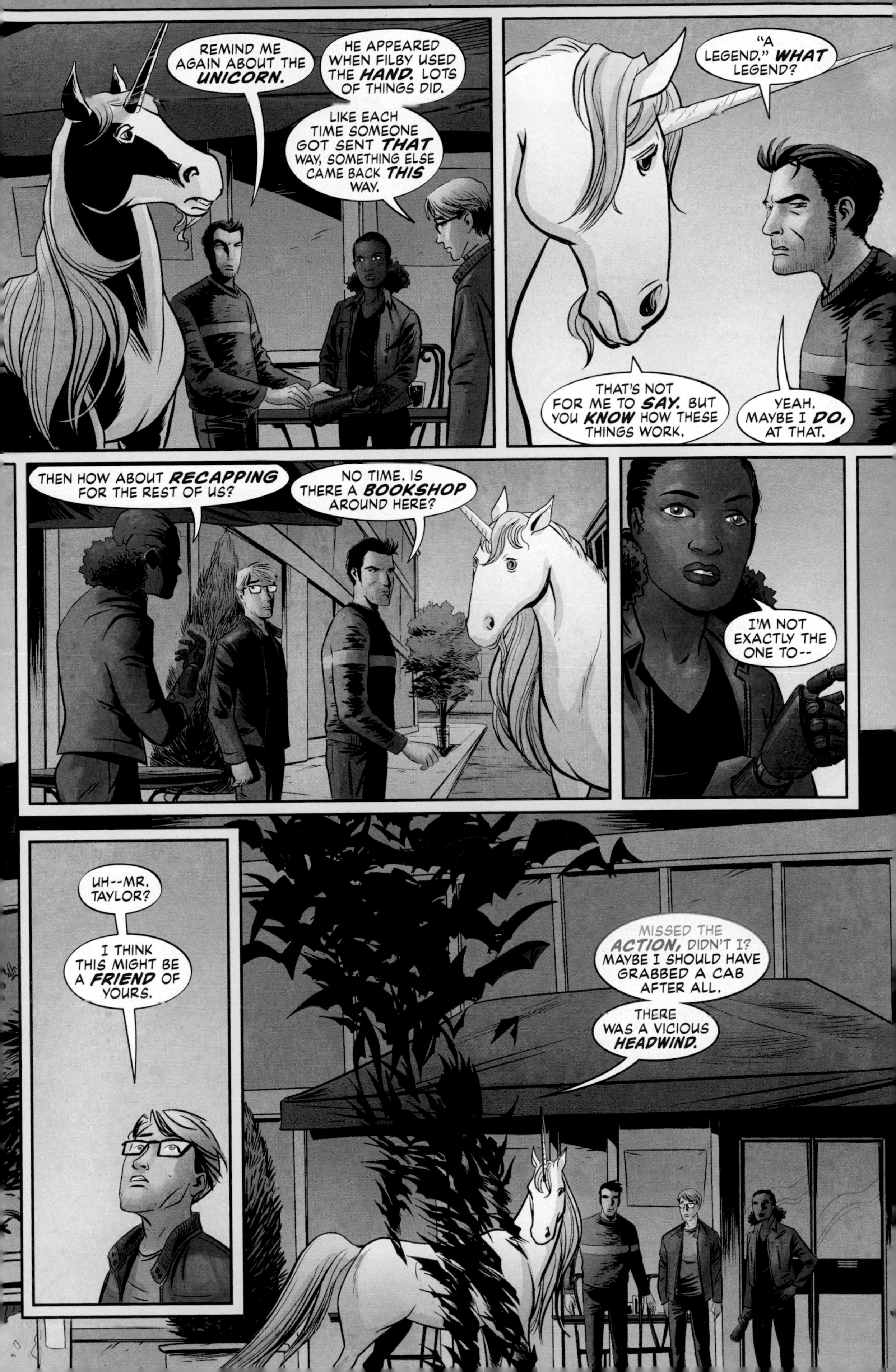
REMIND ME AGAIN ABOUT THE UNICORN.
HE APPEARED WHEN FILBY USED THE HAND. LOTS OF THINGS DID.
LIKE EACH TIME SOMEONE GOT SENT THAT WAY, SOMETHING ELSE CAME BACK THIS WAY.
"A LEGEND." WHAT LEGEND?
THAT'S NOT FOR ME TO SAY. BUT YOU KNOW HOW THESE THINGS WORK.
YEAH. MAYBE I DO, AT THAT.
THEN HOW ABOUT RECAPPING FOR THE REST OF US?
NO TIME. IS THERE A BOOKSHOP AROUND HERE?
I'M NOT EXACTLY THE ONE TO--
UH--MR. TAYLOR?
I THINK THIS MIGHT BE A FRIEND OF YOURS.
MISSED THE ACTION, DIDN'T I? MAYBE I SHOULD HAVE GRABBED A CAB AFTER ALL.
THERE WAS A VICIOUS HEADWIND.

I THOUGHT YOU WERE PRETTY MUCH **DONE** WITH ME, RICHIE. YOU SAID--

KOOKA-BURRA BOOKS

'GOING OUT OF BUSINESS

YOU WANT TO DO THIS **NOW,** TOM? GO BACK OVER ALL THAT SHIT?

OKAY.

HORROR

I'M A **JOURNAL-IST.** I SAY A LOT OF THINGS.

IT USUALLY PAYS TO WAIT FOR THE LATE **EDITION.**

BUT I TURNED YOU INTO--

A BLOODSUCKING **MONSTER.** I KNOW. BEATS BEING TURNED INTO A **CORPSE.**

BESIDES, I **DID** WHAT I SET OUT TO DO. I **WROTE** MYSELF.

AND IT WORKED. I'M A VAMPIRE BY COMMON **CONSENT,** NOW.

BECAUSE A BILLION PEOPLE BELIEVE IT, NOT JUST BECAUSE **YOU** DO.

WHAT ARE WE DOING HERE, BY THE WAY?

WE'RE LOOKING FOR A WAY THROUGH INTO **FICTION.**

THE **DOORKNOB?**

HAVEN'T SEEN IT SINCE OXFORD. AND **TOMMY SPELLS** ARE A RISK I CAN'T AFFORD TO **TAKE.**

ON WILSON'S MAP, THE WHOLE OF AUSTRALIA IS JUST TERRA INCOGNITA.

BUT I FIGURE, ONCE YOU KNOW WHAT THE MAP IS MEANT TO **SHOW**--

PICNIC AT HANGING ROCK

JOAN LINDSAY

--YOU CAN PRETTY MUCH **ROLL** YOUR OWN.

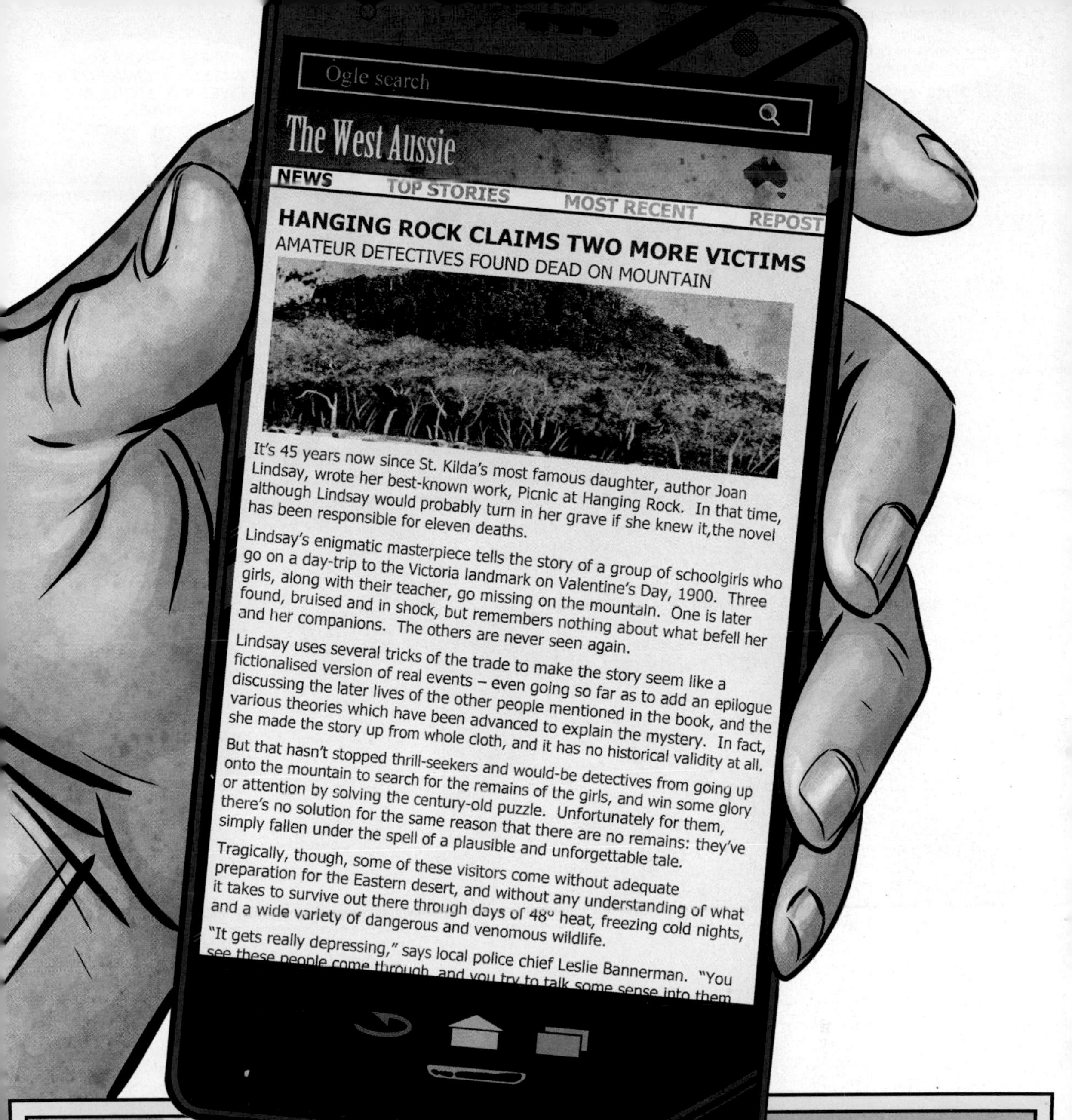
Ogle search
The West Aussie
NEWS
TOP STORIES
MOST RECENT
REPOST
HANGING ROCK CLAIMS TWO MORE VICTIMS
AMATEUR DETECTIVES FOUND DEAD ON MOUNTAIN
It's 45 years now since St. Kilda's most famous daughter, author Joan Lindsay, wrote her best-known work, Picnic at Hanging Rock. In that time, although Lindsay would probably turn in her grave if she knew it,the novel has been responsible for eleven deaths.
Lindsay's enigmatic masterpiece tells the story of a group of schoolgirls who go on a day-trip to the Victoria landmark on Valentine's Day, 1900. Three girls, along with their teacher, go missing on the mountain. One is later found, bruised and in shock, but remembers nothing about what befell her and her companions. The others are never seen again.
Lindsay uses several tricks of the trade to make the story seem like a fictionalised version of real events – even going so far as to add an epilogue discussing the later lives of the other people mentioned in the book, and the various theories which have been advanced to explain the mystery. In fact, she made the story up from whole cloth, and it has no historical validity at all.
But that hasn't stopped thrill-seekers and would-be detectives from going up onto the mountain to search for the remains of the girls, and win some glory or attention by solving the century-old puzzle. Unfortunately for them, there's no solution for the same reason that there are no remains: they've simply fallen under the spell of a plausible and unforgettable tale.
Tragically, though, some of these visitors come without adequate preparation for the Eastern desert, and without any understanding of what it takes to survive out there through days of 48° heat, freezing cold nights, and a wide variety of dangerous and venomous wildlife.
"It gets really depressing," says local police chief Leslie Bannerman. "You

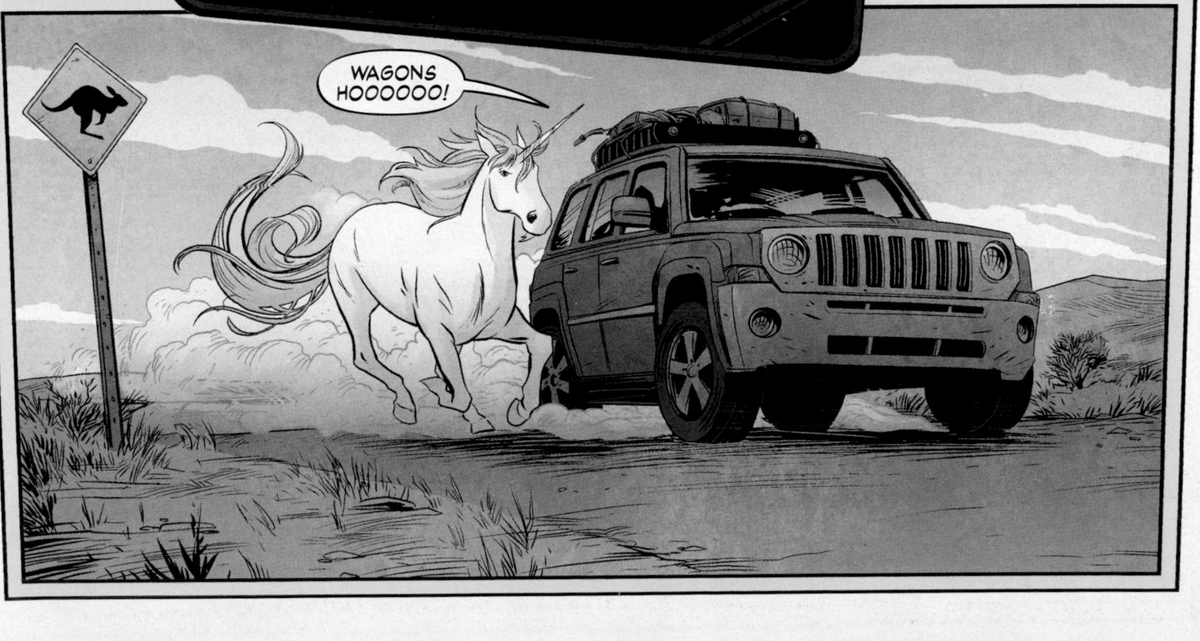
WAGONS HOOOOOO!

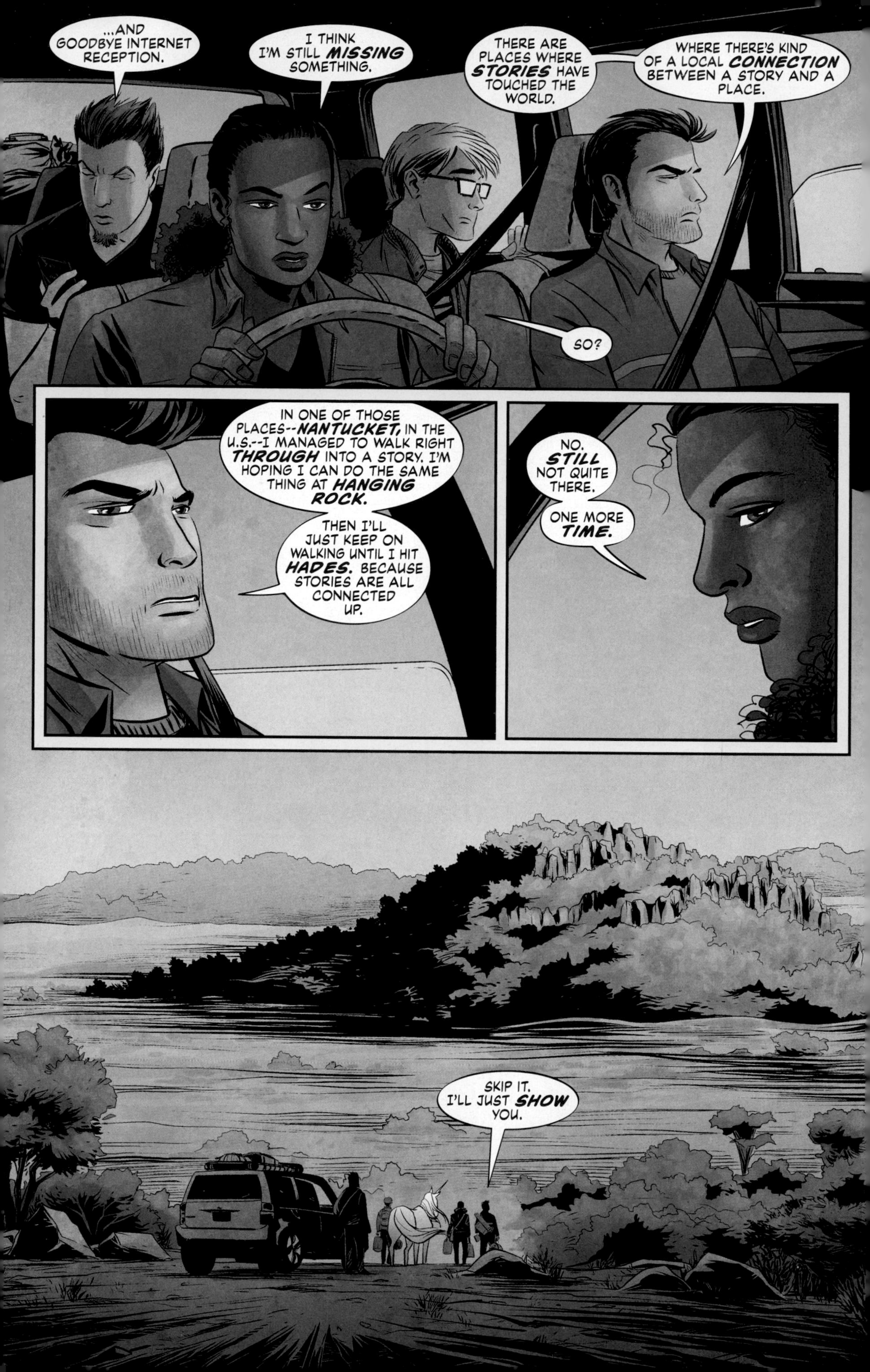
...AND GOODBYE INTERNET RECEPTION.
I THINK I'M STILL MISSING SOMETHING.
THERE ARE PLACES WHERE STORIES HAVE TOUCHED THE WORLD.
WHERE THERE'S KIND OF A LOCAL CONNECTION BETWEEN A STORY AND A PLACE.
SO?
IN ONE OF THOSE PLACES--NANTUCKET, IN THE U.S.--I MANAGED TO WALK RIGHT THROUGH INTO A STORY. I'M HOPING I CAN DO THE SAME THING AT HANGING ROCK.
THEN I'LL JUST KEEP ON WALKING UNTIL I HIT HADES. BECAUSE STORIES ARE ALL CONNECTED UP.
NO. STILL NOT QUITE THERE.
ONE MORE TIME.
SKIP IT. I'LL JUST SHOW YOU.

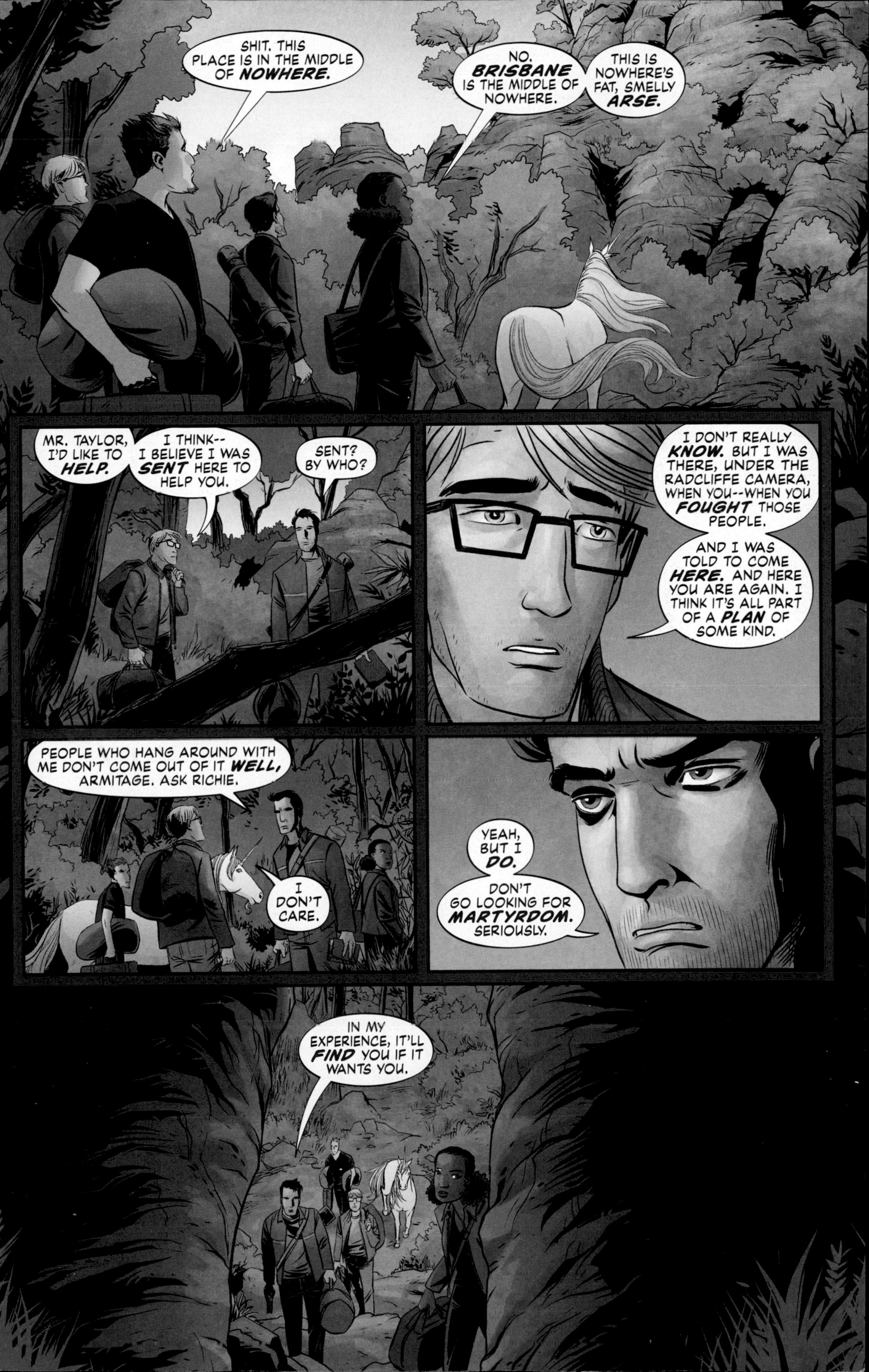
SHIT. THIS PLACE IS IN THE MIDDLE OF NOWHERE.
NO. BRISBANE IS THE MIDDLE OF NOWHERE.
THIS IS NOWHERE'S FAT, SMELLY ARSE.
MR. TAYLOR, I'D LIKE TO HELP.
I THINK-- I BELIEVE I WAS SENT HERE TO HELP YOU.
SENT? BY WHO?
I DON'T REALLY KNOW. BUT I WAS THERE, UNDER THE RADCLIFFE CAMERA, WHEN YOU--WHEN YOU FOUGHT THOSE PEOPLE.
AND I WAS TOLD TO COME HERE. AND HERE YOU ARE AGAIN. I THINK IT'S ALL PART OF A PLAN OF SOME KIND.
PEOPLE WHO HANG AROUND WITH ME DON'T COME OUT OF IT WELL, ARMITAGE. ASK RICHIE.
I DON'T CARE.
YEAH, BUT I DO.
DON'T GO LOOKING FOR MARTYRDOM. SERIOUSLY.
IN MY EXPERIENCE, IT'LL FIND YOU IF IT WANTS YOU.

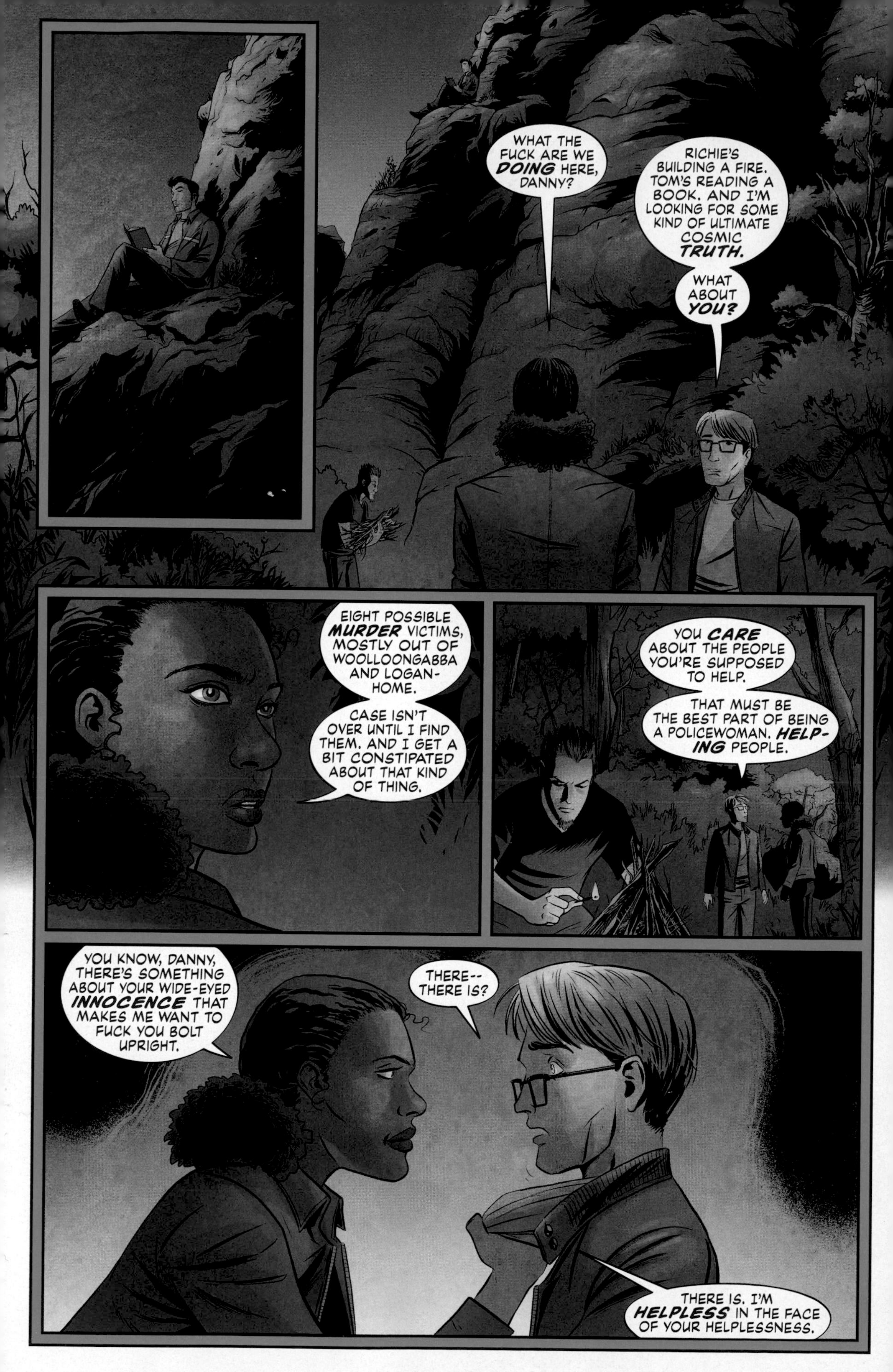

WHAT THE FUCK ARE WE DOING HERE, DANNY?
RICHIE'S BUILDING A FIRE. TOM'S READING A BOOK. AND I'M LOOKING FOR SOME KIND OF ULTIMATE COSMIC TRUTH.
WHAT ABOUT YOU?
EIGHT POSSIBLE MURDER VICTIMS, MOSTLY OUT OF WOOLLOONGABBA AND LOGAN-HOME.
CASE ISN'T OVER UNTIL I FIND THEM. AND I GET A BIT CONSTIPATED ABOUT THAT KIND OF THING.
YOU CARE ABOUT THE PEOPLE YOU'RE SUPPOSED TO HELP.
THAT MUST BE THE BEST PART OF BEING A POLICEWOMAN. HELP-ING PEOPLE.
YOU KNOW, DANNY, THERE'S SOMETHING ABOUT YOUR WIDE-EYED INNOCENCE THAT MAKES ME WANT TO FUCK YOU BOLT UPRIGHT.
THERE-- THERE IS?
THERE IS. I'M HELPLESS IN THE FACE OF YOUR HELPLESSNESS.

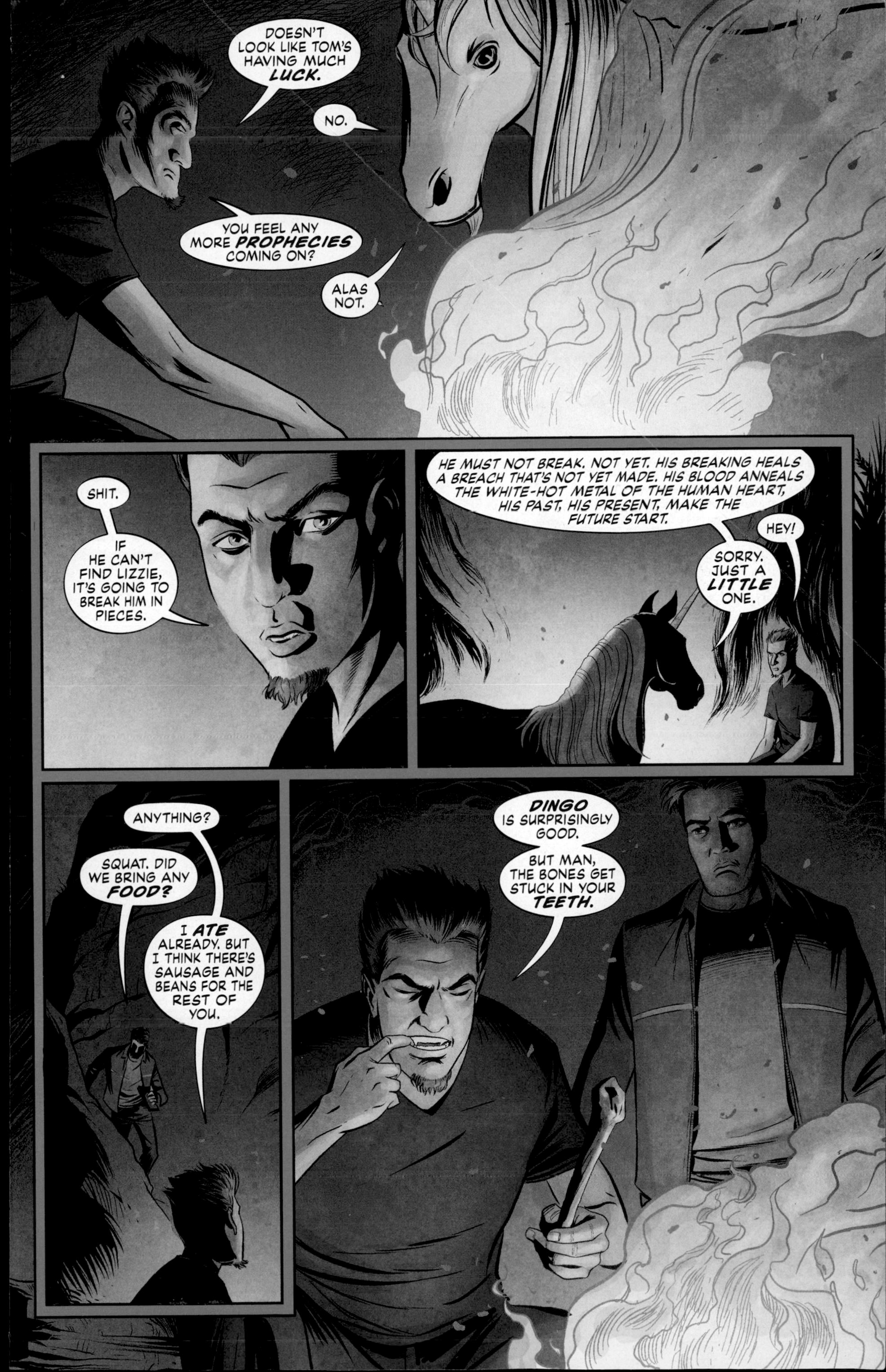
DOESN'T LOOK LIKE TOM'S HAVING MUCH LUCK.
NO.
YOU FEEL ANY MORE PROPHECIES COMING ON?
ALAS NOT.
SHIT.
IF HE CAN'T FIND LIZZIE, IT'S GOING TO BREAK HIM IN PIECES.
HE MUST NOT BREAK. NOT YET. HIS BREAKING HEALS A BREACH THAT'S NOT YET MADE. HIS BLOOD ANNEALS THE WHITE-HOT METAL OF THE HUMAN HEART, HIS PAST, HIS PRESENT, MAKE THE FUTURE START.
HEY!
SORRY. JUST A LITTLE ONE.
ANYTHING?
SQUAT. DID WE BRING ANY FOOD?
I ATE ALREADY. BUT I THINK THERE'S SAUSAGE AND BEANS FOR THE REST OF YOU.
DINGO IS SURPRISINGLY GOOD.
BUT MAN, THE BONES GET STUCK IN YOUR TEETH.

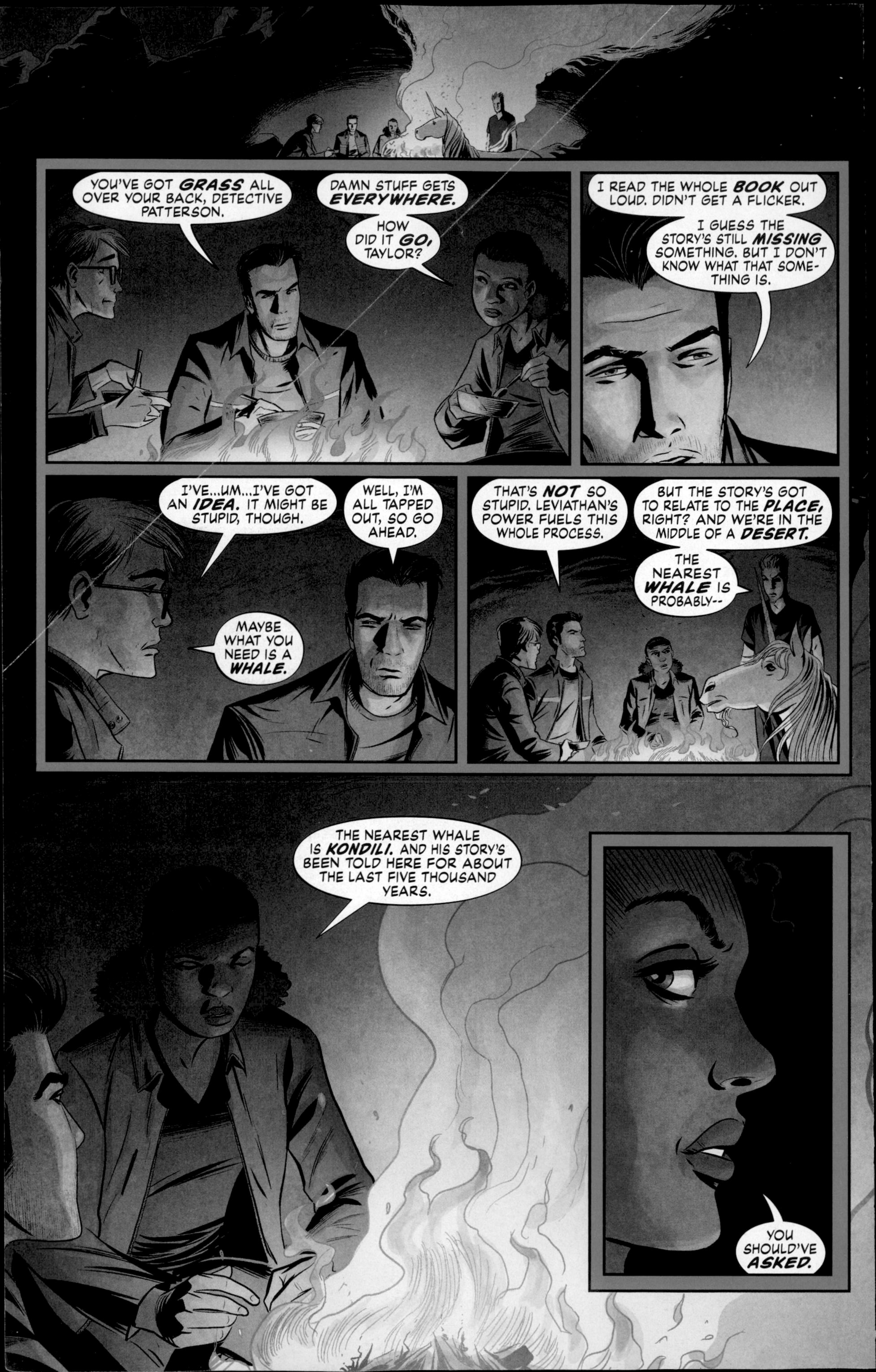
YOU'VE GOT GRASS ALL OVER YOUR BACK, DETECTIVE PATTERSON.
DAMN STUFF GETS EVERYWHERE.
HOW DID IT GO, TAYLOR?
I READ THE WHOLE BOOK OUT LOUD. DIDN'T GET A FLICKER.
I GUESS THE STORY'S STILL MISSING SOMETHING. BUT I DON'T KNOW WHAT THAT SOME-THING IS.
I'VE...UM...I'VE GOT AN IDEA. IT MIGHT BE STUPID, THOUGH.
WELL, I'M ALL TAPPED OUT, SO GO AHEAD.
MAYBE WHAT YOU NEED IS A WHALE.
THAT'S NOT SO STUPID. LEVIATHAN'S POWER FUELS THIS WHOLE PROCESS.
BUT THE STORY'S GOT TO RELATE TO THE PLACE, RIGHT? AND WE'RE IN THE MIDDLE OF A DESERT.
THE NEAREST WHALE IS PROBABLY--
THE NEAREST WHALE IS KONDILI. AND HIS STORY'S BEEN TOLD HERE FOR ABOUT THE LAST FIVE THOUSAND YEARS.
YOU SHOULD'VE ASKED.

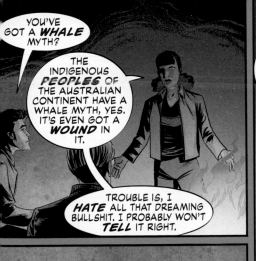

YOU'VE GOT A **WHALE** MYTH?

THE INDIGENOUS **PEOPLES** OF THE AUSTRALIAN CONTINENT HAVE A WHALE MYTH, YES. IT'S EVEN GOT A **WOUND** IN IT.

TROUBLE IS, I **HATE** ALL THAT DREAMING BULLSHIT. I PROBABLY WON'T **TELL** IT RIGHT.

TRUST ME, IF YOU TELL IT AROUND **TOM TAYLOR,** IT WILL PROBABLY TURN OUT FINE.

COULD YOU **TRY,** DIDGE? PLEASE?

WELL, OKAY. I'LL GIVE IT A **SHOT.**

THE **RAMINDJERI** PEOPLE HAD NO **FIRE,** SO THEY COULD ONLY DANCE IN THE DAYTIME.

THIS PISSED THEM OFF TO A **CRAZY** EXTENT.

"SO THE CHIEF COMES UP WITH A **PLAN.**

"'**KONDILI** HAS FIRE. HIS FEET STRIKE **SPARKS** WHEN THEY HIT THE GROUND.

"'WE'LL HOLD A **DANCE.** AND WHEN KONDILI DANCES, WE'LL **STEAL** HIS FIRE.'"

"SO THE RAMINDJERI CALLED A **DANCE MEET.** AND PEOPLE CAME FROM ALL OVER THE PLACE, FOR THE FOOD, FOR THE DANCING.

"ONE OF THE PEOPLE WHO CAME WAS **KONDILI.**"

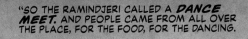

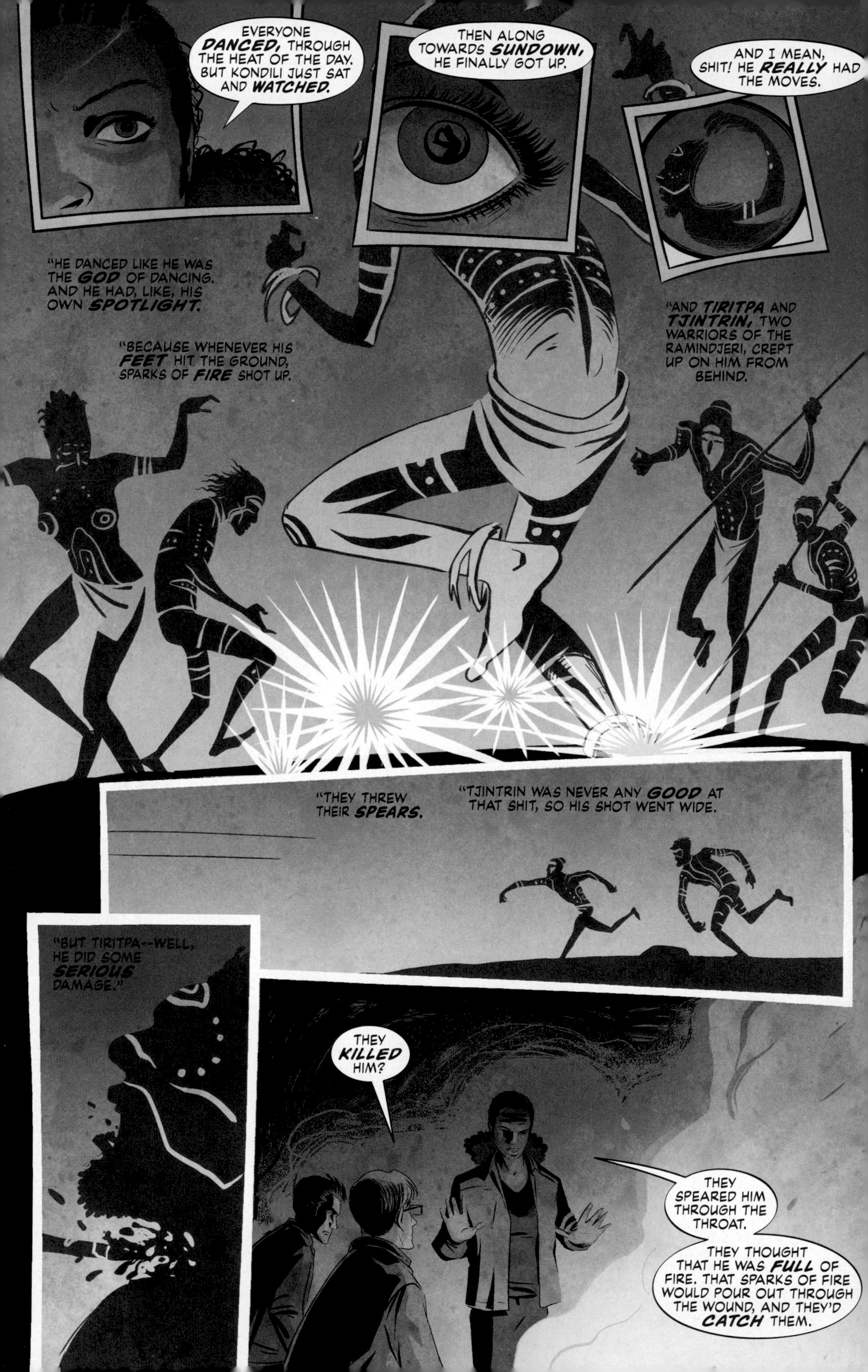
EVERYONE DANCED, THROUGH THE HEAT OF THE DAY. BUT KONDILI JUST SAT AND WATCHED.
THEN ALONG TOWARDS SUNDOWN, HE FINALLY GOT UP.
AND I MEAN, SHIT! HE REALLY HAD THE MOVES.
"HE DANCED LIKE HE WAS THE GOD OF DANCING. AND HE HAD, LIKE, HIS OWN SPOTLIGHT.
"BECAUSE WHENEVER HIS FEET HIT THE GROUND, SPARKS OF FIRE SHOT UP.
"AND TIRITPA AND TJINTRIN, TWO WARRIORS OF THE RAMINDJERI, CREPT UP ON HIM FROM BEHIND.
"THEY THREW THEIR SPEARS.
"TJINTRIN WAS NEVER ANY GOOD AT THAT SHIT, SO HIS SHOT WENT WIDE.
"BUT TIRITPA--WELL, HE DID SOME SERIOUS DAMAGE."
THEY KILLED HIM?
THEY SPEARED HIM THROUGH THE THROAT.
THEY THOUGHT THAT HE WAS FULL OF FIRE. THAT SPARKS OF FIRE WOULD POUR OUT THROUGH THE WOUND, AND THEY'D CATCH THEM.

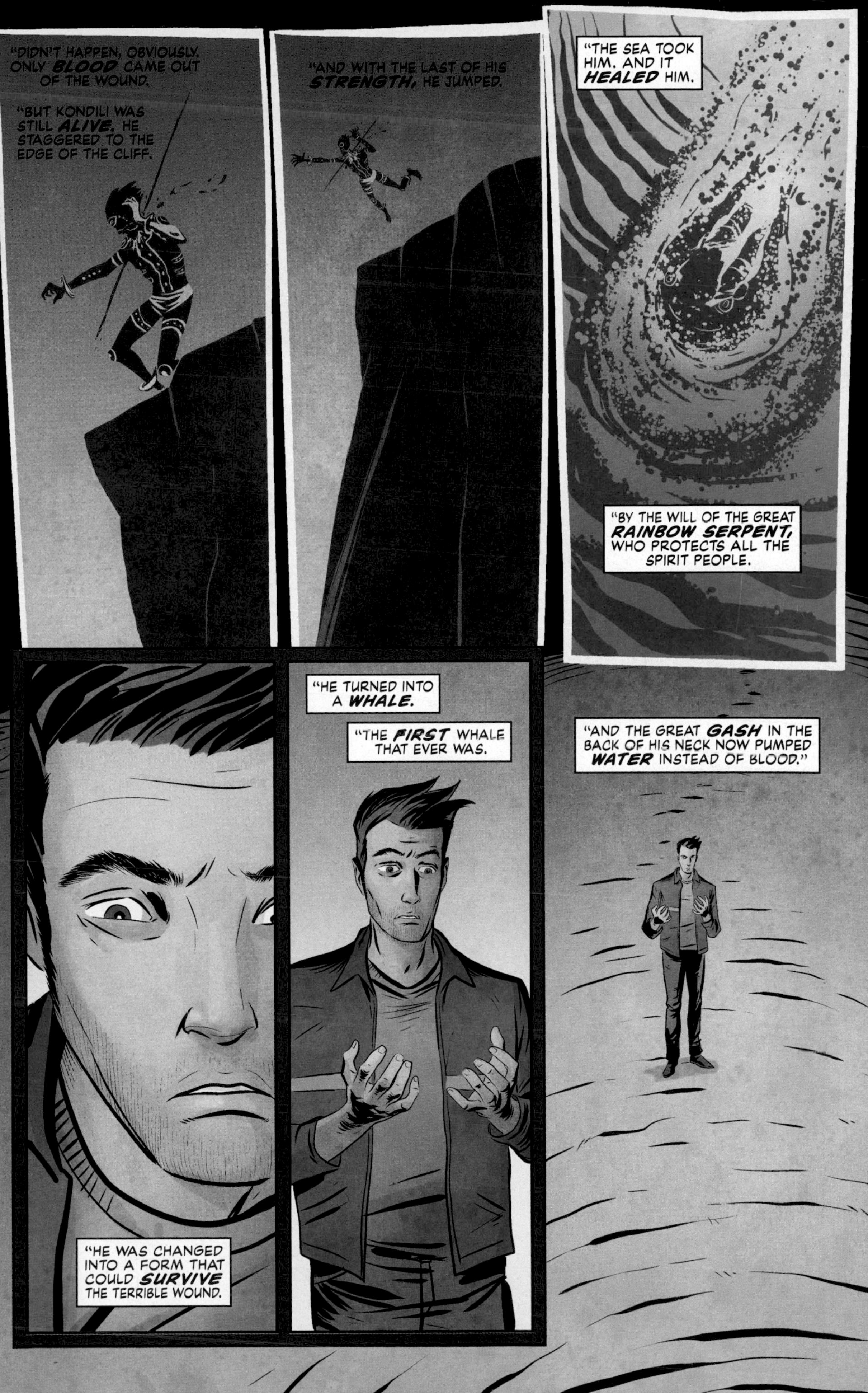
"DIDN'T HAPPEN, OBVIOUSLY. ONLY BLOOD CAME OUT OF THE WOUND.
"BUT KONDILI WAS STILL ALIVE. HE STAGGERED TO THE EDGE OF THE CLIFF.
"AND WITH THE LAST OF HIS STRENGTH, HE JUMPED.
"THE SEA TOOK HIM. AND IT HEALED HIM.
"BY THE WILL OF THE GREAT RAINBOW SERPENT, WHO PROTECTS ALL THE SPIRIT PEOPLE.
"HE WAS CHANGED INTO A FORM THAT COULD SURVIVE THE TERRIBLE WOUND.
"HE TURNED INTO A WHALE.
"THE FIRST WHALE THAT EVER WAS.
"AND THE GREAT GASH IN THE BACK OF HIS NECK NOW PUMPED WATER INSTEAD OF BLOOD."

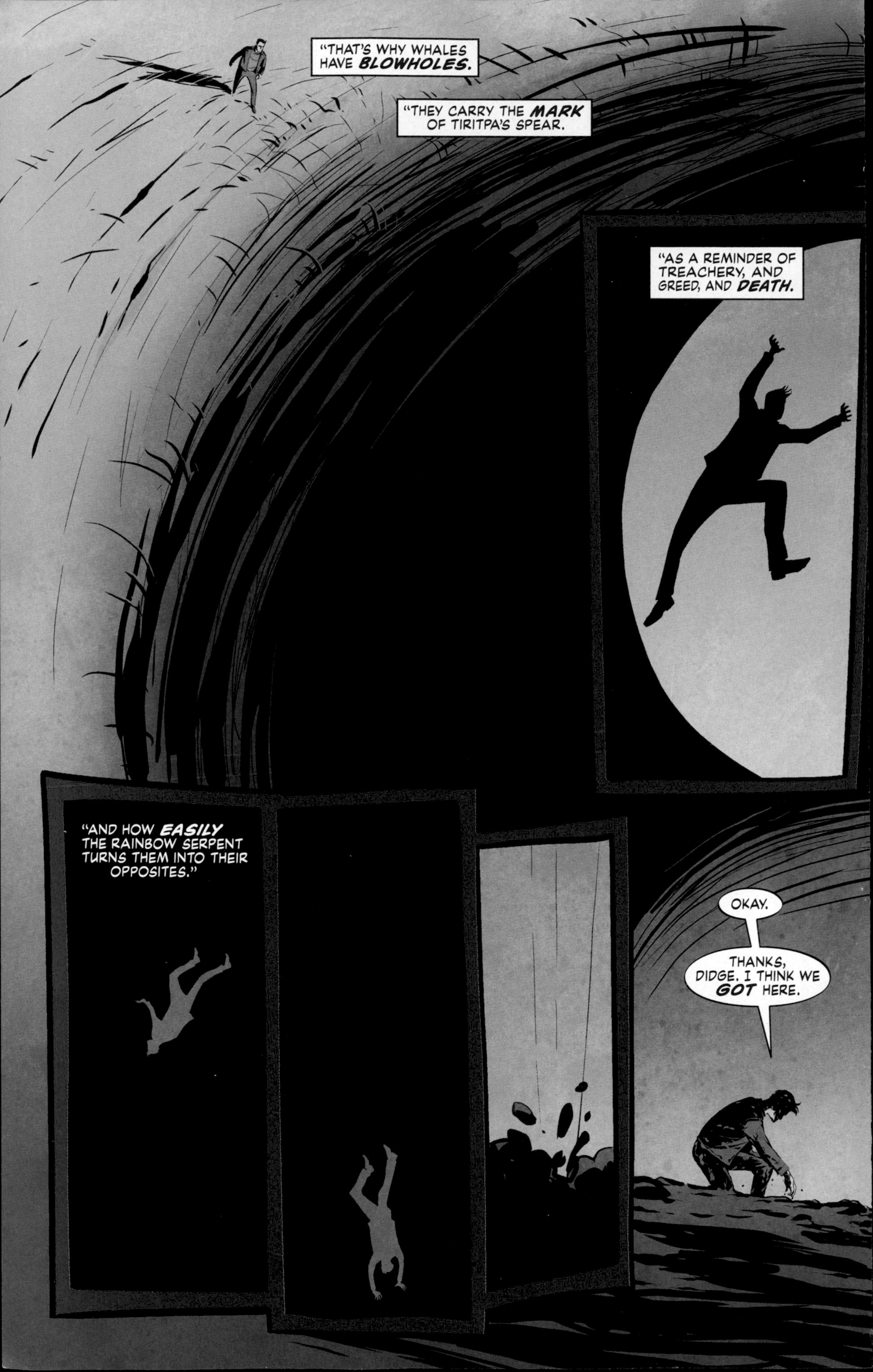
"THAT'S WHY WHALES HAVE **BLOWHOLES.**
"THEY CARRY THE **MARK** OF TIRITPA'S SPEAR.
"AS A REMINDER OF TREACHERY, AND GREED, AND **DEATH.**
"AND HOW **EASILY** THE RAINBOW SERPENT TURNS THEM INTO THEIR OPPOSITES."
OKAY.
THANKS, DIDGE. I THINK WE **GOT** HERE.

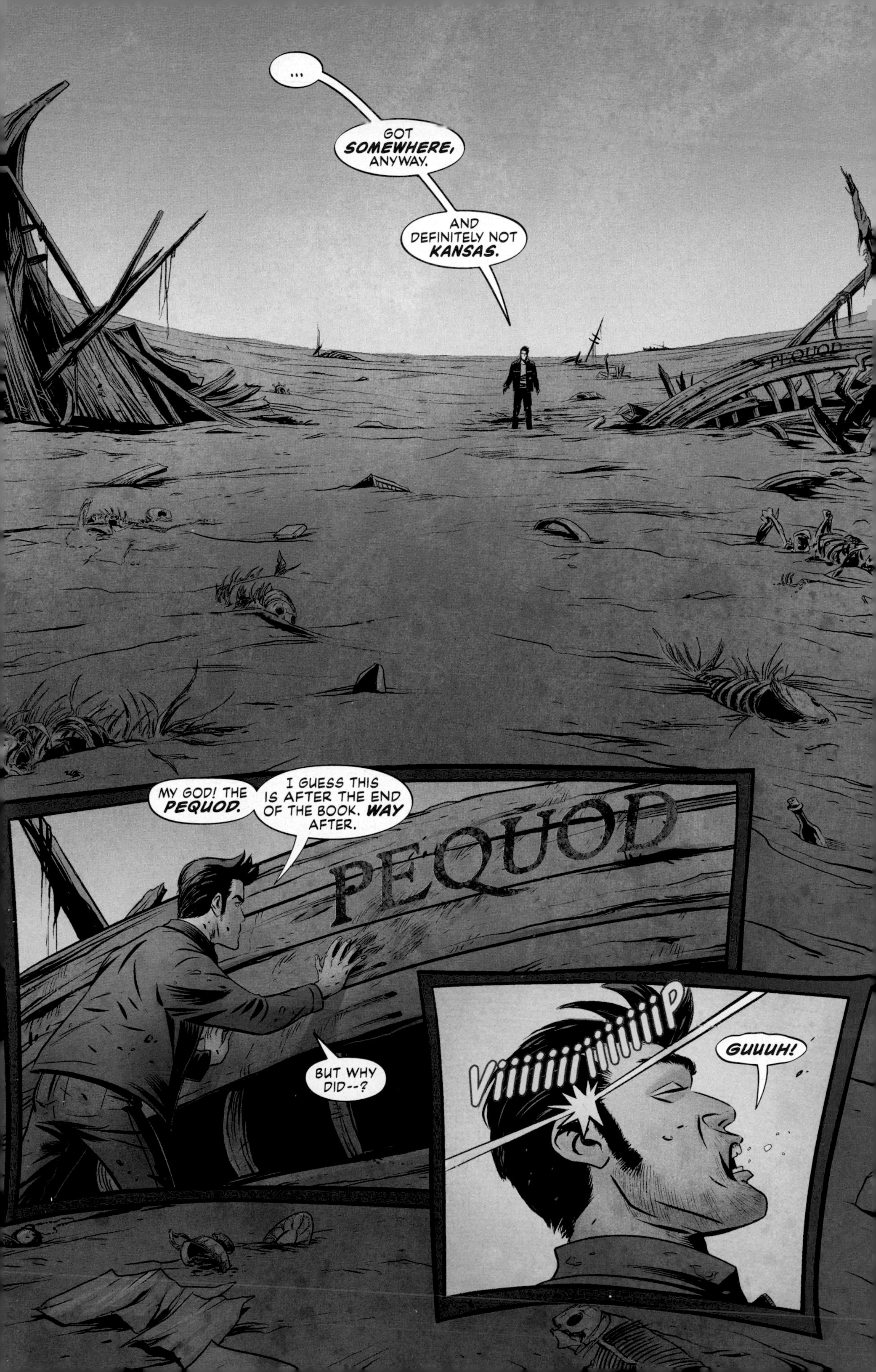
...
GOT SOMEWHERE, ANYWAY.
AND DEFINITELY NOT KANSAS.
PEQUOD
MY GOD! THE PEQUOD.
I GUESS THIS IS AFTER THE END OF THE BOOK. WAY AFTER.
PEQUOD
BUT WHY DID--?
Viiiiiiiiiiiiiiiiip
GUUUH!

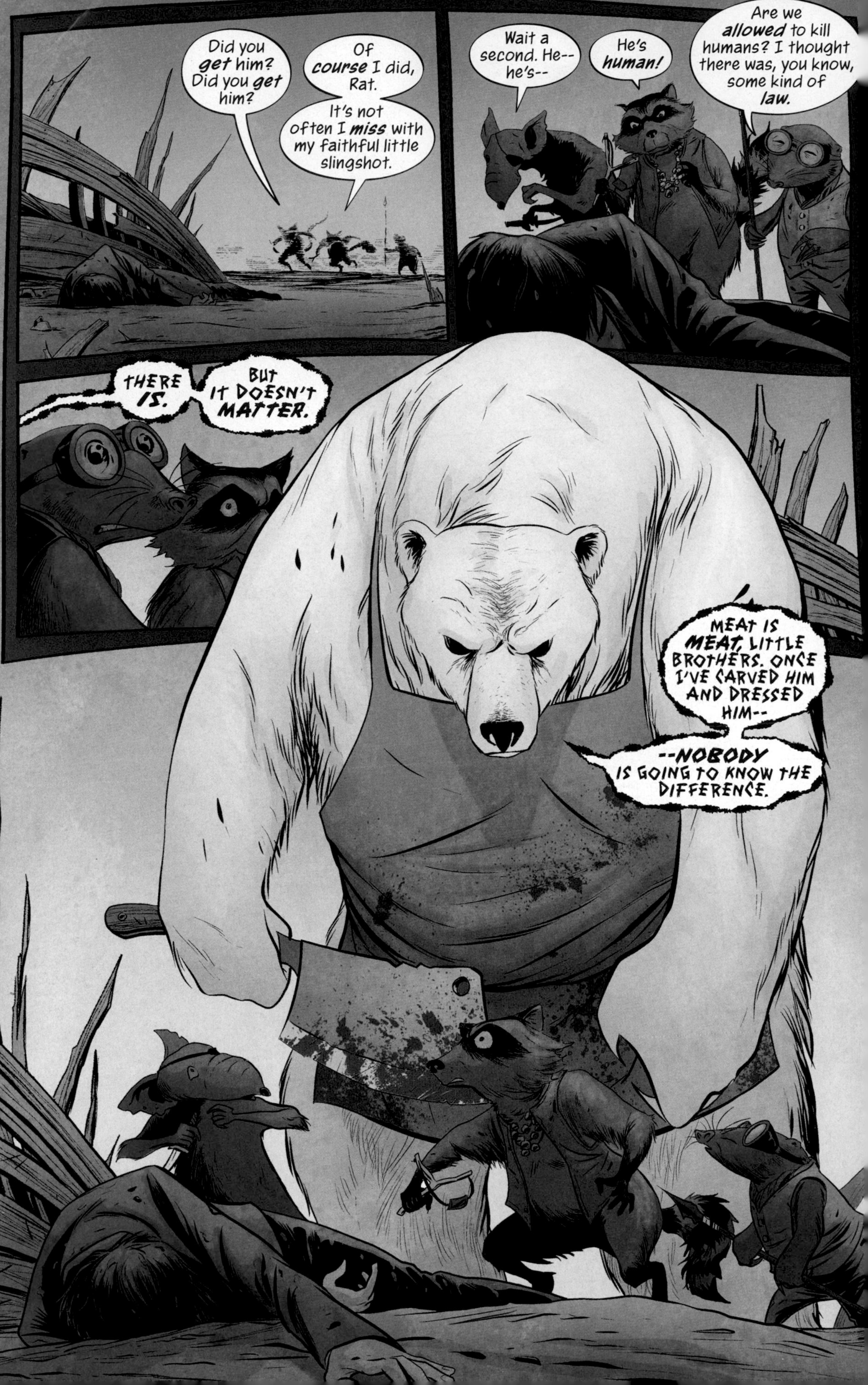
Did you **get** him? Did you **get** him?
Of **course** I did, Rat.
It's not often I **miss** with my faithful little slingshot.
Wait a second. He-- he's--
He's **human!**
Are we **allowed** to kill humans? I thought there was, you know, some kind of **law.**
THERE **IS.**
BUT IT DOESN'T **MATTER.**
MEAT IS **MEAT,** LITTLE BROTHERS. ONCE I'VE CARVED HIM AND DRESSED HIM--
--**NOBODY** IS GOING TO KNOW THE DIFFERENCE.

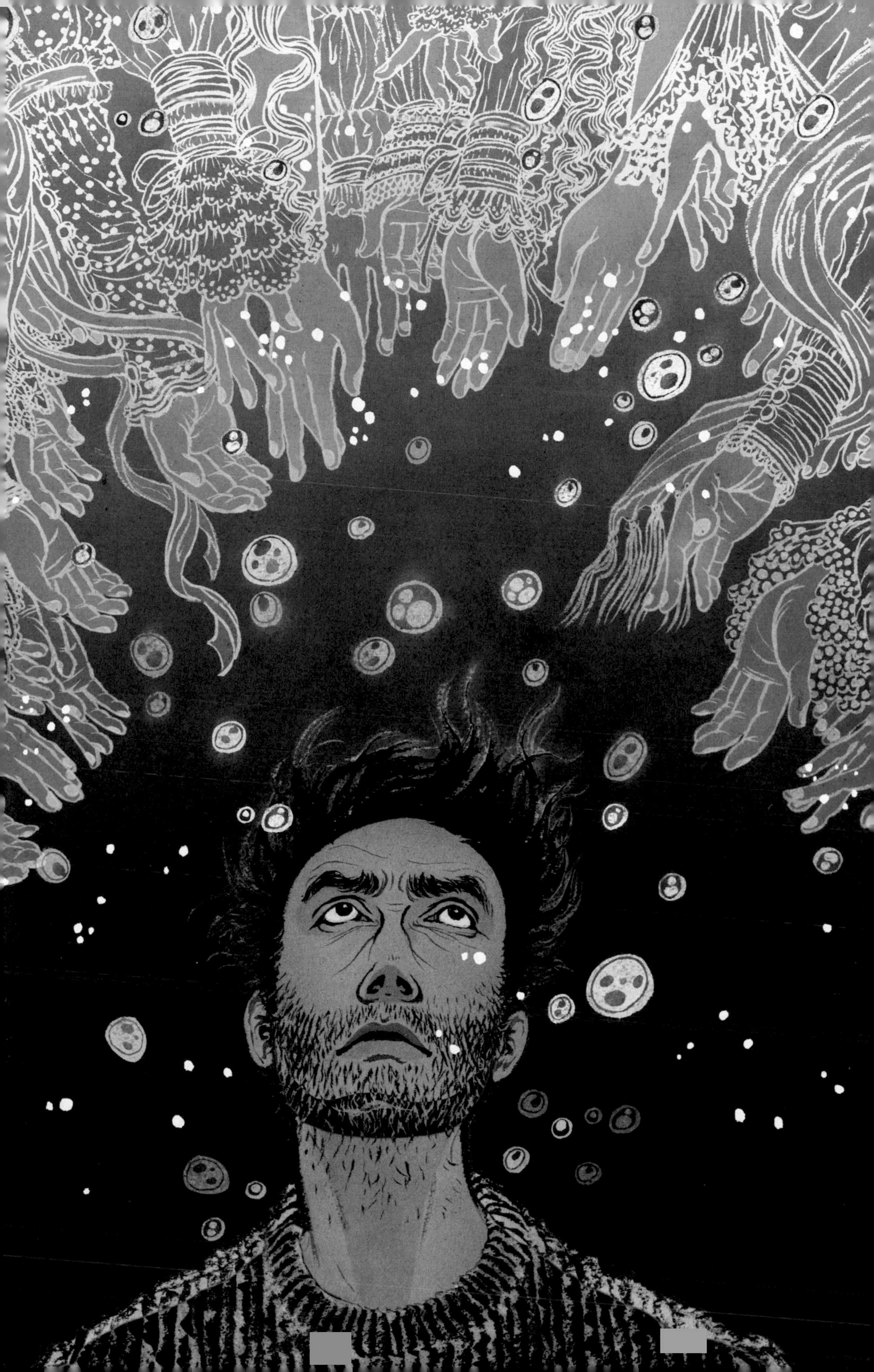

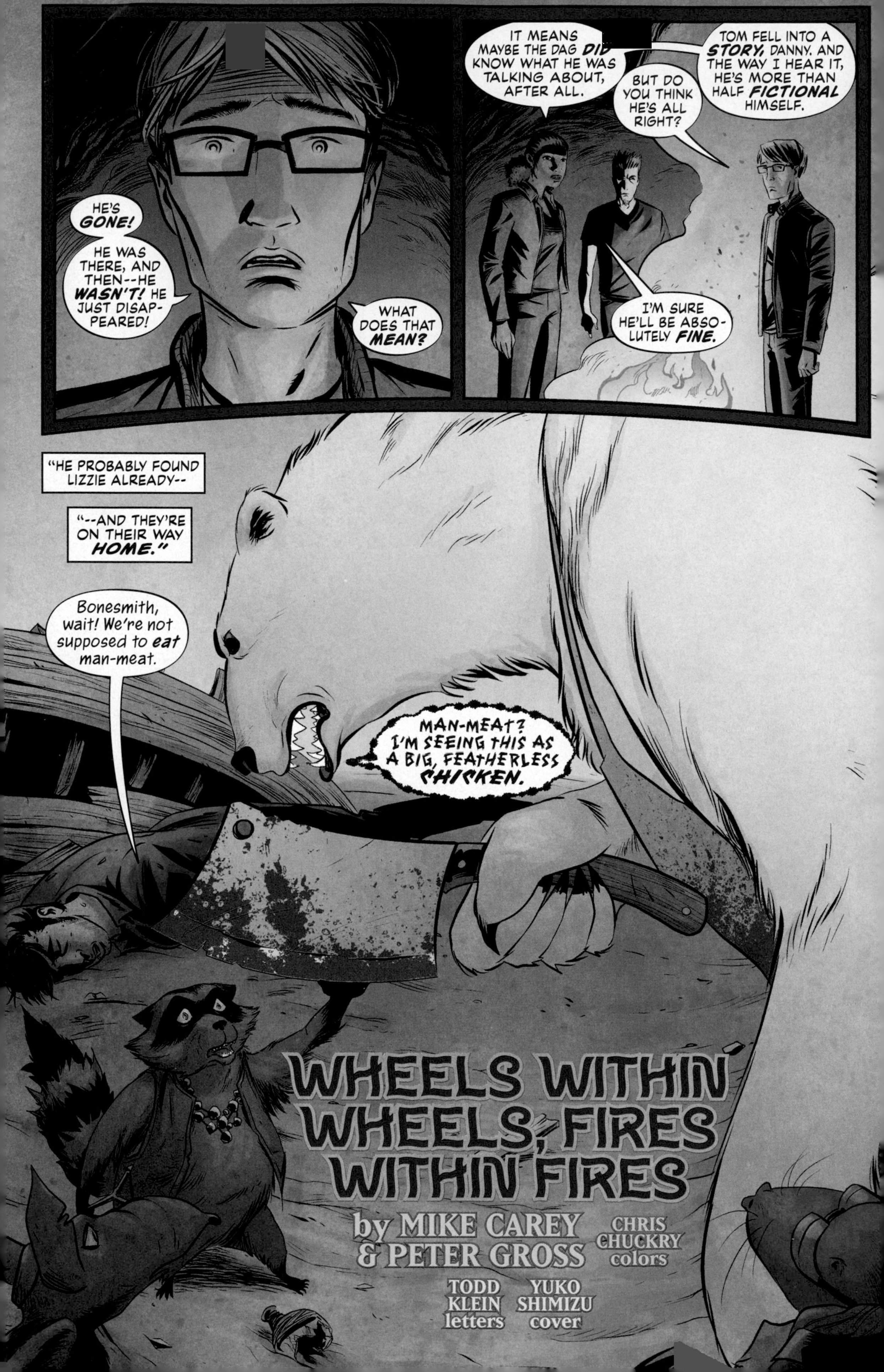
HE'S GONE!
HE WAS THERE, AND THEN--HE WASN'T! HE JUST DISAPPEARED!
WHAT DOES THAT MEAN?
IT MEANS MAYBE THE DAG DID KNOW WHAT HE WAS TALKING ABOUT, AFTER ALL.
BUT DO YOU THINK HE'S ALL RIGHT?
TOM FELL INTO A STORY, DANNY. AND THE WAY I HEAR IT, HE'S MORE THAN HALF FICTIONAL HIMSELF.
I'M SURE HE'LL BE ABSOLUTELY FINE.
"HE PROBABLY FOUND LIZZIE ALREADY--
"--AND THEY'RE ON THEIR WAY HOME."
Bonesmith, wait! We're not supposed to eat man-meat.
MAN-MEAT? I'M SEEING THIS AS A BIG, FEATHERLESS CHICKEN.
WHEELS WITHIN WHEELS, FIRES WITHIN FIRES
by MIKE CAREY & PETER GROSS
CHRIS CHUCKRY colors
TODD KLEIN letters
YUKO SHIMIZU cover

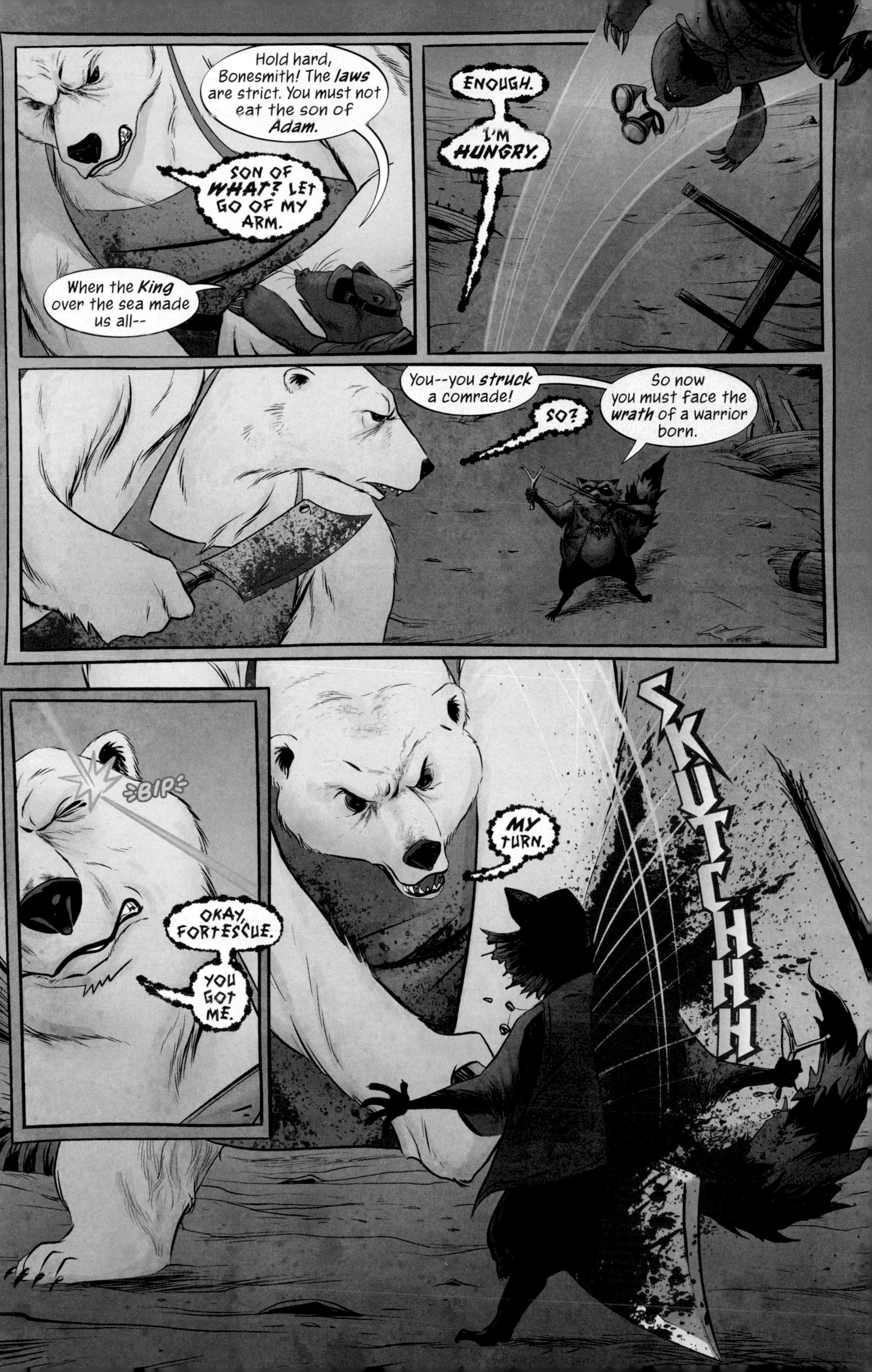

Hold hard, Bonesmith! The *laws* are strict. You must not eat the son of *Adam.*
SON OF *WHAT?* LET GO OF MY ARM.
When the *King* over the sea made us all--
ENOUGH.
I'M *HUNGRY.*
You--you *struck* a comrade!
SO?
So now you must face the *wrath* of a warrior born.
BIP
OKAY, FORTESCUE.
YOU GOT ME.
MY TURN.
SKUTCHHH

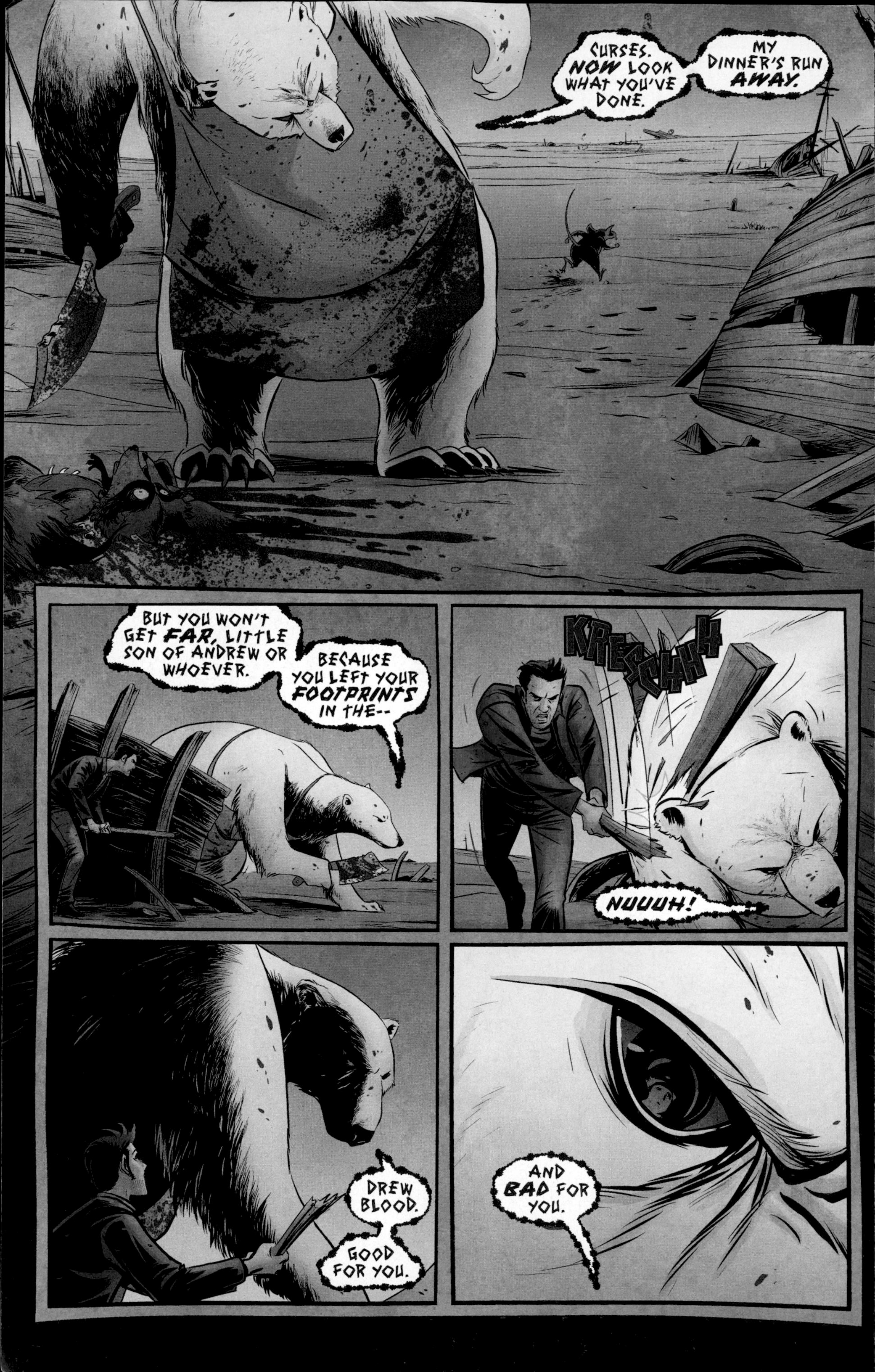
CURSES. NOW LOOK WHAT YOU'VE DONE.
MY DINNER'S RUN AWAY.
BUT YOU WON'T GET FAR, LITTLE SON OF ANDREW OR WHOEVER.
BECAUSE YOU LEFT YOUR FOOTPRINTS IN THE--
KRESCHHH
NUUUH!
DREW BLOOD.
GOOD FOR YOU.
AND BAD FOR YOU.

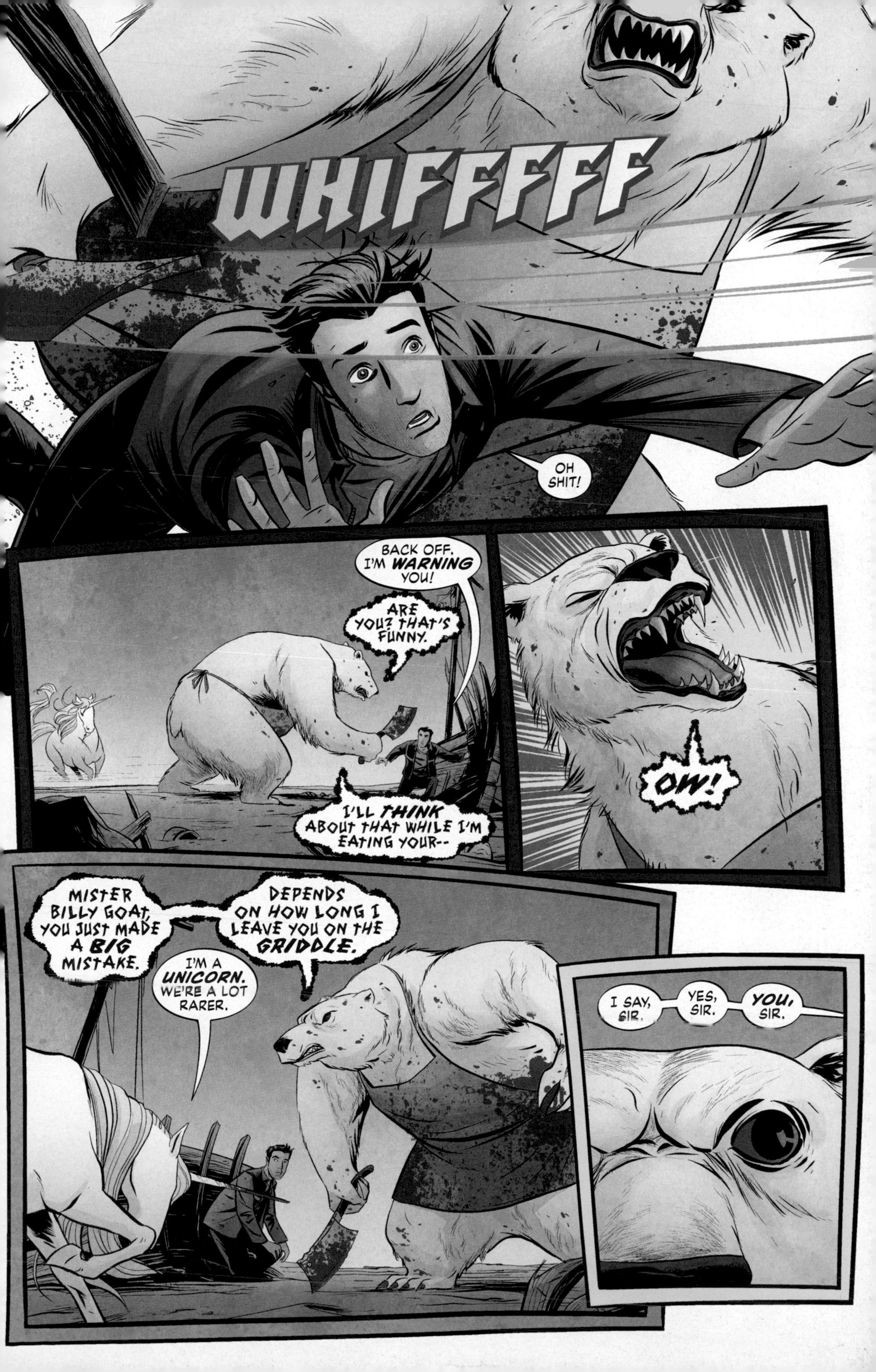

WHIFFFFF
OH SHIT!
BACK OFF. I'M WARNING YOU!
ARE YOU? THAT'S FUNNY.
I'LL THINK ABOUT THAT WHILE I'M EATING YOUR--
OW!
MISTER BILLY GOAT, YOU JUST MADE A BIG MISTAKE.
I'M A UNICORN. WE'RE A LOT RARER.
DEPENDS ON HOW LONG I LEAVE YOU ON THE GRIDDLE.
I SAY, SIR.
YES, SIR.
YOU, SIR.

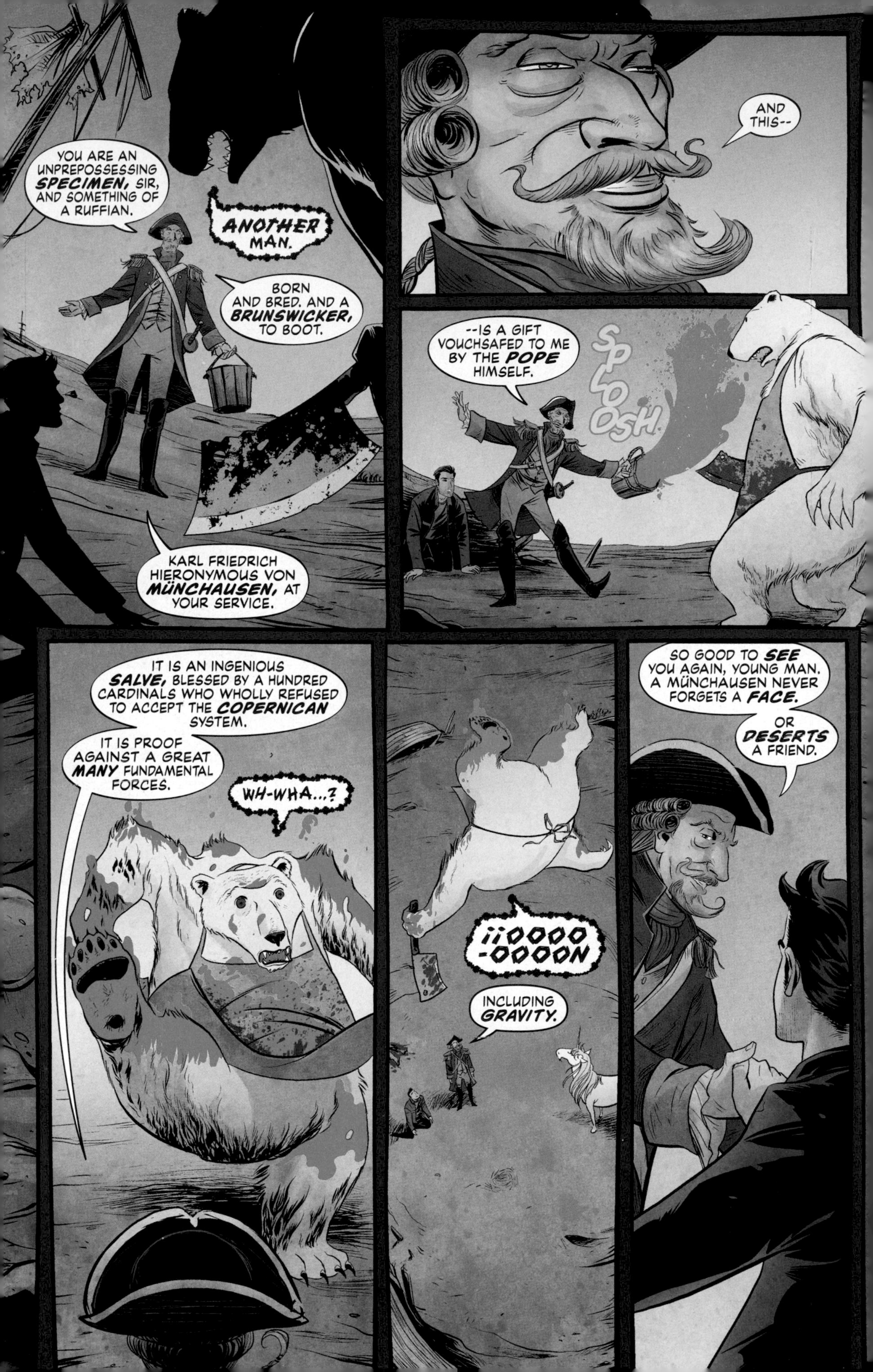
YOU ARE AN UNPREPOSSESSING SPECIMEN, SIR, AND SOMETHING OF A RUFFIAN.
ANOTHER MAN.
BORN AND BRED. AND A BRUNSWICKER, TO BOOT.
KARL FRIEDRICH HIERONYMOUS VON MÜNCHAUSEN, AT YOUR SERVICE.
AND THIS--
--IS A GIFT VOUCHSAFED TO ME BY THE POPE HIMSELF.
SPLOOSH
IT IS AN INGENIOUS SALVE, BLESSED BY A HUNDRED CARDINALS WHO WHOLLY REFUSED TO ACCEPT THE COPERNICAN SYSTEM.
IT IS PROOF AGAINST A GREAT MANY FUNDAMENTAL FORCES.
WH-WHA...?
¡¡OOOO-OOOON
INCLUDING GRAVITY.
SO GOOD TO SEE YOU AGAIN, YOUNG MAN. A MÜNCHAUSEN NEVER FORGETS A FACE.
OR DESERTS A FRIEND.

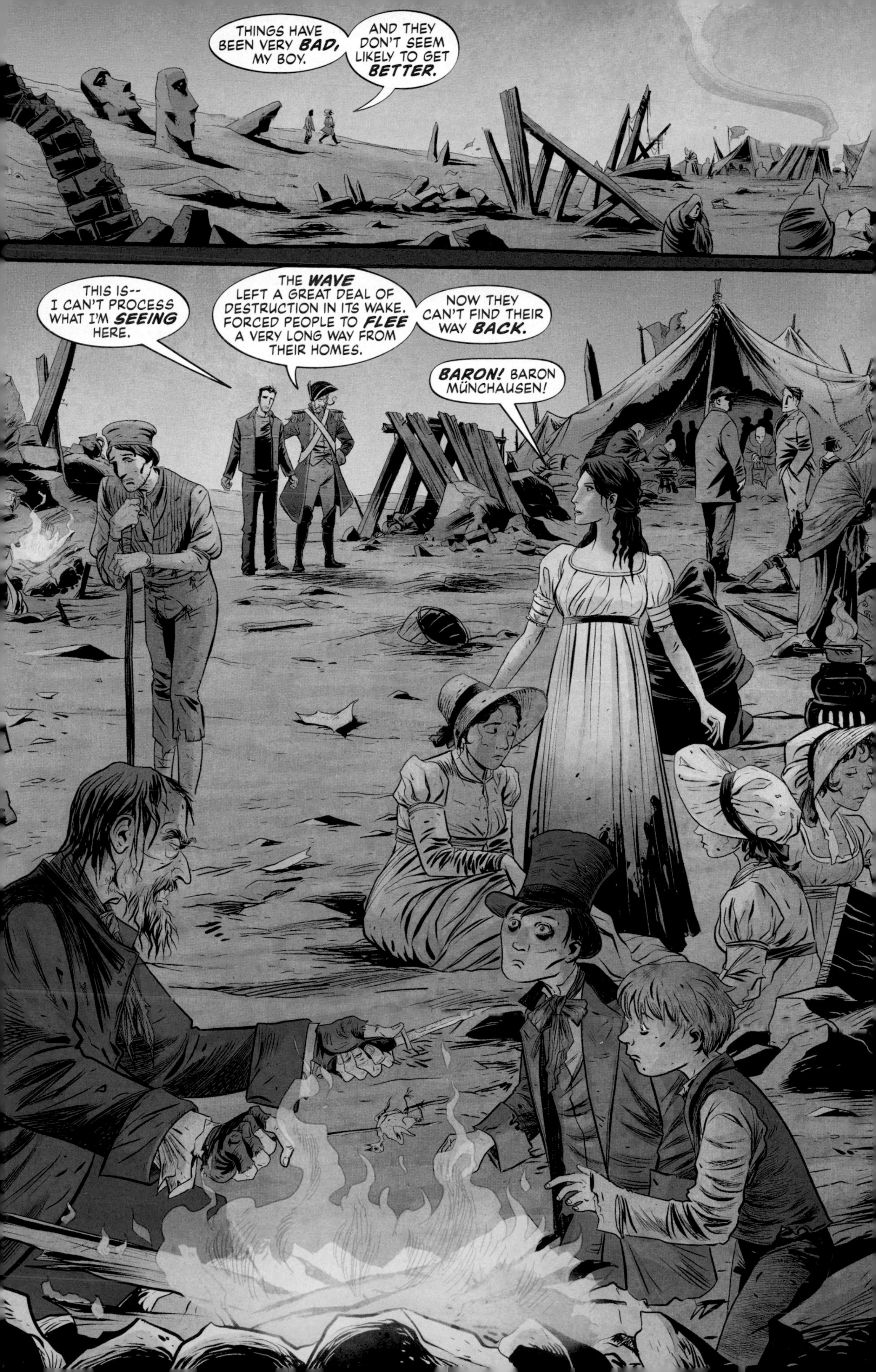
THINGS HAVE BEEN VERY BAD, MY BOY.
AND THEY DON'T SEEM LIKELY TO GET BETTER.
THIS IS-- I CAN'T PROCESS WHAT I'M SEEING HERE.
THE WAVE LEFT A GREAT DEAL OF DESTRUCTION IN ITS WAKE. FORCED PEOPLE TO FLEE A VERY LONG WAY FROM THEIR HOMES.
NOW THEY CAN'T FIND THEIR WAY BACK.
BARON! BARON MÜNCHAUSEN!

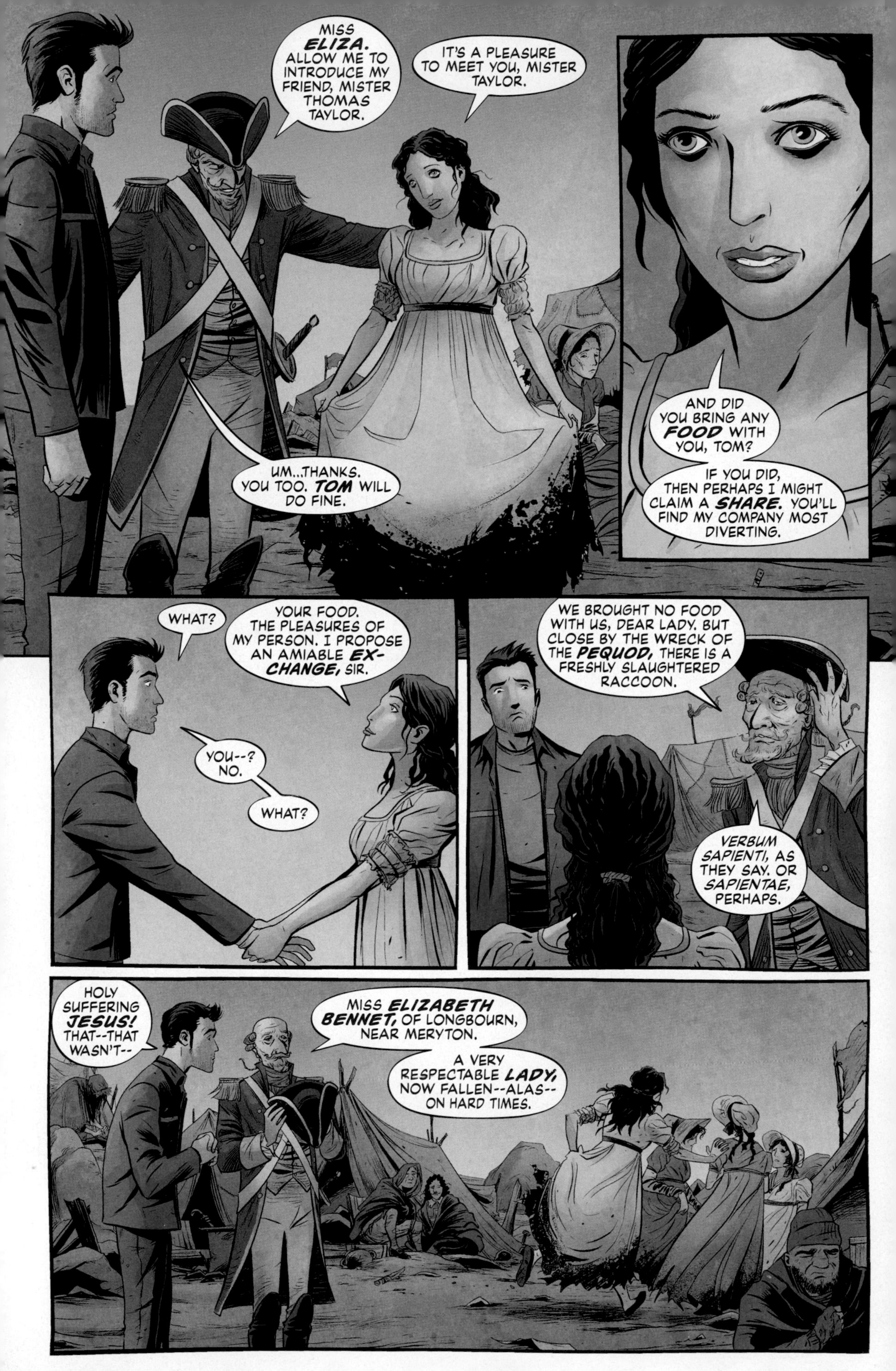
MISS ELIZA. ALLOW ME TO INTRODUCE MY FRIEND, MISTER THOMAS TAYLOR.
IT'S A PLEASURE TO MEET YOU, MISTER TAYLOR.
UM...THANKS. YOU TOO. TOM WILL DO FINE.
AND DID YOU BRING ANY FOOD WITH YOU, TOM?
IF YOU DID, THEN PERHAPS I MIGHT CLAIM A SHARE. YOU'LL FIND MY COMPANY MOST DIVERTING.
WHAT?
YOUR FOOD. THE PLEASURES OF MY PERSON. I PROPOSE AN AMIABLE EX-CHANGE, SIR.
YOU--? NO.
WHAT?
WE BROUGHT NO FOOD WITH US, DEAR LADY. BUT CLOSE BY THE WRECK OF THE PEQUOD, THERE IS A FRESHLY SLAUGHTERED RACCOON.
VERBUM SAPIENTI, AS THEY SAY. OR SAPIENTAE, PERHAPS.
HOLY SUFFERING JESUS! THAT--THAT WASN'T--
MISS ELIZABETH BENNET, OF LONGBOURN, NEAR MERYTON.
A VERY RESPECTABLE LADY, NOW FALLEN--ALAS--ON HARD TIMES.

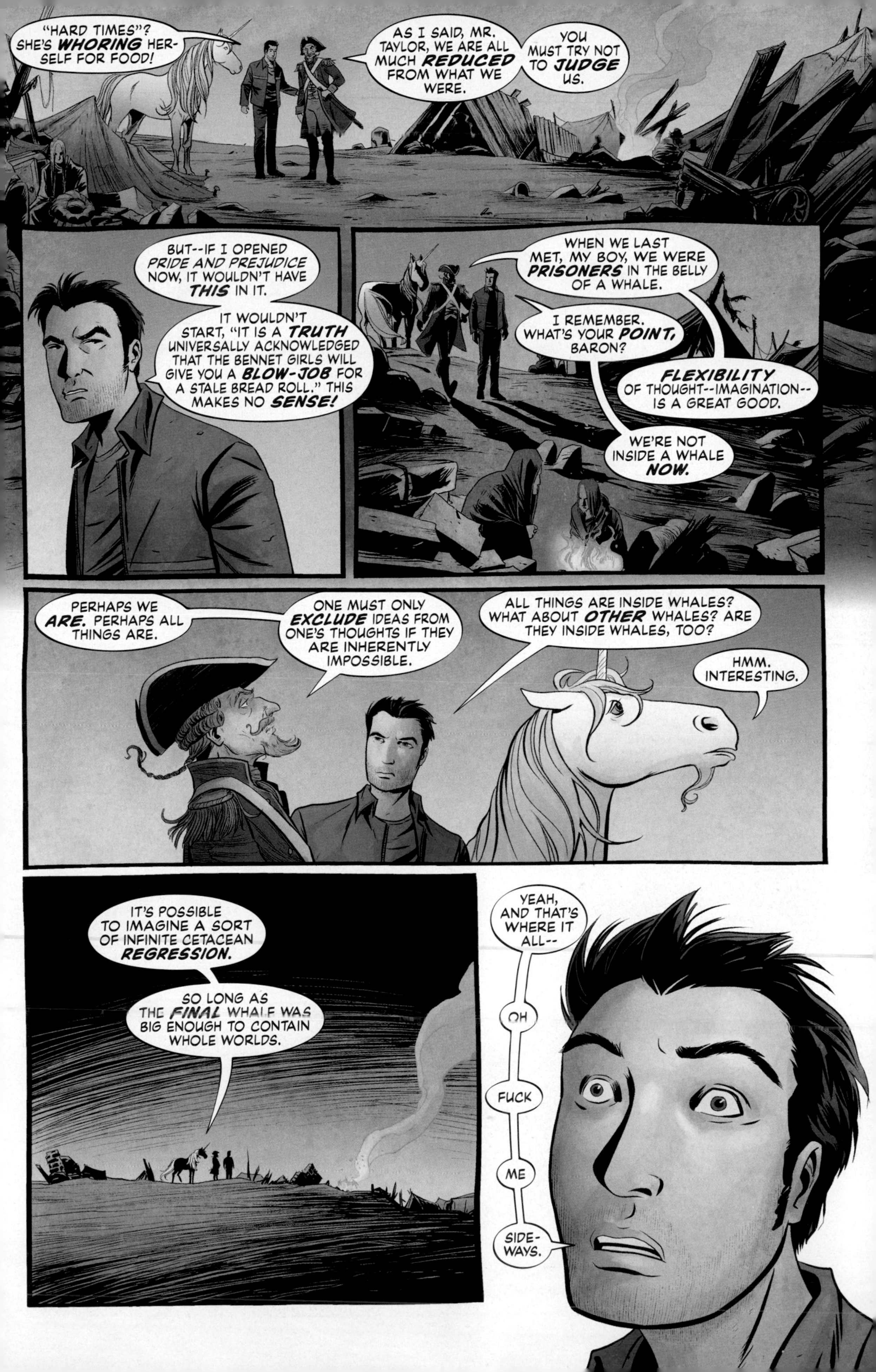
"HARD TIMES"? SHE'S WHORING HER-SELF FOR FOOD!
AS I SAID, MR. TAYLOR, WE ARE ALL MUCH REDUCED FROM WHAT WE WERE.
YOU MUST TRY NOT TO JUDGE US.
BUT--IF I OPENED PRIDE AND PREJUDICE NOW, IT WOULDN'T HAVE THIS IN IT.
IT WOULDN'T START, "IT IS A TRUTH UNIVERSALLY ACKNOWLEDGED THAT THE BENNET GIRLS WILL GIVE YOU A BLOW-JOB FOR A STALE BREAD ROLL." THIS MAKES NO SENSE!
WHEN WE LAST MET, MY BOY, WE WERE PRISONERS IN THE BELLY OF A WHALE.
I REMEMBER. WHAT'S YOUR POINT, BARON?
FLEXIBILITY OF THOUGHT--IMAGINATION--IS A GREAT GOOD.
WE'RE NOT INSIDE A WHALE NOW.
PERHAPS WE ARE. PERHAPS ALL THINGS ARE.
ONE MUST ONLY EXCLUDE IDEAS FROM ONE'S THOUGHTS IF THEY ARE INHERENTLY IMPOSSIBLE.
ALL THINGS ARE INSIDE WHALES? WHAT ABOUT OTHER WHALES? ARE THEY INSIDE WHALES, TOO?
HMM. INTERESTING.
IT'S POSSIBLE TO IMAGINE A SORT OF INFINITE CETACEAN REGRESSION.
SO LONG AS THE FINAL WHALE WAS BIG ENOUGH TO CONTAIN WHOLE WORLDS.
YEAH, AND THAT'S WHERE IT ALL--
OH
FUCK
ME
SIDE-WAYS.

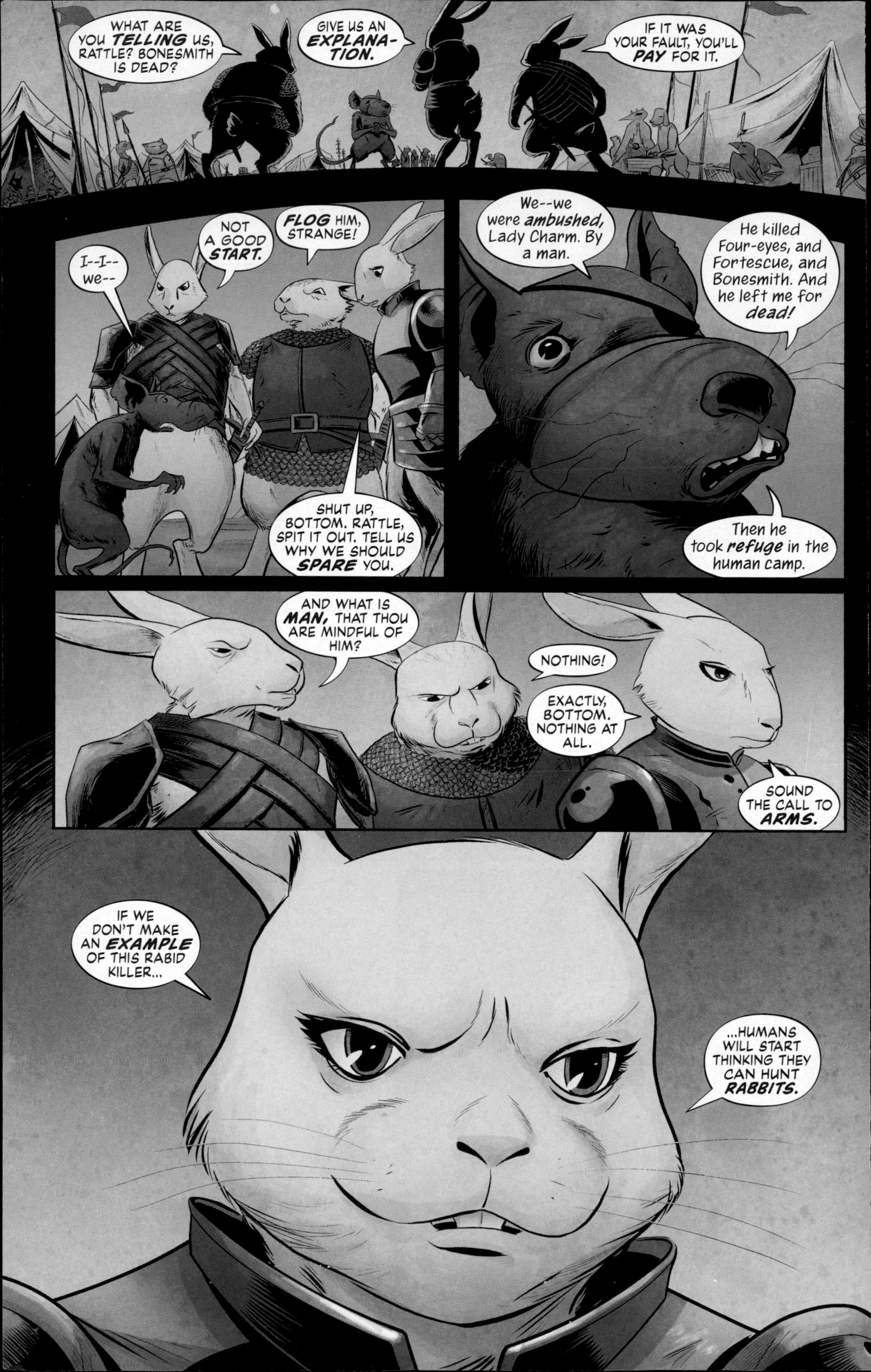
WHAT ARE YOU TELLING US, RATTLE? BONESMITH IS DEAD?
GIVE US AN EXPLANATION.
IF IT WAS YOUR FAULT, YOU'LL PAY FOR IT.
I--I-- we--
NOT A GOOD START.
FLOG HIM, STRANGE!
SHUT UP, BOTTOM. RATTLE, SPIT IT OUT. TELL US WHY WE SHOULD SPARE YOU.
We--we were ambushed, Lady Charm. By a man.
He killed Four-eyes, and Fortescue, and Bonesmith. And he left me for dead!
Then he took refuge in the human camp.
AND WHAT IS MAN, THAT THOU ARE MINDFUL OF HIM?
NOTHING!
EXACTLY, BOTTOM. NOTHING AT ALL.
SOUND THE CALL TO ARMS.
IF WE DON'T MAKE AN EXAMPLE OF THIS RABID KILLER...
...HUMANS WILL START THINKING THEY CAN HUNT RABBITS.

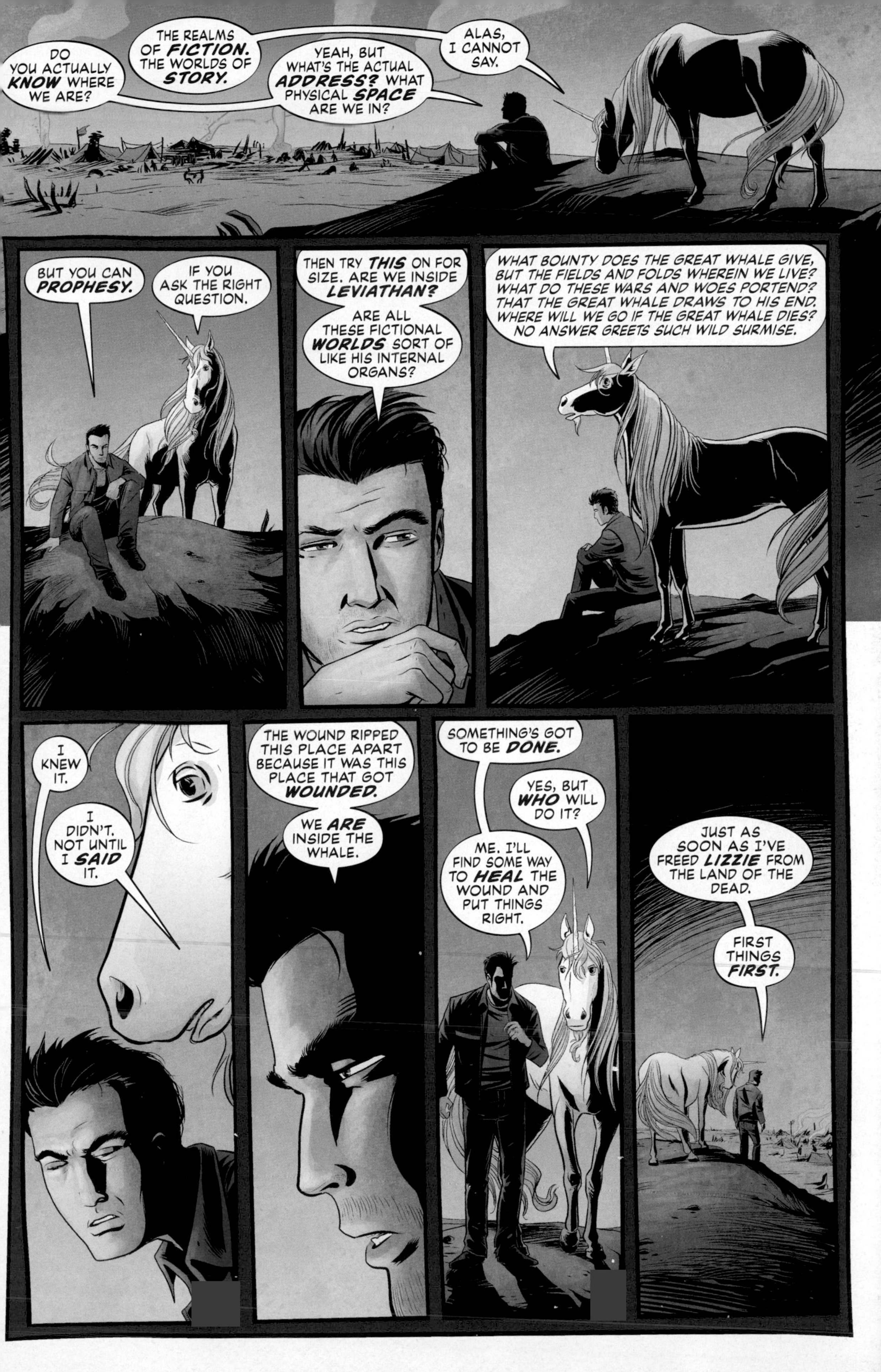
DO YOU ACTUALLY KNOW WHERE WE ARE?
THE REALMS OF FICTION. THE WORLDS OF STORY.
YEAH, BUT WHAT'S THE ACTUAL ADDRESS? WHAT PHYSICAL SPACE ARE WE IN?
ALAS, I CANNOT SAY.
BUT YOU CAN PROPHESY.
IF YOU ASK THE RIGHT QUESTION.
THEN TRY THIS ON FOR SIZE. ARE WE INSIDE LEVIATHAN?
ARE ALL THESE FICTIONAL WORLDS SORT OF LIKE HIS INTERNAL ORGANS?
WHAT BOUNTY DOES THE GREAT WHALE GIVE, BUT THE FIELDS AND FOLDS WHEREIN WE LIVE? WHAT DO THESE WARS AND WOES PORTEND? THAT THE GREAT WHALE DRAWS TO HIS END. WHERE WILL WE GO IF THE GREAT WHALE DIES? NO ANSWER GREETS SUCH WILD SURMISE.
I KNEW IT.
I DIDN'T. NOT UNTIL I SAID IT.
THE WOUND RIPPED THIS PLACE APART BECAUSE IT WAS THIS PLACE THAT GOT WOUNDED.
WE ARE INSIDE THE WHALE.
SOMETHING'S GOT TO BE DONE.
YES, BUT WHO WILL DO IT?
ME. I'LL FIND SOME WAY TO HEAL THE WOUND AND PUT THINGS RIGHT.
JUST AS SOON AS I'VE FREED LIZZIE FROM THE LAND OF THE DEAD.
FIRST THINGS FIRST.

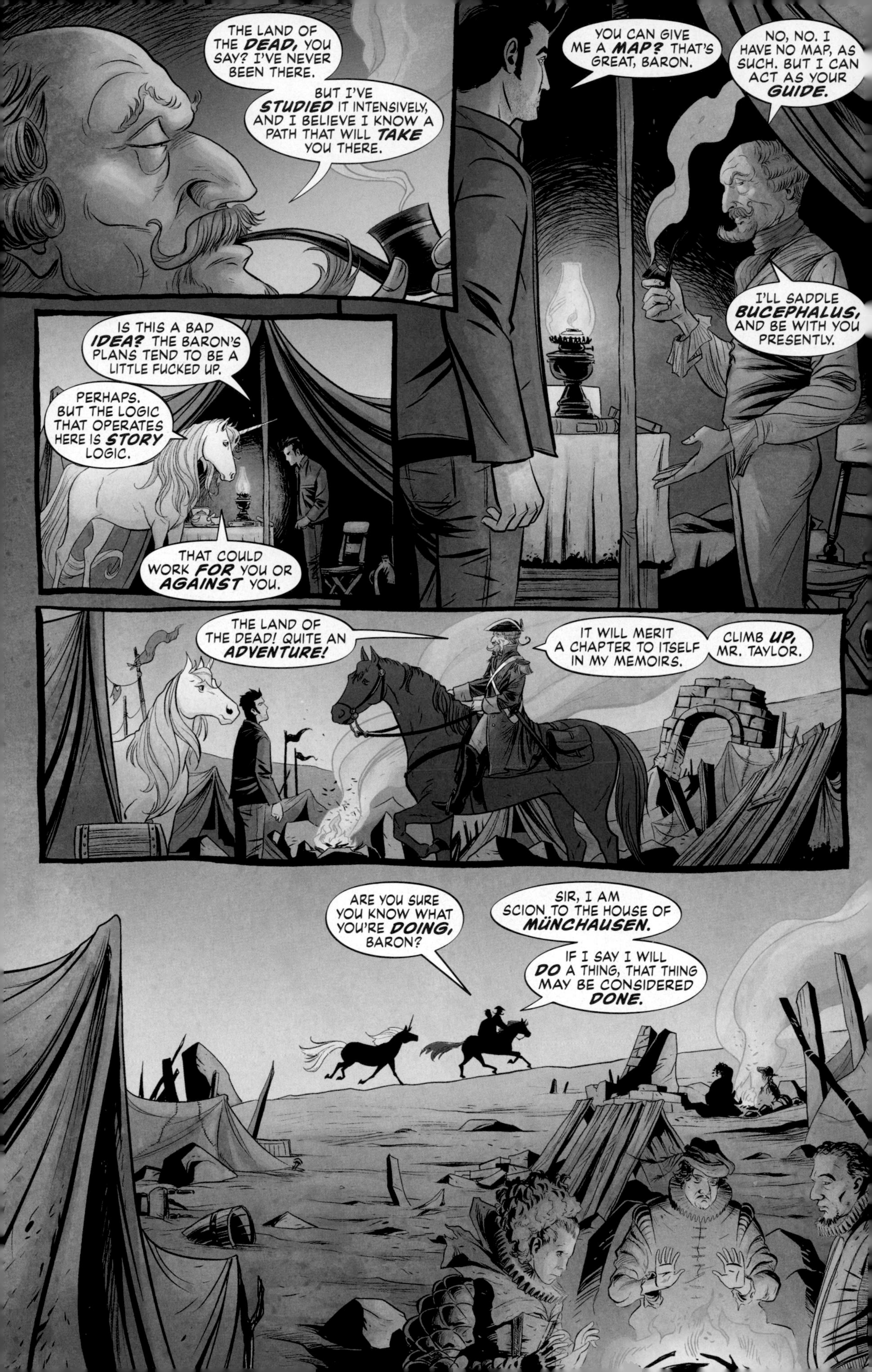
THE LAND OF THE DEAD, YOU SAY? I'VE NEVER BEEN THERE.
BUT I'VE STUDIED IT INTENSIVELY, AND I BELIEVE I KNOW A PATH THAT WILL TAKE YOU THERE.
YOU CAN GIVE ME A MAP? THAT'S GREAT, BARON.
NO, NO. I HAVE NO MAP, AS SUCH. BUT I CAN ACT AS YOUR GUIDE.
I'LL SADDLE BUCEPHALUS, AND BE WITH YOU PRESENTLY.
IS THIS A BAD IDEA? THE BARON'S PLANS TEND TO BE A LITTLE FUCKED UP.
PERHAPS. BUT THE LOGIC THAT OPERATES HERE IS STORY LOGIC.
THAT COULD WORK FOR YOU OR AGAINST YOU.
THE LAND OF THE DEAD! QUITE AN ADVENTURE!
IT WILL MERIT A CHAPTER TO ITSELF IN MY MEMOIRS.
CLIMB UP, MR. TAYLOR.
ARE YOU SURE YOU KNOW WHAT YOU'RE DOING, BARON?
SIR, I AM SCION TO THE HOUSE OF MÜNCHAUSEN.
IF I SAY I WILL DO A THING, THAT THING MAY BE CONSIDERED DONE.

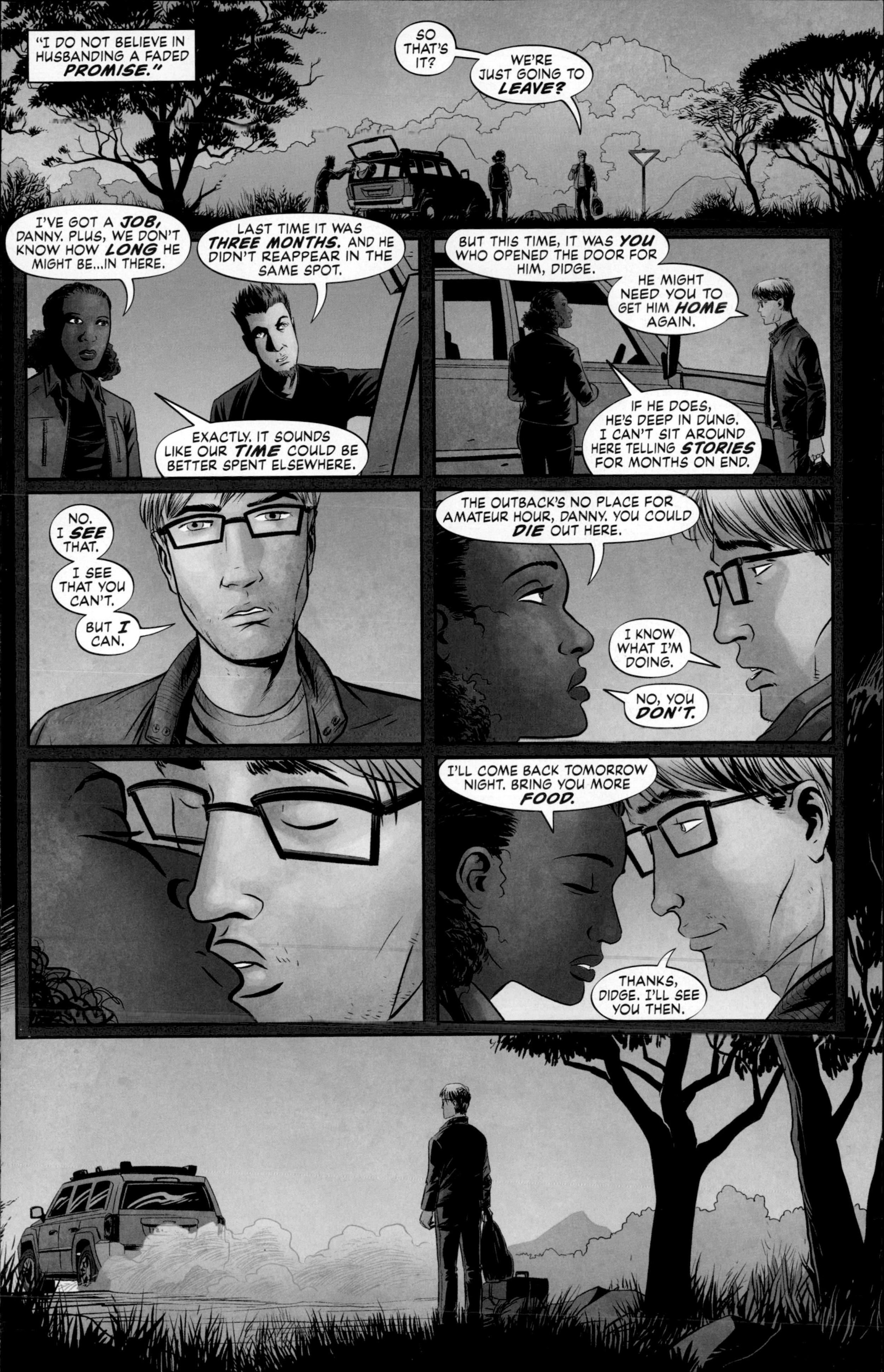
"I DO NOT BELIEVE IN HUSBANDING A FADED PROMISE."
SO THAT'S IT?
WE'RE JUST GOING TO LEAVE?
I'VE GOT A JOB, DANNY. PLUS, WE DON'T KNOW HOW LONG HE MIGHT BE...IN THERE.
LAST TIME IT WAS THREE MONTHS. AND HE DIDN'T REAPPEAR IN THE SAME SPOT.
EXACTLY. IT SOUNDS LIKE OUR TIME COULD BE BETTER SPENT ELSEWHERE.
BUT THIS TIME, IT WAS YOU WHO OPENED THE DOOR FOR HIM, DIDGE.
HE MIGHT NEED YOU TO GET HIM HOME AGAIN.
IF HE DOES, HE'S DEEP IN DUNG. I CAN'T SIT AROUND HERE TELLING STORIES FOR MONTHS ON END.
NO. I SEE THAT.
I SEE THAT YOU CAN'T.
BUT I CAN.
THE OUTBACK'S NO PLACE FOR AMATEUR HOUR, DANNY. YOU COULD DIE OUT HERE.
I KNOW WHAT I'M DOING.
NO, YOU DON'T.
I'LL COME BACK TOMORROW NIGHT. BRING YOU MORE FOOD.
THANKS, DIDGE. I'LL SEE YOU THEN.

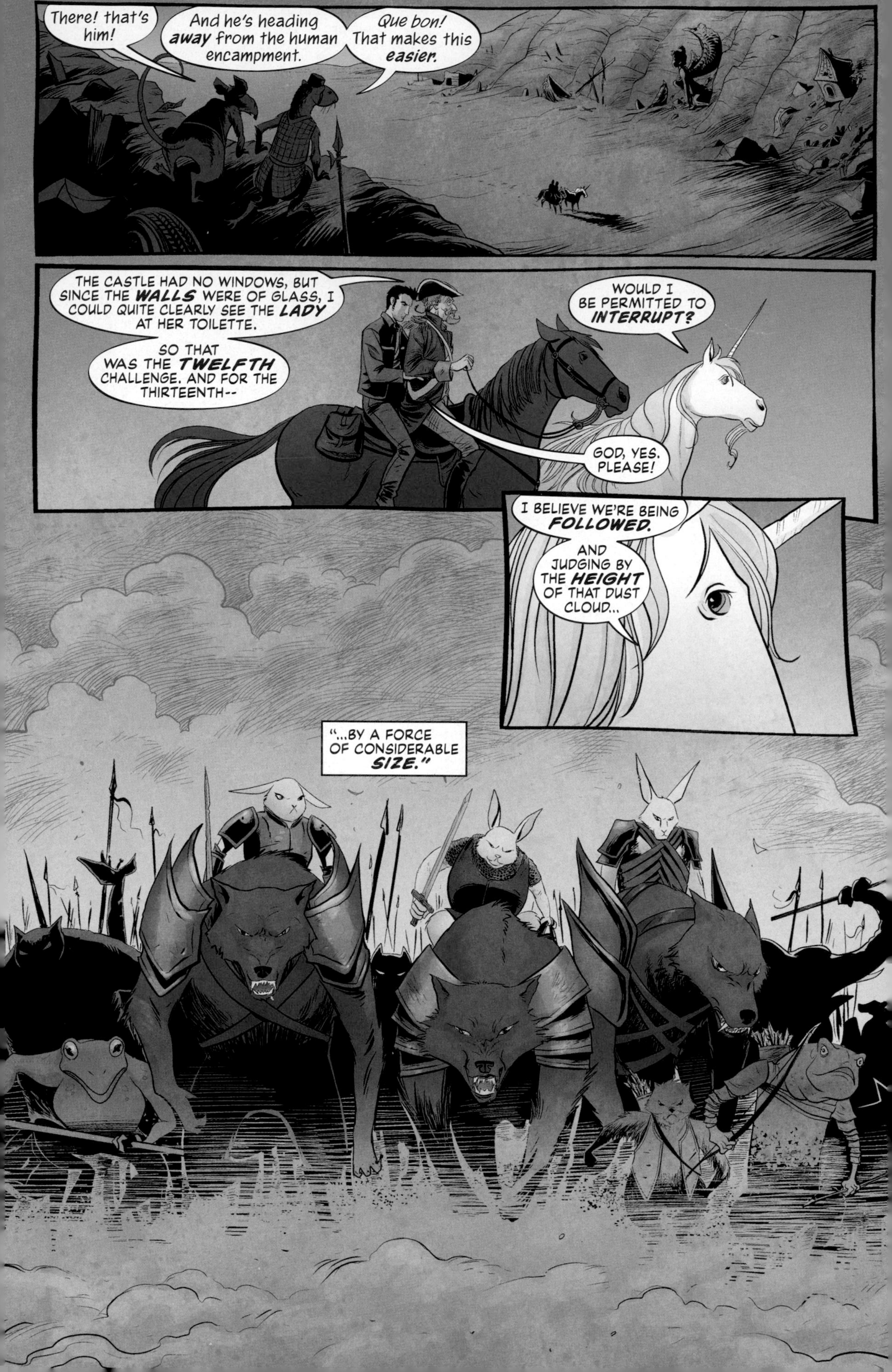
There! that's him!
And he's heading away from the human encampment.
Que bon! That makes this easier.
THE CASTLE HAD NO WINDOWS, BUT SINCE THE WALLS WERE OF GLASS, I COULD QUITE CLEARLY SEE THE LADY AT HER TOILETTE.
SO THAT WAS THE TWELFTH CHALLENGE. AND FOR THE THIRTEENTH--
WOULD I BE PERMITTED TO INTERRUPT?
GOD, YES. PLEASE!
I BELIEVE WE'RE BEING FOLLOWED.
AND JUDGING BY THE HEIGHT OF THAT DUST CLOUD...
"...BY A FORCE OF CONSIDERABLE SIZE."

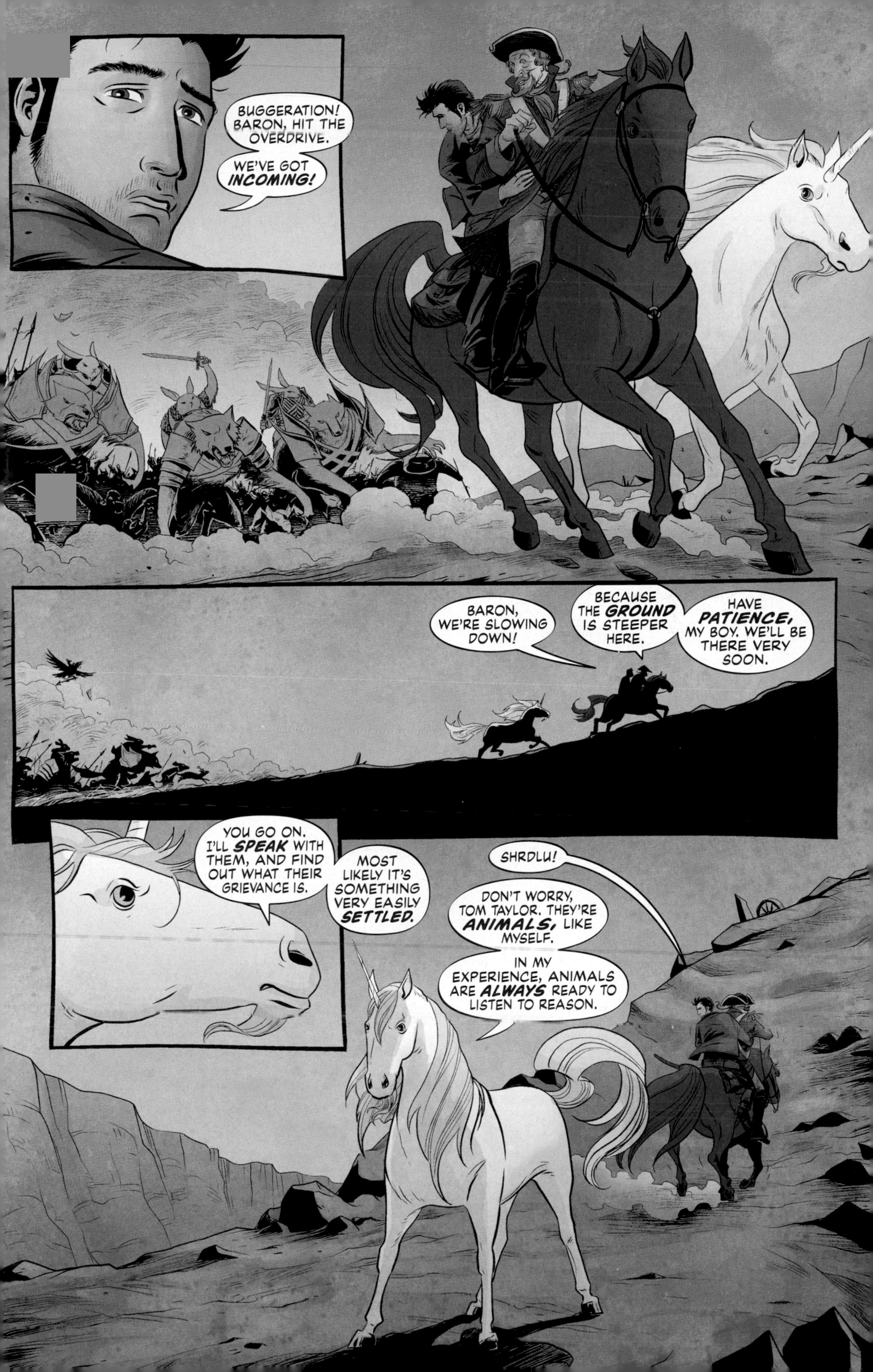

BUGGERATION! BARON, HIT THE OVERDRIVE.
WE'VE GOT INCOMING!
BARON, WE'RE SLOWING DOWN!
BECAUSE THE GROUND IS STEEPER HERE.
HAVE PATIENCE, MY BOY. WE'LL BE THERE VERY SOON.
YOU GO ON. I'LL SPEAK WITH THEM, AND FIND OUT WHAT THEIR GRIEVANCE IS.
MOST LIKELY IT'S SOMETHING VERY EASILY SETTLED.
SHRDLU!
DON'T WORRY, TOM TAYLOR. THEY'RE ANIMALS, LIKE MYSELF.
IN MY EXPERIENCE, ANIMALS ARE ALWAYS READY TO LISTEN TO REASON.

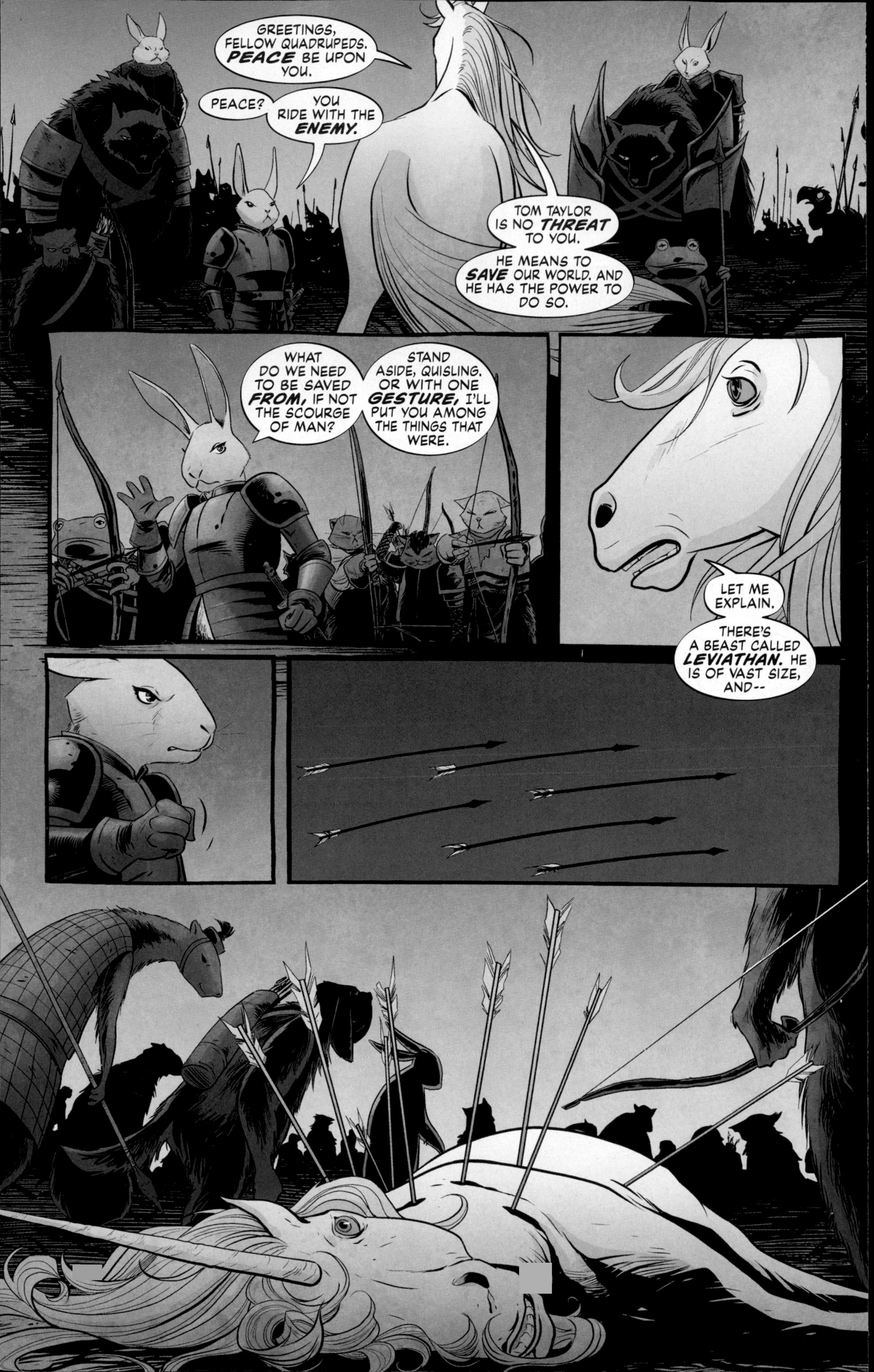
GREETINGS, FELLOW QUADRUPEDS. PEACE BE UPON YOU.
PEACE?
YOU RIDE WITH THE ENEMY.
TOM TAYLOR IS NO THREAT TO YOU.
HE MEANS TO SAVE OUR WORLD. AND HE HAS THE POWER TO DO SO.
WHAT DO WE NEED TO BE SAVED FROM, IF NOT THE SCOURGE OF MAN?
STAND ASIDE, QUISLING. OR WITH ONE GESTURE, I'LL PUT YOU AMONG THE THINGS THAT WERE.
LET ME EXPLAIN.
THERE'S A BEAST CALLED LEVIATHAN. HE IS OF VAST SIZE, AND--

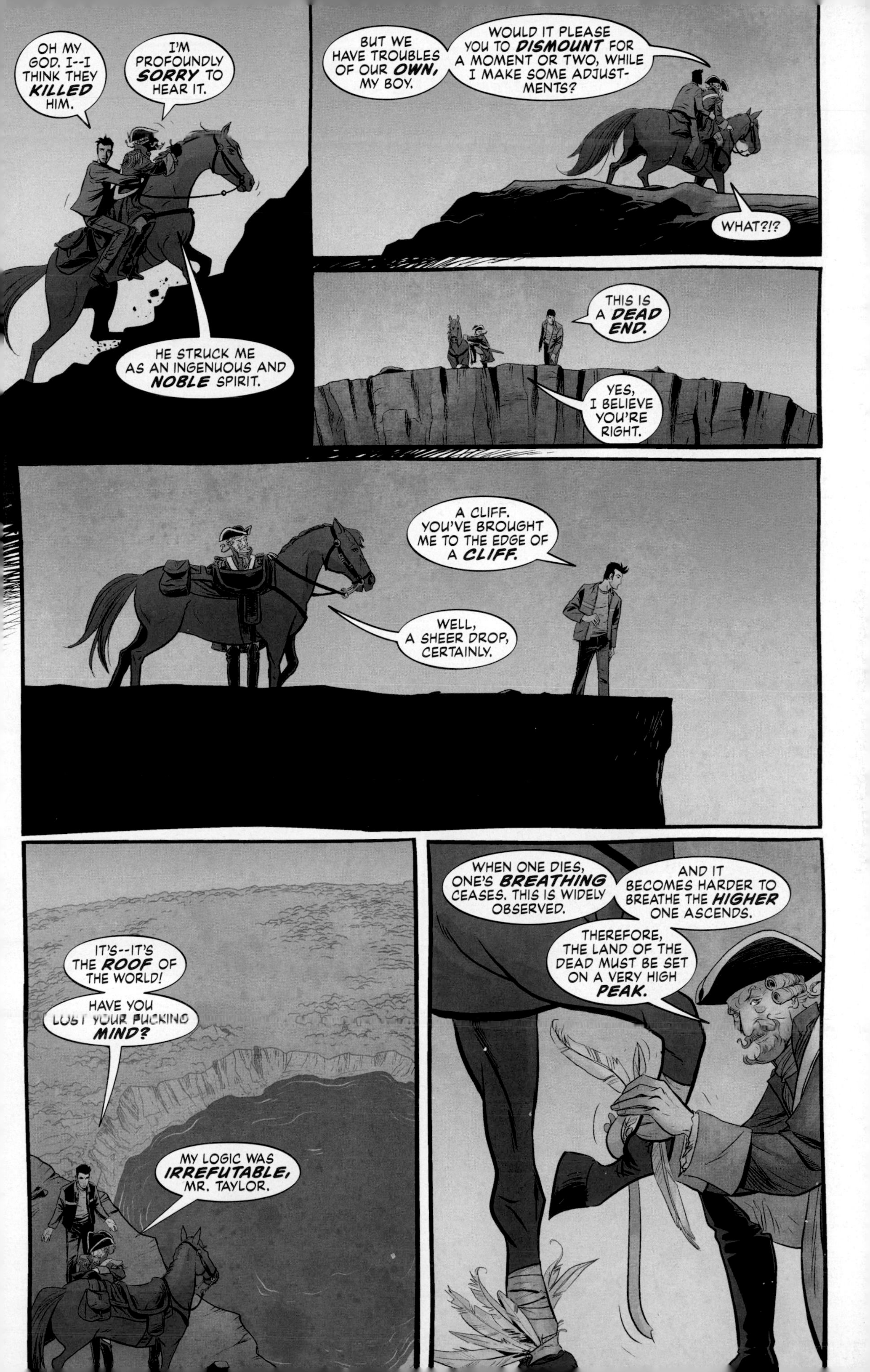
OH MY GOD. I--I THINK THEY KILLED HIM.
I'M PROFOUNDLY SORRY TO HEAR IT.
HE STRUCK ME AS AN INGENUOUS AND NOBLE SPIRIT.
BUT WE HAVE TROUBLES OF OUR OWN, MY BOY.
WOULD IT PLEASE YOU TO DISMOUNT FOR A MOMENT OR TWO, WHILE I MAKE SOME ADJUSTMENTS?
WHAT?!?
THIS IS A DEAD END.
YES, I BELIEVE YOU'RE RIGHT.
A CLIFF. YOU'VE BROUGHT ME TO THE EDGE OF A CLIFF.
WELL, A SHEER DROP, CERTAINLY.
IT'S--IT'S THE ROOF OF THE WORLD!
HAVE YOU LOST YOUR FUCKING MIND?
MY LOGIC WAS IRREFUTABLE, MR. TAYLOR.
WHEN ONE DIES, ONE'S BREATHING CEASES. THIS IS WIDELY OBSERVED.
AND IT BECOMES HARDER TO BREATHE THE HIGHER ONE ASCENDS.
THEREFORE, THE LAND OF THE DEAD MUST BE SET ON A VERY HIGH PEAK.

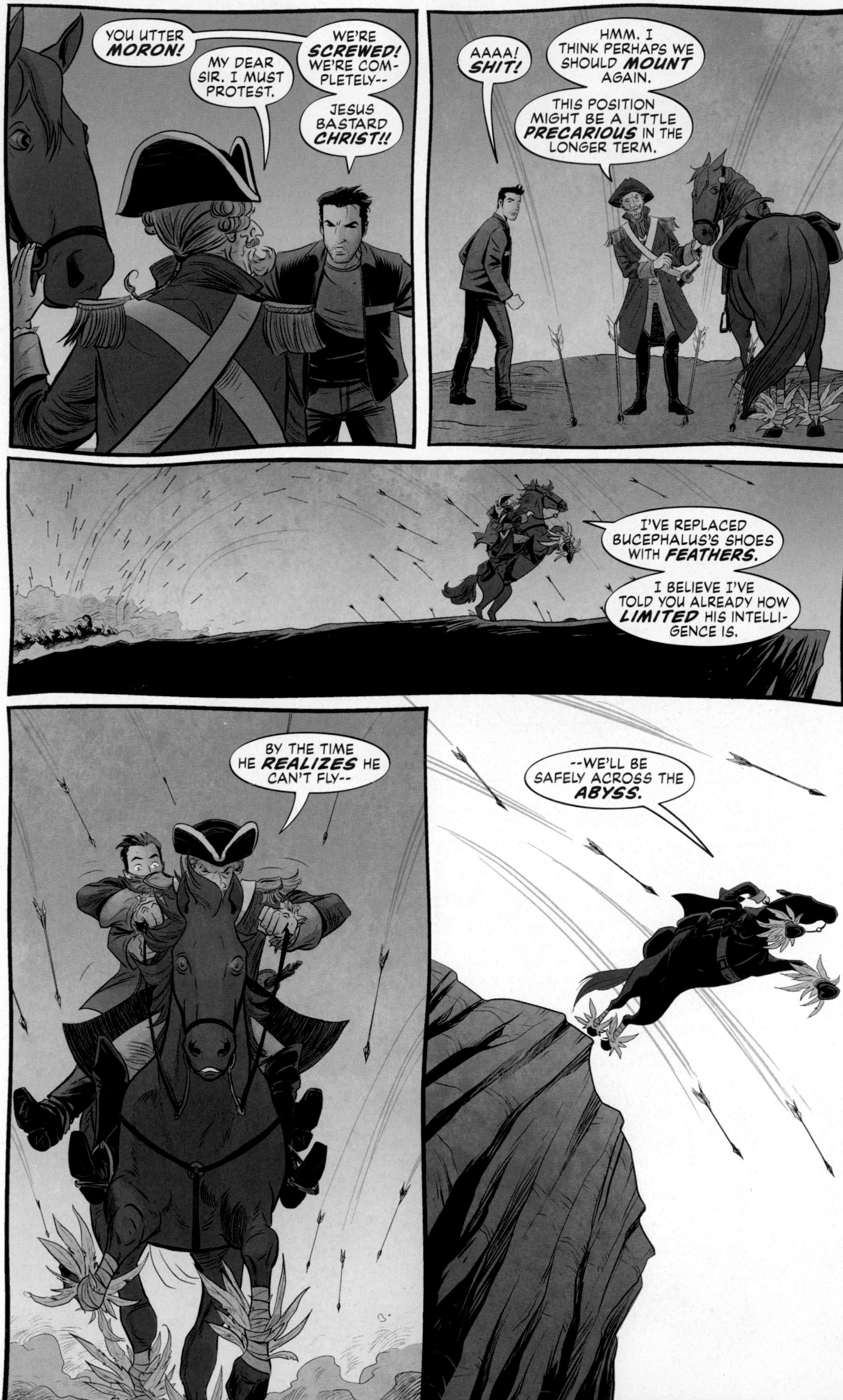
YOU UTTER MORON!
WE'RE SCREWED! WE'RE COMPLETELY--
MY DEAR SIR. I MUST PROTEST.
JESUS BASTARD CHRIST!!
AAAA! SHIT!
HMM. I THINK PERHAPS WE SHOULD MOUNT AGAIN.
THIS POSITION MIGHT BE A LITTLE PRECARIOUS IN THE LONGER TERM.
I'VE REPLACED BUCEPHALUS'S SHOES WITH FEATHERS.
I BELIEVE I'VE TOLD YOU ALREADY HOW LIMITED HIS INTELLIGENCE IS.
BY THE TIME HE REALIZES HE CAN'T FLY--
--WE'LL BE SAFELY ACROSS THE ABYSS.

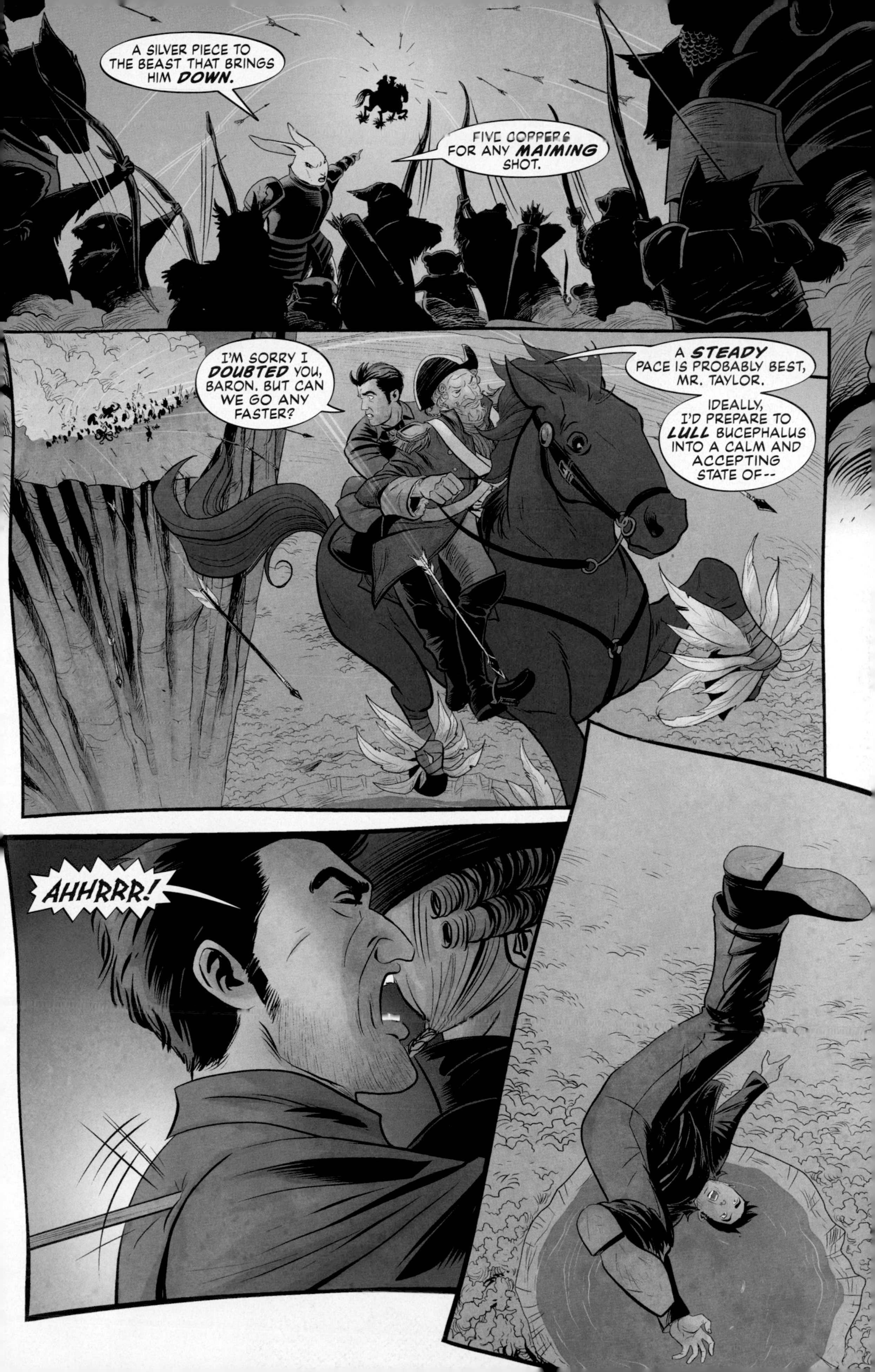
A SILVER PIECE TO THE BEAST THAT BRINGS HIM DOWN.
FIVE COPPERS FOR ANY MAIMING SHOT.
I'M SORRY I DOUBTED YOU, BARON. BUT CAN WE GO ANY FASTER?
A STEADY PACE IS PROBABLY BEST, MR. TAYLOR.
IDEALLY, I'D PREPARE TO LULL BUCEPHALUS INTO A CALM AND ACCEPTING STATE OF--
AHHRRR!

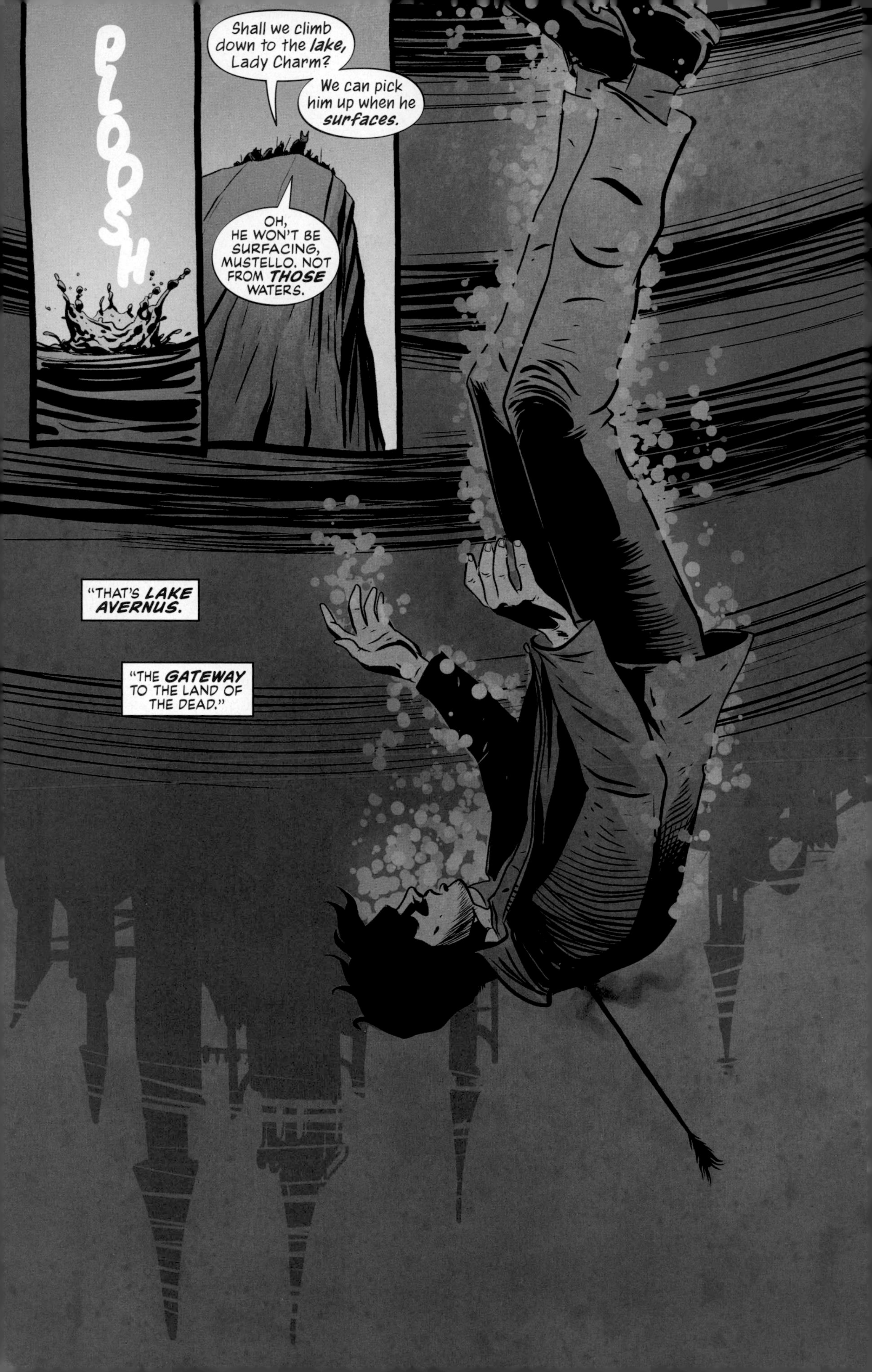
PLOOSH
Shall we climb down to the *lake*, Lady Charm?
We can pick him up when he ***surfaces.***
OH, HE WON'T BE SURFACING, MUSTELLO. NOT FROM ***THOSE*** WATERS.
"THAT'S ***LAKE AVERNUS.***
"THE ***GATEWAY*** TO THE LAND OF THE DEAD."

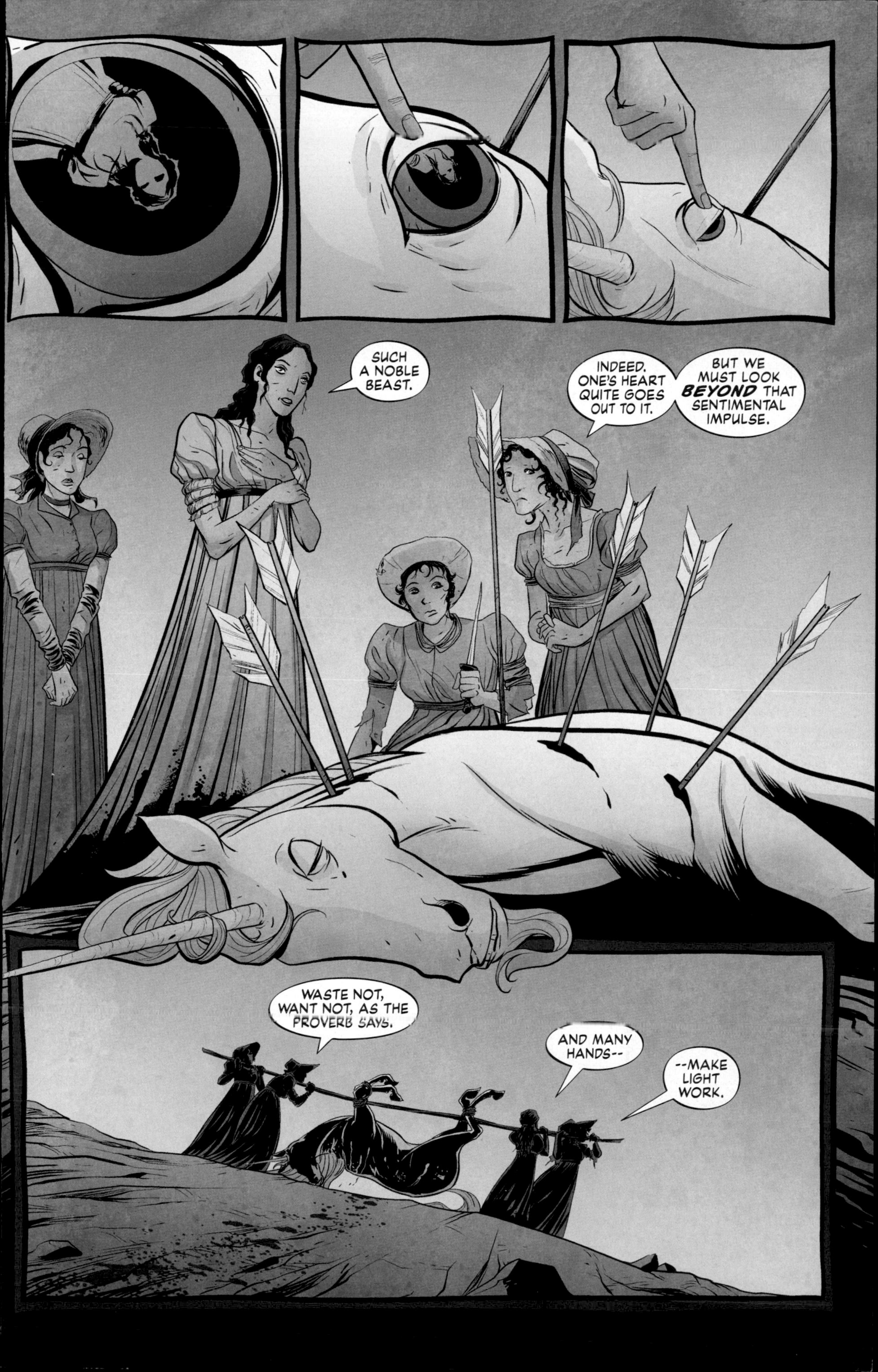
SUCH A NOBLE BEAST.
INDEED. ONE'S HEART QUITE GOES OUT TO IT.
BUT WE MUST LOOK BEYOND THAT SENTIMENTAL IMPULSE.
WASTE NOT, WANT NOT, AS THE PROVERB SAYS.
AND MANY HANDS--
--MAKE LIGHT WORK.

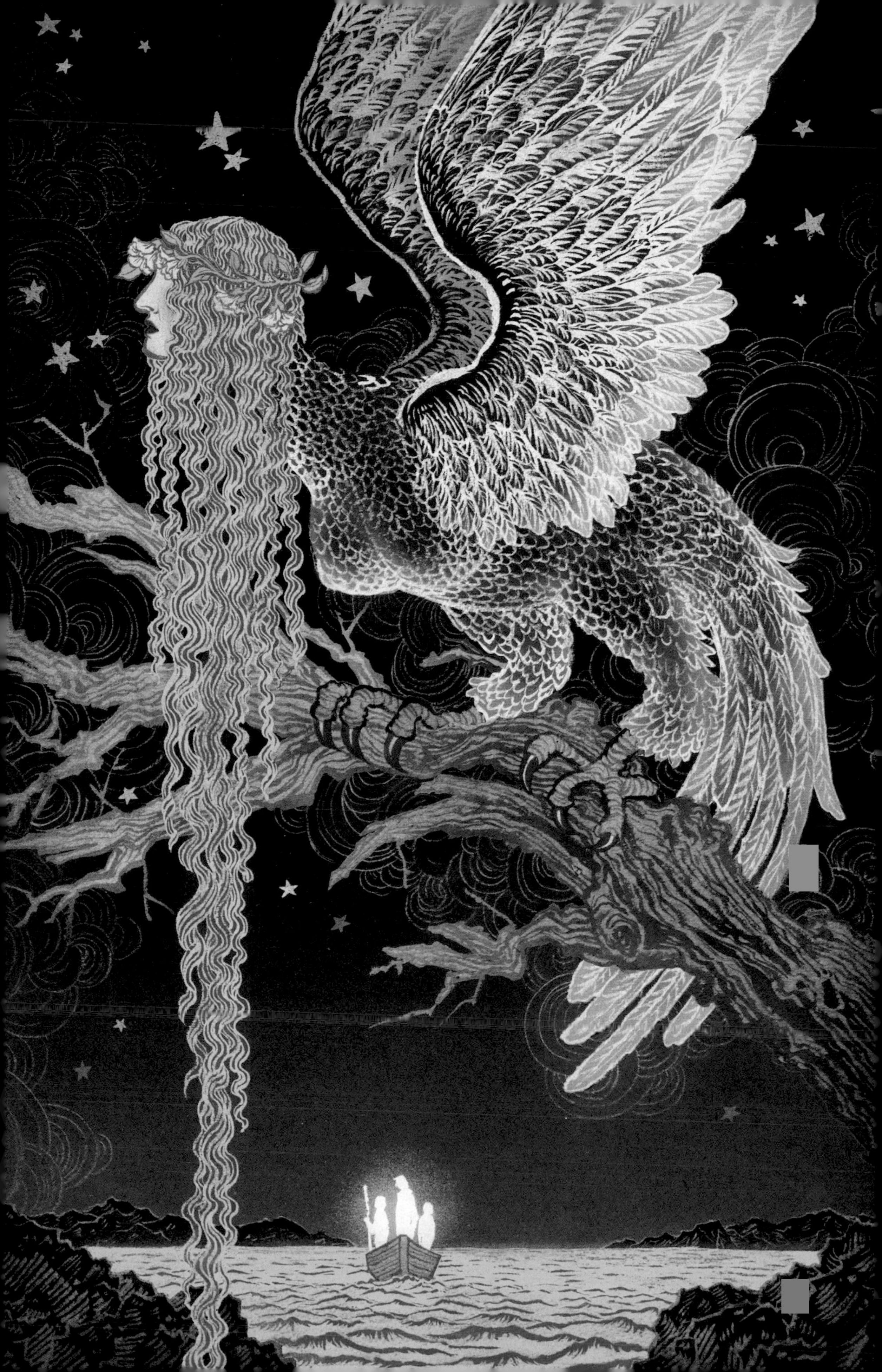

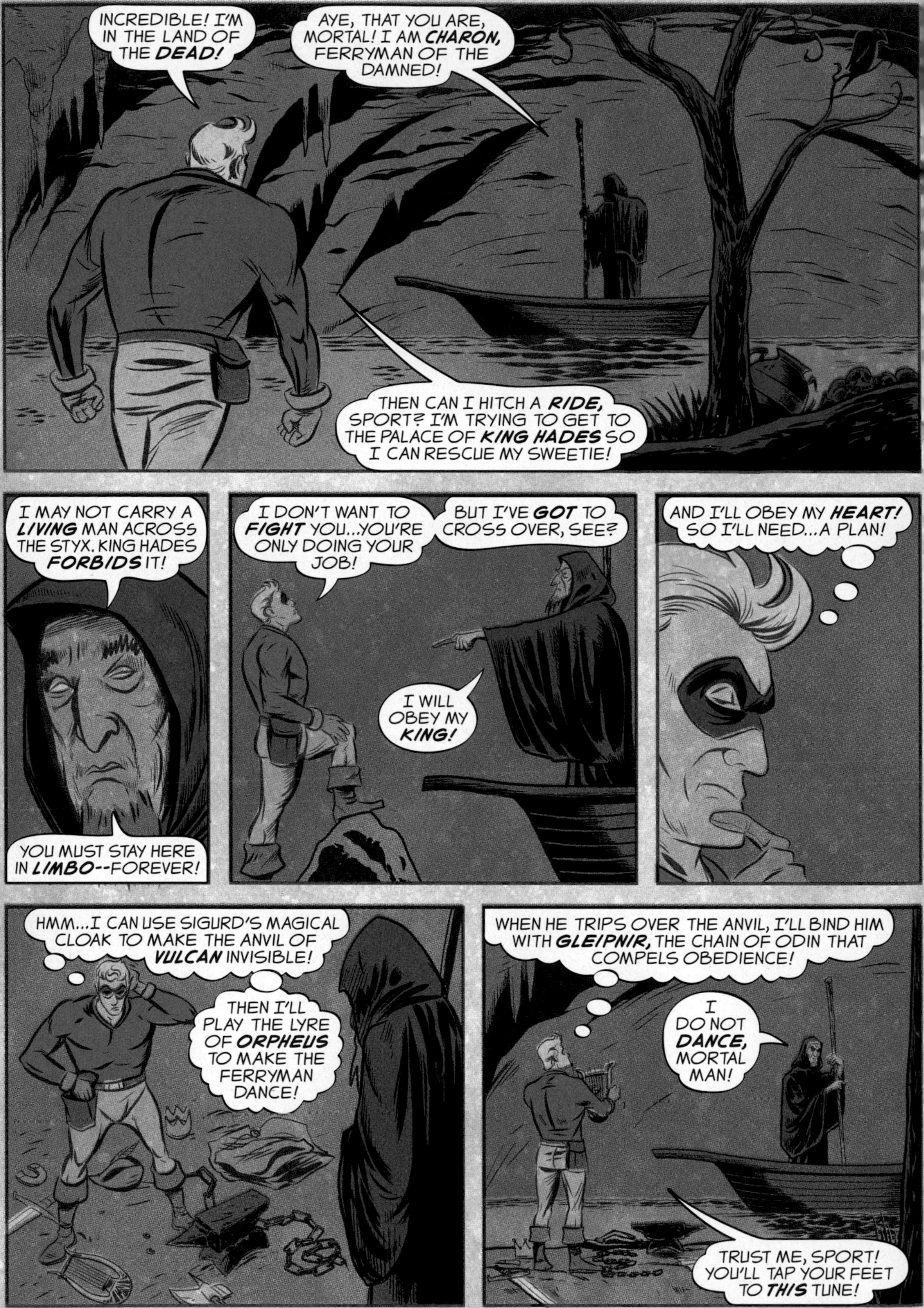
INCREDIBLE! I'M IN THE LAND OF THE DEAD!
AYE, THAT YOU ARE, MORTAL! I AM CHARON, FERRYMAN OF THE DAMNED!
THEN CAN I HITCH A RIDE, SPORT? I'M TRYING TO GET TO THE PALACE OF KING HADES SO I CAN RESCUE MY SWEETIE!
I MAY NOT CARRY A LIVING MAN ACROSS THE STYX. KING HADES FORBIDS IT!
YOU MUST STAY HERE IN LIMBO--FOREVER!
I DON'T WANT TO FIGHT YOU...YOU'RE ONLY DOING YOUR JOB!
BUT I'VE GOT TO CROSS OVER, SEE?
I WILL OBEY MY KING!
AND I'LL OBEY MY HEART! SO I'LL NEED...A PLAN!
HMM...I CAN USE SIGURD'S MAGICAL CLOAK TO MAKE THE ANVIL OF VULCAN INVISIBLE!
THEN I'LL PLAY THE LYRE OF ORPHEUS TO MAKE THE FERRYMAN DANCE!
WHEN HE TRIPS OVER THE ANVIL, I'LL BIND HIM WITH GLEIPNIR, THE CHAIN OF ODIN THAT COMPELS OBEDIENCE!
I DO NOT DANCE, MORTAL MAN!
TRUST ME, SPORT! YOU'LL TAP YOUR FEET TO THIS TUNE!

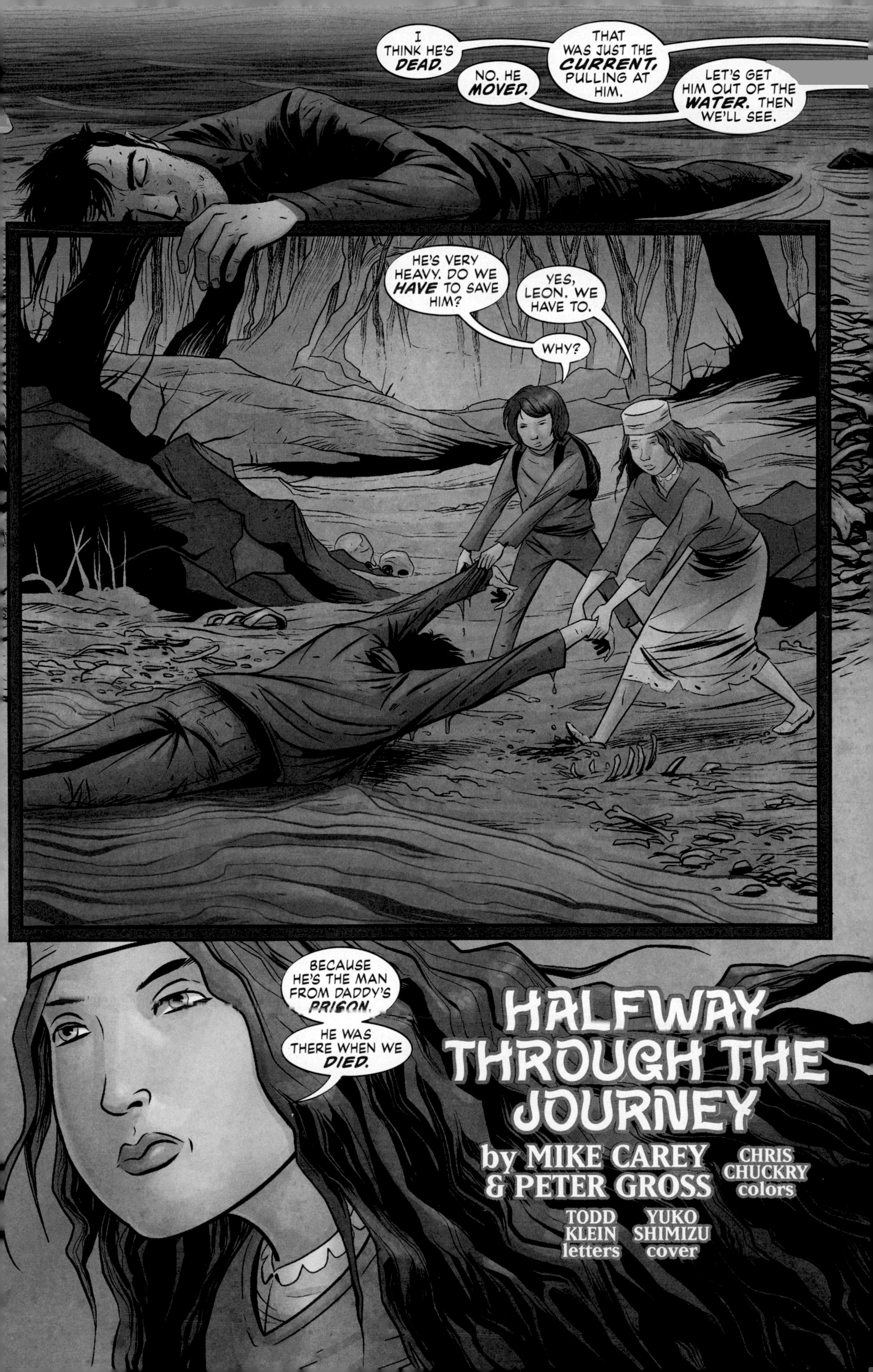
I THINK HE'S *DEAD.*
NO. HE *MOVED.*
THAT WAS JUST THE *CURRENT,* PULLING AT HIM.
LET'S GET HIM OUT OF THE *WATER.* THEN WE'LL SEE.
HE'S VERY HEAVY. DO WE *HAVE* TO SAVE HIM?
YES, LEON. WE HAVE TO.
WHY?
BECAUSE HE'S THE MAN FROM DADDY'S *PRISON.*
HE WAS THERE WHEN WE *DIED.*
HALFWAY THROUGH THE JOURNEY
by MIKE CAREY & PETER GROSS
CHRIS CHUCKRY colors
TODD KLEIN letters
YUKO SHIMIZU cover

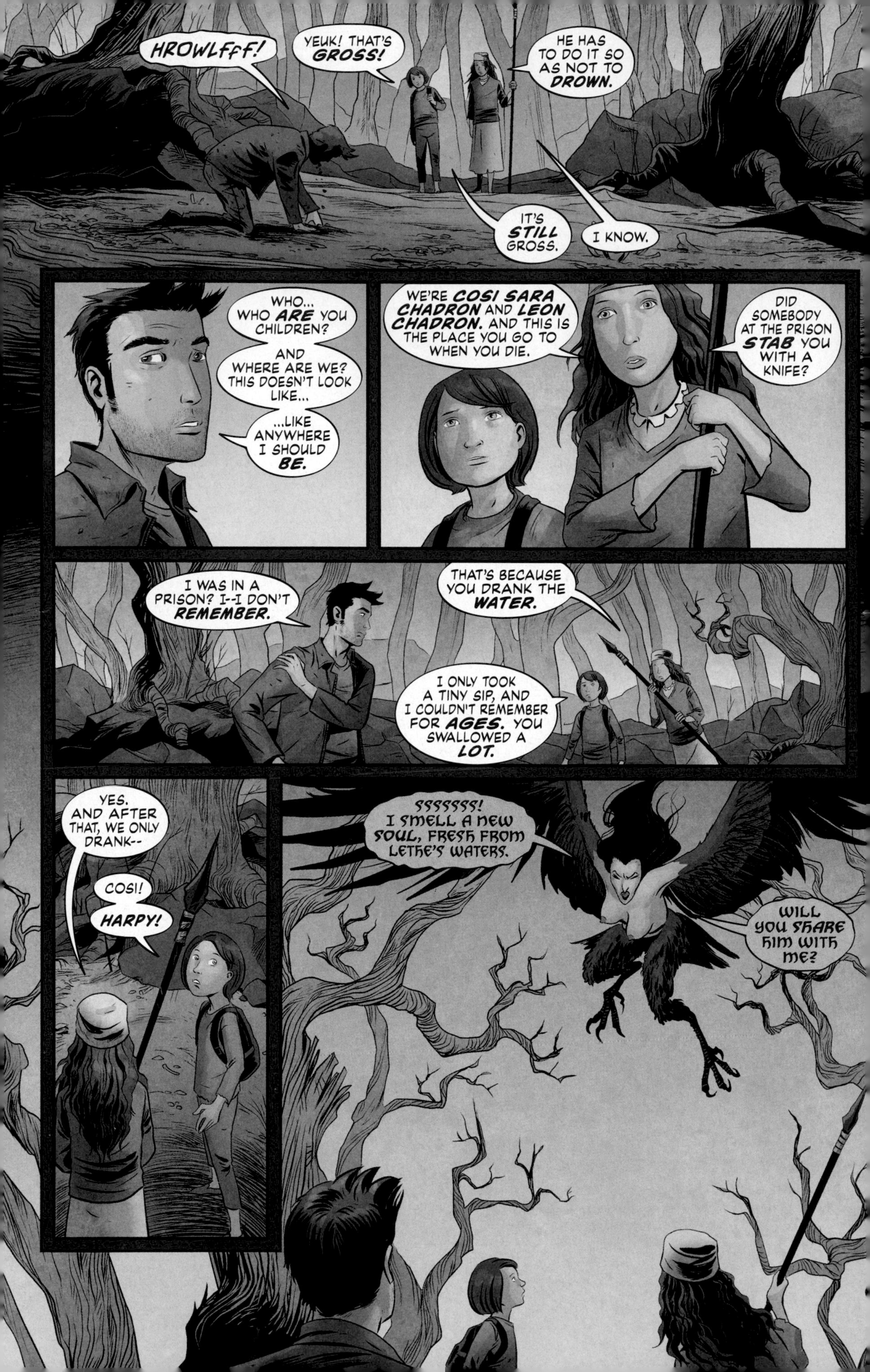
HROWLFFF!
YEUK! THAT'S GROSS!
HE HAS TO DO IT SO AS NOT TO DROWN.
IT'S STILL GROSS.
I KNOW.
WHO... WHO ARE YOU CHILDREN?
AND WHERE ARE WE? THIS DOESN'T LOOK LIKE...
...LIKE ANYWHERE I SHOULD BE.
WE'RE COSI SARA CHADRON AND LEON CHADRON. AND THIS IS THE PLACE YOU GO TO WHEN YOU DIE.
DID SOMEBODY AT THE PRISON STAB YOU WITH A KNIFE?
I WAS IN A PRISON? I--I DON'T REMEMBER.
THAT'S BECAUSE YOU DRANK THE WATER.
I ONLY TOOK A TINY SIP, AND I COULDN'T REMEMBER FOR AGES. YOU SWALLOWED A LOT.
YES. AND AFTER THAT, WE ONLY DRANK--
COSI!
HARPY!
SSSSSSS! I SMELL A NEW SOUL, FRESH FROM LETHE'S WATERS.
WILL YOU SHARE HIM WITH ME?

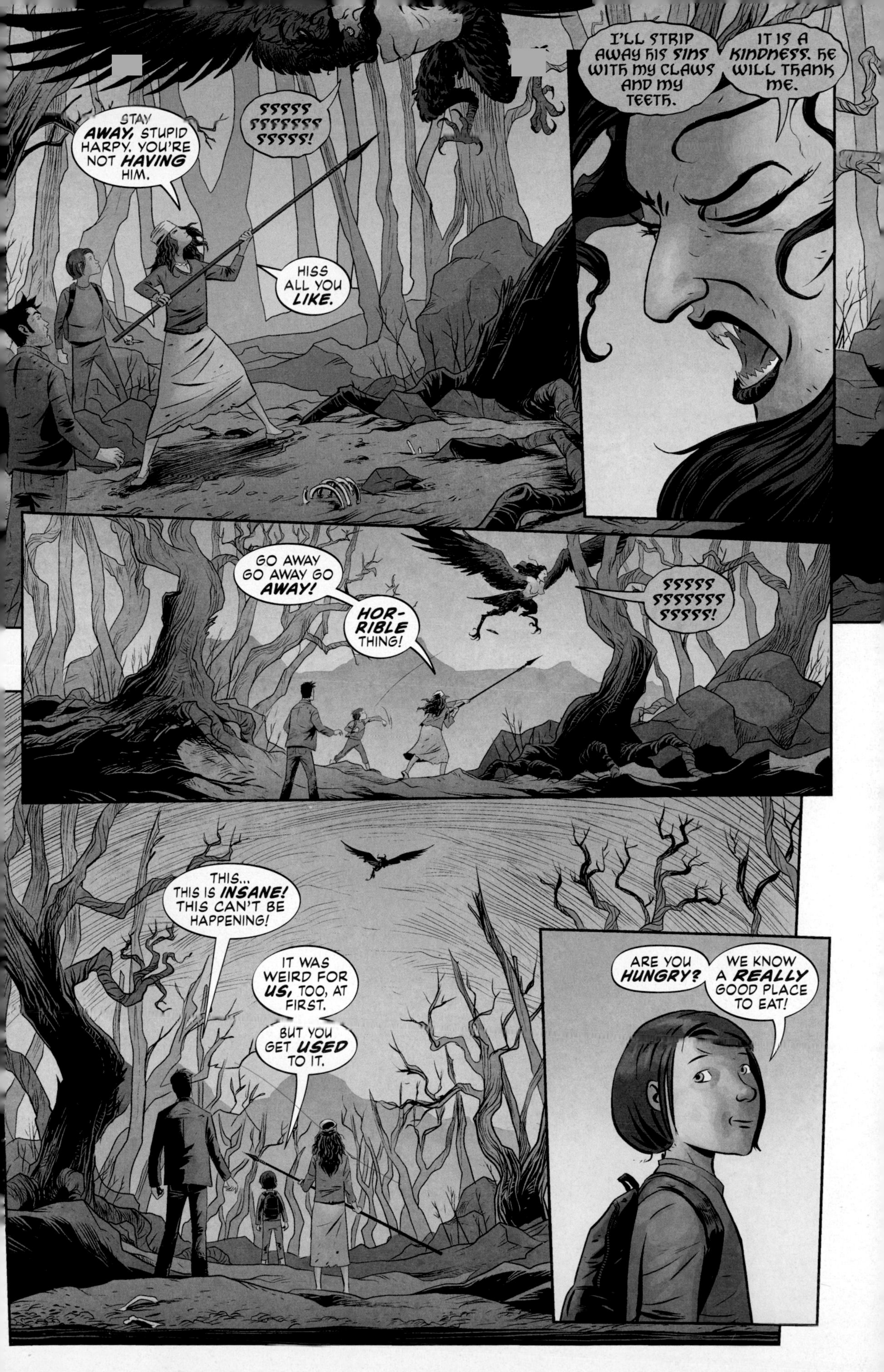
STAY AWAY, STUPID HARPY. YOU'RE NOT HAVING HIM.
SSSSS SSSSSSS SSSSS!
HISS ALL YOU LIKE.
I'LL STRIP AWAY HIS SINS WITH MY CLAWS AND MY TEETH.
IT IS A KINDNESS. HE WILL THANK ME.
GO AWAY GO AWAY GO AWAY!
HORRIBLE THING!
SSSSS SSSSSSS SSSSS!
THIS... THIS IS INSANE! THIS CAN'T BE HAPPENING!
IT WAS WEIRD FOR US, TOO, AT FIRST.
BUT YOU GET USED TO IT.
ARE YOU HUNGRY?
WE KNOW A REALLY GOOD PLACE TO EAT!

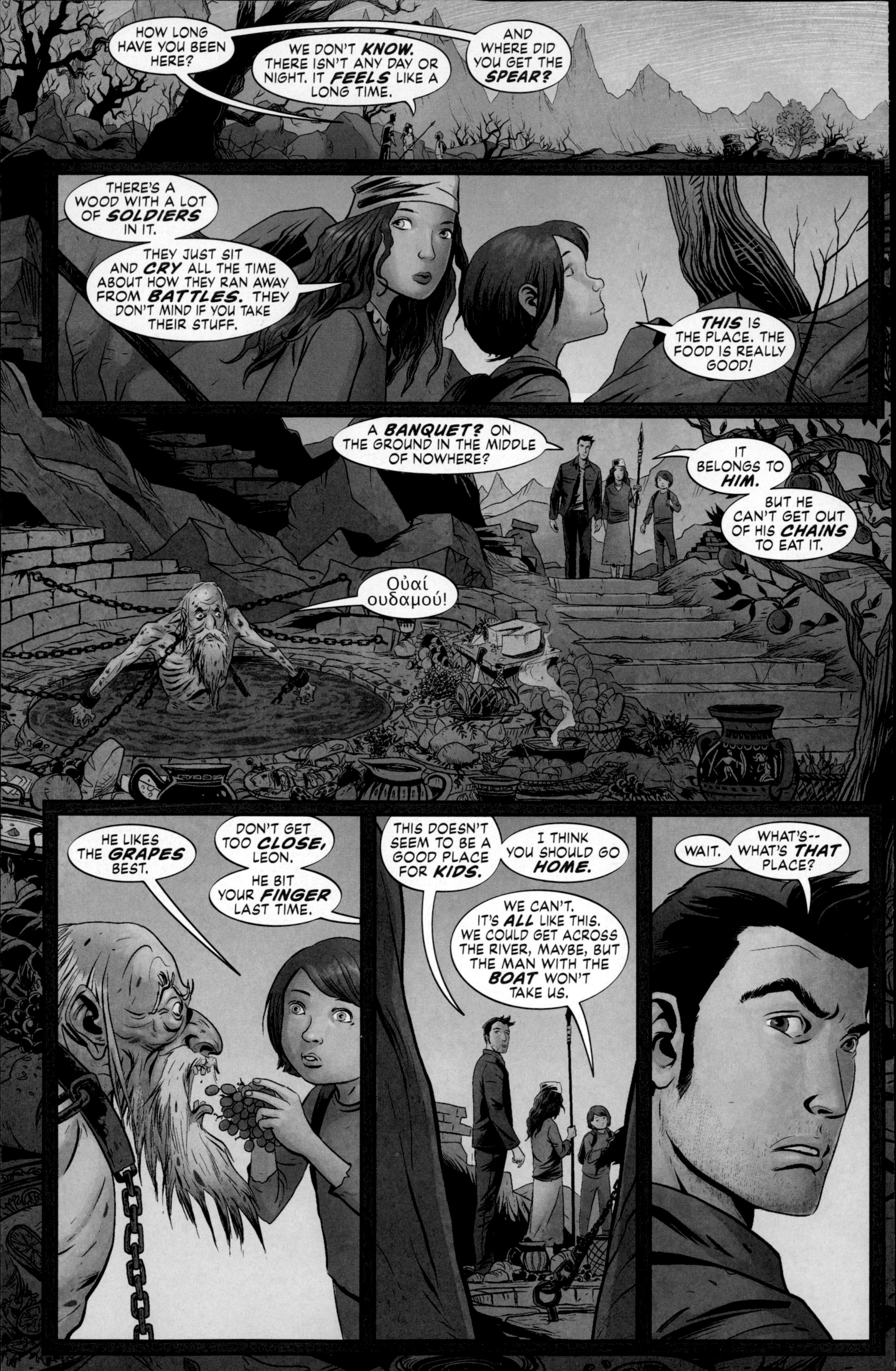

HOW LONG HAVE YOU BEEN HERE?
WE DON'T KNOW. THERE ISN'T ANY DAY OR NIGHT. IT FEELS LIKE A LONG TIME.
AND WHERE DID YOU GET THE SPEAR?
THERE'S A WOOD WITH A LOT OF SOLDIERS IN IT.
THEY JUST SIT AND CRY ALL THE TIME ABOUT HOW THEY RAN AWAY FROM BATTLES. THEY DON'T MIND IF YOU TAKE THEIR STUFF.
THIS IS THE PLACE. THE FOOD IS REALLY GOOD!
A BANQUET? ON THE GROUND IN THE MIDDLE OF NOWHERE?
IT BELONGS TO HIM.
BUT HE CAN'T GET OUT OF HIS CHAINS TO EAT IT.
Ουαί ουδαμού!
HE LIKES THE GRAPES BEST.
DON'T GET TOO CLOSE, LEON.
HE BIT YOUR FINGER LAST TIME.
THIS DOESN'T SEEM TO BE A GOOD PLACE FOR KIDS.
I THINK YOU SHOULD GO HOME.
WE CAN'T. IT'S ALL LIKE THIS. WE COULD GET ACROSS THE RIVER, MAYBE, BUT THE MAN WITH THE BOAT WON'T TAKE US.
WAIT.
WHAT'S-- WHAT'S THAT PLACE?

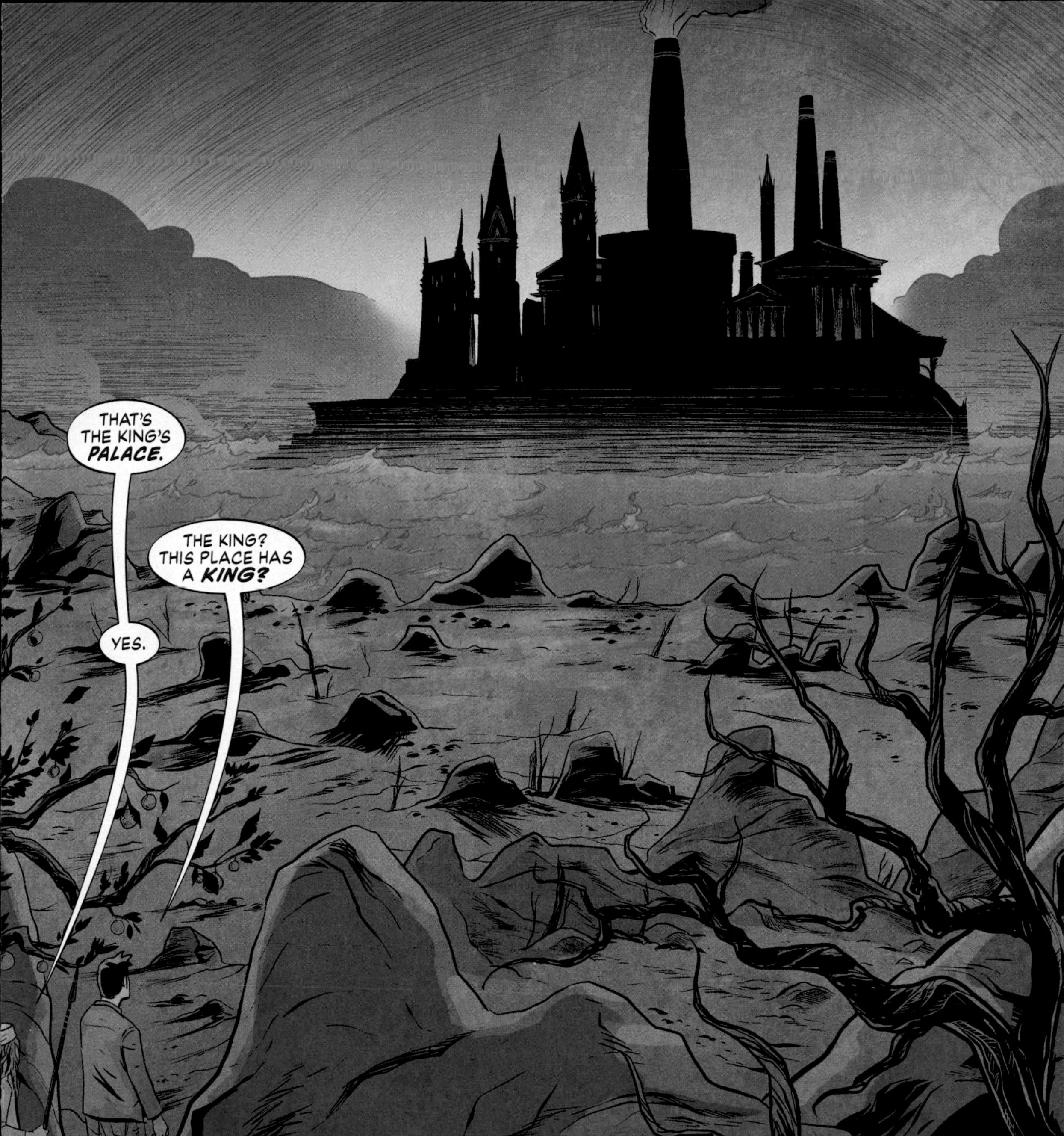
THAT'S THE KING'S PALACE.
THE KING? THIS PLACE HAS A KING?
YES.

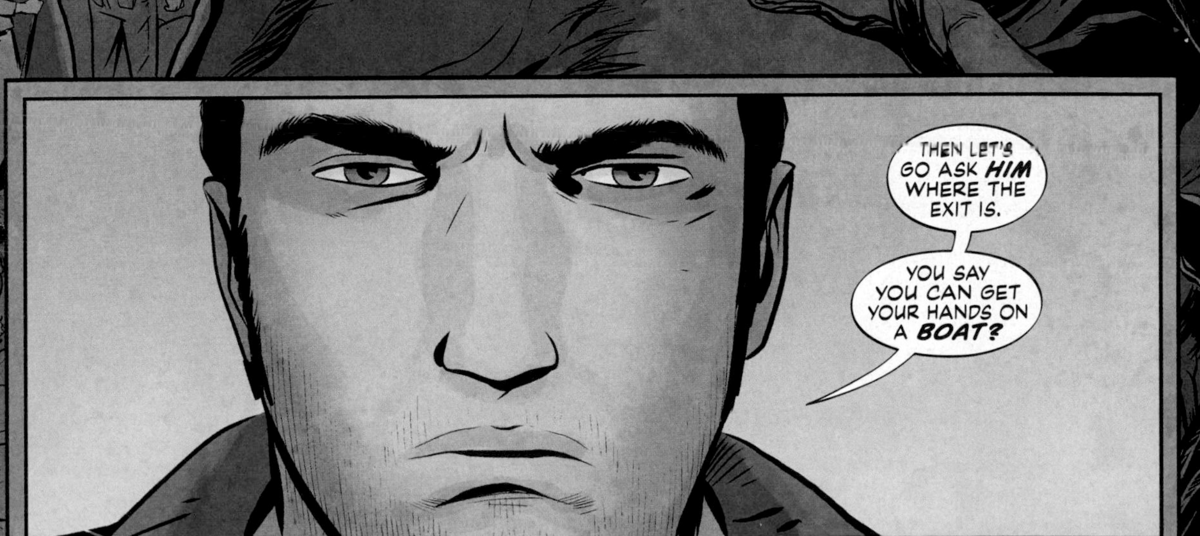
THEN LET'S GO ASK HIM WHERE THE EXIT IS.
YOU SAY YOU CAN GET YOUR HANDS ON A BOAT?

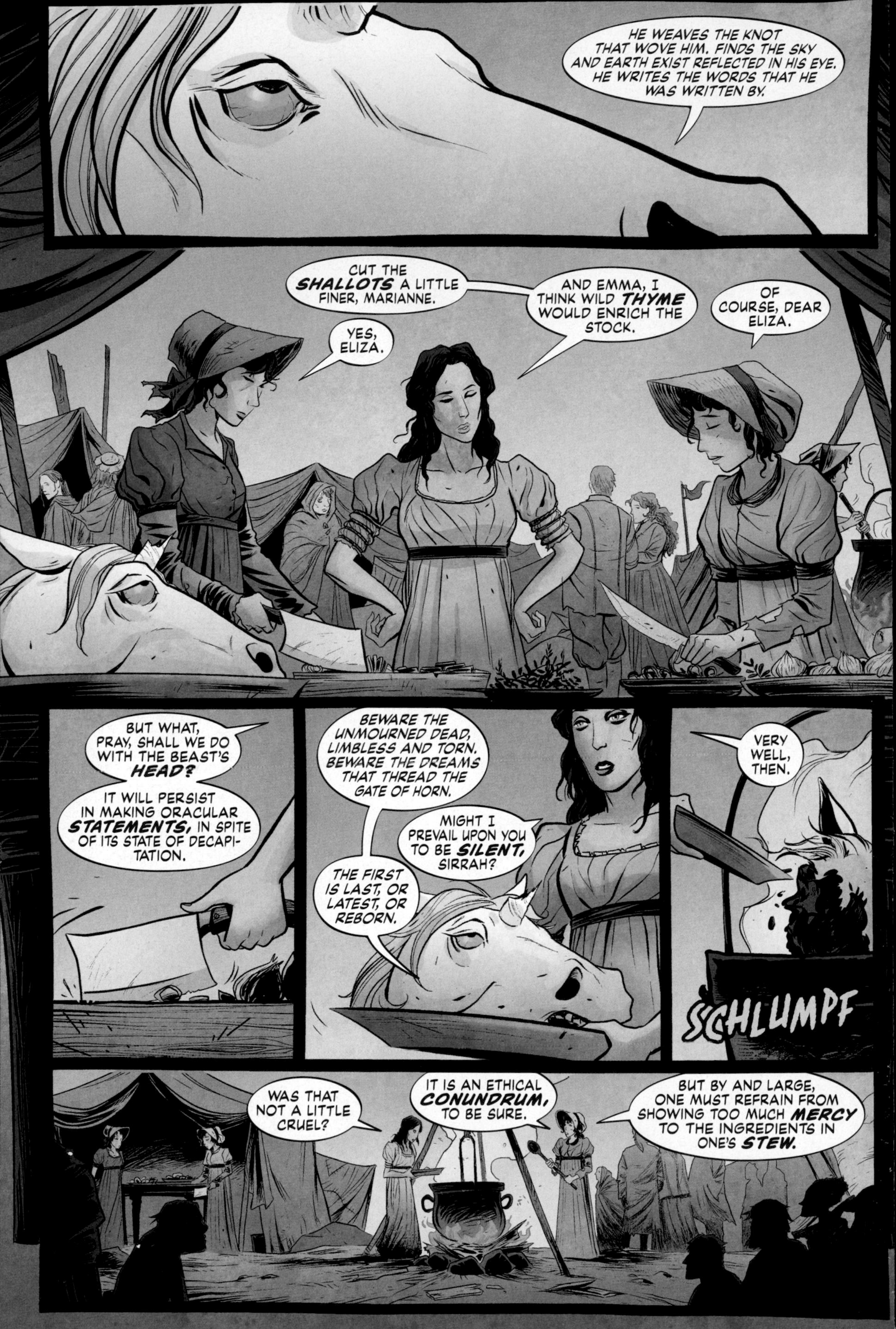
HE WEAVES THE KNOT THAT WOVE HIM. FINDS THE SKY AND EARTH EXIST REFLECTED IN HIS EYE. HE WRITES THE WORDS THAT HE WAS WRITTEN BY.
CUT THE SHALLOTS A LITTLE FINER, MARIANNE.
YES, ELIZA.
AND EMMA, I THINK WILD THYME WOULD ENRICH THE STOCK.
OF COURSE, DEAR ELIZA.
BUT WHAT, PRAY, SHALL WE DO WITH THE BEAST'S HEAD?
IT WILL PERSIST IN MAKING ORACULAR STATEMENTS, IN SPITE OF ITS STATE OF DECAPI-TATION.
BEWARE THE UNMOURNED DEAD, LIMBLESS AND TORN. BEWARE THE DREAMS THAT THREAD THE GATE OF HORN.
MIGHT I PREVAIL UPON YOU TO BE SILENT, SIRRAH?
THE FIRST IS LAST, OR LATEST, OR REBORN.
VERY WELL, THEN.
SCHLUMPF
WAS THAT NOT A LITTLE CRUEL?
IT IS AN ETHICAL CONUNDRUM, TO BE SURE.
BUT BY AND LARGE, ONE MUST REFRAIN FROM SHOWING TOO MUCH MERCY TO THE INGREDIENTS IN ONE'S STEW.

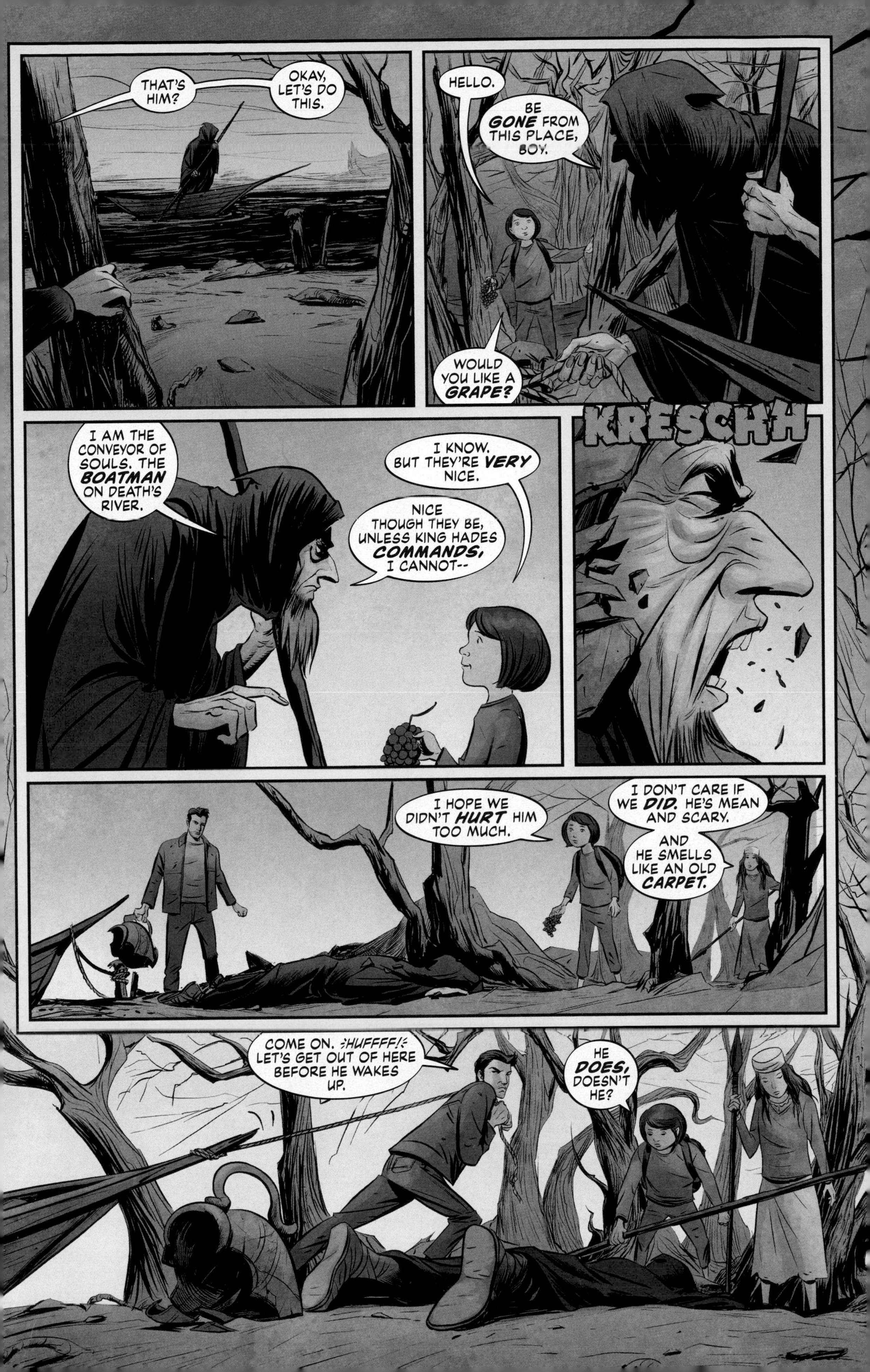
THAT'S HIM?
OKAY, LET'S DO THIS.
HELLO.
BE GONE FROM THIS PLACE, BOY.
WOULD YOU LIKE A GRAPE?
I AM THE CONVEYOR OF SOULS. THE BOATMAN ON DEATH'S RIVER.
I KNOW. BUT THEY'RE VERY NICE.
NICE THOUGH THEY BE, UNLESS KING HADES COMMANDS, I CANNOT--
KRESCHH
I HOPE WE DIDN'T HURT HIM TOO MUCH.
I DON'T CARE IF WE DID. HE'S MEAN AND SCARY.
AND HE SMELLS LIKE AN OLD CARPET.
COME ON. HUFFFFF! LET'S GET OUT OF HERE BEFORE HE WAKES UP.
HE DOES, DOESN'T HE?

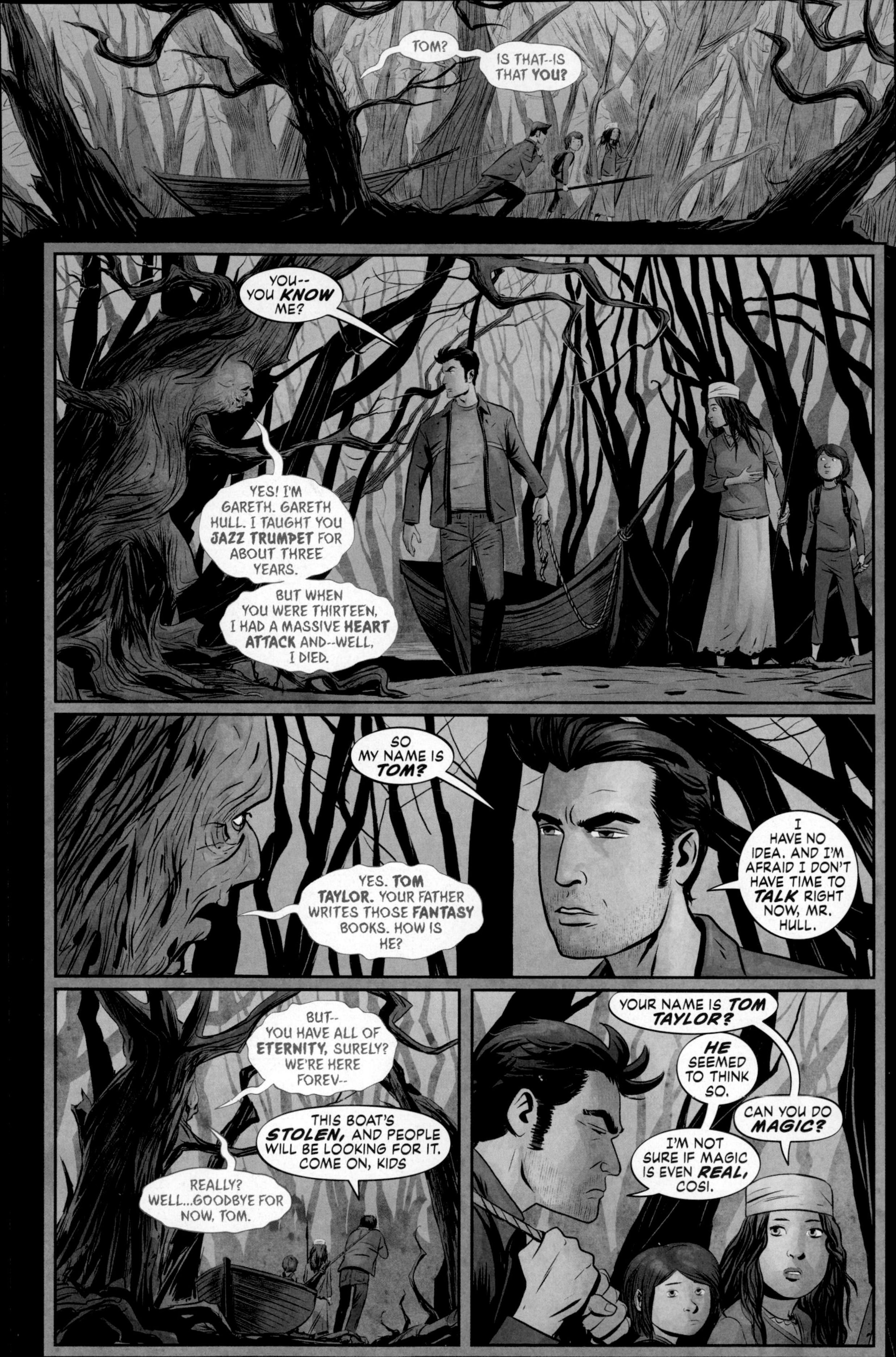
TOM?
IS THAT--IS THAT YOU?
YOU--YOU KNOW ME?
YES! I'M GARETH. GARETH HULL. I TAUGHT YOU JAZZ TRUMPET FOR ABOUT THREE YEARS.
BUT WHEN YOU WERE THIRTEEN, I HAD A MASSIVE HEART ATTACK AND--WELL, I DIED.
SO MY NAME IS TOM?
YES. TOM TAYLOR. YOUR FATHER WRITES THOSE FANTASY BOOKS. HOW IS HE?
I HAVE NO IDEA. AND I'M AFRAID I DON'T HAVE TIME TO TALK RIGHT NOW, MR. HULL.
BUT--YOU HAVE ALL OF ETERNITY, SURELY? WE'RE HERE FOREV--
THIS BOAT'S STOLEN, AND PEOPLE WILL BE LOOKING FOR IT. COME ON, KIDS
REALLY? WELL...GOODBYE FOR NOW, TOM.
YOUR NAME IS TOM TAYLOR?
HE SEEMED TO THINK SO.
CAN YOU DO MAGIC?
I'M NOT SURE IF MAGIC IS EVEN REAL, COSI.

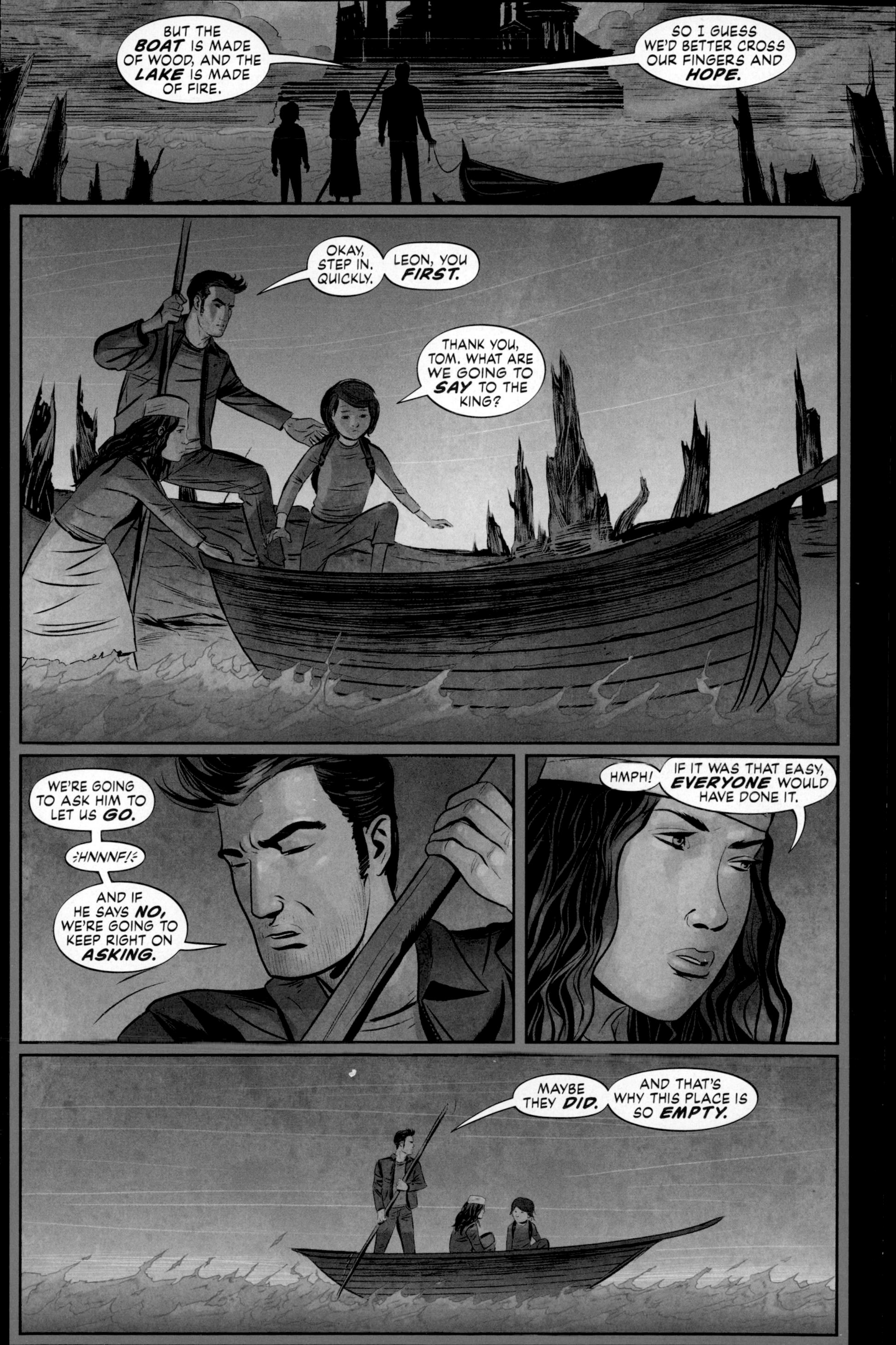
BUT THE BOAT IS MADE OF WOOD, AND THE LAKE IS MADE OF FIRE.
SO I GUESS WE'D BETTER CROSS OUR FINGERS AND HOPE.
OKAY, STEP IN. QUICKLY.
LEON, YOU FIRST.
THANK YOU, TOM. WHAT ARE WE GOING TO SAY TO THE KING?
WE'RE GOING TO ASK HIM TO LET US GO.
HNNNF!
AND IF HE SAYS NO, WE'RE GOING TO KEEP RIGHT ON ASKING.
HMPH!
IF IT WAS THAT EASY, EVERYONE WOULD HAVE DONE IT.
MAYBE THEY DID.
AND THAT'S WHY THIS PLACE IS SO EMPTY.

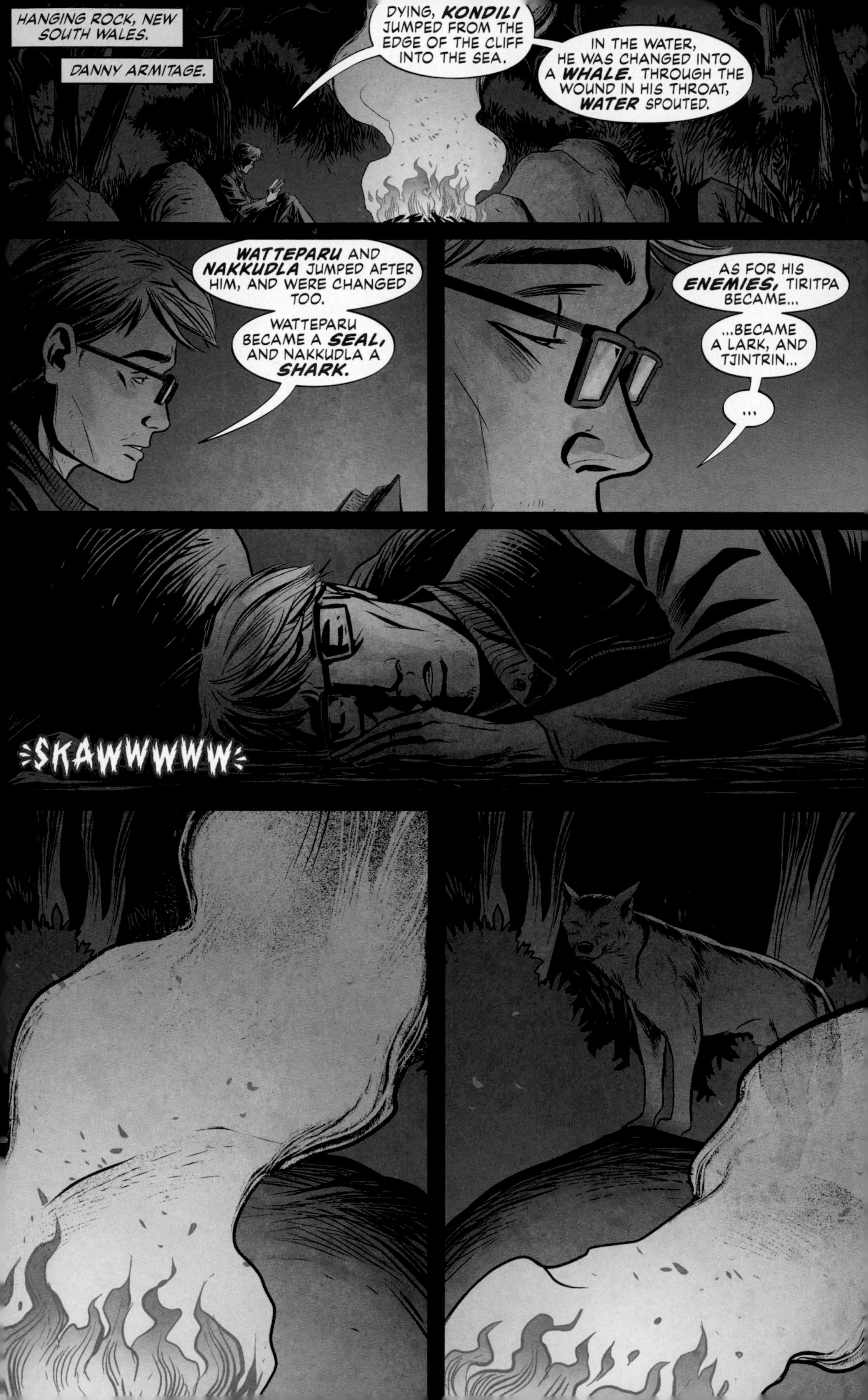
HANGING ROCK, NEW SOUTH WALES.
DANNY ARMITAGE.
DYING, KONDILI JUMPED FROM THE EDGE OF THE CLIFF INTO THE SEA.
IN THE WATER, HE WAS CHANGED INTO A WHALE. THROUGH THE WOUND IN HIS THROAT, WATER SPOUTED.
WATTEPARU AND NAKKUDLA JUMPED AFTER HIM, AND WERE CHANGED TOO.
WATTEPARU BECAME A SEAL, AND NAKKUDLA A SHARK.
AS FOR HIS ENEMIES, TIRITPA BECAME...
...BECAME A LARK, AND TJINTRIN...
...
SKAWWWWW

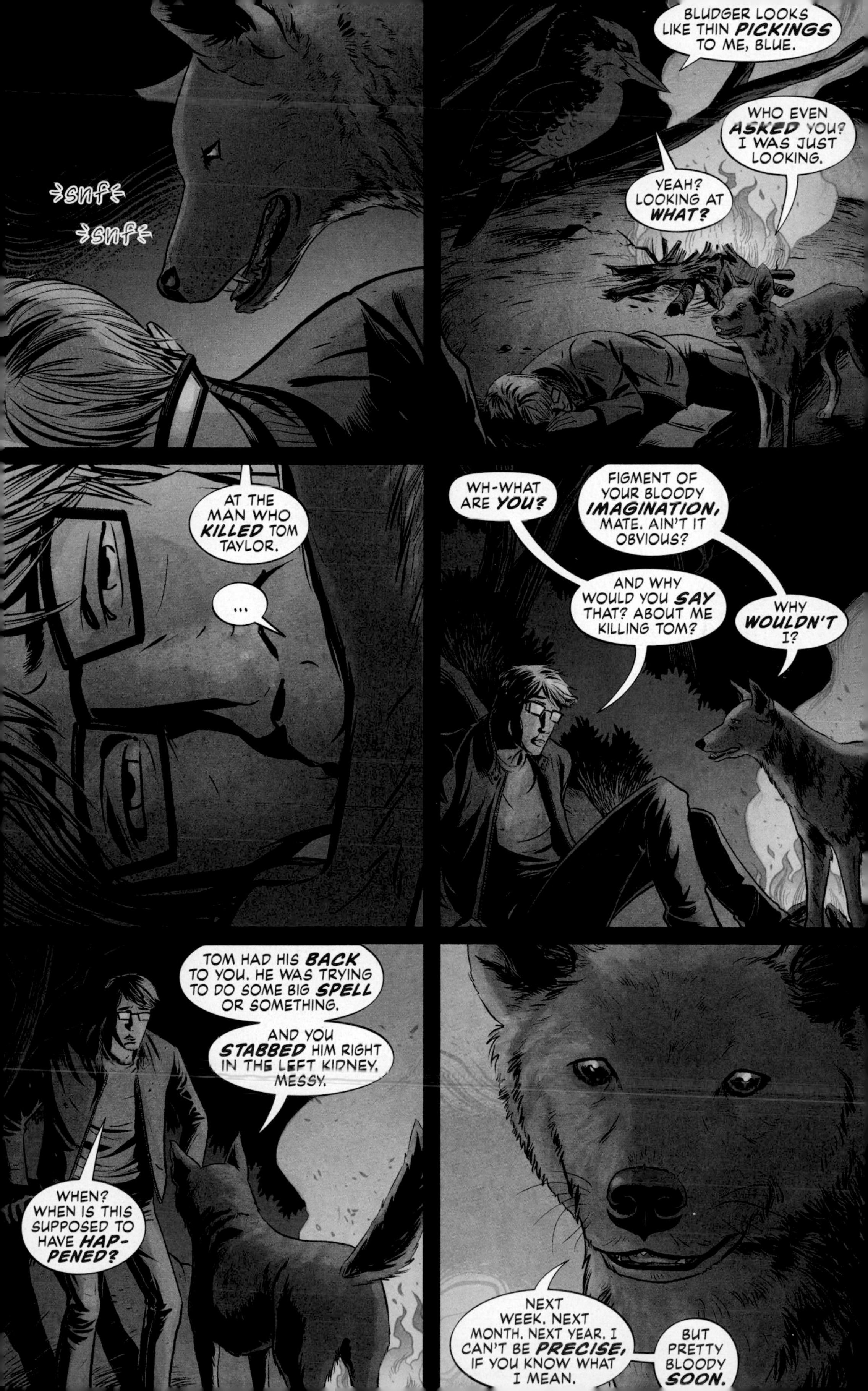

SNF
SNF
BLUDGER LOOKS LIKE THIN PICKINGS TO ME, BLUE.
WHO EVEN ASKED YOU? I WAS JUST LOOKING.
YEAH? LOOKING AT WHAT?
AT THE MAN WHO KILLED TOM TAYLOR.
...
WH-WHAT ARE YOU?
FIGMENT OF YOUR BLOODY IMAGINATION, MATE. AIN'T IT OBVIOUS?
AND WHY WOULD YOU SAY THAT? ABOUT ME KILLING TOM?
WHY WOULDN'T I?
TOM HAD HIS BACK TO YOU. HE WAS TRYING TO DO SOME BIG SPELL OR SOMETHING.
AND YOU STABBED HIM RIGHT IN THE LEFT KIDNEY. MESSY.
WHEN? WHEN IS THIS SUPPOSED TO HAVE HAP-PENED?
NEXT WEEK. NEXT MONTH. NEXT YEAR. I CAN'T BE PRECISE, IF YOU KNOW WHAT I MEAN.
BUT PRETTY BLOODY SOON.

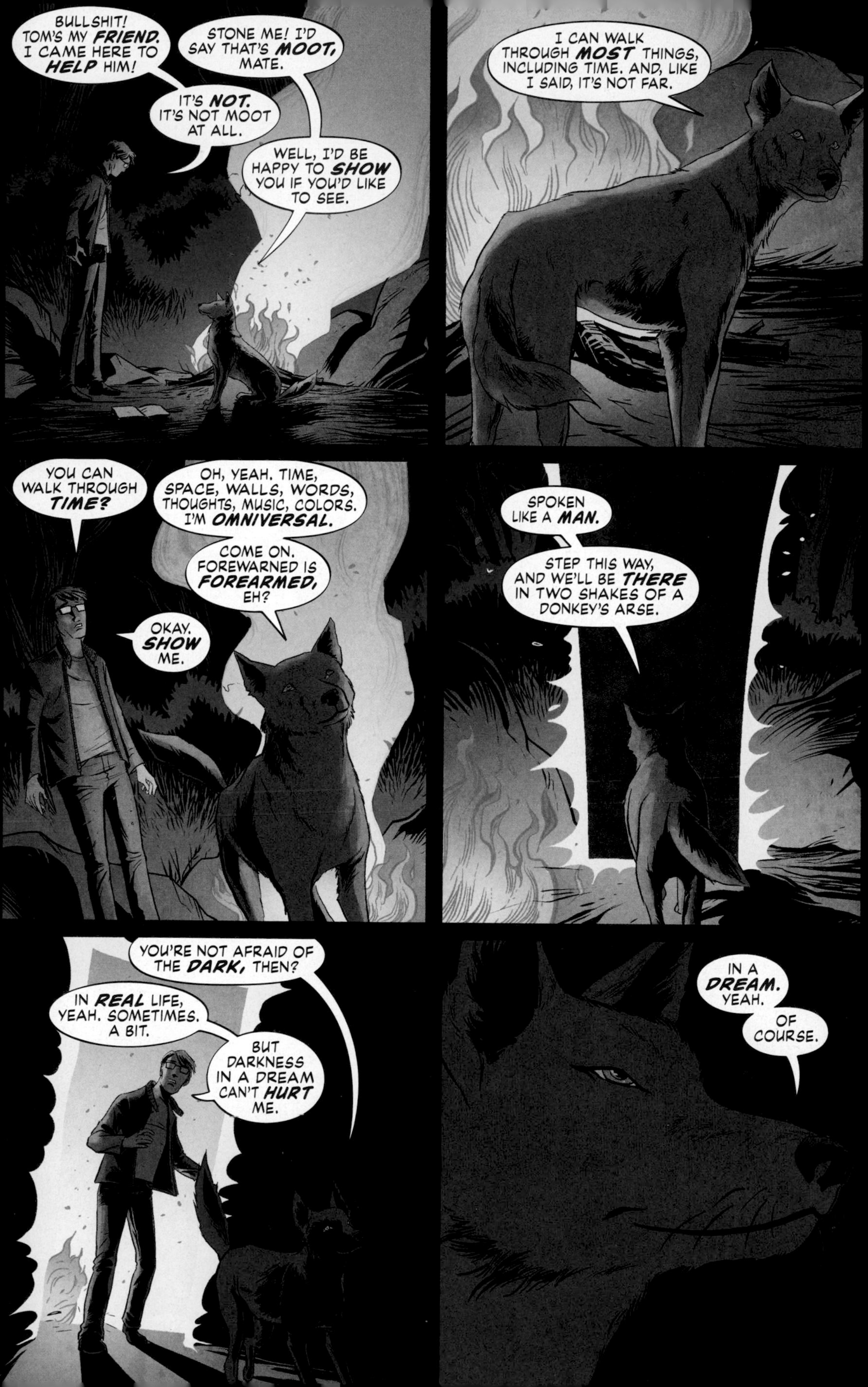
BULLSHIT! TOM'S MY FRIEND. I CAME HERE TO HELP HIM!
STONE ME! I'D SAY THAT'S MOOT, MATE.
IT'S NOT. IT'S NOT MOOT AT ALL.
WELL, I'D BE HAPPY TO SHOW YOU IF YOU'D LIKE TO SEE.
I CAN WALK THROUGH MOST THINGS, INCLUDING TIME. AND, LIKE I SAID, IT'S NOT FAR.
YOU CAN WALK THROUGH TIME?
OH, YEAH. TIME, SPACE, WALLS, WORDS, THOUGHTS, MUSIC, COLORS. I'M OMNIVERSAL.
COME ON. FOREWARNED IS FOREARMED, EH?
OKAY. SHOW ME.
SPOKEN LIKE A MAN.
STEP THIS WAY, AND WE'LL BE THERE IN TWO SHAKES OF A DONKEY'S ARSE.
YOU'RE NOT AFRAID OF THE DARK, THEN?
IN REAL LIFE, YEAH. SOMETIMES. A BIT.
BUT DARKNESS IN A DREAM CAN'T HURT ME.
IN A DREAM. YEAH.
OF COURSE.

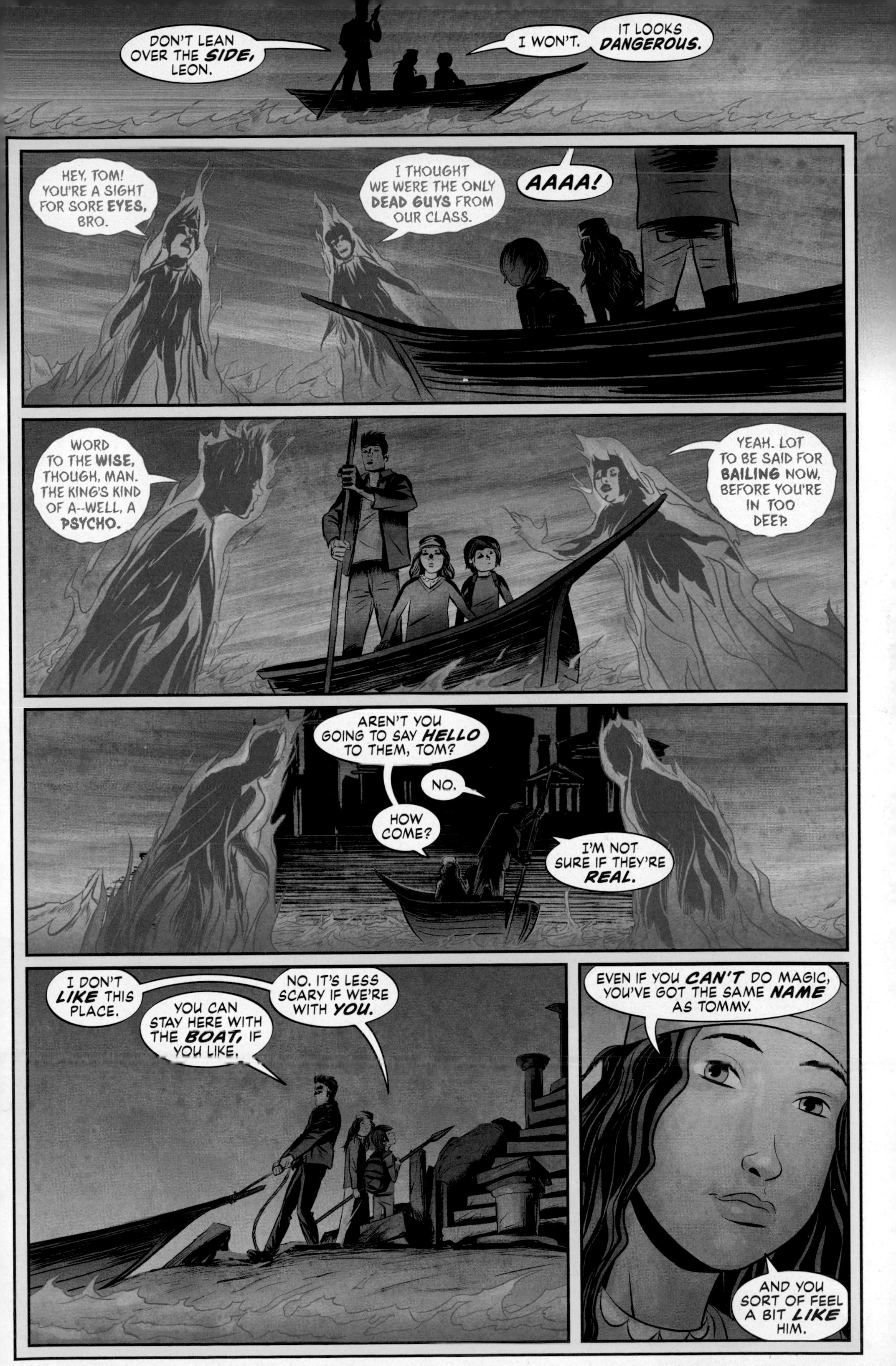

DON'T LEAN OVER THE SIDE, LEON.
I WON'T.
IT LOOKS DANGEROUS.
HEY, TOM! YOU'RE A SIGHT FOR SORE EYES, BRO.
I THOUGHT WE WERE THE ONLY DEAD GUYS FROM OUR CLASS.
AAAA!
WORD TO THE WISE, THOUGH, MAN. THE KING'S KIND OF A--WELL, A PSYCHO.
YEAH. LOT TO BE SAID FOR BAILING NOW, BEFORE YOU'RE IN TOO DEEP.
AREN'T YOU GOING TO SAY HELLO TO THEM, TOM?
NO.
HOW COME?
I'M NOT SURE IF THEY'RE REAL.
I DON'T LIKE THIS PLACE.
YOU CAN STAY HERE WITH THE BOAT, IF YOU LIKE.
NO. IT'S LESS SCARY IF WE'RE WITH YOU.
EVEN IF YOU CAN'T DO MAGIC, YOU'VE GOT THE SAME NAME AS TOMMY.
AND YOU SORT OF FEEL A BIT LIKE HIM.

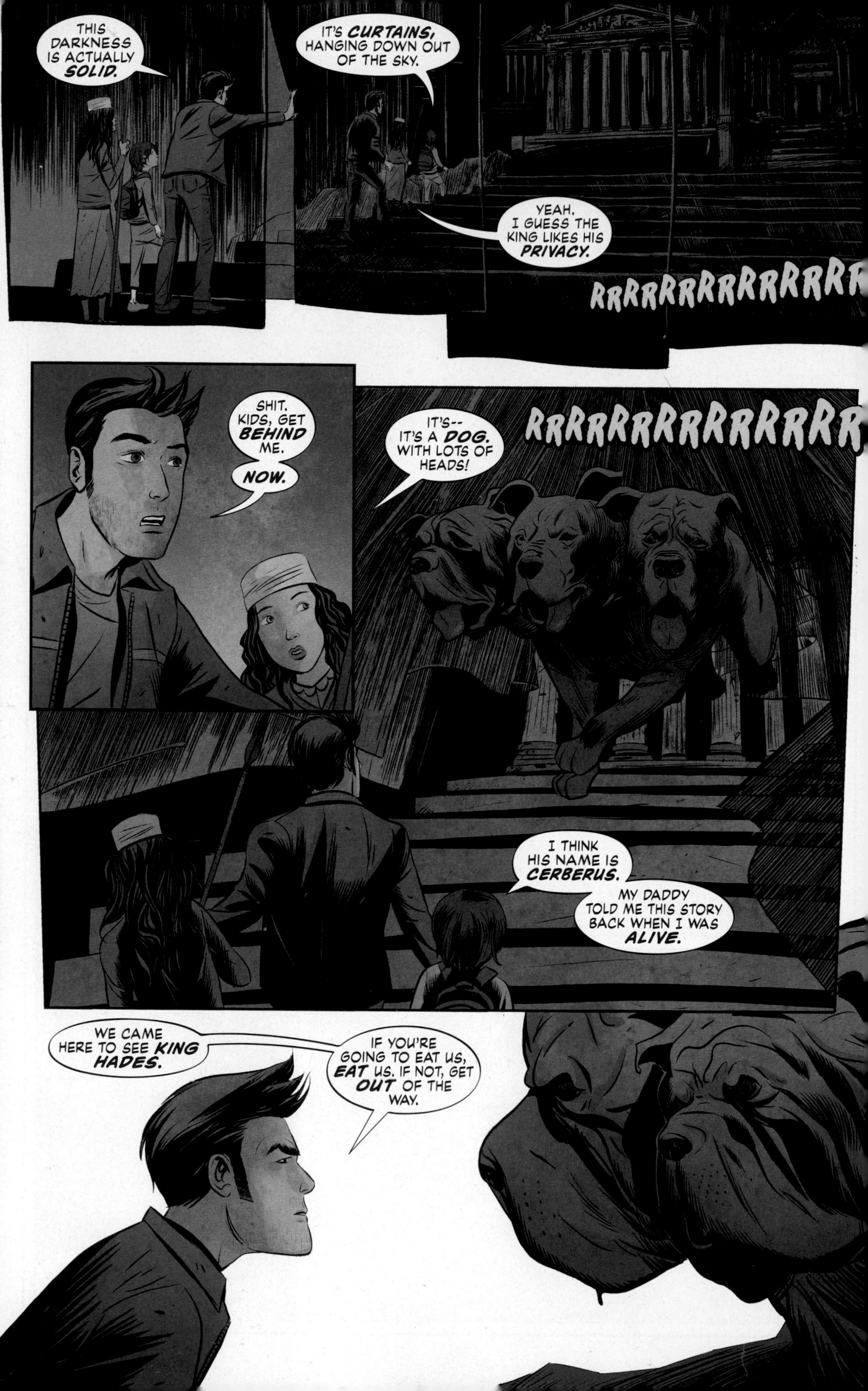

THIS DARKNESS IS ACTUALLY SOLID.
IT'S CURTAINS, HANGING DOWN OUT OF THE SKY.
YEAH. I GUESS THE KING LIKES HIS PRIVACY.
RRRRRRRRRRRRRRR
SHIT. KIDS, GET BEHIND ME.
NOW.
IT'S-- IT'S A DOG. WITH LOTS OF HEADS!
RRRRRRRRRRRRRRR
I THINK HIS NAME IS CERBERUS.
MY DADDY TOLD ME THIS STORY BACK WHEN I WAS ALIVE.
WE CAME HERE TO SEE KING HADES.
IF YOU'RE GOING TO EAT US, EAT US. IF NOT, GET OUT OF THE WAY.

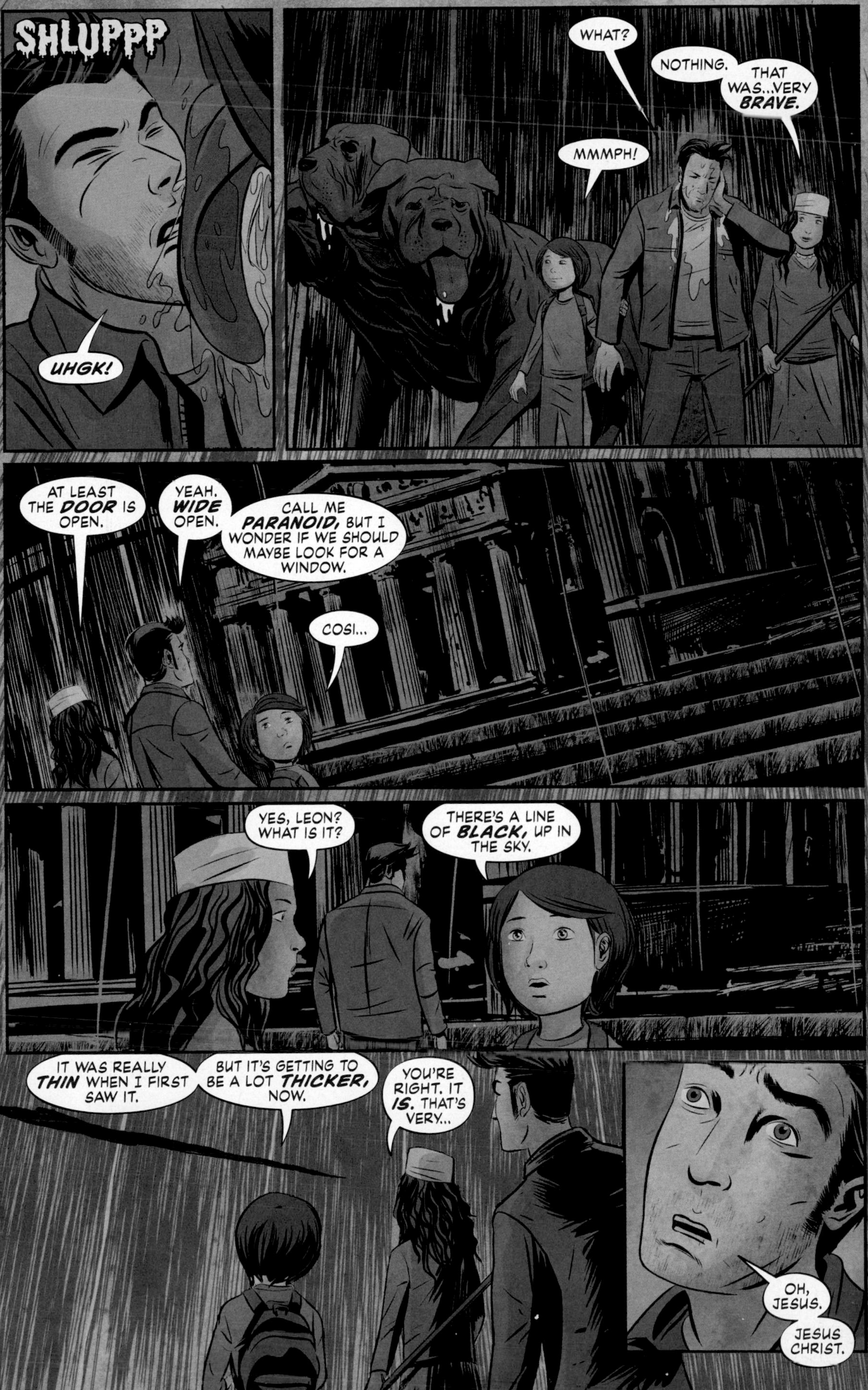
SHLUPPP
UHGK!
WHAT?
NOTHING.
THAT WAS...VERY BRAVE.
MMMPH!
AT LEAST THE DOOR IS OPEN.
YEAH. WIDE OPEN.
CALL ME PARANOID, BUT I WONDER IF WE SHOULD MAYBE LOOK FOR A WINDOW.
COSI...
YES, LEON? WHAT IS IT?
THERE'S A LINE OF BLACK, UP IN THE SKY.
IT WAS REALLY THIN WHEN I FIRST SAW IT.
BUT IT'S GETTING TO BE A LOT THICKER, NOW.
YOU'RE RIGHT. IT IS. THAT'S VERY...
OH, JESUS.
JESUS CHRIST.

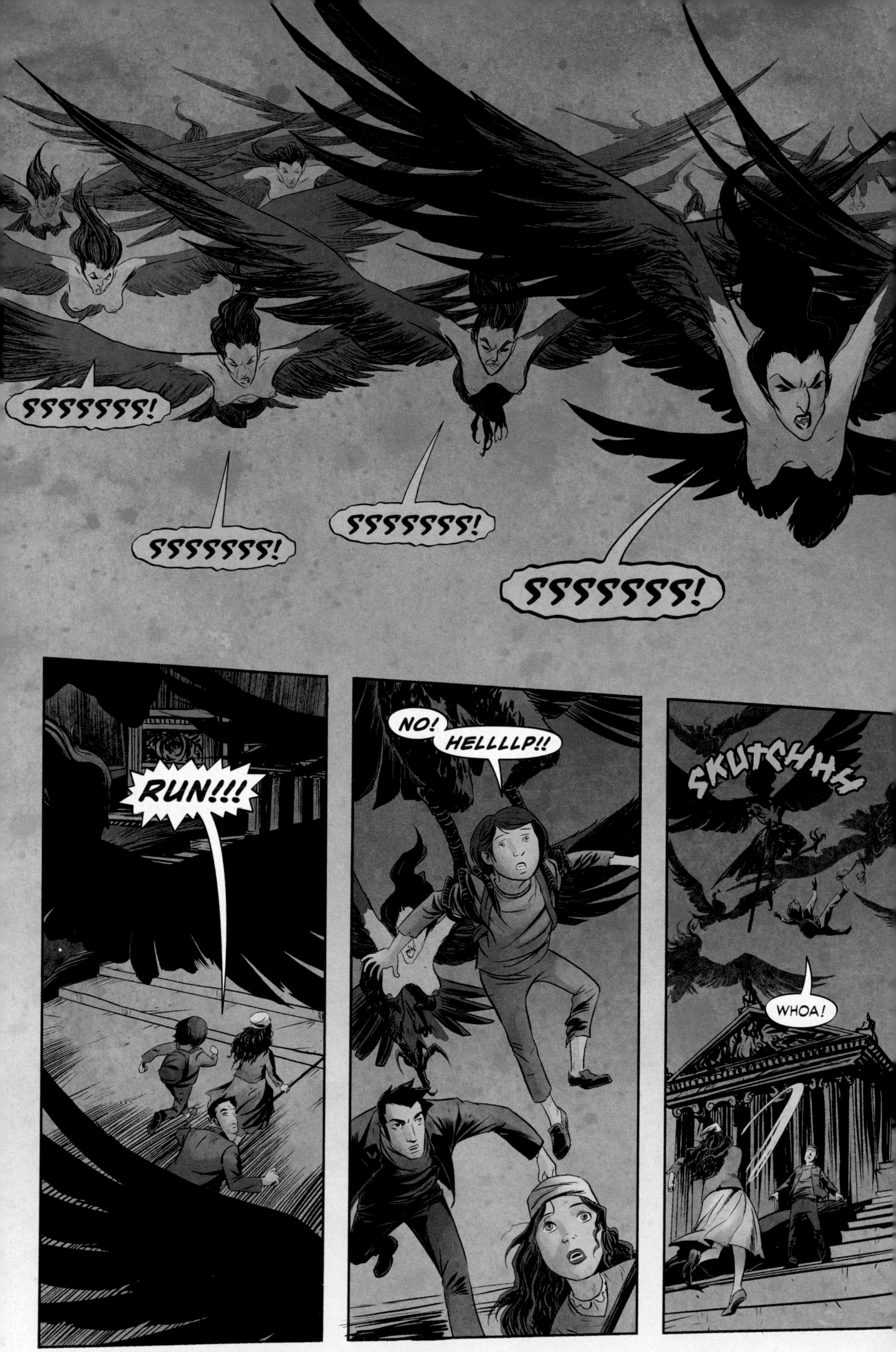
SSSSSSS!
SSSSSSS!
SSSSSSS!
SSSSSSS!
RUN!!!
NO!
HELLLLP!!
SKUTCHHH
WHOA!

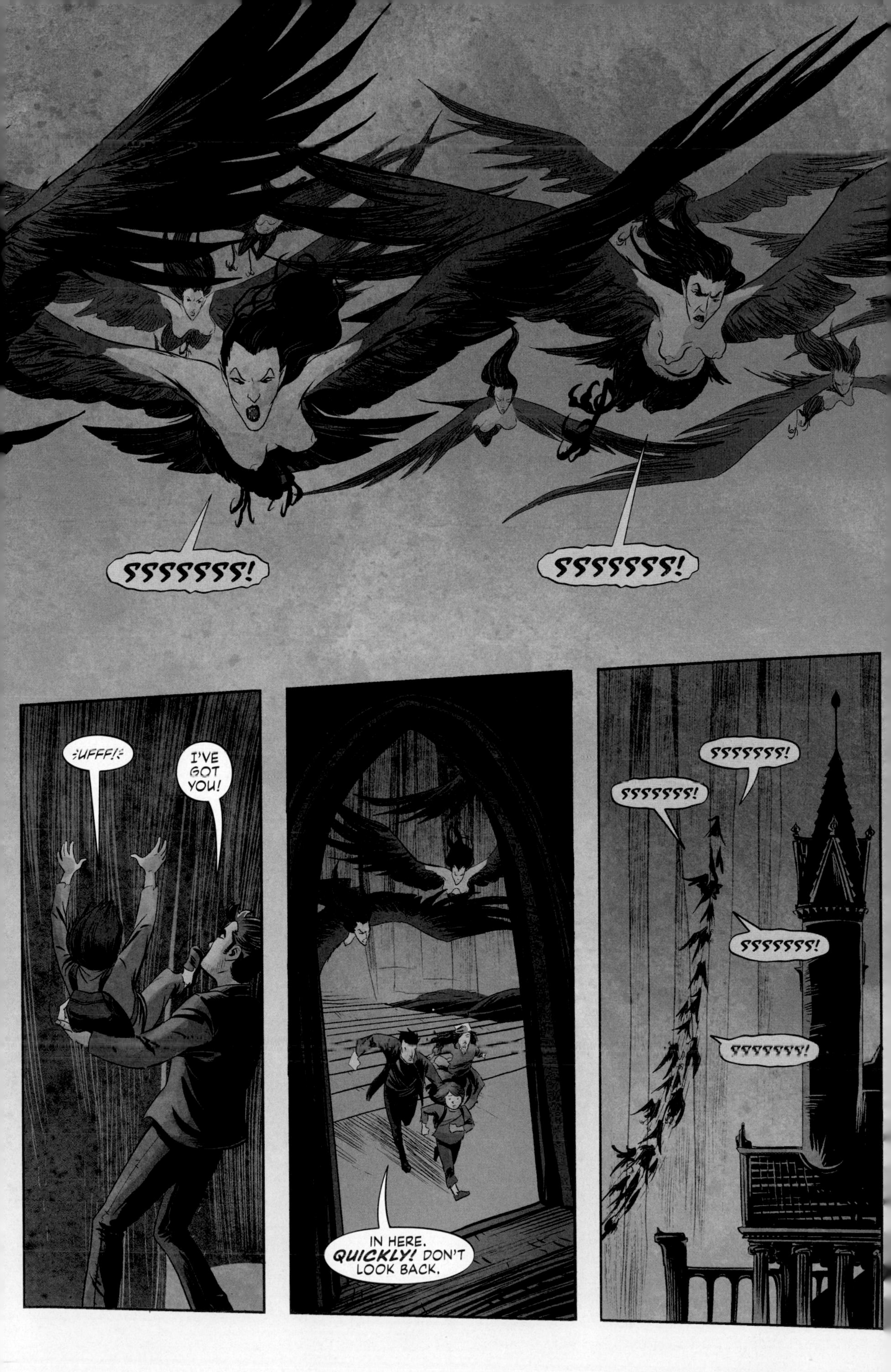
SSSSSSS!
SSSSSSS!
UFFF!
I'VE GOT YOU!
IN HERE. QUICKLY! DON'T LOOK BACK.
SSSSSSS!
SSSSSSS!
SSSSSSS!
SSSSSSS!

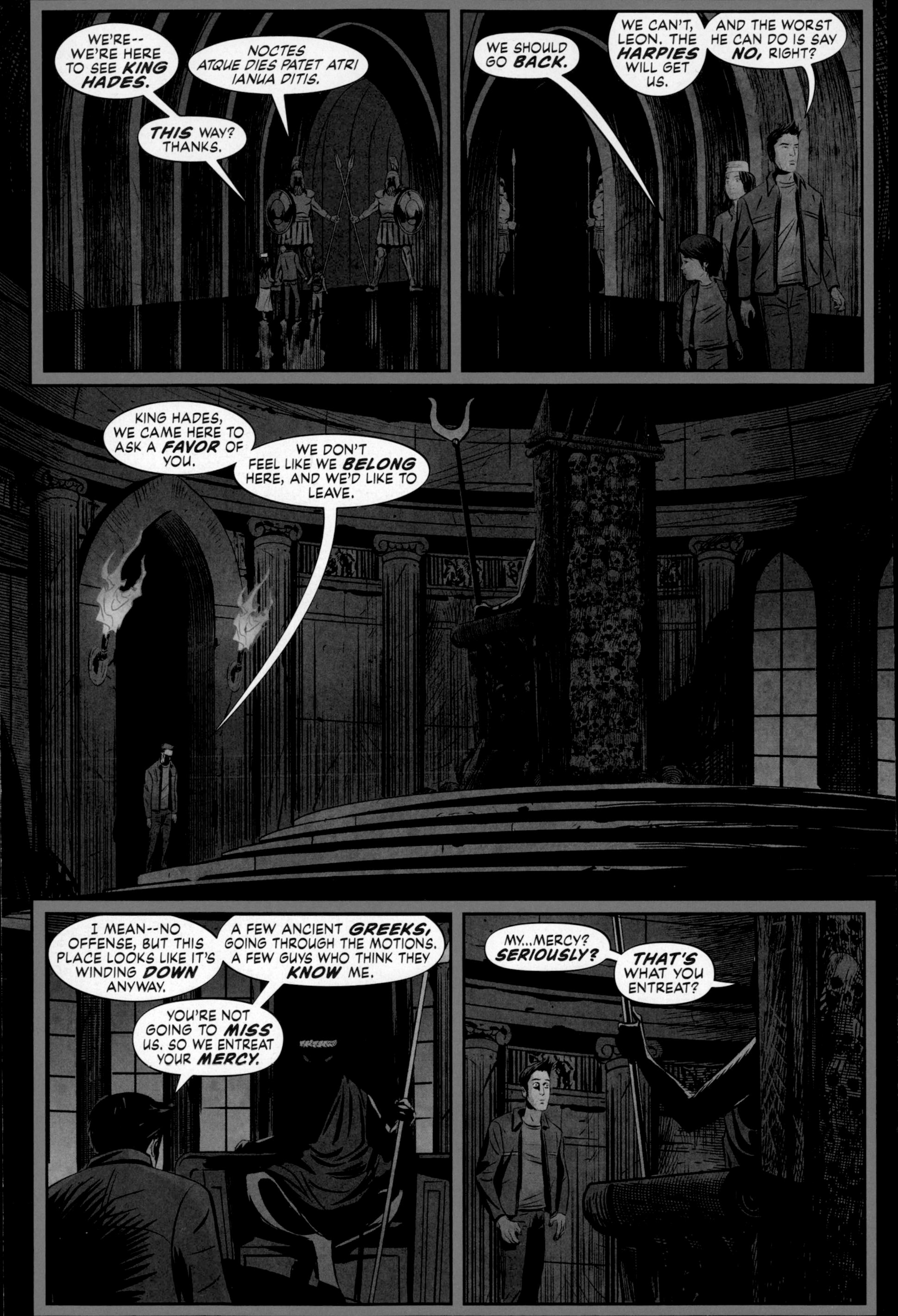
WE'RE--
WE'RE HERE TO SEE KING HADES.
NOCTES ATQUE DIES PATET ATRI IANUA DITIS.
THIS WAY? THANKS.
WE SHOULD GO BACK.
WE CAN'T, LEON. THE HARPIES WILL GET US.
AND THE WORST HE CAN DO IS SAY NO, RIGHT?
KING HADES, WE CAME HERE TO ASK A FAVOR OF YOU.
WE DON'T FEEL LIKE WE BELONG HERE, AND WE'D LIKE TO LEAVE.
I MEAN--NO OFFENSE, BUT THIS PLACE LOOKS LIKE IT'S WINDING DOWN ANYWAY.
A FEW ANCIENT GREEKS, GOING THROUGH THE MOTIONS. A FEW GUYS WHO THINK THEY KNOW ME.
YOU'RE NOT GOING TO MISS US. SO WE ENTREAT YOUR MERCY.
MY...MERCY? SERIOUSLY?
THAT'S WHAT YOU ENTREAT?

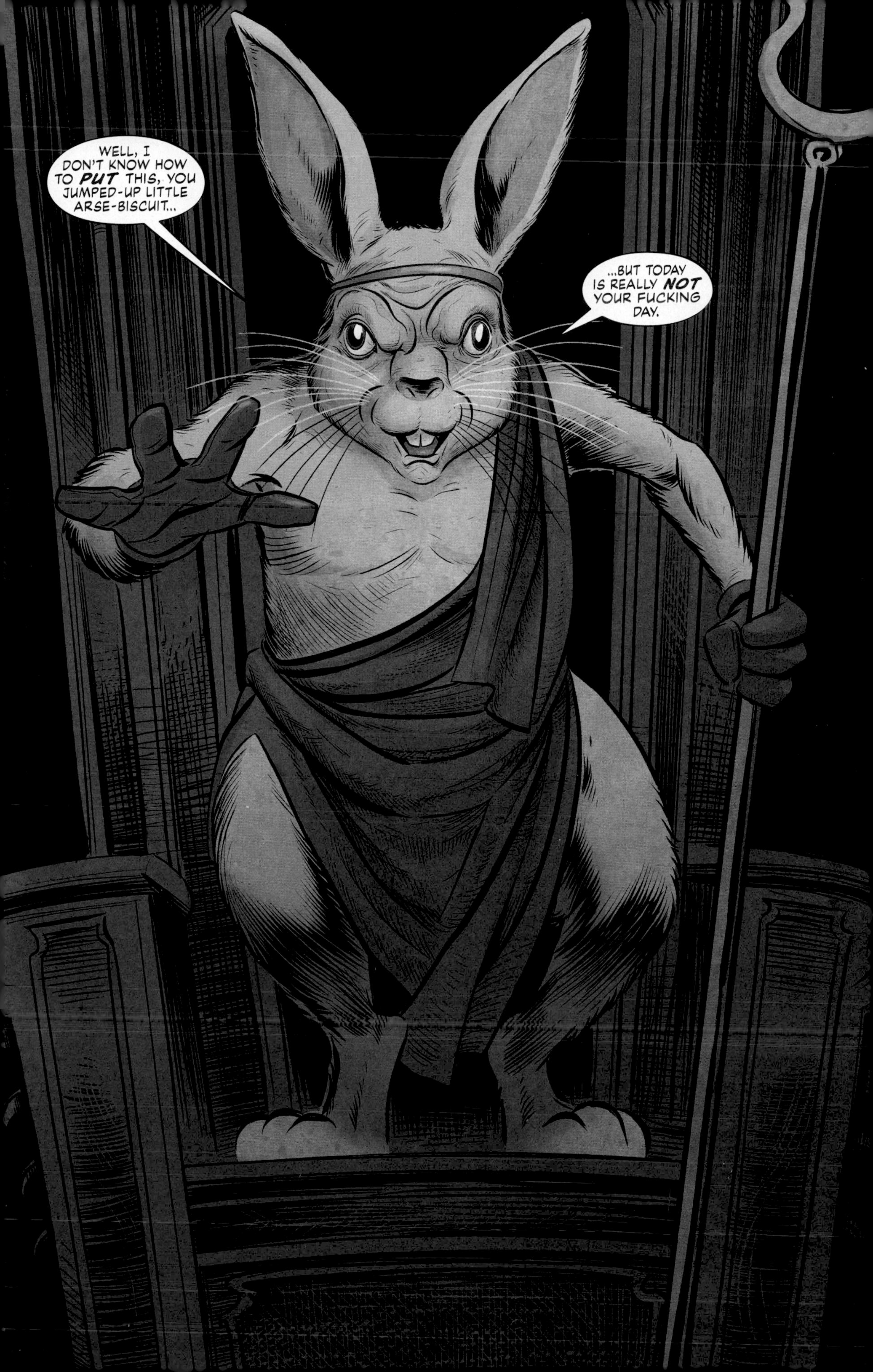
WELL, I DON'T KNOW HOW TO PUT THIS, YOU JUMPED-UP LITTLE ARSE-BISCUIT...
...BUT TODAY IS REALLY NOT YOUR FUCKING DAY.

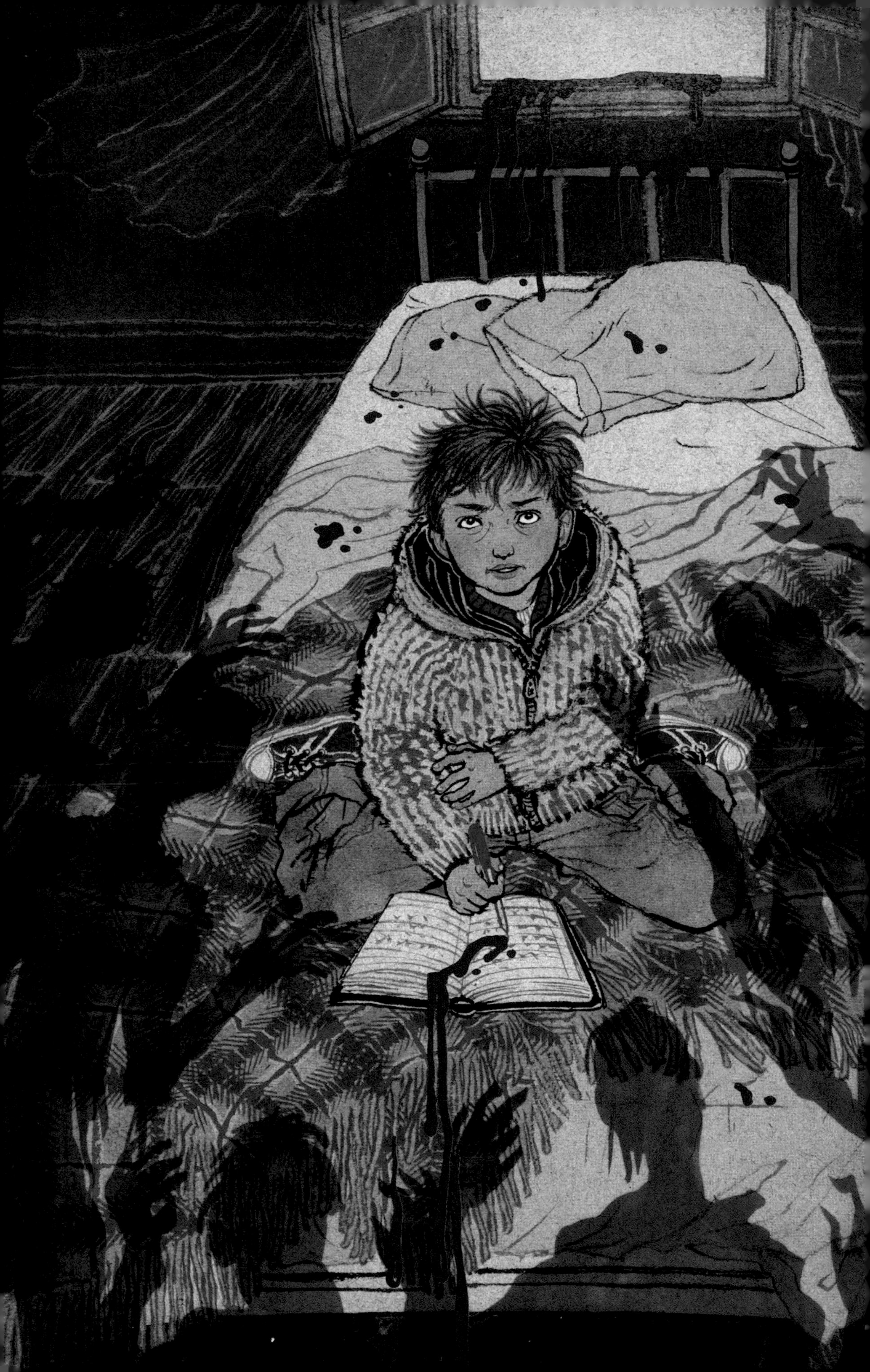

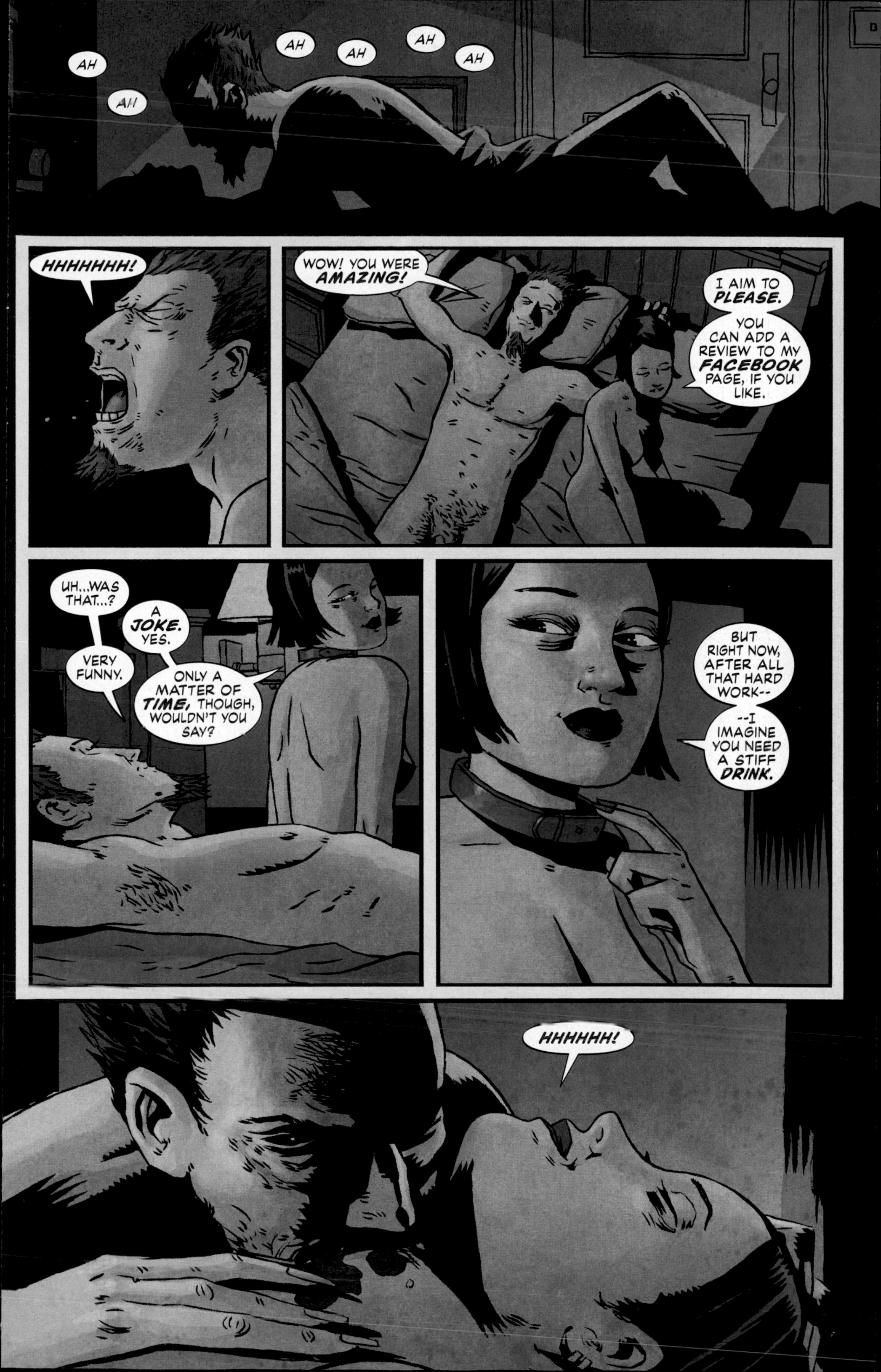
AH
AH
AH
AH
AH
AH
HHHHHHH!
WOW! YOU WERE AMAZING!
I AIM TO PLEASE.
YOU CAN ADD A REVIEW TO MY FACEBOOK PAGE, IF YOU LIKE.
UH...WAS THAT...?
A JOKE. YES.
VERY FUNNY.
ONLY A MATTER OF TIME, THOUGH, WOULDN'T YOU SAY?
BUT RIGHT NOW, AFTER ALL THAT HARD WORK--
--I IMAGINE YOU NEED A STIFF DRINK.
HHHHHH!

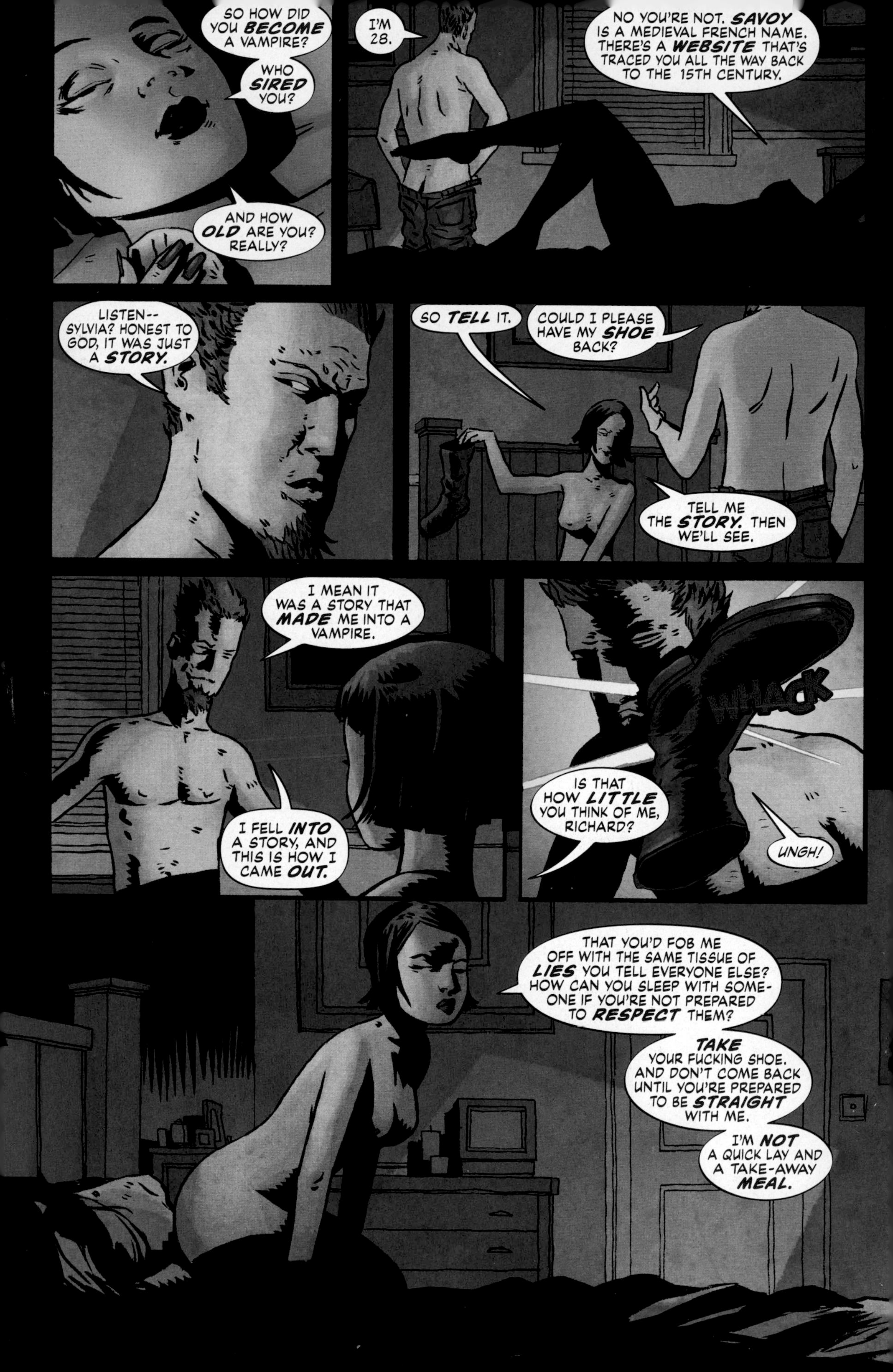
SO HOW DID YOU BECOME A VAMPIRE?
WHO SIRED YOU?
AND HOW OLD ARE YOU? REALLY?
I'M 28.
NO YOU'RE NOT. SAVOY IS A MEDIEVAL FRENCH NAME. THERE'S A WEBSITE THAT'S TRACED YOU ALL THE WAY BACK TO THE 15TH CENTURY.
LISTEN-- SYLVIA? HONEST TO GOD, IT WAS JUST A STORY.
SO TELL IT.
COULD I PLEASE HAVE MY SHOE BACK?
TELL ME THE STORY. THEN WE'LL SEE.
I MEAN IT WAS A STORY THAT MADE ME INTO A VAMPIRE.
I FELL INTO A STORY, AND THIS IS HOW I CAME OUT.
WHACK
IS THAT HOW LITTLE YOU THINK OF ME, RICHARD?
UNGH!
THAT YOU'D FOB ME OFF WITH THE SAME TISSUE OF LIES YOU TELL EVERYONE ELSE? HOW CAN YOU SLEEP WITH SOME-ONE IF YOU'RE NOT PREPARED TO RESPECT THEM?
TAKE YOUR FUCKING SHOE. AND DON'T COME BACK UNTIL YOU'RE PREPARED TO BE STRAIGHT WITH ME.
I'M NOT A QUICK LAY AND A TAKE-AWAY MEAL.

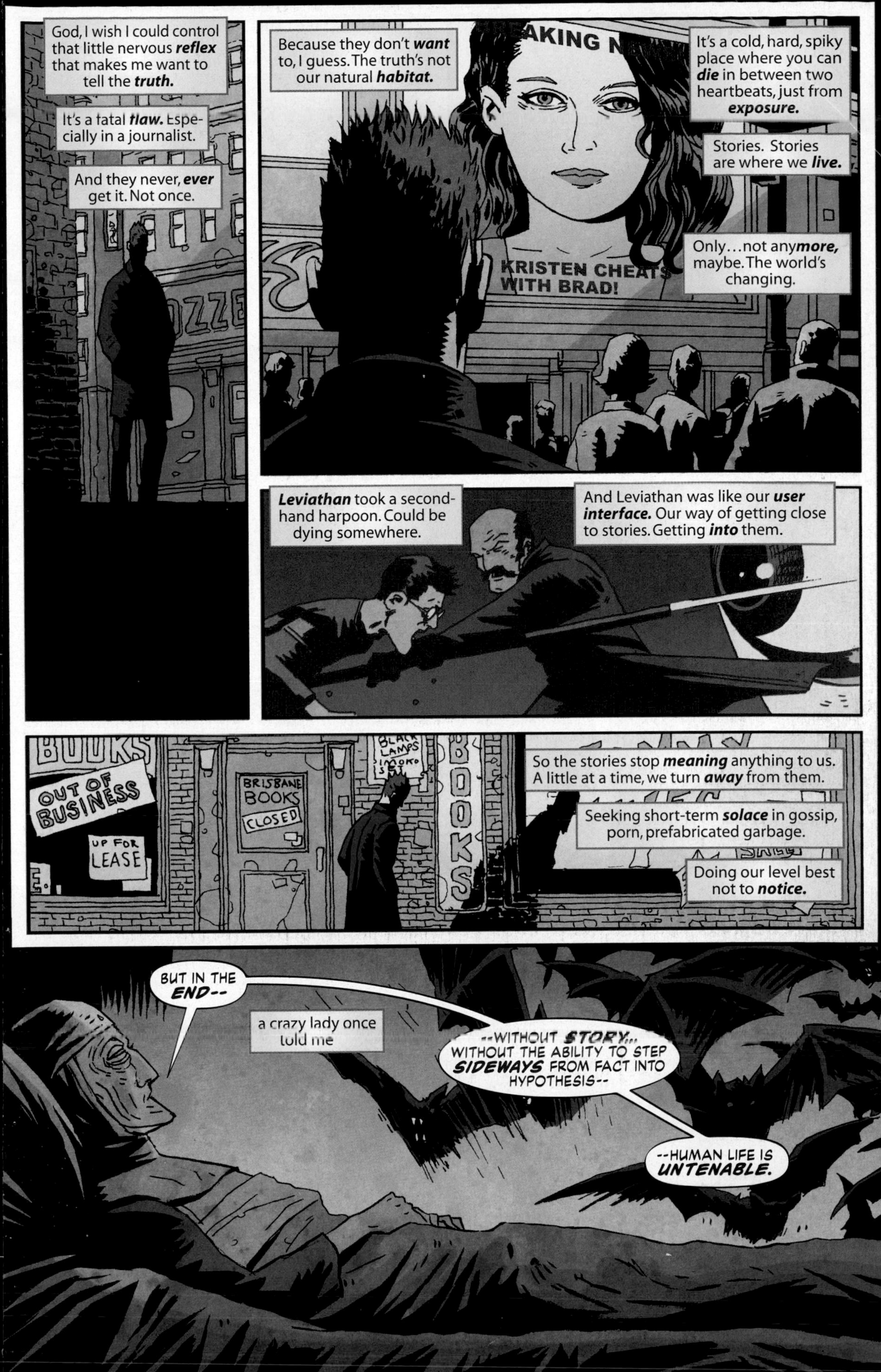
God, I wish I could control that little nervous *reflex* that makes me want to tell the *truth.*
It's a fatal *flaw.* Especially in a journalist.
And they never, *ever* get it. Not once.
Because they don't *want* to, I guess. The truth's not our natural *habitat.*
KRISTEN CHEATS WITH BRAD!
It's a cold, hard, spiky place where you can *die* in between two heartbeats, just from *exposure.*
Stories. Stories are where we *live.*
Only... not any*more,* maybe. The world's changing.
*Leviathan* took a second-hand harpoon. Could be dying somewhere.
And Leviathan was like our *user interface.* Our way of getting close to stories. Getting *into* them.
BOOKS
OUT OF BUSINESS
UP FOR LEASE
BRISBANE BOOKS
CLOSED
BOOKS
So the stories stop *meaning* anything to us. A little at a time, we turn *away* from them.
Seeking short-term *solace* in gossip, porn, prefabricated garbage.
Doing our level best not to *notice.*
BUT IN THE *END--*
a crazy lady once told me
--WITHOUT *STORY...* WITHOUT THE ABILITY TO STEP *SIDEWAYS* FROM FACT INTO HYPOTHESIS--
--HUMAN LIFE IS *UNTENABLE.*

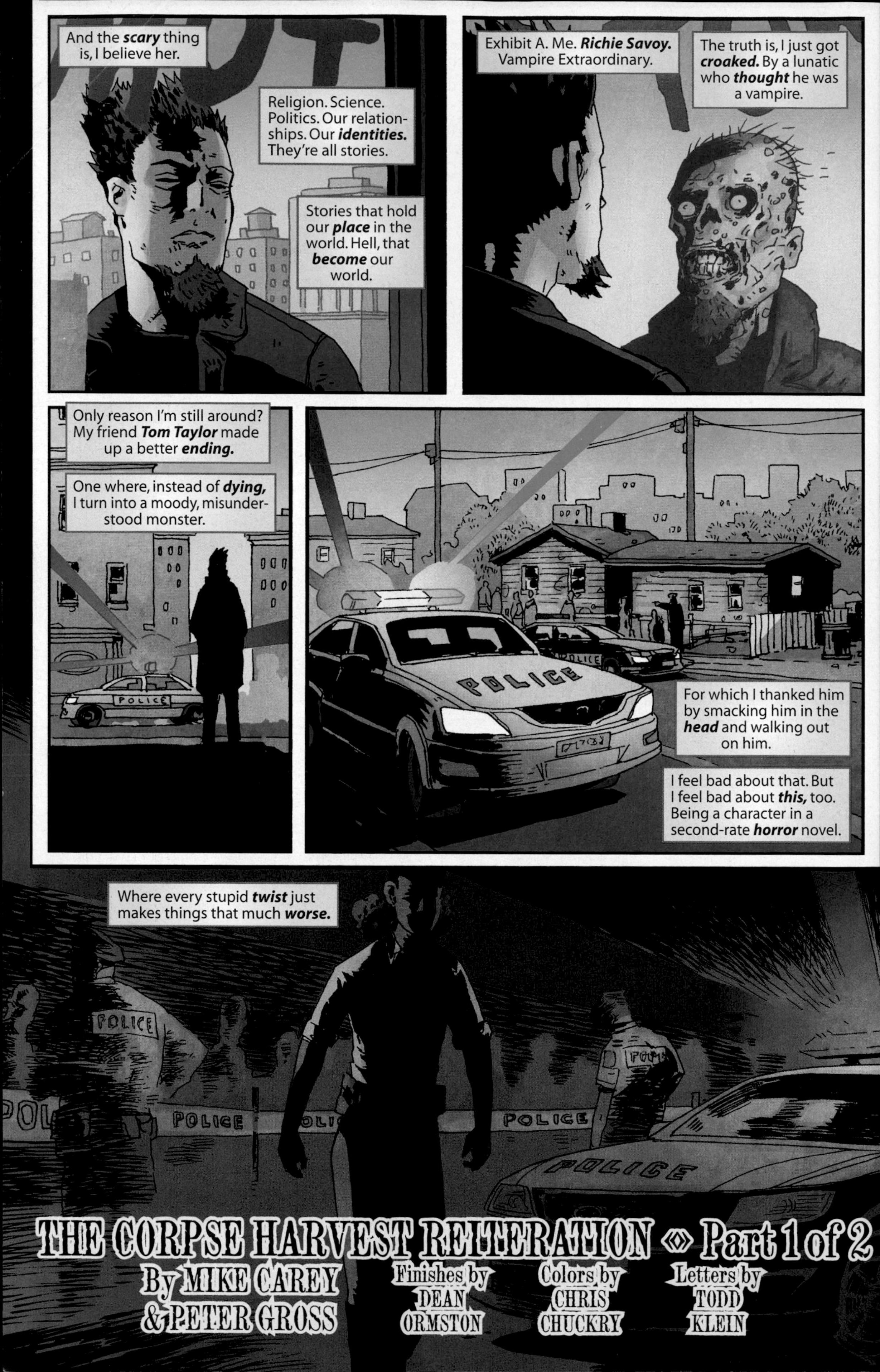

And the scary thing is, I believe her.
Religion. Science. Politics. Our relationships. Our identities. They're all stories.
Stories that hold our place in the world. Hell, that become our world.
Exhibit A. Me. Richie Savoy. Vampire Extraordinary.
The truth is, I just got croaked. By a lunatic who thought he was a vampire.
Only reason I'm still around? My friend Tom Taylor made up a better ending.
One where, instead of dying, I turn into a moody, misunderstood monster.
POLICE
POLICE
POLICE
For which I thanked him by smacking him in the head and walking out on him.
I feel bad about that. But I feel bad about this, too. Being a character in a second-rate horror novel.
Where every stupid twist just makes things that much worse.
POLICE
POLICE
POLICE
POLICE
THE CORPSE HARVEST REITERATION « Part 1 of 2
By MIKE CAREY & PETER GROSS
Finishes by DEAN ORMSTON
Colors by CHRIS CHUCKRY
Letters by TODD KLEIN

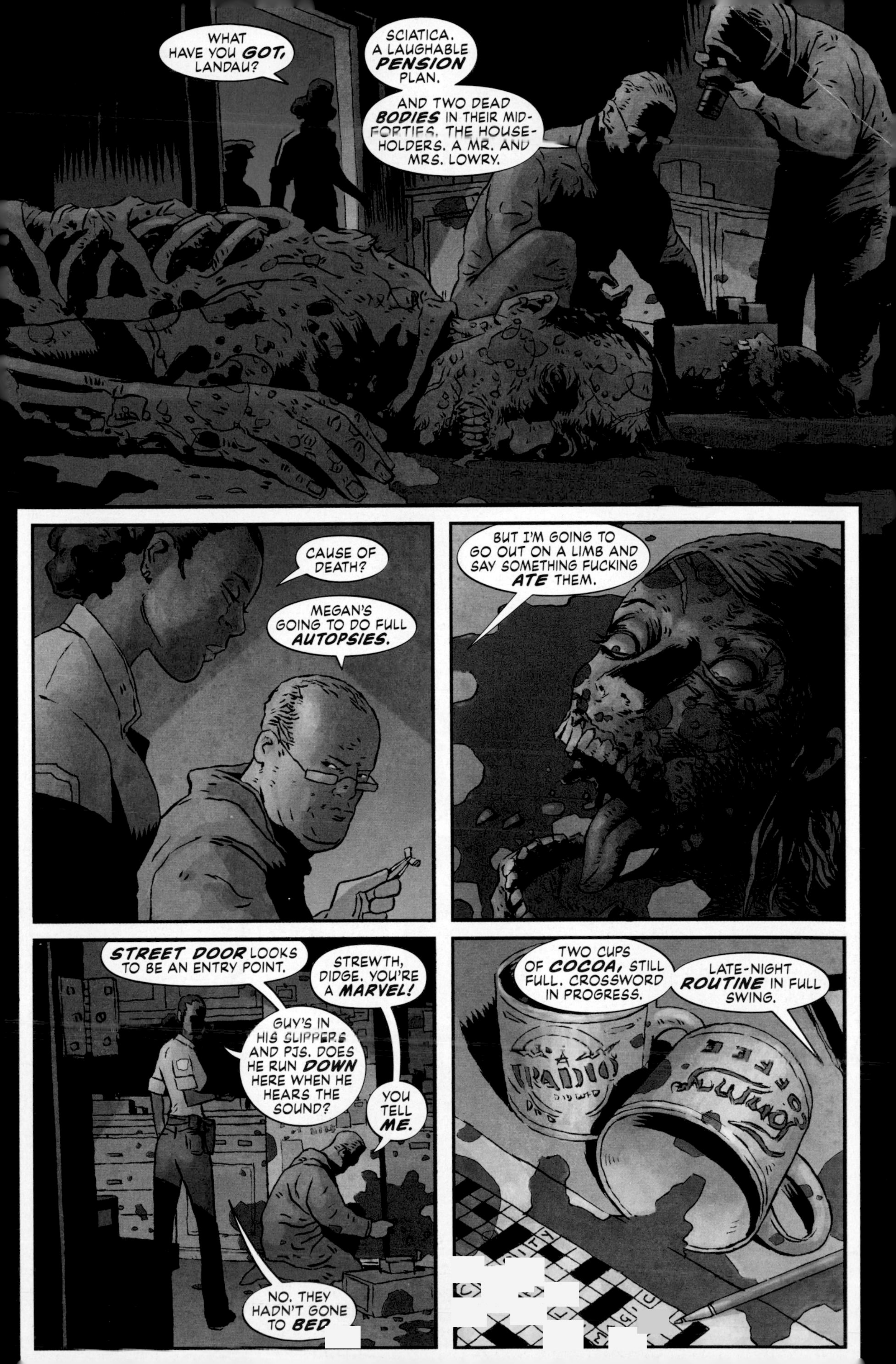
WHAT HAVE YOU GOT, LANDAU?
SCIATICA. A LAUGHABLE PENSION PLAN.
AND TWO DEAD BODIES IN THEIR MID-FORTIES. THE HOUSEHOLDERS. A MR. AND MRS. LOWRY.
CAUSE OF DEATH?
MEGAN'S GOING TO DO FULL AUTOPSIES.
BUT I'M GOING TO GO OUT ON A LIMB AND SAY SOMETHING FUCKING ATE THEM.
STREET DOOR LOOKS TO BE AN ENTRY POINT.
STREWTH, DIDGE. YOU'RE A MARVEL!
GUY'S IN HIS SLIPPERS AND PJS. DOES HE RUN DOWN HERE WHEN HE HEARS THE SOUND?
YOU TELL ME.
NO. THEY HADN'T GONE TO BED.
TWO CUPS OF COCOA, STILL FULL. CROSSWORD IN PROGRESS.
LATE-NIGHT ROUTINE IN FULL SWING.

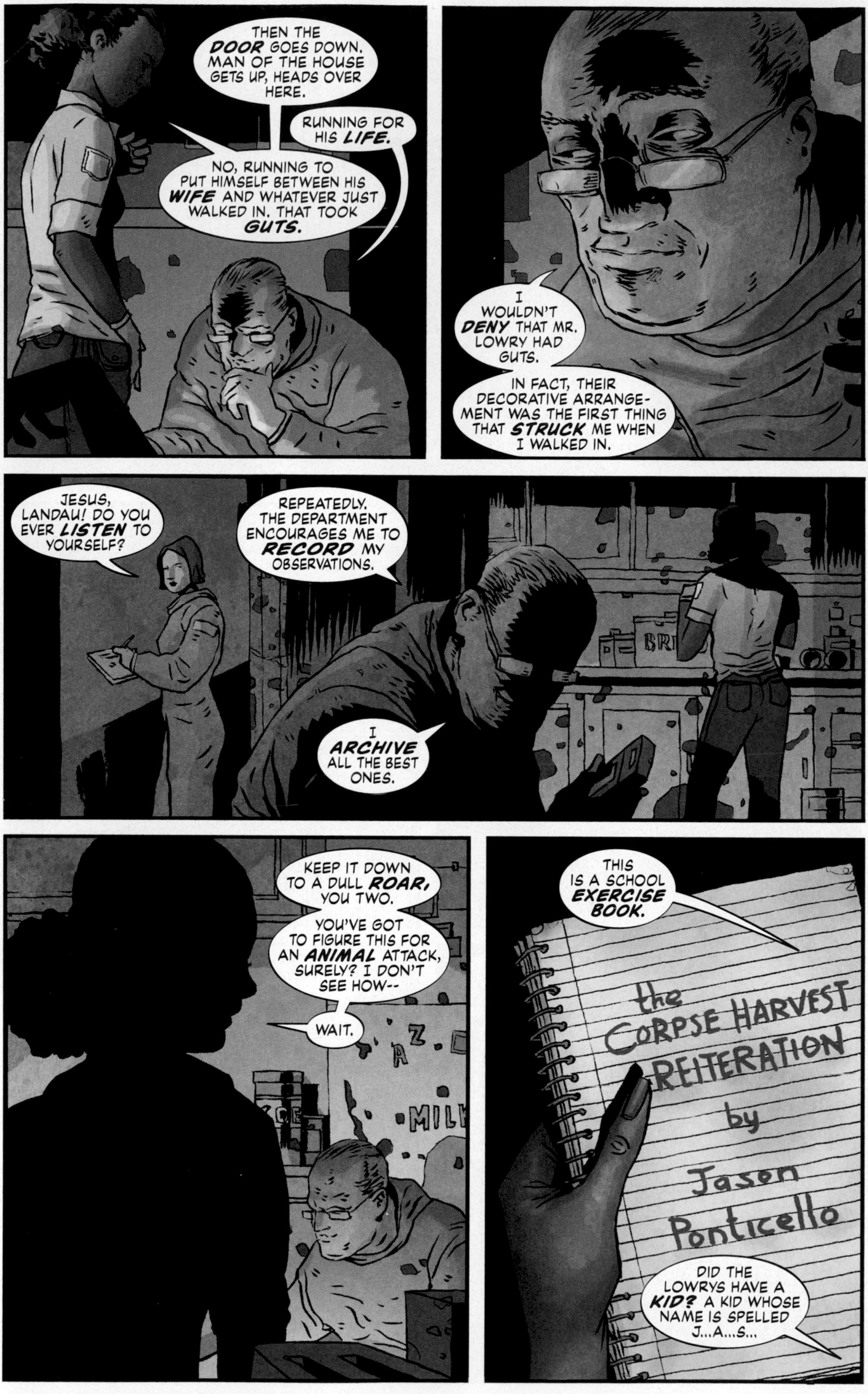
THEN THE DOOR GOES DOWN. MAN OF THE HOUSE GETS UP, HEADS OVER HERE.
RUNNING FOR HIS LIFE.
NO, RUNNING TO PUT HIMSELF BETWEEN HIS WIFE AND WHATEVER JUST WALKED IN. THAT TOOK GUTS.
I WOULDN'T DENY THAT MR. LOWRY HAD GUTS.
IN FACT, THEIR DECORATIVE ARRANGE-MENT WAS THE FIRST THING THAT STRUCK ME WHEN I WALKED IN.
JESUS, LANDAU! DO YOU EVER LISTEN TO YOURSELF?
REPEATEDLY. THE DEPARTMENT ENCOURAGES ME TO RECORD MY OBSERVATIONS.
I ARCHIVE ALL THE BEST ONES.
KEEP IT DOWN TO A DULL ROAR, YOU TWO.
YOU'VE GOT TO FIGURE THIS FOR AN ANIMAL ATTACK, SURELY? I DON'T SEE HOW--
WAIT.
THIS IS A SCHOOL EXERCISE BOOK.
the CORPSE HARVEST REITERATION by Jason Ponticello
DID THE LOWRYS HAVE A KID? A KID WHOSE NAME IS SPELLED J...A...S...

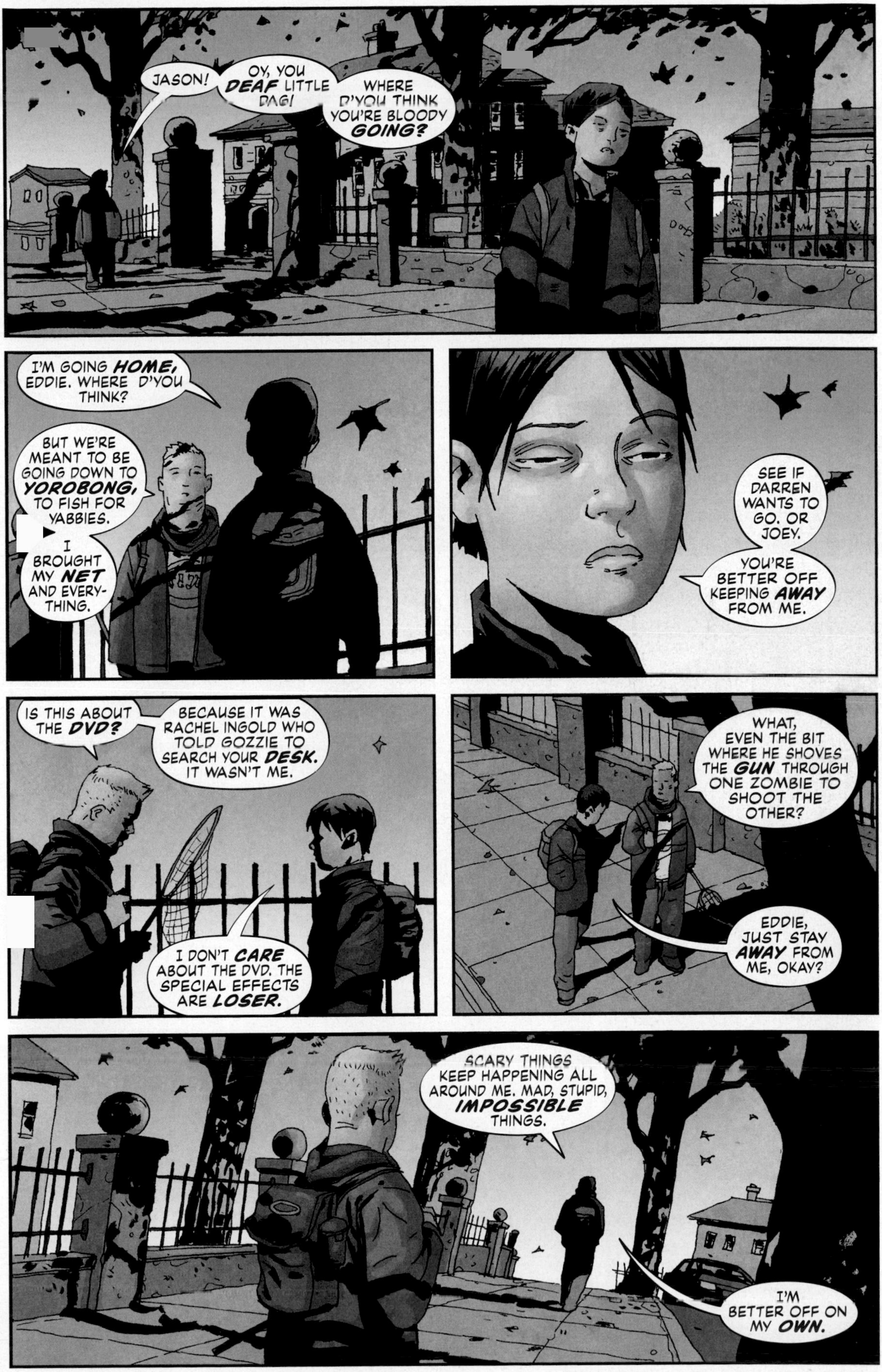
JASON!
OY, YOU DEAF LITTLE DAG!
WHERE D'YOU THINK YOU'RE BLOODY GOING?
I'M GOING HOME, EDDIE. WHERE D'YOU THINK?
BUT WE'RE MEANT TO BE GOING DOWN TO YOROBONG, TO FISH FOR YABBIES.
I BROUGHT MY NET AND EVERY-THING.
SEE IF DARREN WANTS TO GO. OR JOEY.
YOU'RE BETTER OFF KEEPING AWAY FROM ME.
IS THIS ABOUT THE DVD?
BECAUSE IT WAS RACHEL INGOLD WHO TOLD GOZZIE TO SEARCH YOUR DESK. IT WASN'T ME.
I DON'T CARE ABOUT THE DVD. THE SPECIAL EFFECTS ARE LOSER.
WHAT, EVEN THE BIT WHERE HE SHOVES THE GUN THROUGH ONE ZOMBIE TO SHOOT THE OTHER?
EDDIE, JUST STAY AWAY FROM ME, OKAY?
SCARY THINGS KEEP HAPPENING ALL AROUND ME. MAD, STUPID, IMPOSSIBLE THINGS.
I'M BETTER OFF ON MY OWN.

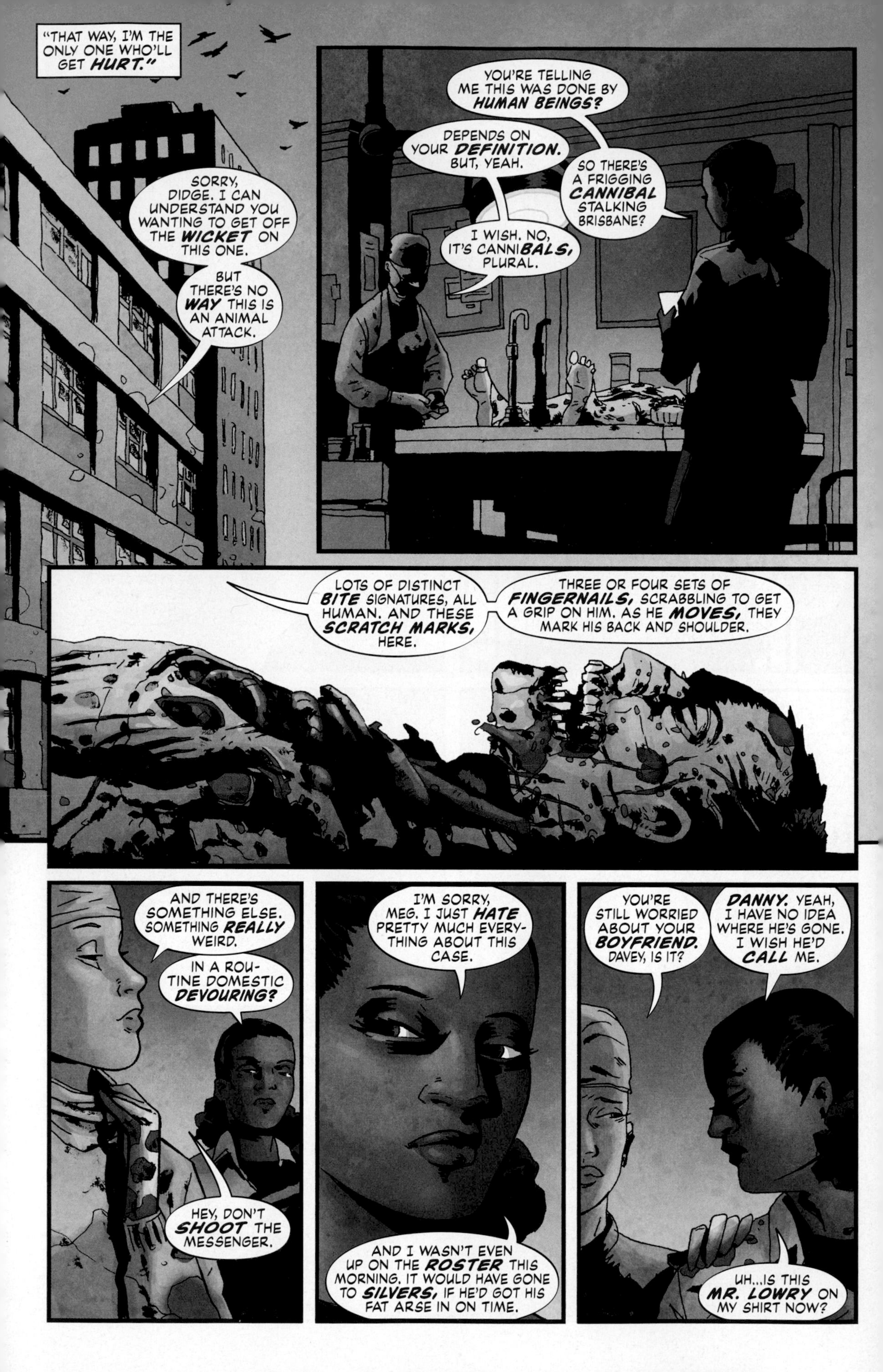
"THAT WAY, I'M THE ONLY ONE WHO'LL GET HURT."
SORRY, DIDGE. I CAN UNDERSTAND YOU WANTING TO GET OFF THE WICKET ON THIS ONE.
BUT THERE'S NO WAY THIS IS AN ANIMAL ATTACK.
YOU'RE TELLING ME THIS WAS DONE BY HUMAN BEINGS?
DEPENDS ON YOUR DEFINITION. BUT, YEAH.
SO THERE'S A FRIGGING CANNIBAL STALKING BRISBANE?
I WISH. NO, IT'S CANNIBALS, PLURAL.
LOTS OF DISTINCT BITE SIGNATURES, ALL HUMAN. AND THESE SCRATCH MARKS, HERE.
THREE OR FOUR SETS OF FINGERNAILS, SCRABBLING TO GET A GRIP ON HIM. AS HE MOVES, THEY MARK HIS BACK AND SHOULDER.
AND THERE'S SOMETHING ELSE. SOMETHING REALLY WEIRD.
IN A ROUTINE DOMESTIC DEVOURING?
HEY, DON'T SHOOT THE MESSENGER.
I'M SORRY, MEG. I JUST HATE PRETTY MUCH EVERYTHING ABOUT THIS CASE.
AND I WASN'T EVEN UP ON THE ROSTER THIS MORNING. IT WOULD HAVE GONE TO SILVERS, IF HE'D GOT HIS FAT ARSE IN ON TIME.
YOU'RE STILL WORRIED ABOUT YOUR BOYFRIEND. DAVEY, IS IT?
DANNY. YEAH, I HAVE NO IDEA WHERE HE'S GONE. I WISH HE'D CALL ME.
UH...IS THIS MR. LOWRY ON MY SHIRT NOW?

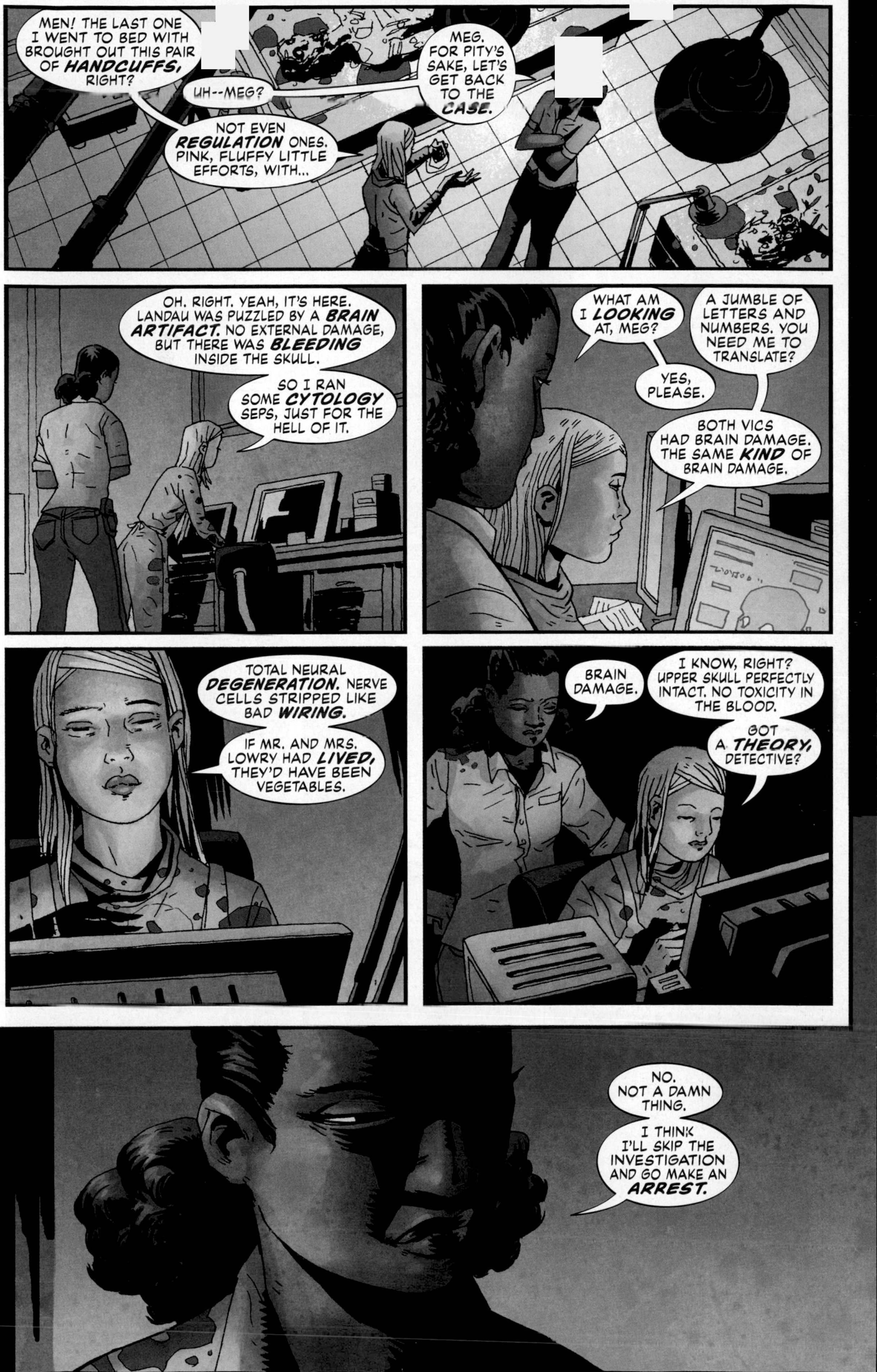
MEN! THE LAST ONE I WENT TO BED WITH BROUGHT OUT THIS PAIR OF HANDCUFFS, RIGHT?
UH--MEG?
NOT EVEN REGULATION ONES. PINK, FLUFFY LITTLE EFFORTS, WITH...
MEG. FOR PITY'S SAKE, LET'S GET BACK TO THE CASE.
OH. RIGHT. YEAH, IT'S HERE. LANDAU WAS PUZZLED BY A BRAIN ARTIFACT. NO EXTERNAL DAMAGE, BUT THERE WAS BLEEDING INSIDE THE SKULL.
SO I RAN SOME CYTOLOGY SEPS, JUST FOR THE HELL OF IT.
WHAT AM I LOOKING AT, MEG?
A JUMBLE OF LETTERS AND NUMBERS. YOU NEED ME TO TRANSLATE?
YES, PLEASE.
BOTH VICS HAD BRAIN DAMAGE. THE SAME KIND OF BRAIN DAMAGE.
TOTAL NEURAL DEGENERATION. NERVE CELLS STRIPPED LIKE BAD WIRING.
IF MR. AND MRS. LOWRY HAD LIVED, THEY'D HAVE BEEN VEGETABLES.
BRAIN DAMAGE.
I KNOW, RIGHT? UPPER SKULL PERFECTLY INTACT. NO TOXICITY IN THE BLOOD.
GOT A THEORY, DETECTIVE?
NO. NOT A DAMN THING.
I THINK I'LL SKIP THE INVESTIGATION AND GO MAKE AN ARREST.

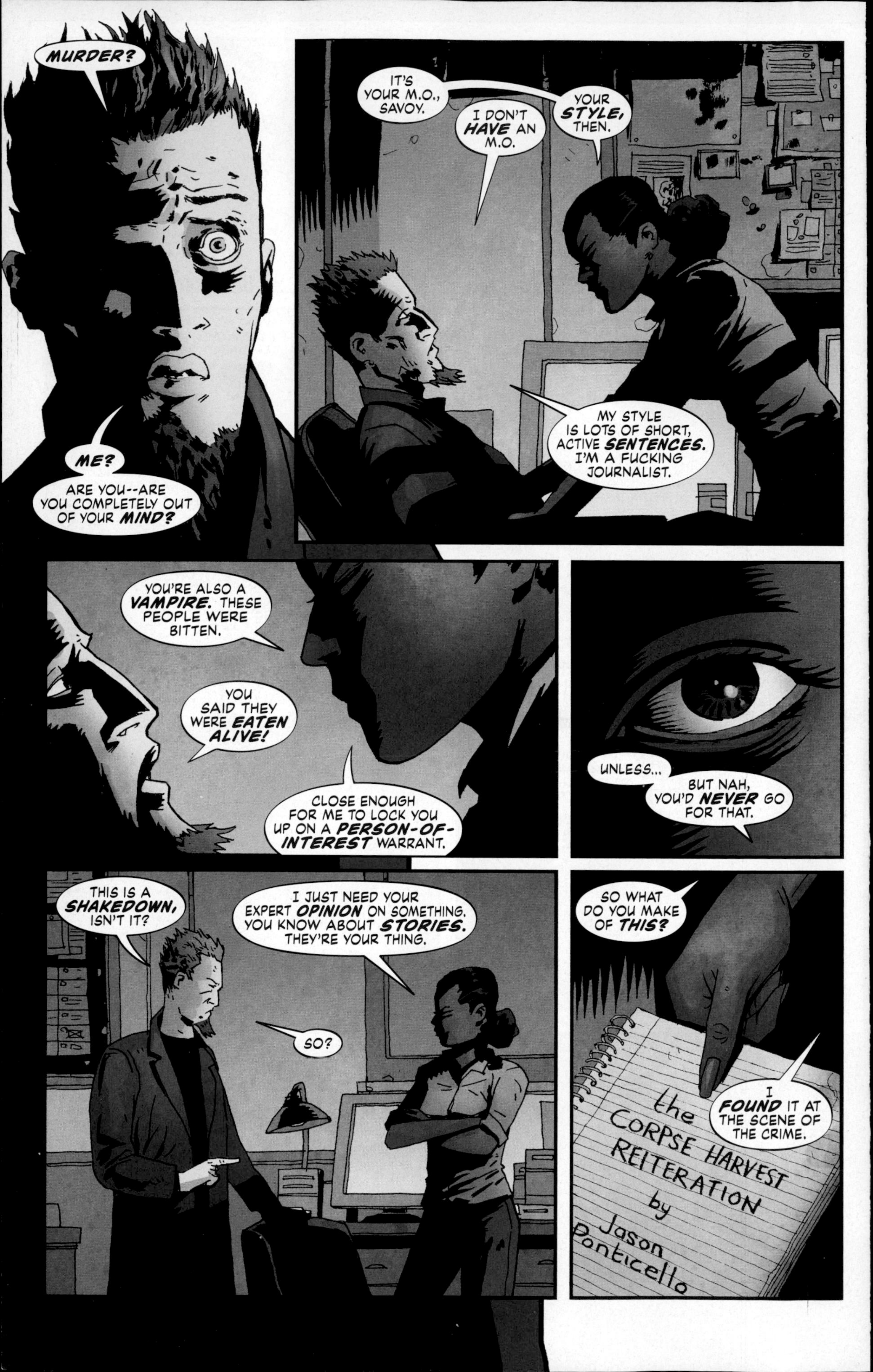
MURDER?
ME?
ARE YOU--ARE YOU COMPLETELY OUT OF YOUR MIND?
IT'S YOUR M.O., SAVOY.
I DON'T HAVE AN M.O.
YOUR STYLE, THEN.
MY STYLE IS LOTS OF SHORT, ACTIVE SENTENCES. I'M A FUCKING JOURNALIST.
YOU'RE ALSO A VAMPIRE. THESE PEOPLE WERE BITTEN.
YOU SAID THEY WERE EATEN ALIVE!
CLOSE ENOUGH FOR ME TO LOCK YOU UP ON A PERSON-OF-INTEREST WARRANT.
UNLESS...
BUT NAH, YOU'D NEVER GO FOR THAT.
THIS IS A SHAKEDOWN, ISN'T IT?
I JUST NEED YOUR EXPERT OPINION ON SOMETHING. YOU KNOW ABOUT STORIES. THEY'RE YOUR THING.
SO?
SO WHAT DO YOU MAKE OF THIS?
I FOUND IT AT THE SCENE OF THE CRIME.
the CORPSE HARVEST REITERATION by Jason Ponticello

not posibly hold against the battering it was getting now. The dead things had smeled blood, and now they wanted flesh. It was the one undeniable law of their nature. "Stay behind me," Nick told Andrea. "And if you get a chance run for it. I'll hold them off as long as I can." The gorgeous long-leged blonde knew he meant it. She didnt waste words. She just kissed him hard on the lips. Then she picked up the machete, and threw him his well-worn AK-47. "This has everything going for it," she told him. "If we win, that bitch Lubek will finally give me my promotion. And if we lose..." she ran a hand down her perfect body "...you get to remember me like this." Nick opened his mouth to speak, but at that moment the door was riped off its hinges and fell into the room, shatered into matchwood.

The zombies at the front of the massed horde were also destroyed, mashed against the doorframe by the crush of those presing forward from behind. But there were plenty more to take their place.Nick aimed low, the machine gun rounds riping into the legs of the zombies. Dozens fell. But Nick was losing ground, and in the narow room that culd only end one way. A zombie fastened its teeth into his sholder and he screamed in agony. Blood sperted like red wine.

"NO!" Andrea yeled. She swung the machete in a wild arc, as thogh she was carving the Sunday joint at the devils own dinner table. A zombie head bounced into the corner of the room, it's jaws still moving. What a woman, Nick thoght. He jamed the gun barrel under the zombies jaw and fired. It was too late for him now but at least he could save Andrea. But Andrea sliped in the blood that was thick on the floor. Zombies poured over her slow but neverending like treacle from a can, more than you could ever count.

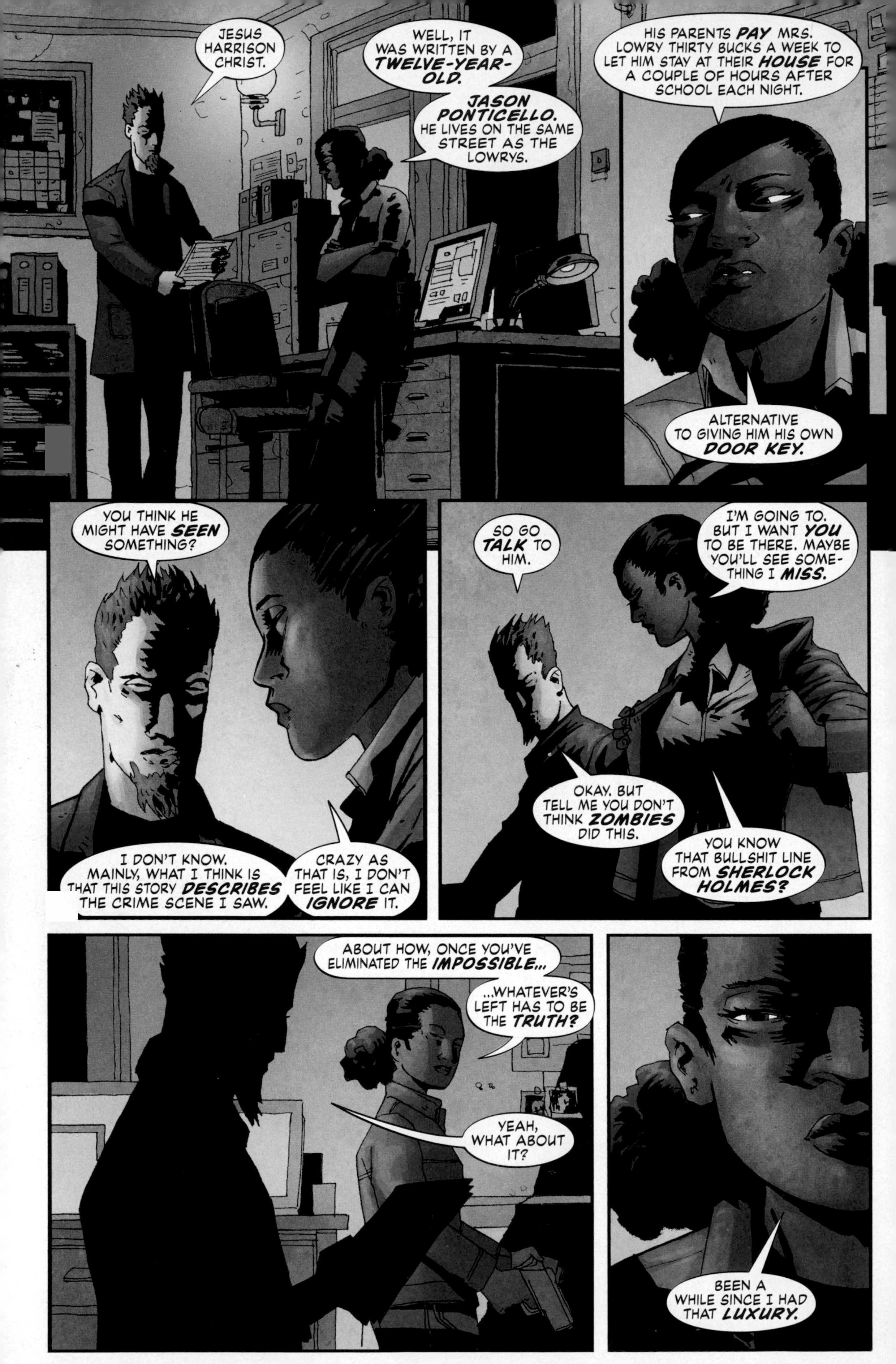
JESUS HARRISON CHRIST.
WELL, IT WAS WRITTEN BY A TWELVE-YEAR-OLD.
JASON PONTICELLO. HE LIVES ON THE SAME STREET AS THE LOWRYS.
HIS PARENTS PAY MRS. LOWRY THIRTY BUCKS A WEEK TO LET HIM STAY AT THEIR HOUSE FOR A COUPLE OF HOURS AFTER SCHOOL EACH NIGHT.
ALTERNATIVE TO GIVING HIM HIS OWN DOOR KEY.
YOU THINK HE MIGHT HAVE SEEN SOMETHING?
I DON'T KNOW. MAINLY, WHAT I THINK IS THAT THIS STORY DESCRIBES THE CRIME SCENE I SAW.
CRAZY AS THAT IS, I DON'T FEEL LIKE I CAN IGNORE IT.
SO GO TALK TO HIM.
I'M GOING TO. BUT I WANT YOU TO BE THERE. MAYBE YOU'LL SEE SOME-THING I MISS.
OKAY. BUT TELL ME YOU DON'T THINK ZOMBIES DID THIS.
YOU KNOW THAT BULLSHIT LINE FROM SHERLOCK HOLMES?
ABOUT HOW, ONCE YOU'VE ELIMINATED THE IMPOSSIBLE...
...WHATEVER'S LEFT HAS TO BE THE TRUTH?
YEAH, WHAT ABOUT IT?
BEEN A WHILE SINCE I HAD THAT LUXURY.

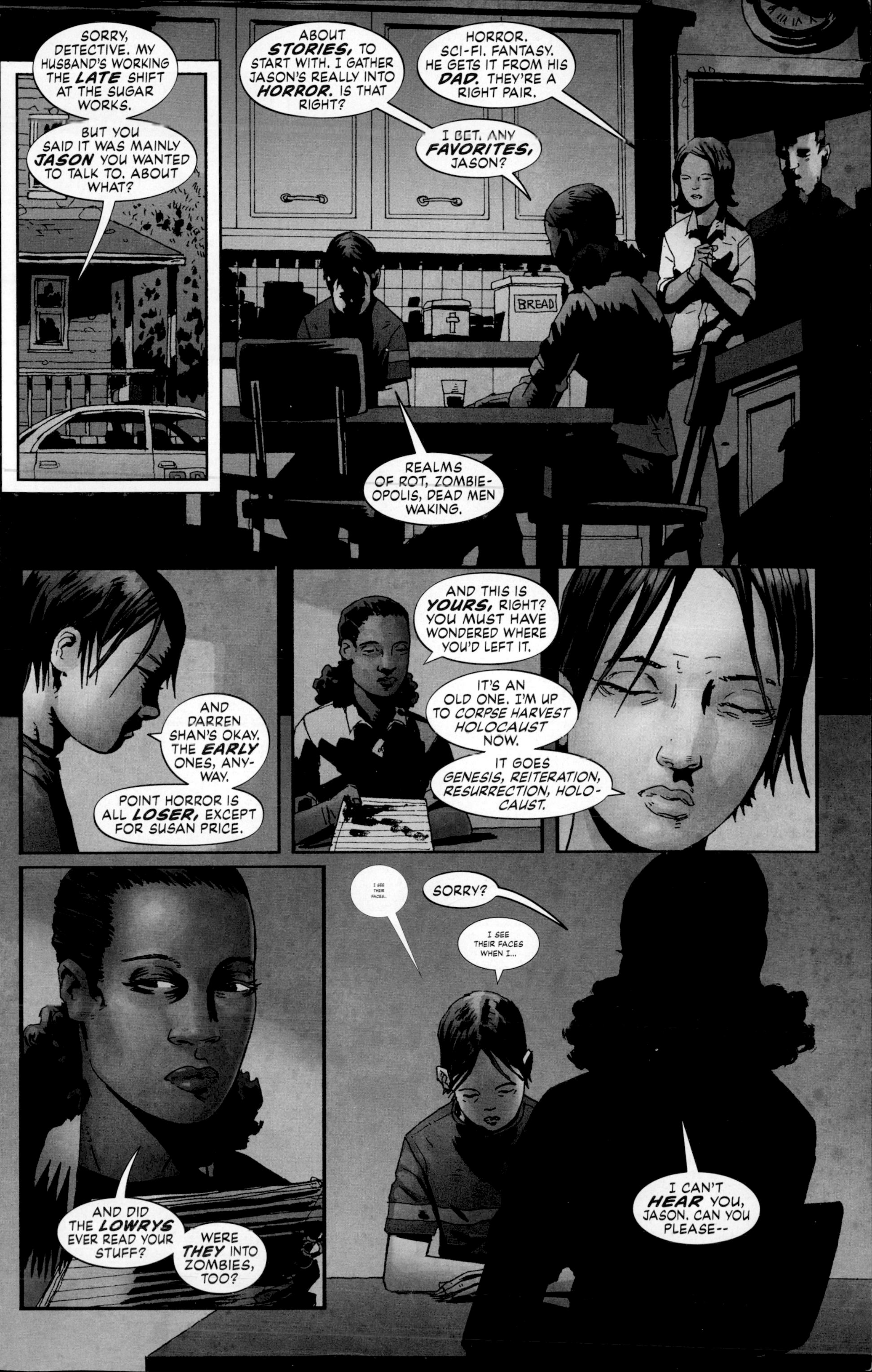
SORRY, DETECTIVE. MY HUSBAND'S WORKING THE LATE SHIFT AT THE SUGAR WORKS.
BUT YOU SAID IT WAS MAINLY JASON YOU WANTED TO TALK TO. ABOUT WHAT?
ABOUT STORIES, TO START WITH. I GATHER JASON'S REALLY INTO HORROR. IS THAT RIGHT?
HORROR. SCI-FI. FANTASY. HE GETS IT FROM HIS DAD. THEY'RE A RIGHT PAIR.
I BET. ANY FAVORITES, JASON?
BREAD
REALMS OF ROT, ZOMBIE-OPOLIS, DEAD MEN WAKING.
AND DARREN SHAN'S OKAY. THE EARLY ONES, ANYWAY.
POINT HORROR IS ALL LOSER, EXCEPT FOR SUSAN PRICE.
AND THIS IS YOURS, RIGHT? YOU MUST HAVE WONDERED WHERE YOU'D LEFT IT.
IT'S AN OLD ONE. I'M UP TO CORPSE HARVEST HOLOCAUST NOW.
IT GOES GENESIS, REITERATION, RESURRECTION, HOLOCAUST.
AND DID THE LOWRYS EVER READ YOUR STUFF?
WERE THEY INTO ZOMBIES, TOO?
I SEE THEIR FACES...
SORRY?
I SEE THEIR FACES WHEN I...
I CAN'T HEAR YOU, JASON. CAN YOU PLEASE--

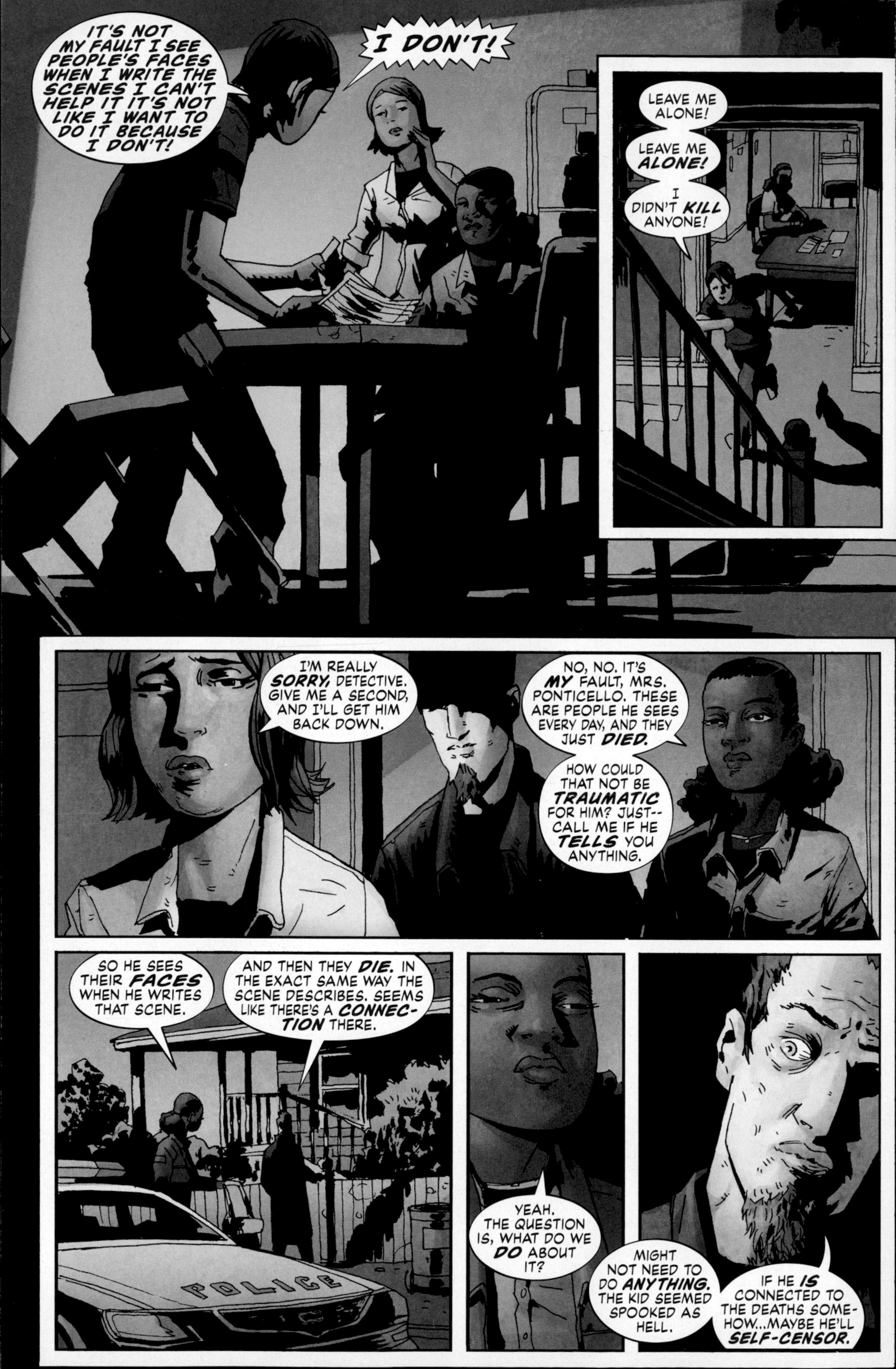
IT'S NOT MY FAULT I SEE PEOPLE'S FACES WHEN I WRITE THE SCENES I CAN'T HELP IT IT'S NOT LIKE I WANT TO DO IT BECAUSE I DON'T!
I DON'T!
LEAVE ME ALONE!
LEAVE ME ALONE!
I DIDN'T KILL ANYONE!
I'M REALLY SORRY, DETECTIVE. GIVE ME A SECOND, AND I'LL GET HIM BACK DOWN.
NO, NO. IT'S MY FAULT, MRS. PONTICELLO. THESE ARE PEOPLE HE SEES EVERY DAY, AND THEY JUST DIED.
HOW COULD THAT NOT BE TRAUMATIC FOR HIM? JUST-- CALL ME IF HE TELLS YOU ANYTHING.
SO HE SEES THEIR FACES WHEN HE WRITES THAT SCENE.
AND THEN THEY DIE. IN THE EXACT SAME WAY THE SCENE DESCRIBES. SEEMS LIKE THERE'S A CONNECTION THERE.
POLICE
YEAH. THE QUESTION IS, WHAT DO WE DO ABOUT IT?
MIGHT NOT NEED TO DO ANYTHING. THE KID SEEMED SPOOKED AS HELL.
IF HE IS CONNECTED TO THE DEATHS SOMEHOW...MAYBE HE'LL SELF-CENSOR.

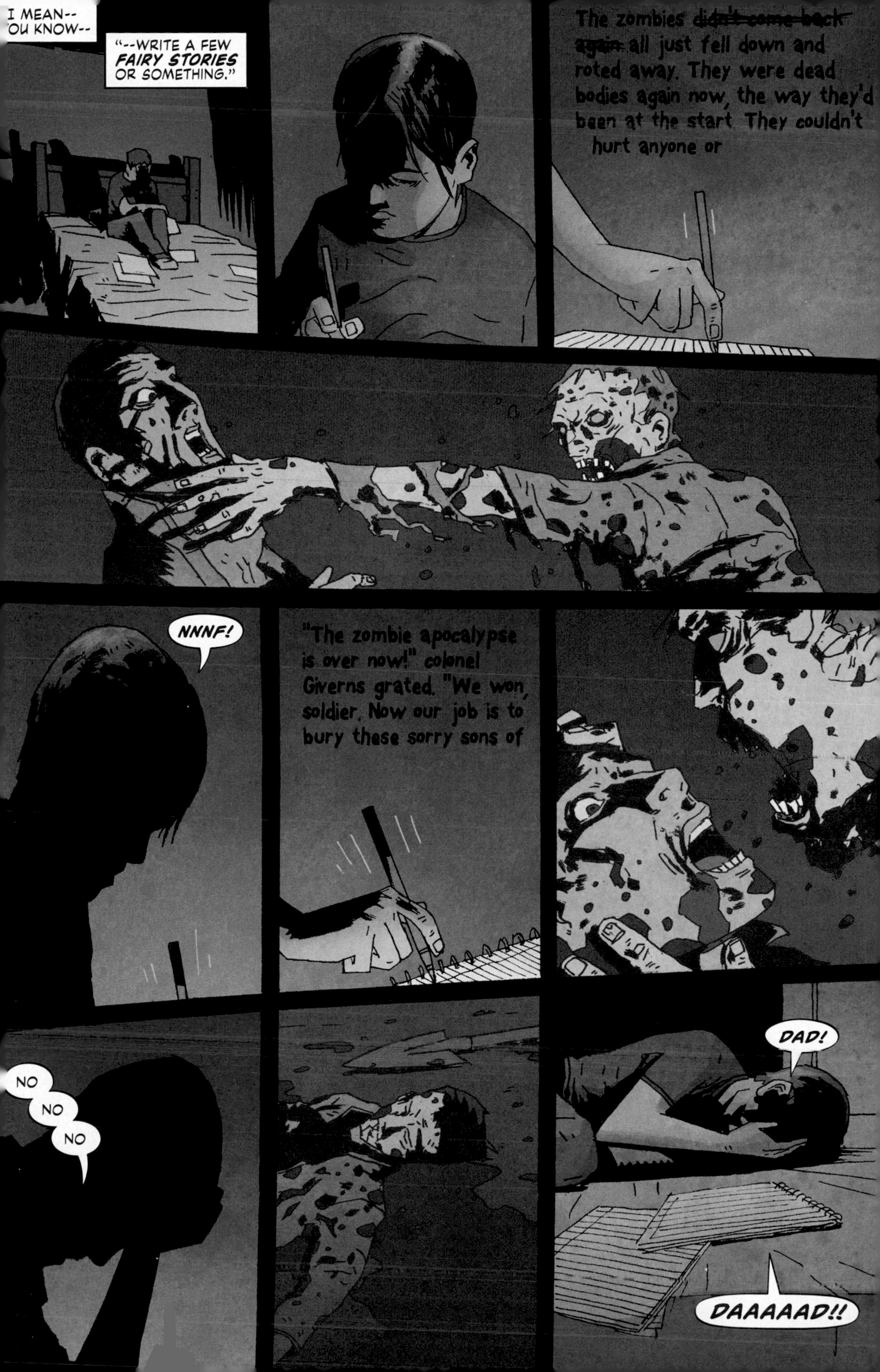

I MEAN--
OU KNOW--
"--WRITE A FEW *FAIRY STORIES* OR SOMETHING."
The zombies ~~didn't come back again~~ all just fell down and roted away. They were dead bodies again now, the way they'd been at the start. They couldn't hurt anyone or
NNNF!
"The zombie apocalypse is over now!" colonel Giverns grated. "We won, soldier. Now our job is to bury these sorry sons of
NO
NO
NO
DAD!
DAAAAAD!!

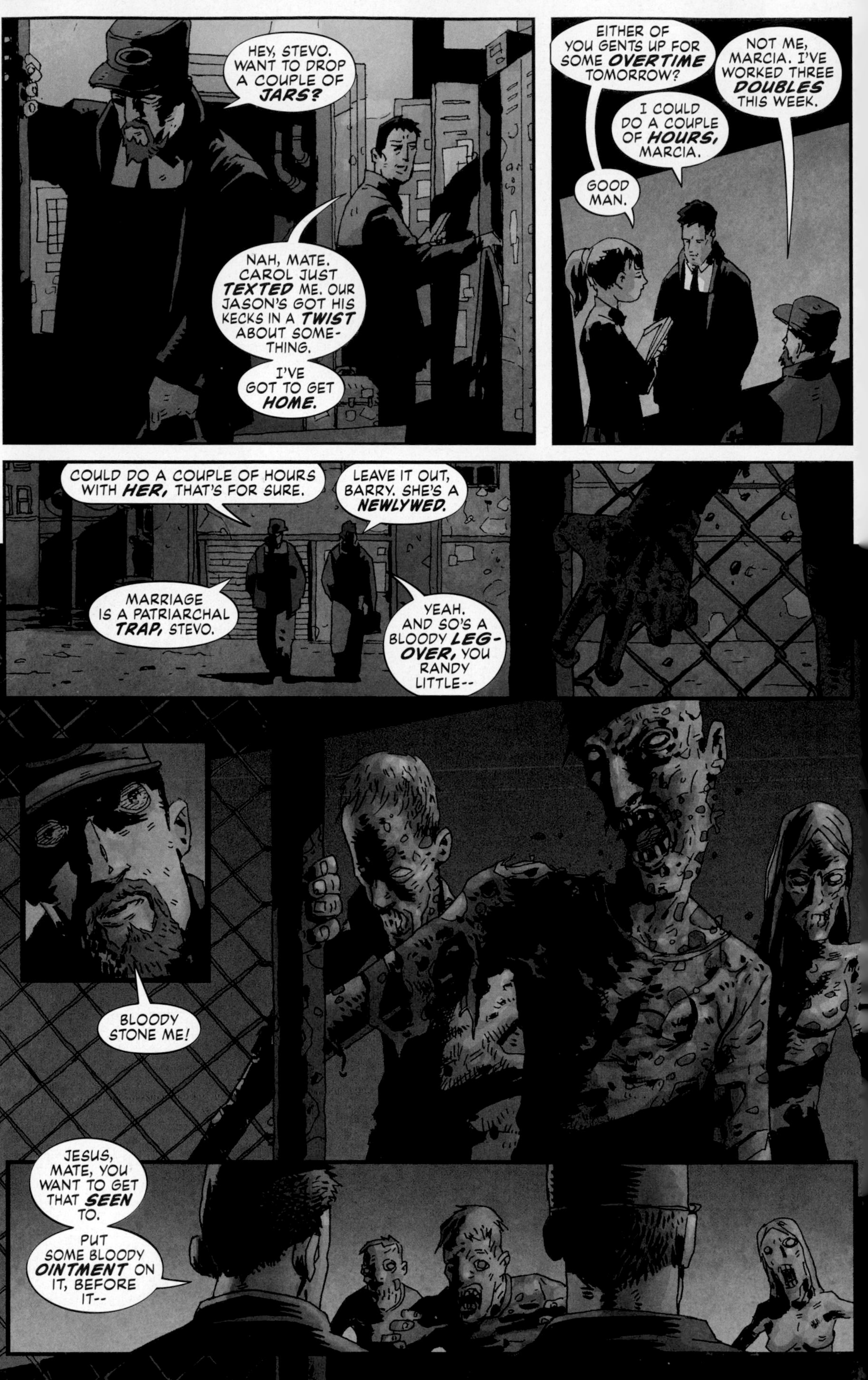
HEY, STEVO. WANT TO DROP A COUPLE OF JARS?
NAH, MATE. CAROL JUST TEXTED ME. OUR JASON'S GOT HIS KECKS IN A TWIST ABOUT SOMETHING.
I'VE GOT TO GET HOME.
EITHER OF YOU GENTS UP FOR SOME OVERTIME TOMORROW?
NOT ME, MARCIA. I'VE WORKED THREE DOUBLES THIS WEEK.
I COULD DO A COUPLE OF HOURS, MARCIA.
GOOD MAN.
COULD DO A COUPLE OF HOURS WITH HER, THAT'S FOR SURE.
LEAVE IT OUT, BARRY. SHE'S A NEWLYWED.
MARRIAGE IS A PATRIARCHAL TRAP, STEVO.
YEAH. AND SO'S A BLOODY LEG-OVER, YOU RANDY LITTLE--
BLOODY STONE ME!
JESUS, MATE, YOU WANT TO GET THAT SEEN TO.
PUT SOME BLOODY OINTMENT ON IT, BEFORE IT--

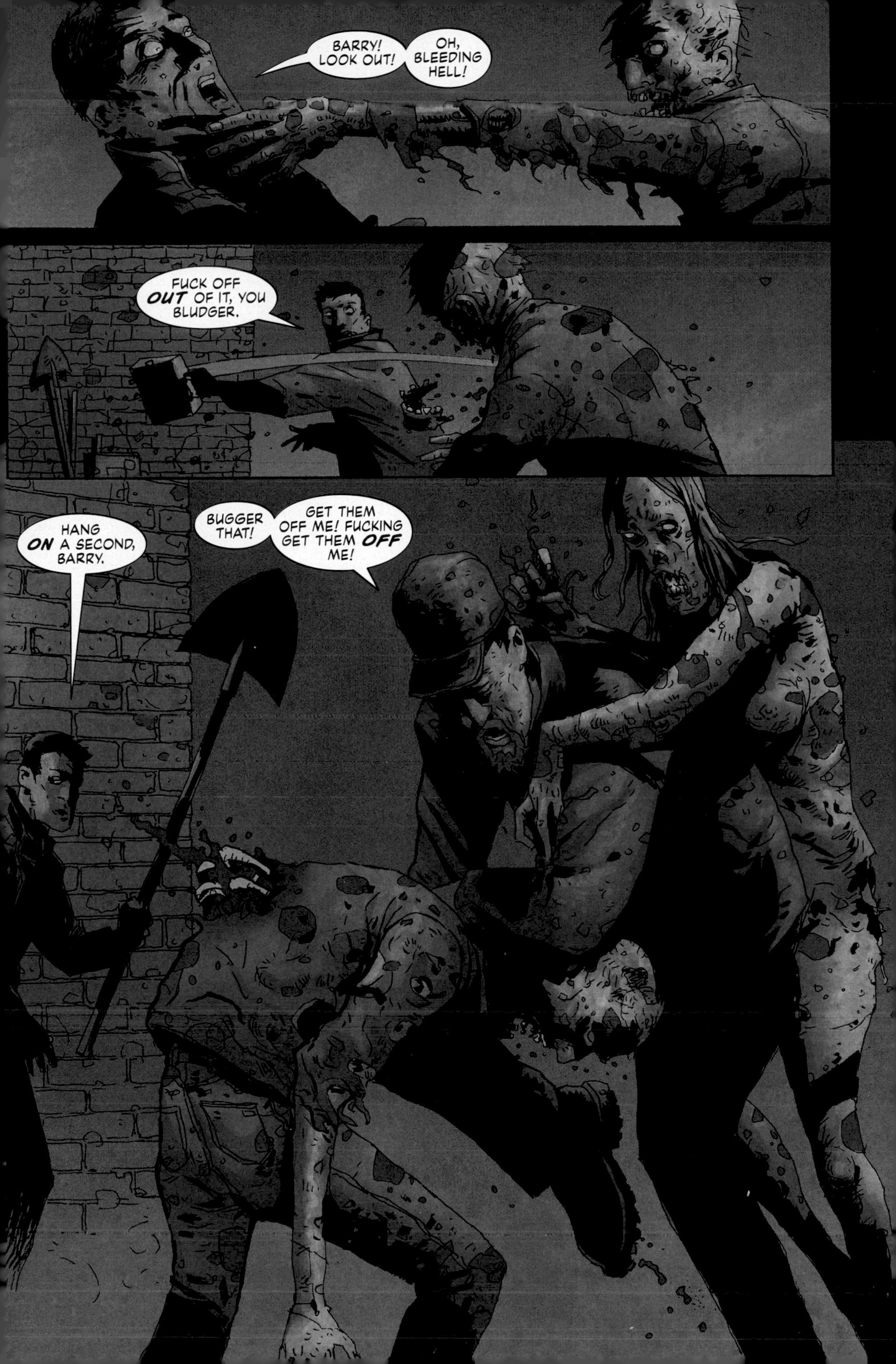
BARRY! LOOK OUT!
OH, BLEEDING HELL!
FUCK OFF OUT OF IT, YOU BLUDGER.
HANG ON A SECOND, BARRY.
BUGGER THAT!
GET THEM OFF ME! FUCKING GET THEM OFF ME!

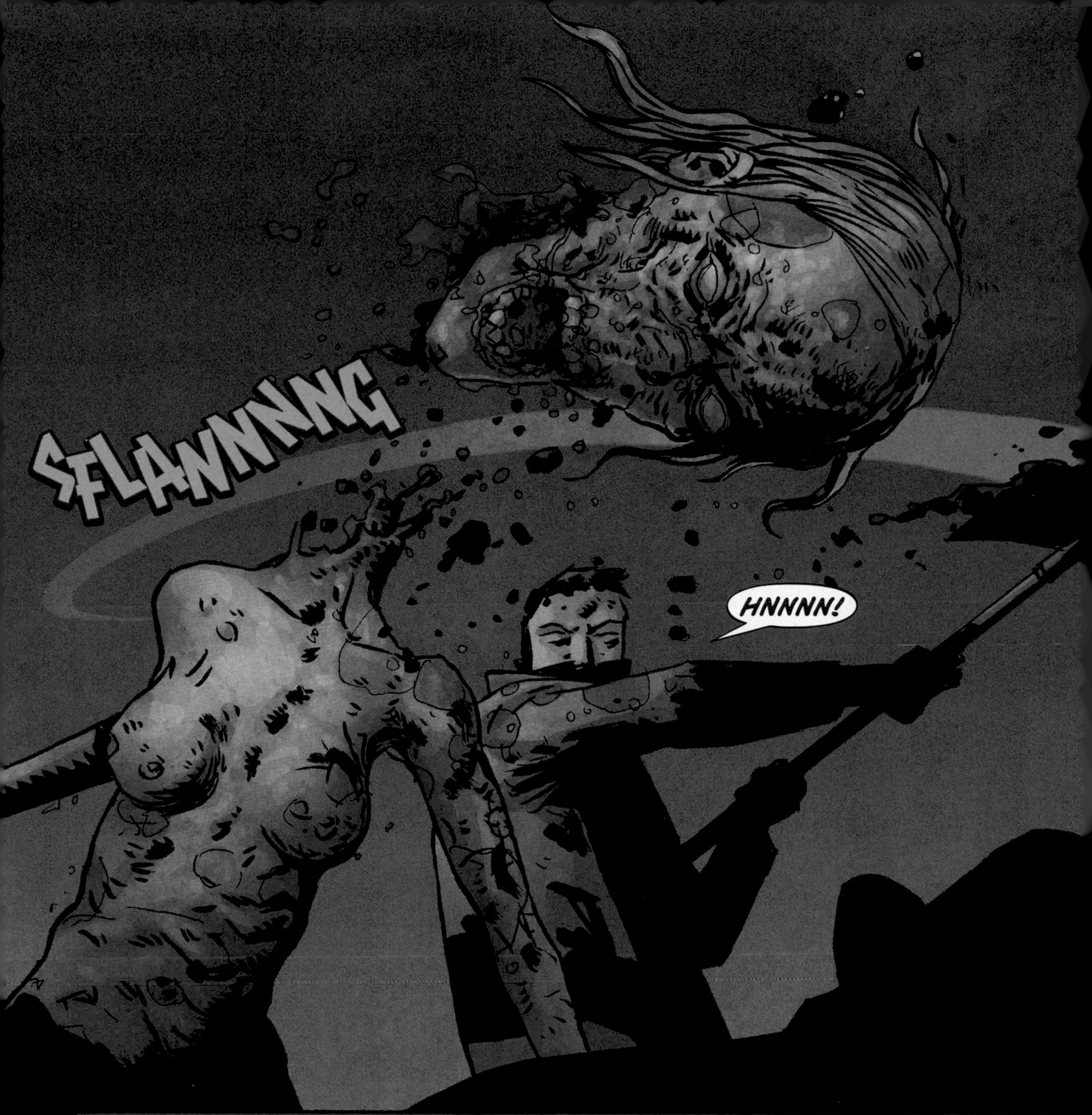
SFLANNNNG
HNNNN!

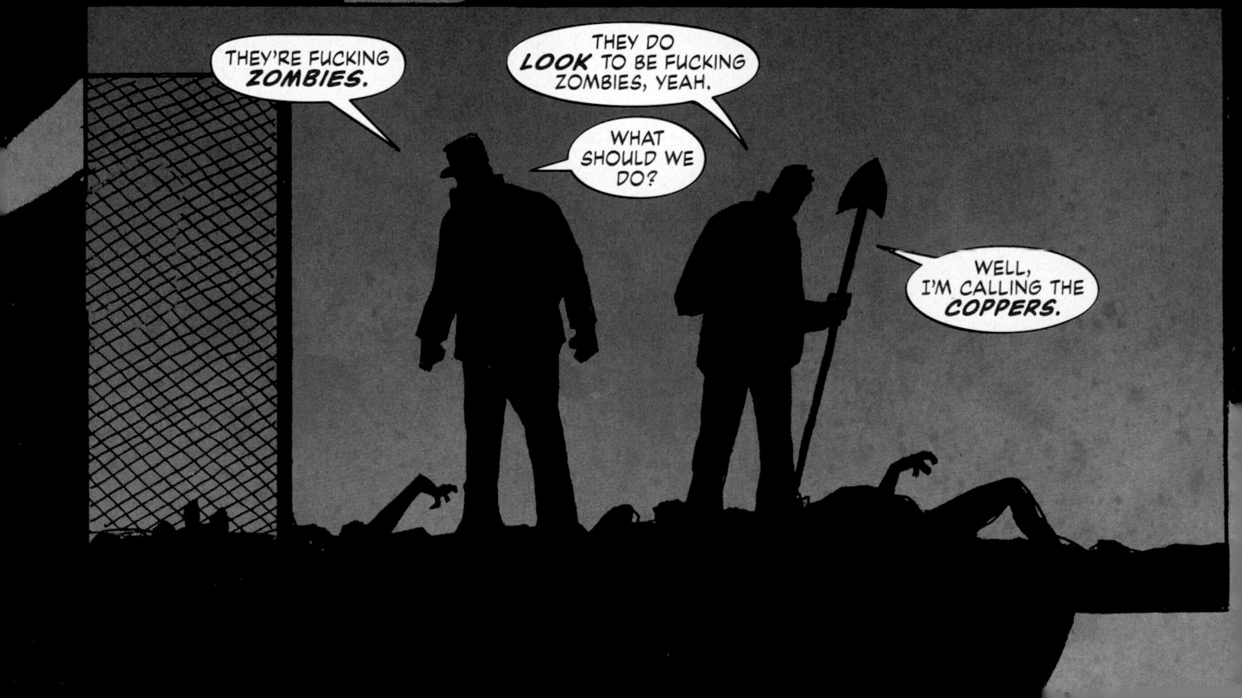
THEY'RE FUCKING ZOMBIES.
THEY DO LOOK TO BE FUCKING ZOMBIES, YEAH.
WHAT SHOULD WE DO?
WELL, I'M CALLING THE COPPERS.

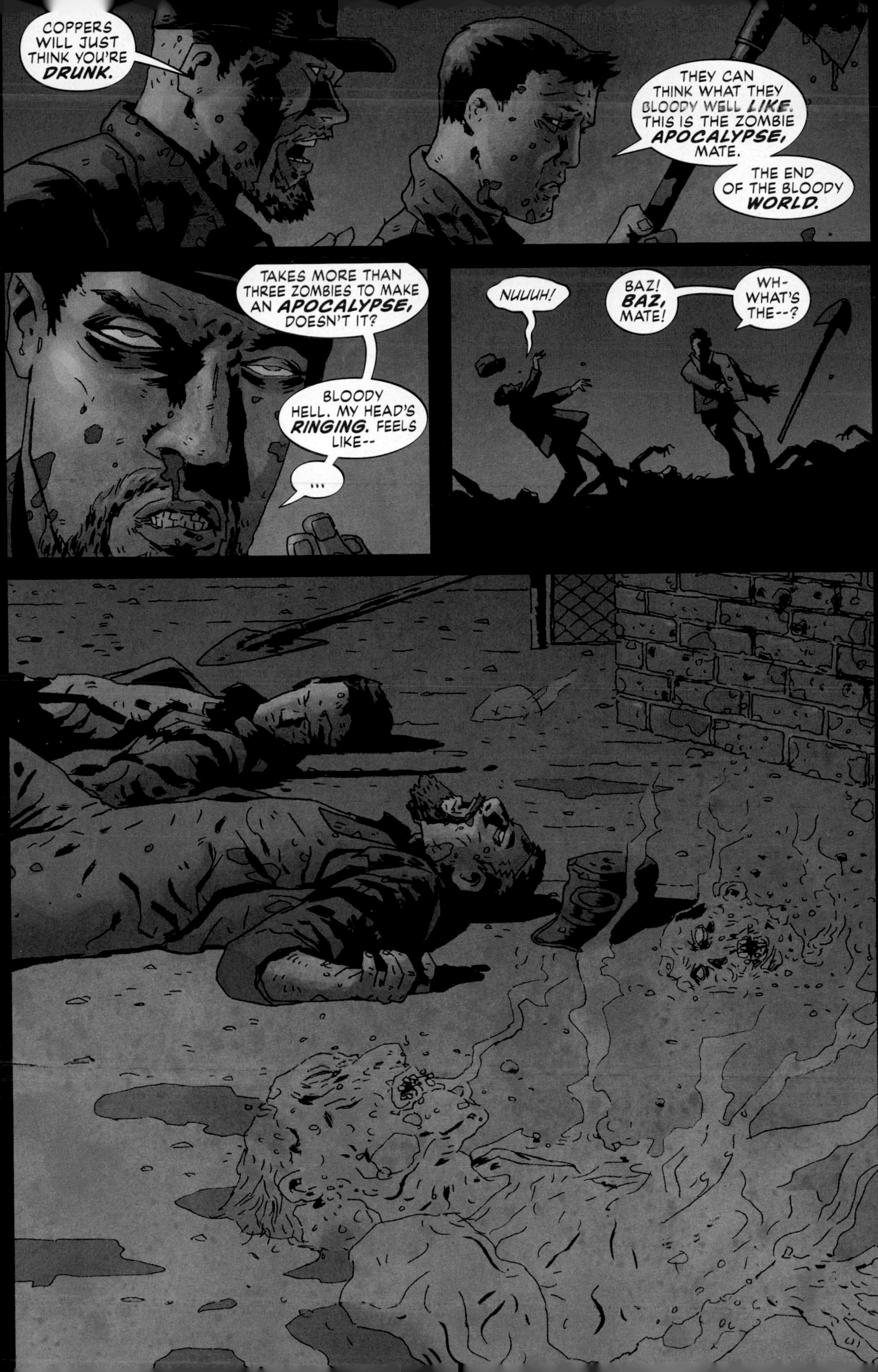
COPPERS WILL JUST THINK YOU'RE DRUNK.
THEY CAN THINK WHAT THEY BLOODY WELL LIKE. THIS IS THE ZOMBIE APOCALYPSE, MATE.
THE END OF THE BLOODY WORLD.
TAKES MORE THAN THREE ZOMBIES TO MAKE AN APOCALYPSE, DOESN'T IT?
BLOODY HELL. MY HEAD'S RINGING. FEELS LIKE--
...
NUUUH!
BAZ! BAZ, MATE!
WH-WHAT'S THE--?

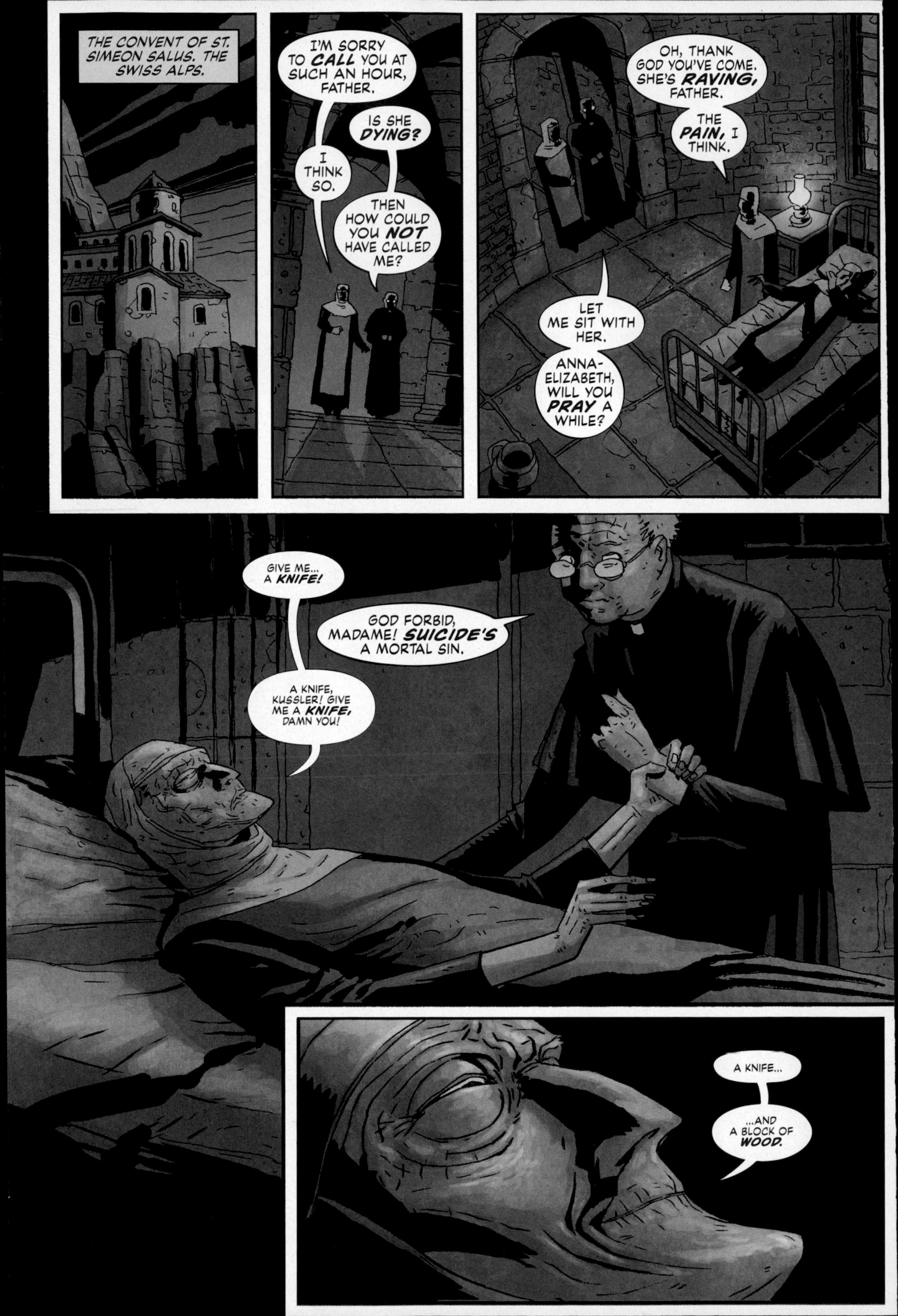
THE CONVENT OF ST. SIMEON SALUS. THE SWISS ALPS.
I'M SORRY TO CALL YOU AT SUCH AN HOUR, FATHER.
IS SHE DYING?
I THINK SO.
THEN HOW COULD YOU NOT HAVE CALLED ME?
OH, THANK GOD YOU'VE COME. SHE'S RAVING, FATHER.
THE PAIN, I THINK.
LET ME SIT WITH HER.
ANNA-ELIZABETH, WILL YOU PRAY A WHILE?
GIVE ME... A KNIFE!
GOD FORBID, MADAME! SUICIDE'S A MORTAL SIN.
A KNIFE, KUSSLER! GIVE ME A KNIFE, DAMN YOU!
A KNIFE...
...AND A BLOCK OF WOOD.

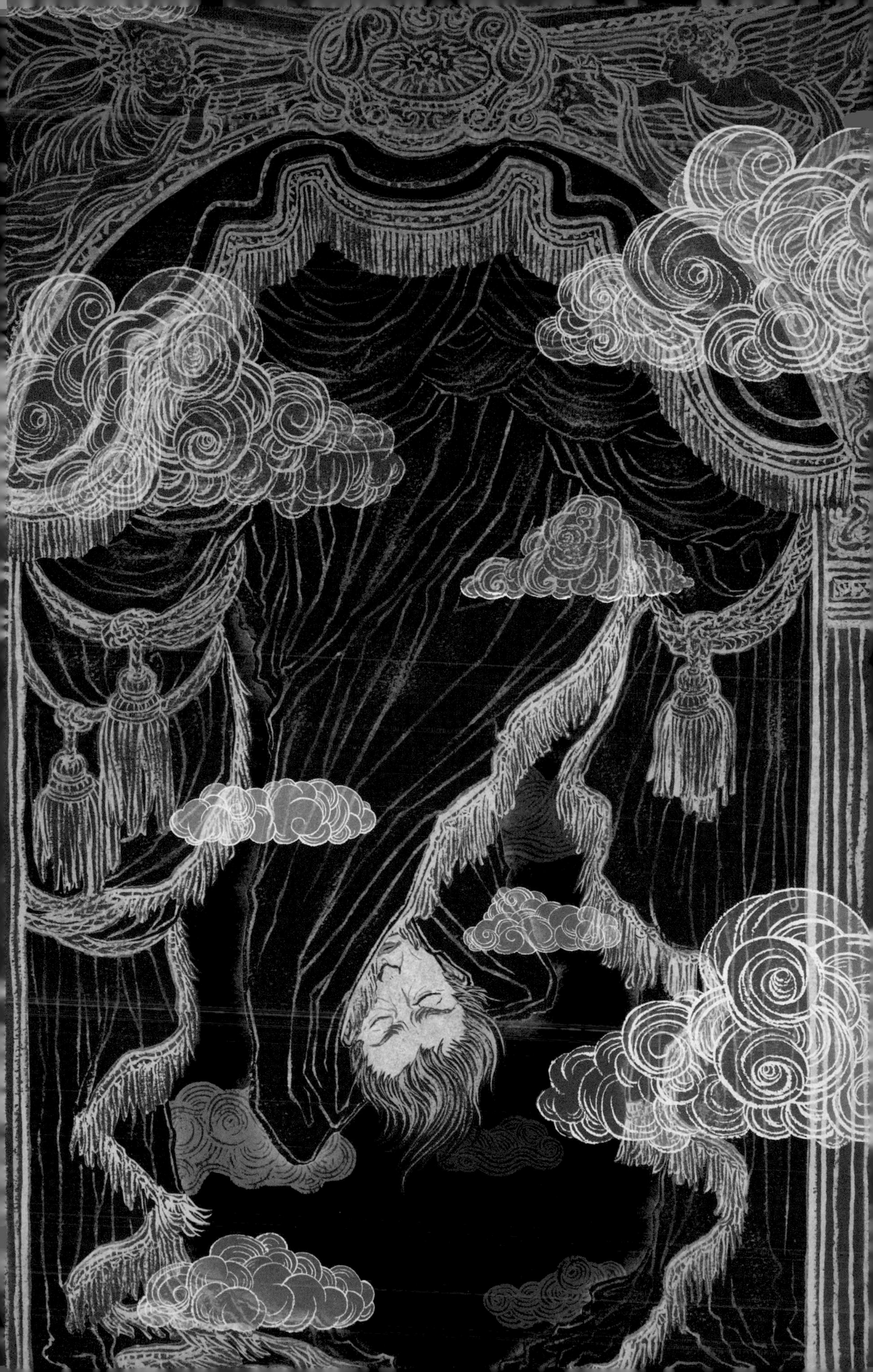

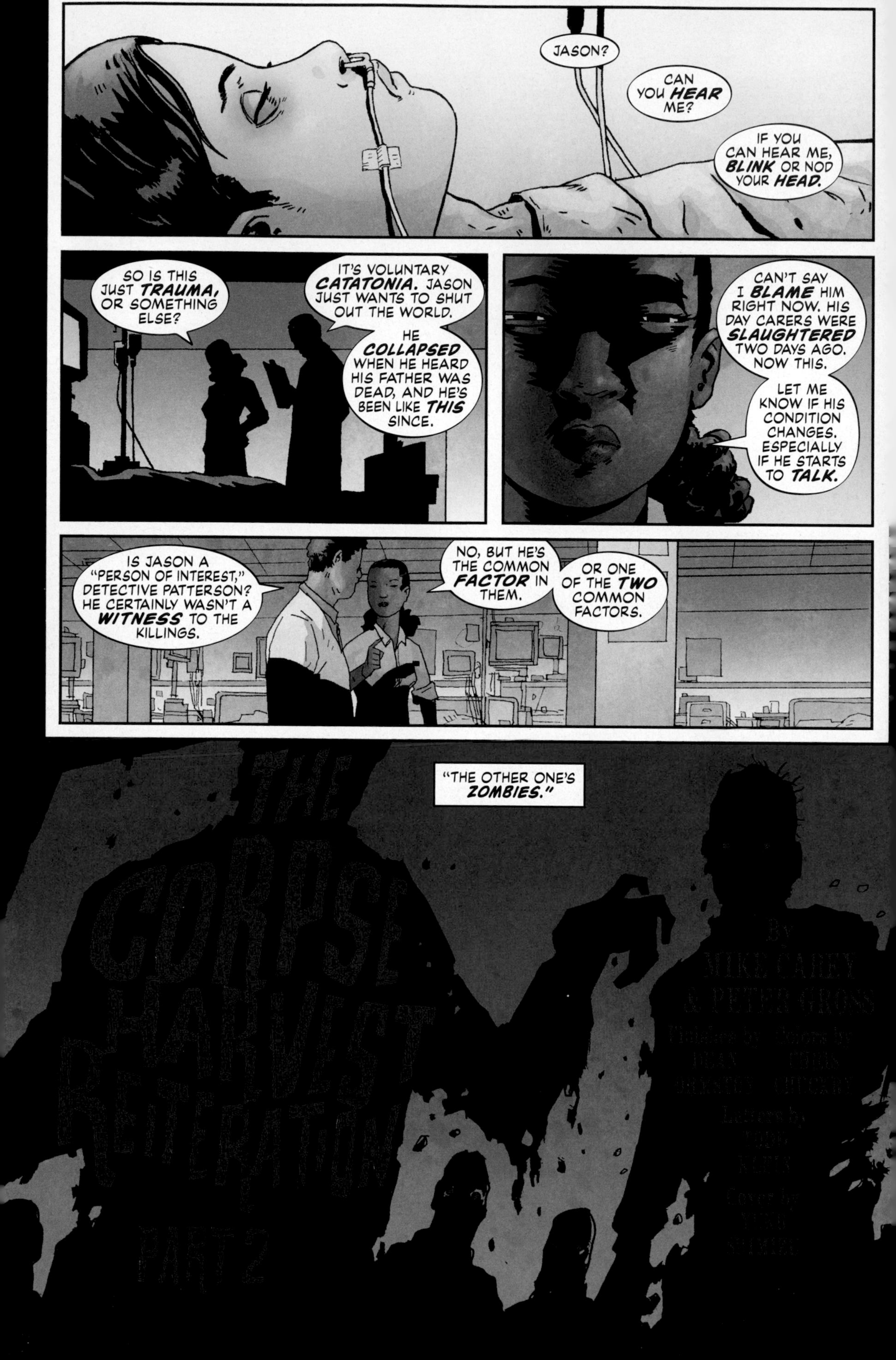
JASON?
CAN YOU HEAR ME?
IF YOU CAN HEAR ME, BLINK OR NOD YOUR HEAD.
SO IS THIS JUST TRAUMA, OR SOMETHING ELSE?
IT'S VOLUNTARY CATATONIA. JASON JUST WANTS TO SHUT OUT THE WORLD.
HE COLLAPSED WHEN HE HEARD HIS FATHER WAS DEAD, AND HE'S BEEN LIKE THIS SINCE.
CAN'T SAY I BLAME HIM RIGHT NOW. HIS DAY CARERS WERE SLAUGHTERED TWO DAYS AGO. NOW THIS.
LET ME KNOW IF HIS CONDITION CHANGES. ESPECIALLY IF HE STARTS TO TALK.
IS JASON A "PERSON OF INTEREST," DETECTIVE PATTERSON? HE CERTAINLY WASN'T A WITNESS TO THE KILLINGS.
NO, BUT HE'S THE COMMON FACTOR IN THEM.
OR ONE OF THE TWO COMMON FACTORS.
"THE OTHER ONE'S ZOMBIES."
THE
CORPSE
HARVEST
PART 2
By
MIKE CAREY
& PETER GROSS

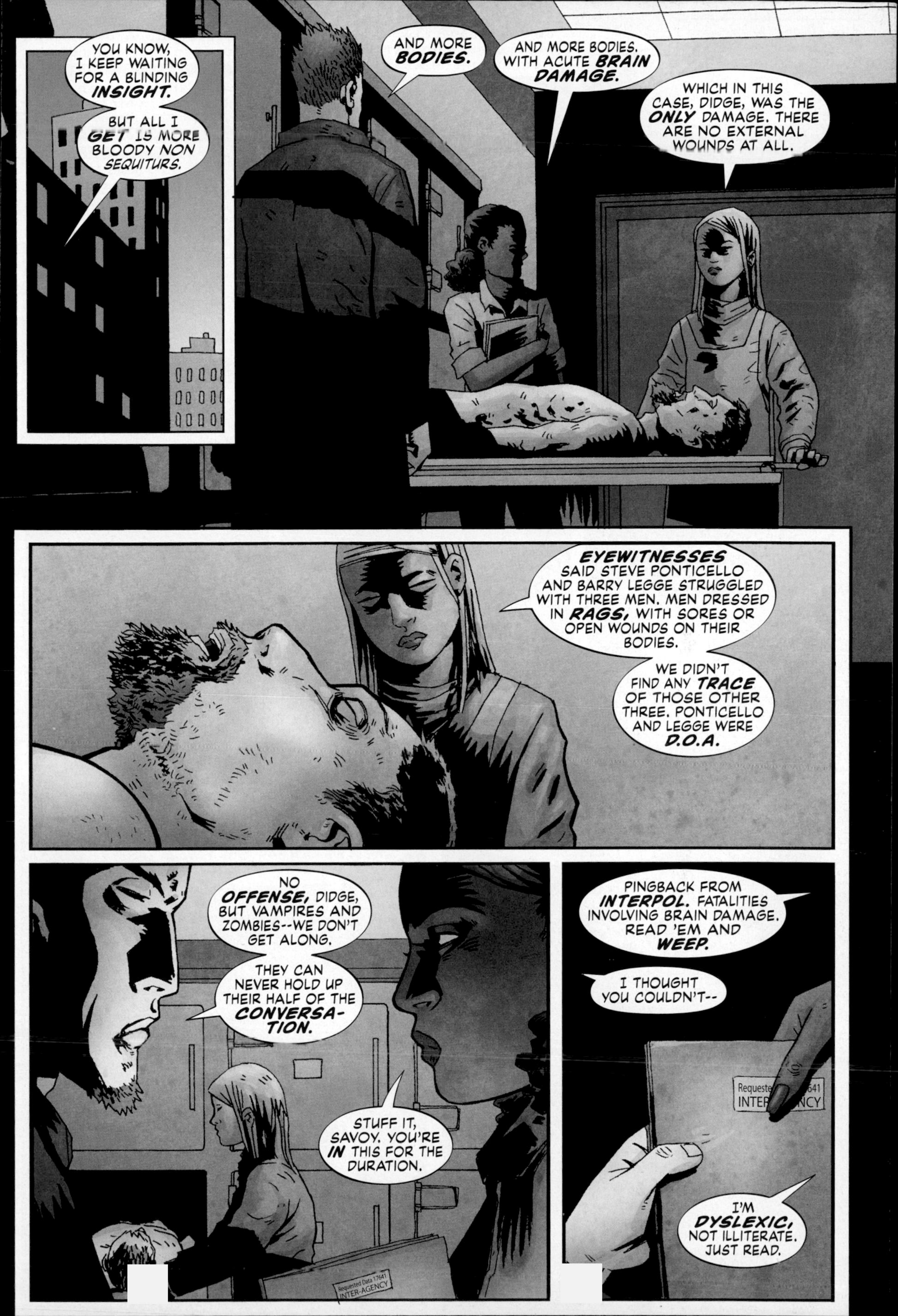
YOU KNOW, I KEEP WAITING FOR A BLINDING INSIGHT.
BUT ALL I GET IS MORE BLOODY NON SEQUITURS.
AND MORE BODIES.
AND MORE BODIES. WITH ACUTE BRAIN DAMAGE.
WHICH IN THIS CASE, DIDGE, WAS THE ONLY DAMAGE. THERE ARE NO EXTERNAL WOUNDS AT ALL.
EYEWITNESSES SAID STEVE PONTICELLO AND BARRY LEGGE STRUGGLED WITH THREE MEN. MEN DRESSED IN RAGS, WITH SORES OR OPEN WOUNDS ON THEIR BODIES.
WE DIDN'T FIND ANY TRACE OF THOSE OTHER THREE. PONTICELLO AND LEGGE WERE D.O.A.
NO OFFENSE, DIDGE, BUT VAMPIRES AND ZOMBIES--WE DON'T GET ALONG.
THEY CAN NEVER HOLD UP THEIR HALF OF THE CONVERSA-TION.
STUFF IT, SAVOY. YOU'RE IN THIS FOR THE DURATION.
Requested Data 17641
INTER-AGENCY
PINGBACK FROM INTERPOL. FATALITIES INVOLVING BRAIN DAMAGE. READ 'EM AND WEEP.
I THOUGHT YOU COULDN'T--
I'M DYSLEXIC, NOT ILLITERATE. JUST READ.

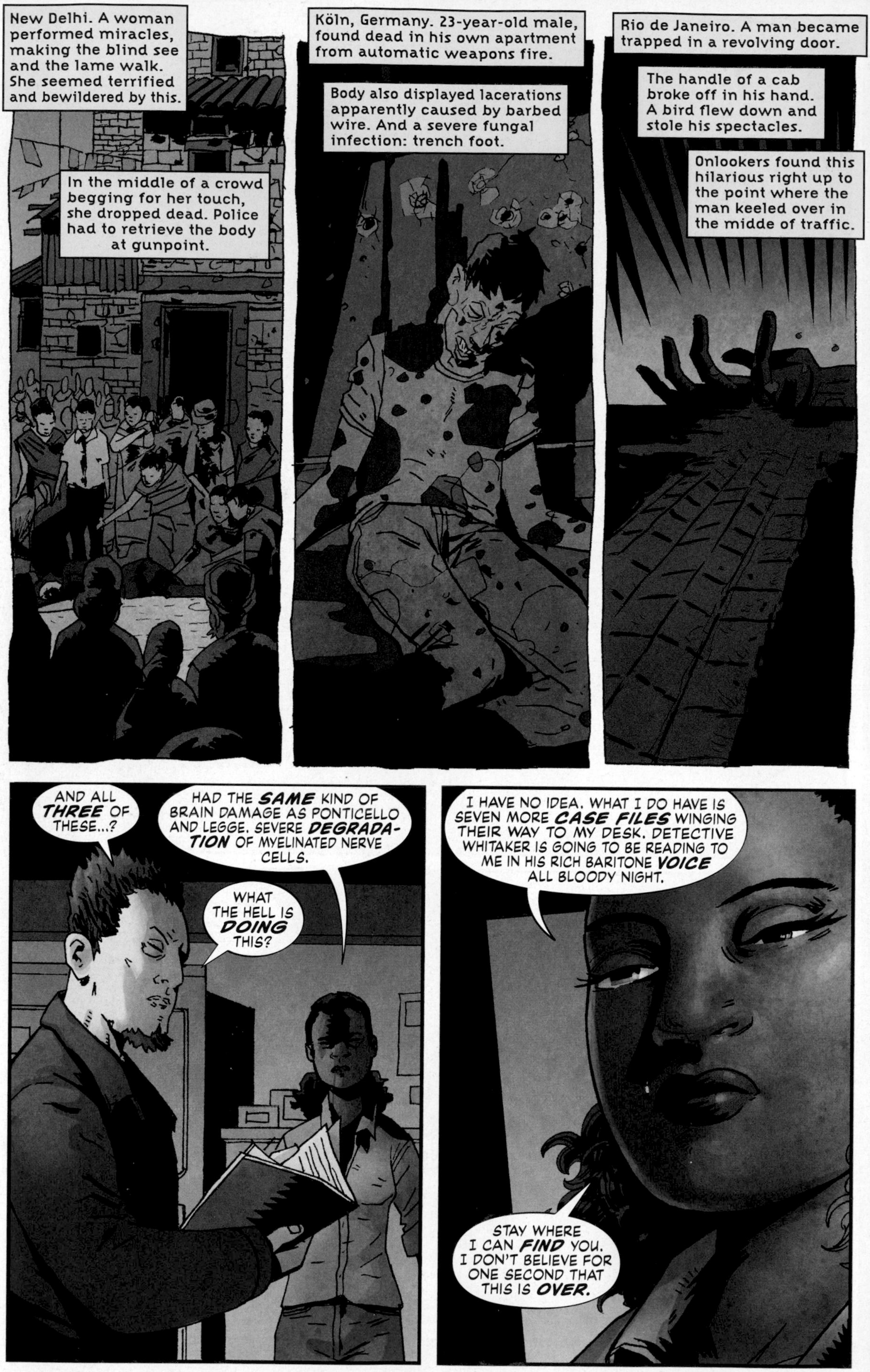
New Delhi. A woman performed miracles, making the blind see and the lame walk. She seemed terrified and bewildered by this.
In the middle of a crowd begging for her touch, she dropped dead. Police had to retrieve the body at gunpoint.
Köln, Germany. 23-year-old male, found dead in his own apartment from automatic weapons fire.
Body also displayed lacerations apparently caused by barbed wire. And a severe fungal infection: trench foot.
Rio de Janeiro. A man became trapped in a revolving door.
The handle of a cab broke off in his hand. A bird flew down and stole his spectacles.
Onlookers found this hilarious right up to the point where the man keeled over in the midde of traffic.
AND ALL THREE OF THESE...?
HAD THE SAME KIND OF BRAIN DAMAGE AS PONTICELLO AND LEGGE. SEVERE DEGRADATION OF MYELINATED NERVE CELLS.
WHAT THE HELL IS DOING THIS?
I HAVE NO IDEA. WHAT I DO HAVE IS SEVEN MORE CASE FILES WINGING THEIR WAY TO MY DESK. DETECTIVE WHITAKER IS GOING TO BE READING TO ME IN HIS RICH BARITONE VOICE ALL BLOODY NIGHT.
STAY WHERE I CAN FIND YOU. I DON'T BELIEVE FOR ONE SECOND THAT THIS IS OVER.

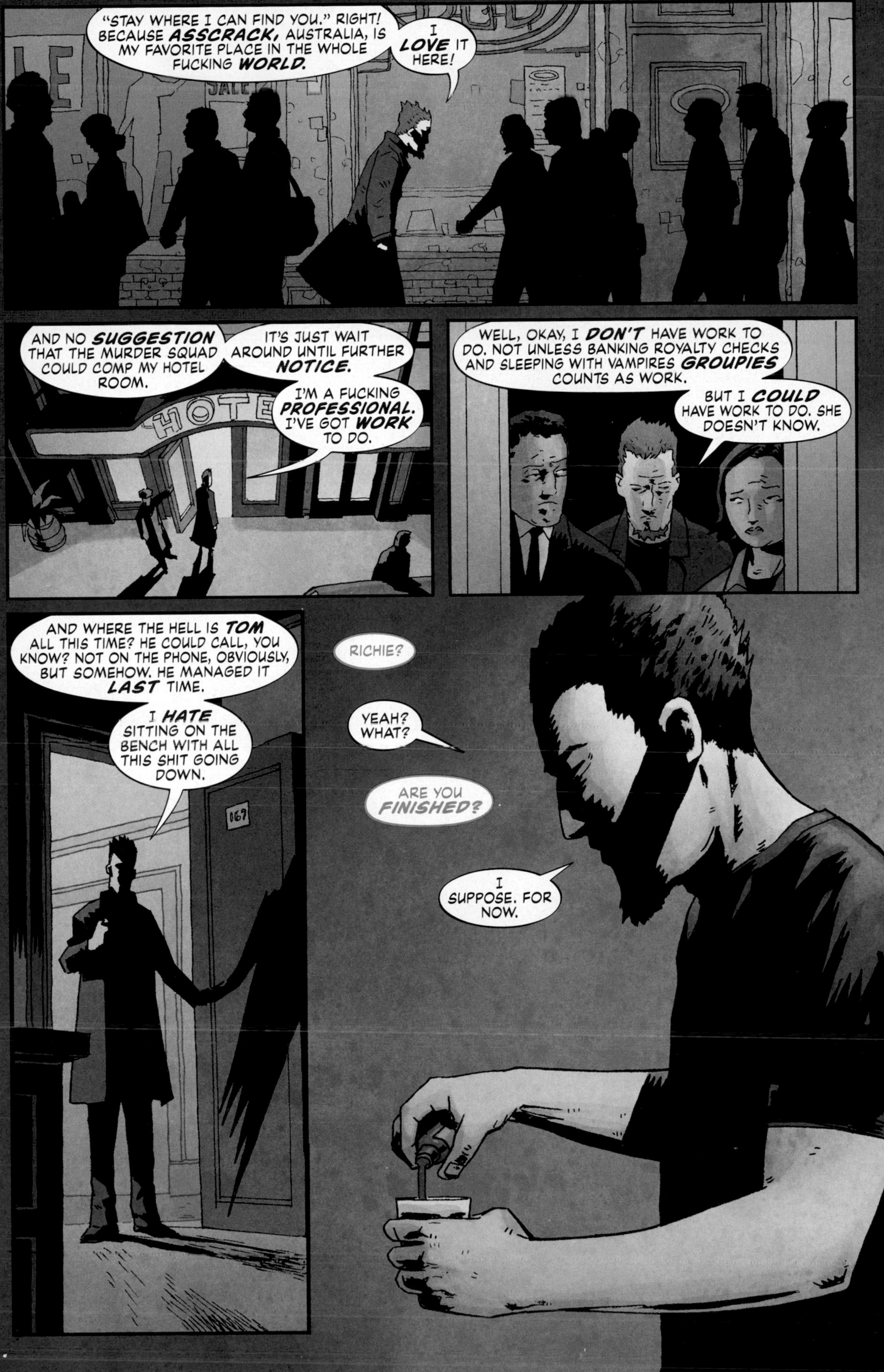
"STAY WHERE I CAN FIND YOU." RIGHT! BECAUSE ASSCRACK, AUSTRALIA, IS MY FAVORITE PLACE IN THE WHOLE FUCKING WORLD.
I LOVE IT HERE!
AND NO SUGGESTION THAT THE MURDER SQUAD COULD COMP MY HOTEL ROOM.
IT'S JUST WAIT AROUND UNTIL FURTHER NOTICE.
I'M A FUCKING PROFESSIONAL. I'VE GOT WORK TO DO.
WELL, OKAY, I DON'T HAVE WORK TO DO. NOT UNLESS BANKING ROYALTY CHECKS AND SLEEPING WITH VAMPIRES GROUPIES COUNTS AS WORK.
BUT I COULD HAVE WORK TO DO. SHE DOESN'T KNOW.
AND WHERE THE HELL IS TOM ALL THIS TIME? HE COULD CALL, YOU KNOW? NOT ON THE PHONE, OBVIOUSLY, BUT SOMEHOW. HE MANAGED IT LAST TIME.
I HATE SITTING ON THE BENCH WITH ALL THIS SHIT GOING DOWN.
RICHIE?
YEAH? WHAT?
ARE YOU FINISHED?
I SUPPOSE. FOR NOW.

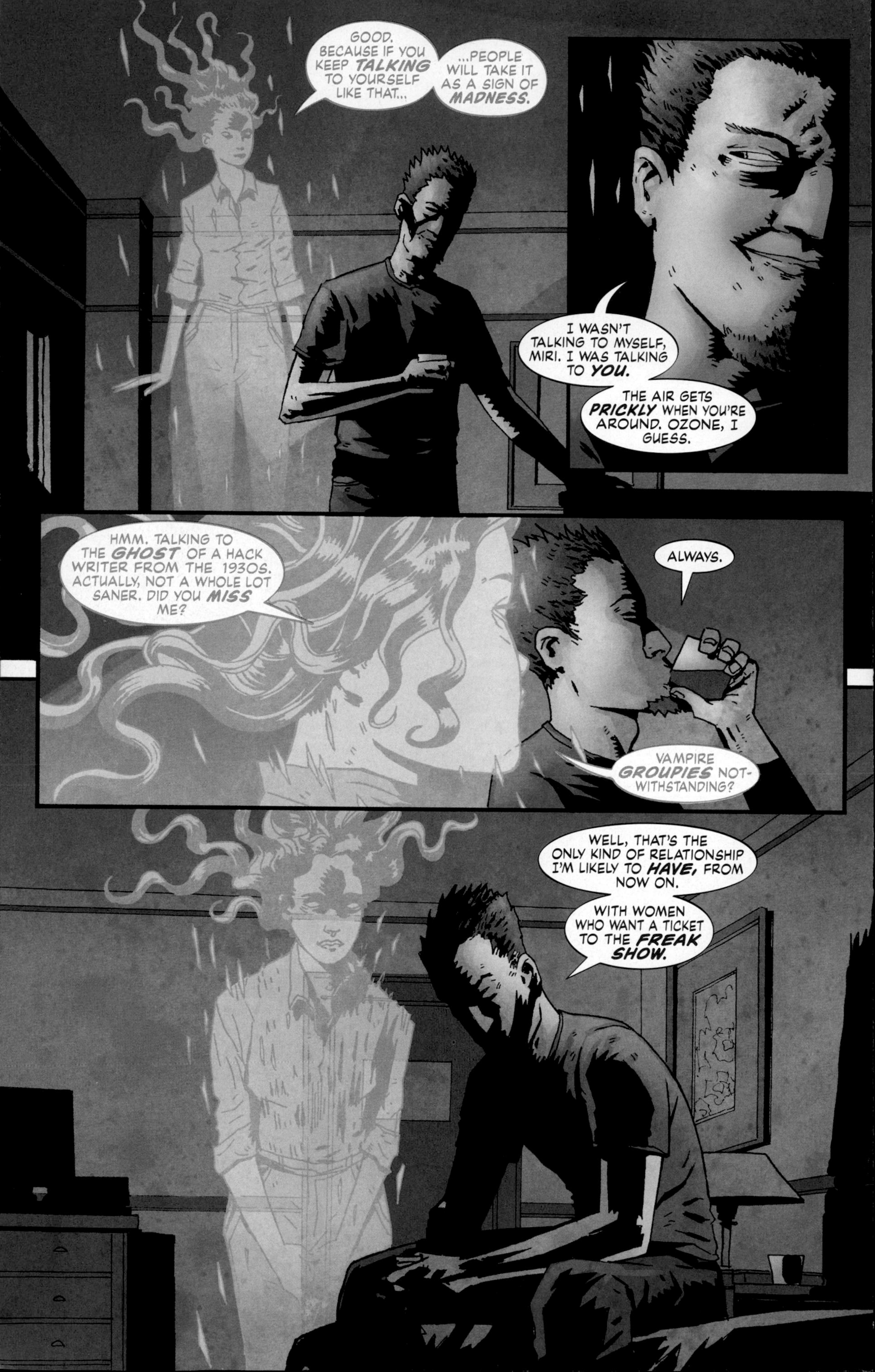
GOOD. BECAUSE IF YOU KEEP TALKING TO YOURSELF LIKE THAT...
...PEOPLE WILL TAKE IT AS A SIGN OF MADNESS.
I WASN'T TALKING TO MYSELF, MIRI. I WAS TALKING TO YOU.
THE AIR GETS PRICKLY WHEN YOU'RE AROUND. OZONE, I GUESS.
HMM. TALKING TO THE GHOST OF A HACK WRITER FROM THE 1930S. ACTUALLY, NOT A WHOLE LOT SANER. DID YOU MISS ME?
ALWAYS.
VAMPIRE GROUPIES NOT-WITHSTANDING?
WELL, THAT'S THE ONLY KIND OF RELATIONSHIP I'M LIKELY TO HAVE, FROM NOW ON.
WITH WOMEN WHO WANT A TICKET TO THE FREAK SHOW.

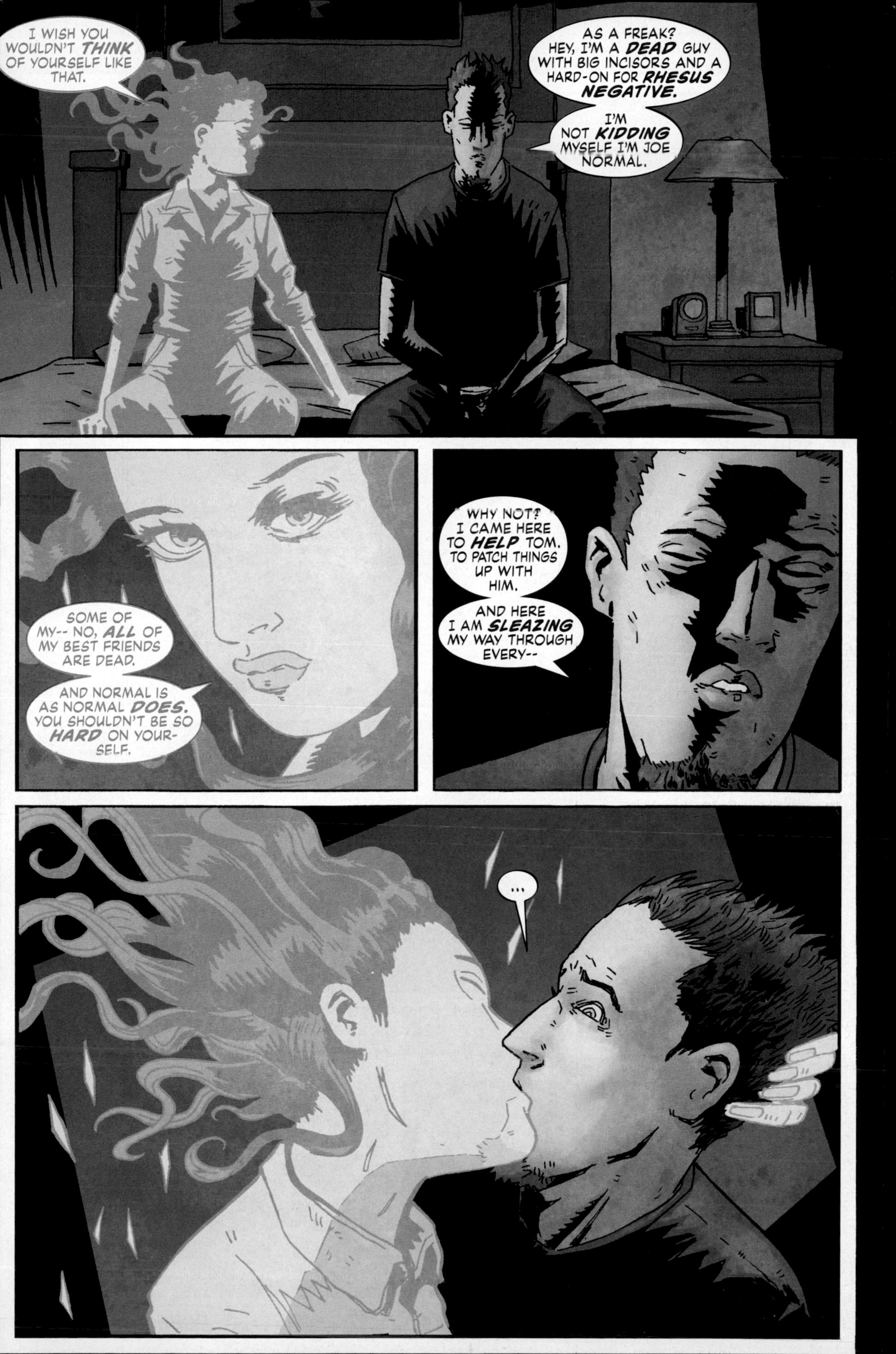
I WISH YOU WOULDN'T THINK OF YOURSELF LIKE THAT.
AS A FREAK? HEY, I'M A DEAD GUY WITH BIG INCISORS AND A HARD-ON FOR RHESUS NEGATIVE.
I'M NOT KIDDING MYSELF I'M JOE NORMAL.
SOME OF MY-- NO, ALL OF MY BEST FRIENDS ARE DEAD.
AND NORMAL IS AS NORMAL DOES. YOU SHOULDN'T BE SO HARD ON YOURSELF.
WHY NOT? I CAME HERE TO HELP TOM. TO PATCH THINGS UP WITH HIM.
AND HERE I AM SLEAZING MY WAY THROUGH EVERY--
...

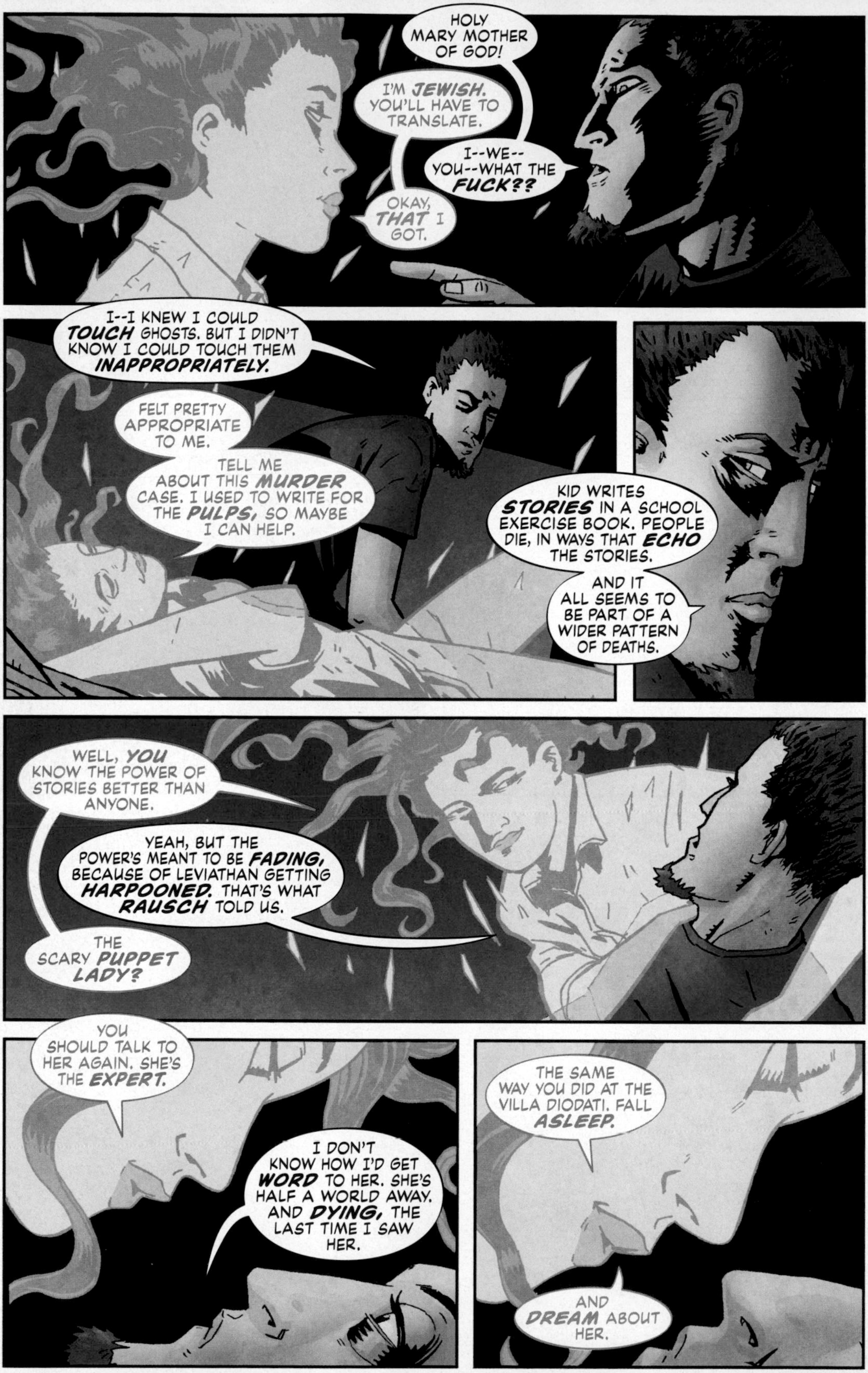
HOLY MARY MOTHER OF GOD!
I'M JEWISH. YOU'LL HAVE TO TRANSLATE.
I--WE-- YOU--WHAT THE FUCK??
OKAY, THAT I GOT.
I--I KNEW I COULD TOUCH GHOSTS. BUT I DIDN'T KNOW I COULD TOUCH THEM INAPPROPRIATELY.
FELT PRETTY APPROPRIATE TO ME.
TELL ME ABOUT THIS MURDER CASE. I USED TO WRITE FOR THE PULPS, SO MAYBE I CAN HELP.
KID WRITES STORIES IN A SCHOOL EXERCISE BOOK. PEOPLE DIE, IN WAYS THAT ECHO THE STORIES.
AND IT ALL SEEMS TO BE PART OF A WIDER PATTERN OF DEATHS.
WELL, YOU KNOW THE POWER OF STORIES BETTER THAN ANYONE.
YEAH, BUT THE POWER'S MEANT TO BE FADING, BECAUSE OF LEVIATHAN GETTING HARPOONED. THAT'S WHAT RAUSCH TOLD US.
THE SCARY PUPPET LADY?
YOU SHOULD TALK TO HER AGAIN. SHE'S THE EXPERT.
I DON'T KNOW HOW I'D GET WORD TO HER. SHE'S HALF A WORLD AWAY. AND DYING, THE LAST TIME I SAW HER.
THE SAME WAY YOU DID AT THE VILLA DIODATI. FALL ASLEEP.
AND DREAM ABOUT HER.

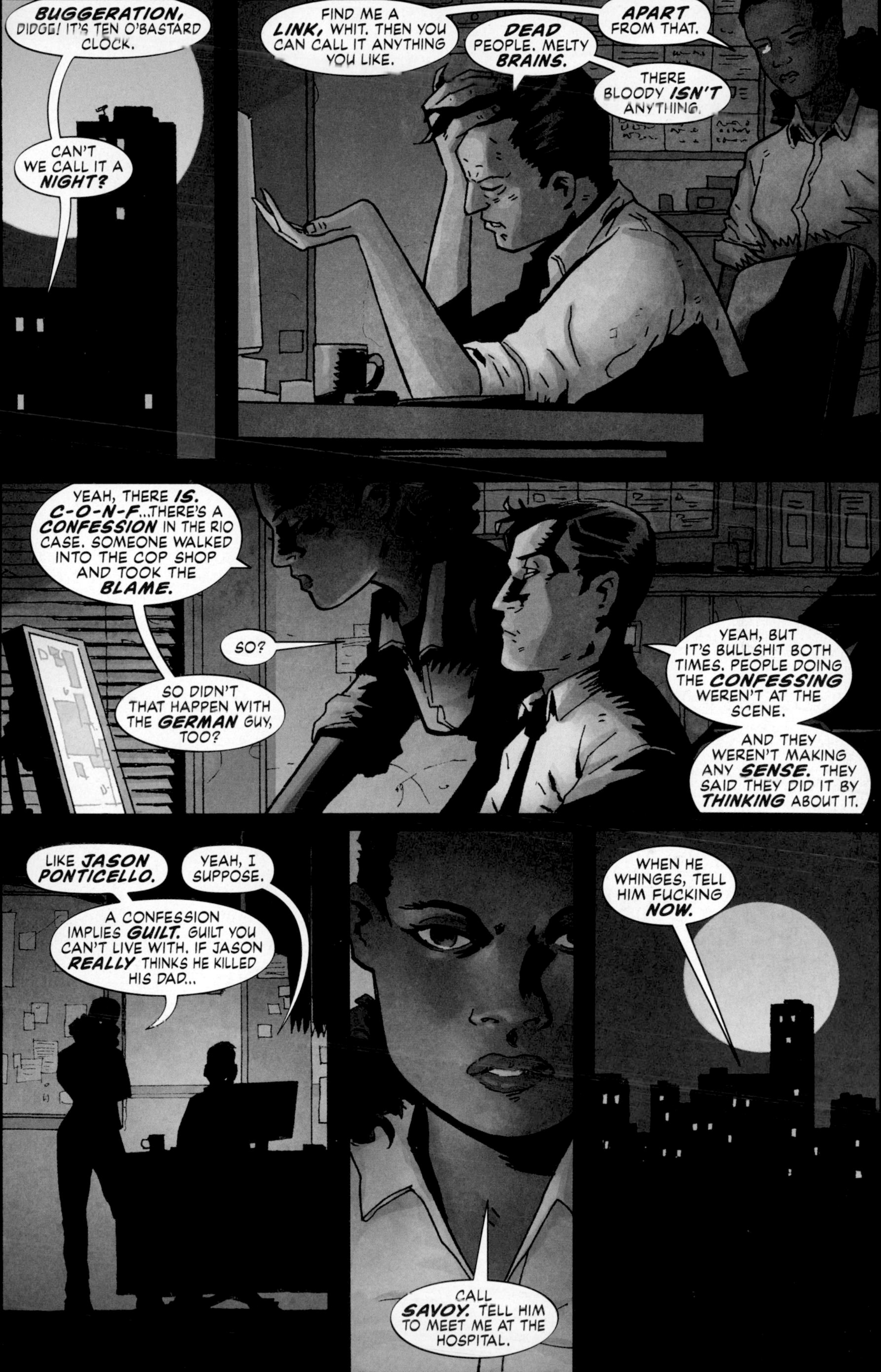
BUGGERATION, DIDGE! IT'S TEN O'BASTARD CLOCK.
CAN'T WE CALL IT A NIGHT?
FIND ME A LINK, WHIT. THEN YOU CAN CALL IT ANYTHING YOU LIKE.
DEAD PEOPLE. MELTY BRAINS.
APART FROM THAT.
THERE BLOODY ISN'T ANYTHING.
YEAH, THERE IS. C-O-N-F...THERE'S A CONFESSION IN THE RIO CASE. SOMEONE WALKED INTO THE COP SHOP AND TOOK THE BLAME.
SO?
SO DIDN'T THAT HAPPEN WITH THE GERMAN GUY, TOO?
YEAH, BUT IT'S BULLSHIT BOTH TIMES. PEOPLE DOING THE CONFESSING WEREN'T AT THE SCENE.
AND THEY WEREN'T MAKING ANY SENSE. THEY SAID THEY DID IT BY THINKING ABOUT IT.
LIKE JASON PONTICELLO.
YEAH, I SUPPOSE.
A CONFESSION IMPLIES GUILT. GUILT YOU CAN'T LIVE WITH. IF JASON REALLY THINKS HE KILLED HIS DAD...
CALL SAVOY. TELL HIM TO MEET ME AT THE HOSPITAL.
WHEN HE WHINGES, TELL HIM FUCKING NOW.

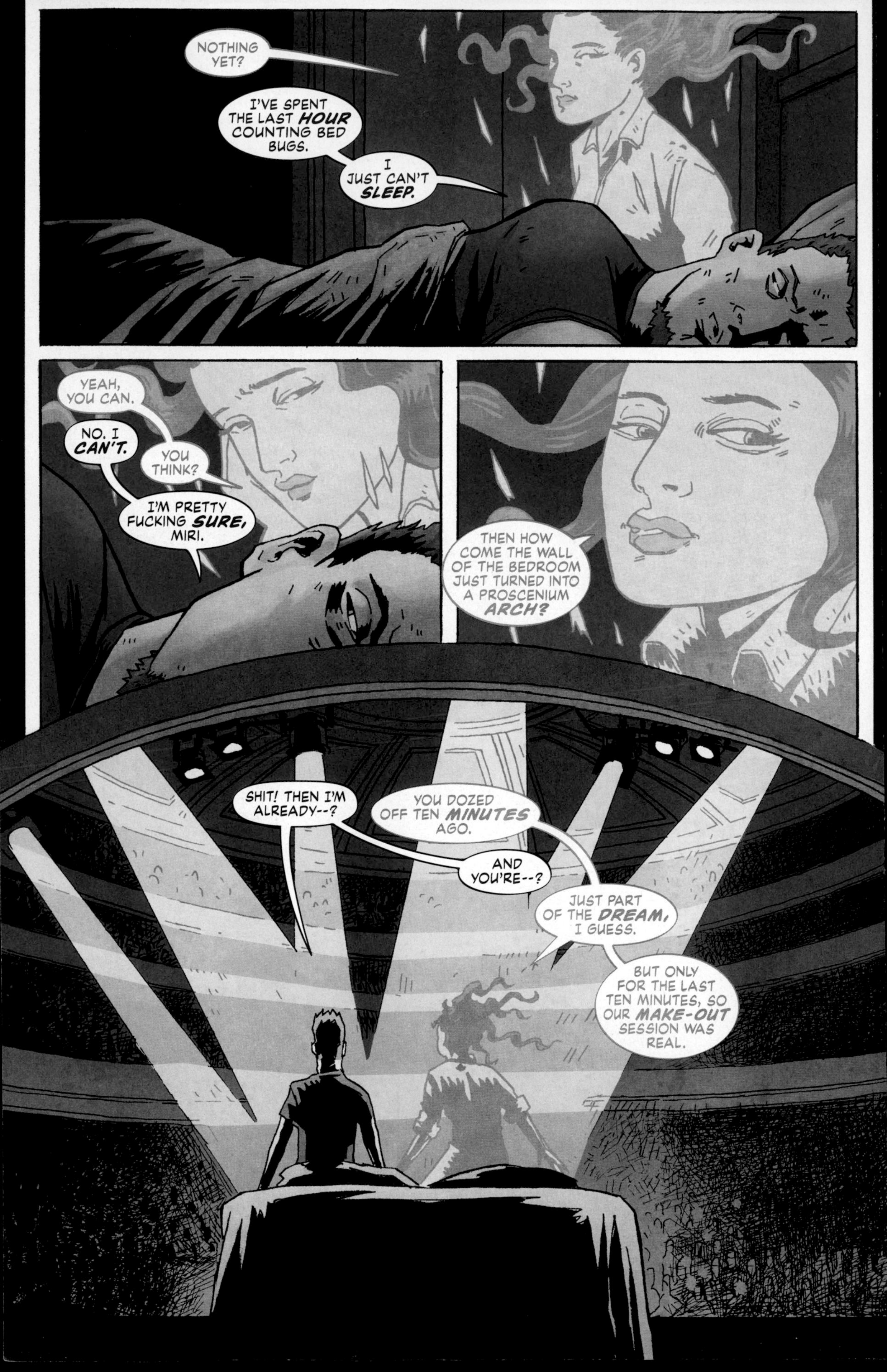
NOTHING YET?
I'VE SPENT THE LAST HOUR COUNTING BED BUGS.
I JUST CAN'T SLEEP.
YEAH, YOU CAN.
NO. I CAN'T.
YOU THINK?
I'M PRETTY FUCKING SURE, MIRI.
THEN HOW COME THE WALL OF THE BEDROOM JUST TURNED INTO A PROSCENIUM ARCH?
SHIT! THEN I'M ALREADY--?
YOU DOZED OFF TEN MINUTES AGO.
AND YOU'RE--?
JUST PART OF THE DREAM, I GUESS.
BUT ONLY FOR THE LAST TEN MINUTES, SO OUR MAKE-OUT SESSION WAS REAL.

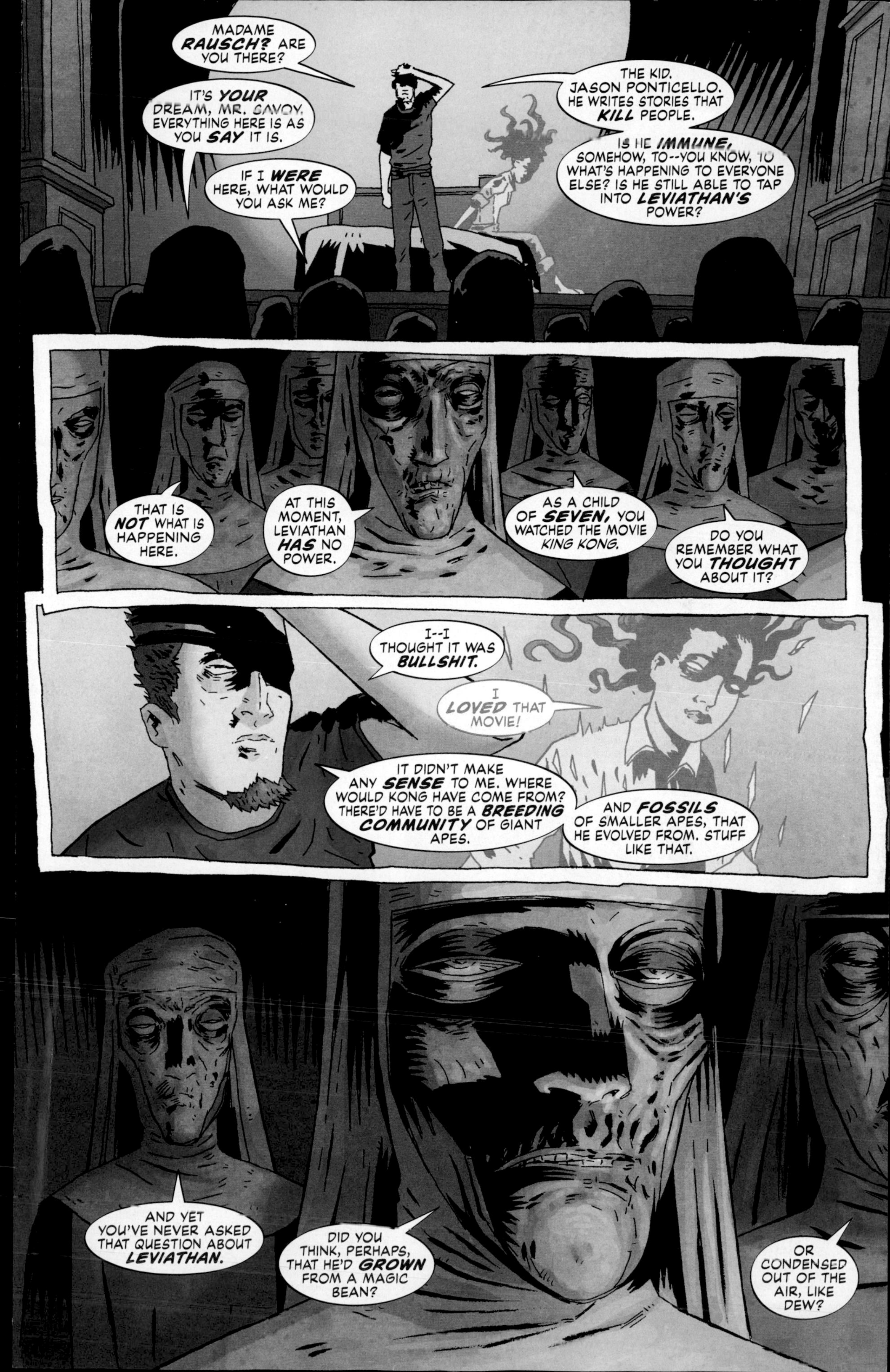
MADAME RAUSCH? ARE YOU THERE?
IT'S YOUR DREAM, MR. SAVOY. EVERYTHING HERE IS AS YOU SAY IT IS.
IF I WERE HERE, WHAT WOULD YOU ASK ME?
THE KID. JASON PONTICELLO. HE WRITES STORIES THAT KILL PEOPLE.
IS HE IMMUNE, SOMEHOW, TO--YOU KNOW, TO WHAT'S HAPPENING TO EVERYONE ELSE? IS HE STILL ABLE TO TAP INTO LEVIATHAN'S POWER?
THAT IS NOT WHAT IS HAPPENING HERE.
AT THIS MOMENT, LEVIATHAN HAS NO POWER.
AS A CHILD OF SEVEN, YOU WATCHED THE MOVIE KING KONG.
DO YOU REMEMBER WHAT YOU THOUGHT ABOUT IT?
I--I THOUGHT IT WAS BULLSHIT.
I LOVED THAT MOVIE!
IT DIDN'T MAKE ANY SENSE TO ME. WHERE WOULD KONG HAVE COME FROM? THERE'D HAVE TO BE A BREEDING COMMUNITY OF GIANT APES.
AND FOSSILS OF SMALLER APES, THAT HE EVOLVED FROM. STUFF LIKE THAT.
AND YET YOU'VE NEVER ASKED THAT QUESTION ABOUT LEVIATHAN.
DID YOU THINK, PERHAPS, THAT HE'D GROWN FROM A MAGIC BEAN?
OR CONDENSED OUT OF THE AIR, LIKE DEW?

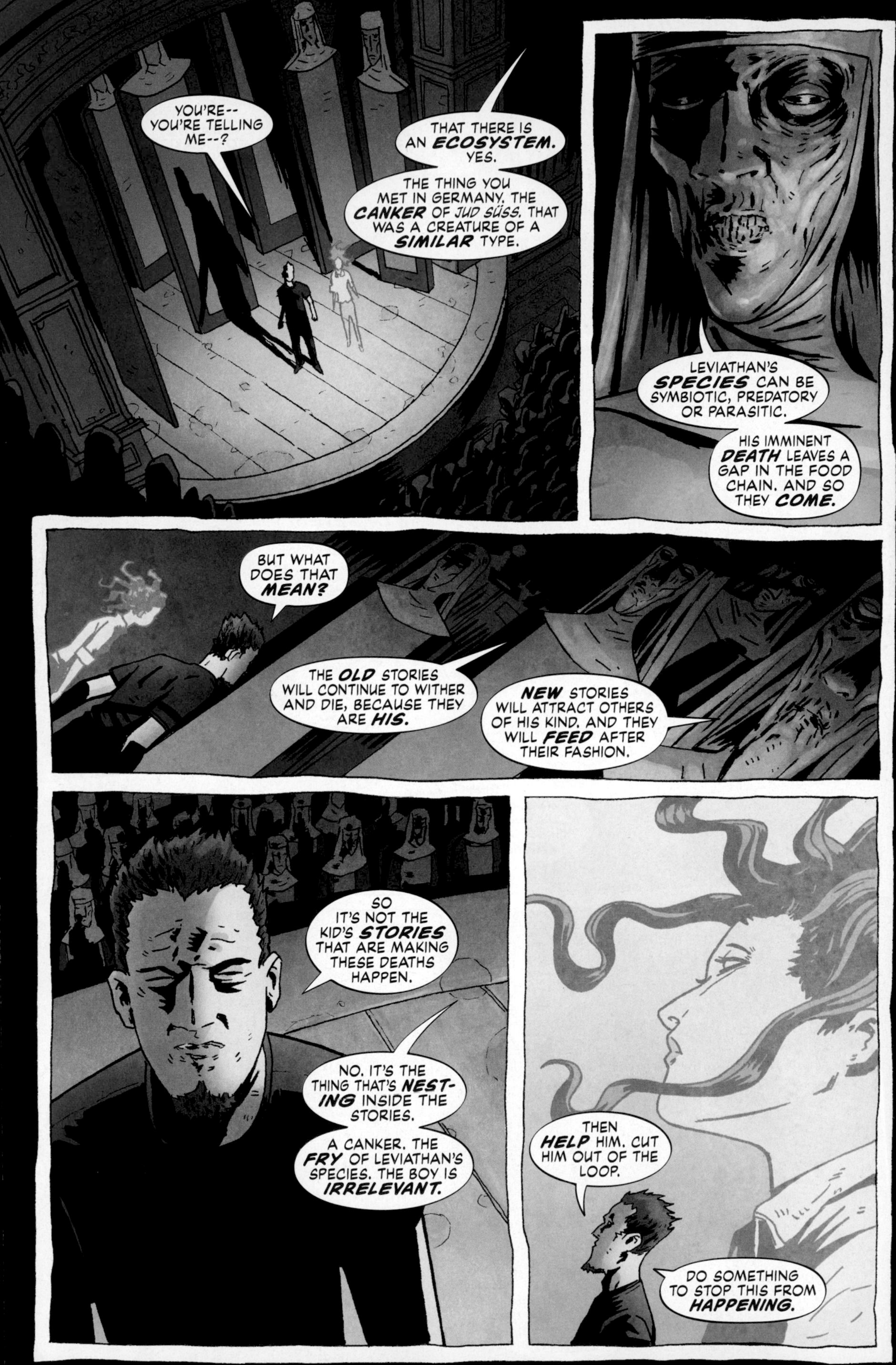
YOU'RE-- YOU'RE TELLING ME--?
THAT THERE IS AN ECOSYSTEM. YES.
THE THING YOU MET IN GERMANY. THE CANKER OF JUD SÜSS. THAT WAS A CREATURE OF A SIMILAR TYPE.
LEVIATHAN'S SPECIES CAN BE SYMBIOTIC, PREDATORY OR PARASITIC.
HIS IMMINENT DEATH LEAVES A GAP IN THE FOOD CHAIN. AND SO THEY COME.
BUT WHAT DOES THAT MEAN?
THE OLD STORIES WILL CONTINUE TO WITHER AND DIE, BECAUSE THEY ARE HIS.
NEW STORIES WILL ATTRACT OTHERS OF HIS KIND. AND THEY WILL FEED AFTER THEIR FASHION.
SO IT'S NOT THE KID'S STORIES THAT ARE MAKING THESE DEATHS HAPPEN.
NO. IT'S THE THING THAT'S NEST-ING INSIDE THE STORIES.
A CANKER. THE FRY OF LEVIATHAN'S SPECIES. THE BOY IS IRRELEVANT.
THEN HELP HIM. CUT HIM OUT OF THE LOOP.
DO SOMETHING TO STOP THIS FROM HAPPENING.

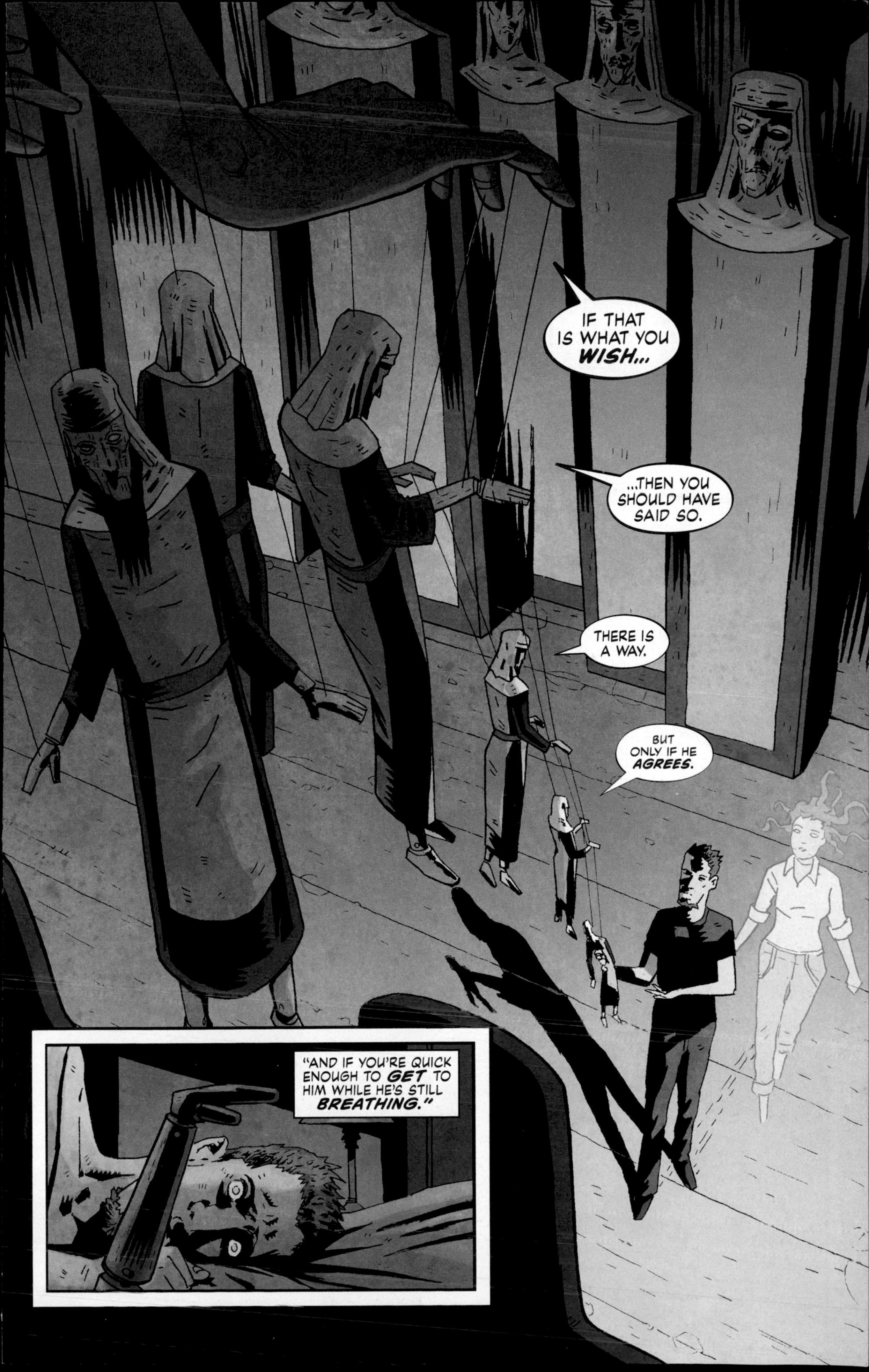
IF THAT IS WHAT YOU *WISH*...
...THEN YOU SHOULD HAVE SAID SO.
THERE IS A WAY.
BUT ONLY IF HE *AGREES*.
"AND IF YOU'RE QUICK ENOUGH TO *GET* TO HIM WHILE HE'S STILL *BREATHING*."

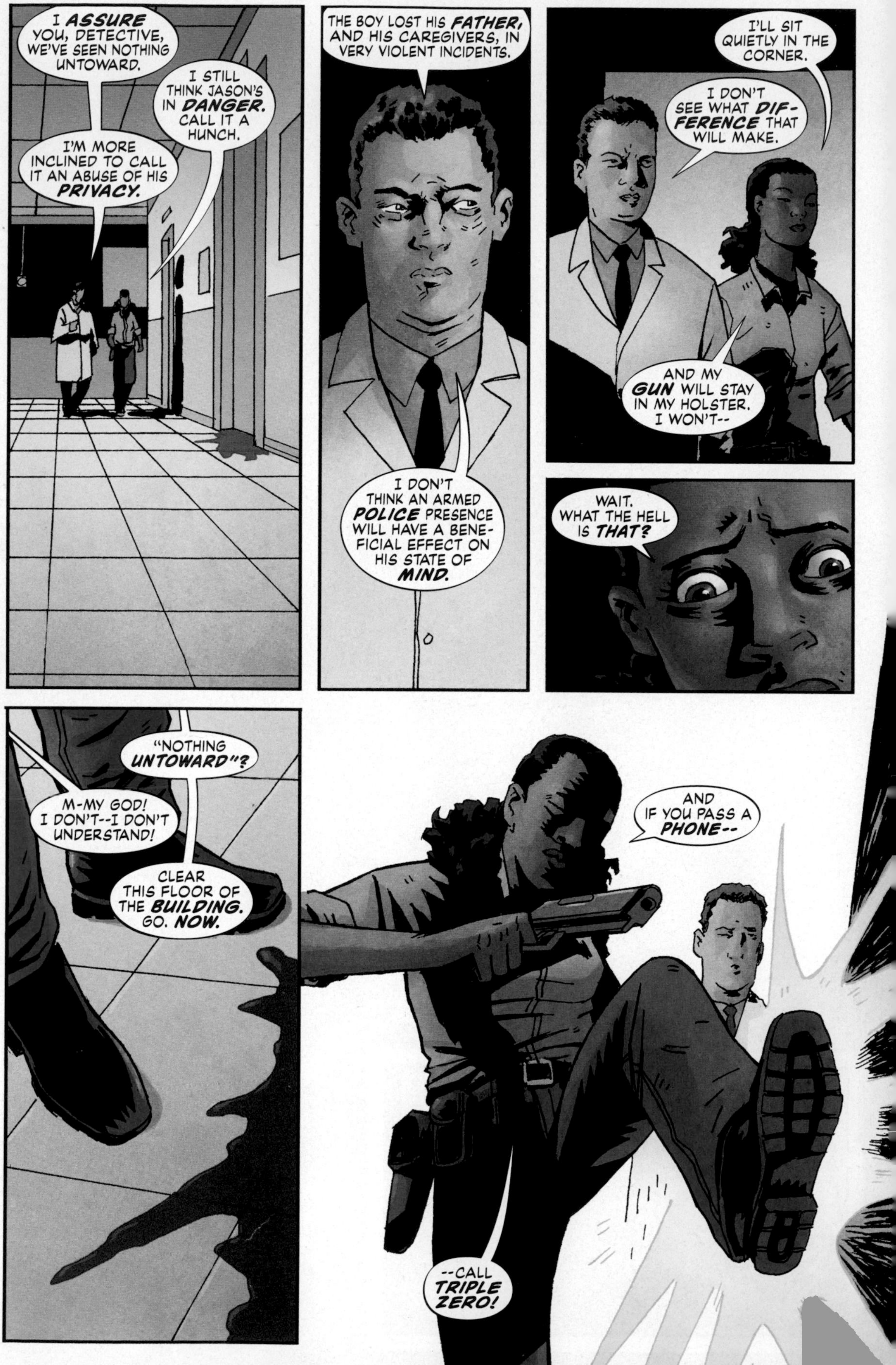
I ASSURE YOU, DETECTIVE, WE'VE SEEN NOTHING UNTOWARD.
I STILL THINK JASON'S IN DANGER. CALL IT A HUNCH.
I'M MORE INCLINED TO CALL IT AN ABUSE OF HIS PRIVACY.
THE BOY LOST HIS FATHER, AND HIS CAREGIVERS, IN VERY VIOLENT INCIDENTS.
I DON'T THINK AN ARMED POLICE PRESENCE WILL HAVE A BENEFICIAL EFFECT ON HIS STATE OF MIND.
I'LL SIT QUIETLY IN THE CORNER.
I DON'T SEE WHAT DIFFERENCE THAT WILL MAKE.
AND MY GUN WILL STAY IN MY HOLSTER. I WON'T--
WAIT. WHAT THE HELL IS THAT?
"NOTHING UNTOWARD"?
M-MY GOD! I DON'T--I DON'T UNDERSTAND!
CLEAR THIS FLOOR OF THE BUILDING. GO. NOW.
AND IF YOU PASS A PHONE--
--CALL TRIPLE ZERO!

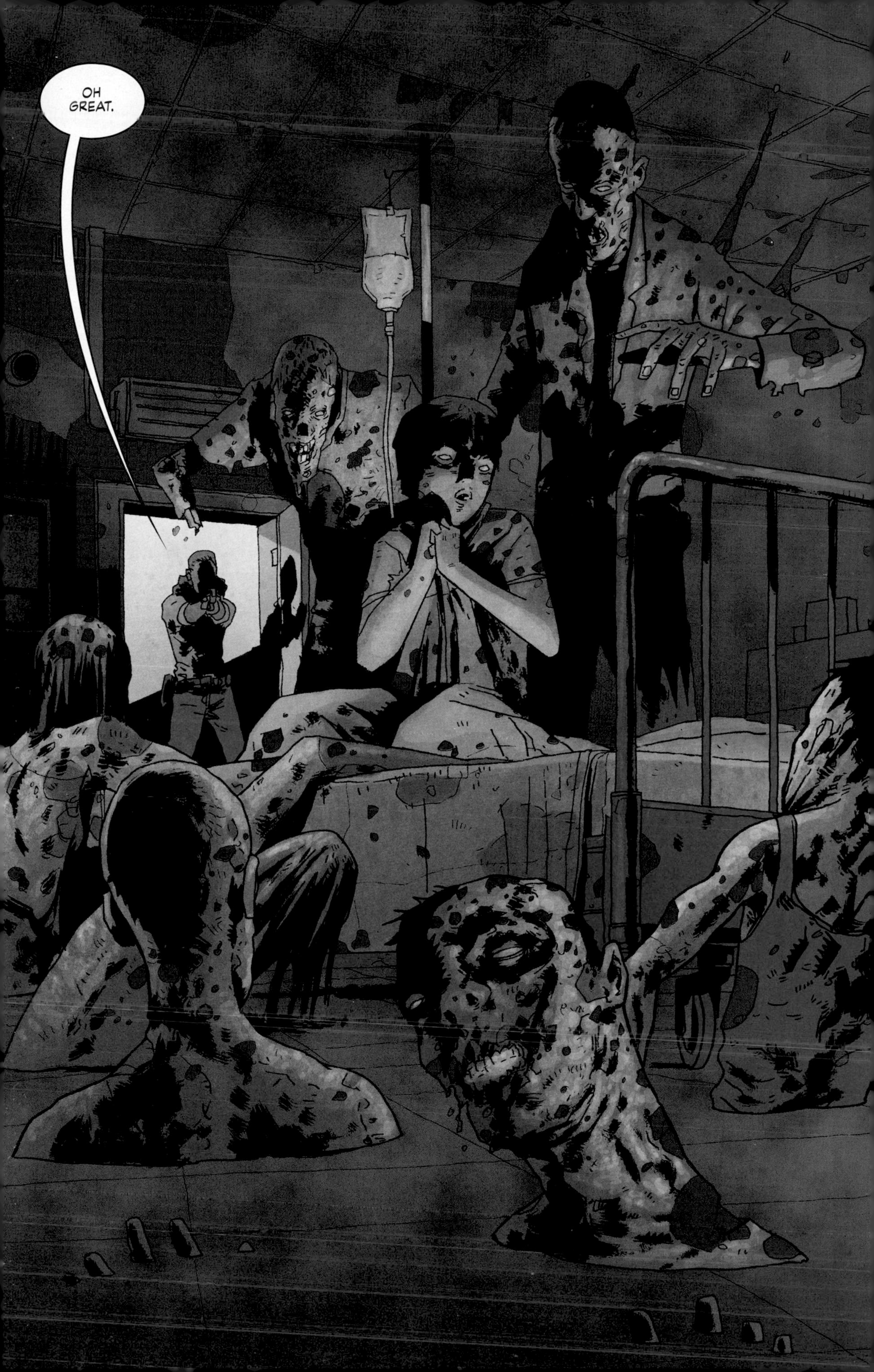
OH GREAT.

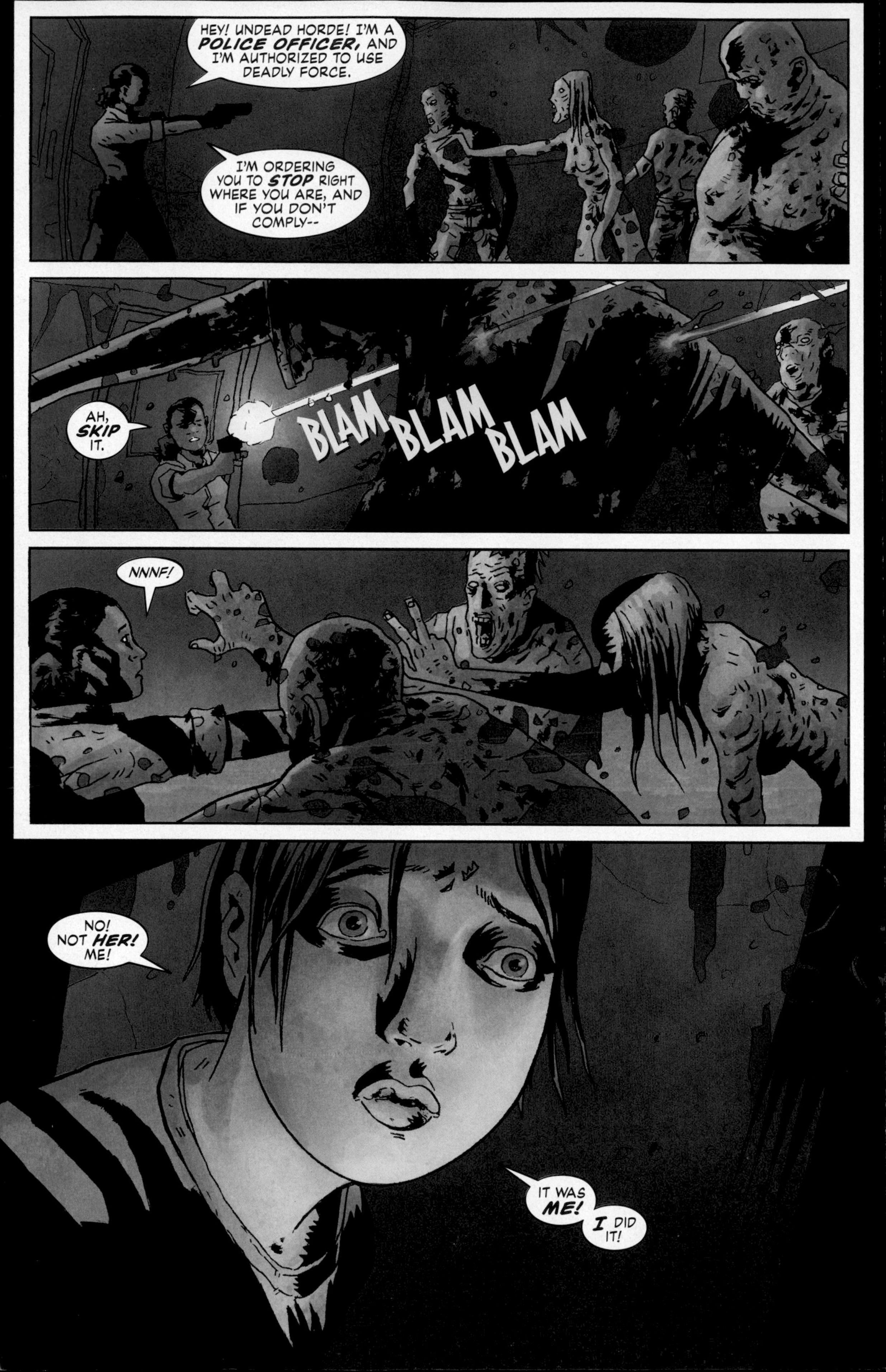
HEY! UNDEAD HORDE! I'M A POLICE OFFICER, AND I'M AUTHORIZED TO USE DEADLY FORCE.
I'M ORDERING YOU TO STOP RIGHT WHERE YOU ARE, AND IF YOU DON'T COMPLY--
AH, SKIP IT.
BLAM BLAM BLAM
NNNF!
NO! NOT HER! ME!
IT WAS ME!
I DID IT!

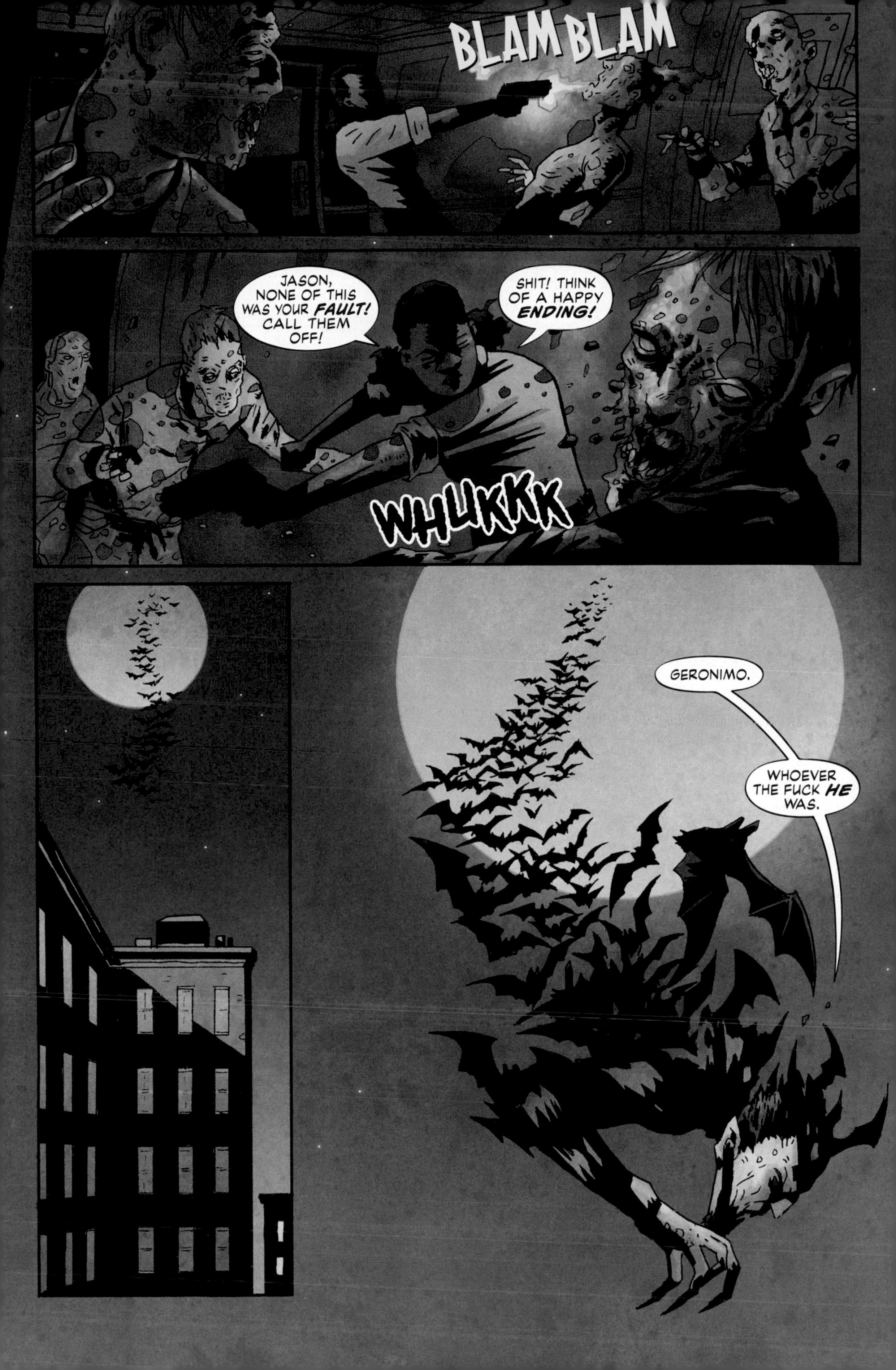
BLAM BLAM
JASON, NONE OF THIS WAS YOUR FAULT! CALL THEM OFF!
SHIT! THINK OF A HAPPY ENDING!
WHLIKKK
GERONIMO.
WHOEVER THE FUCK HE WAS.

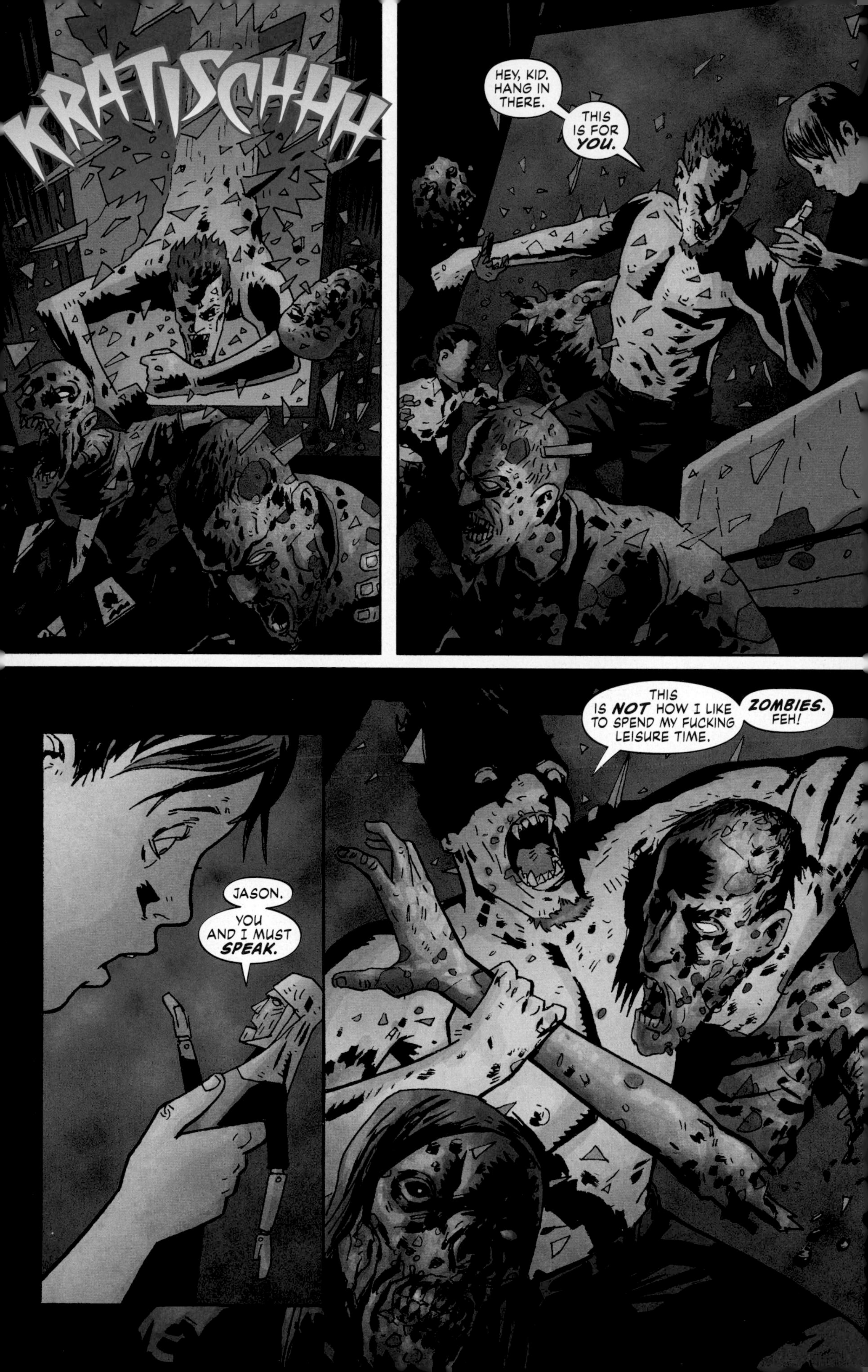
KRATISCHHH
HEY, KID. HANG IN THERE.
THIS IS FOR YOU.
THIS IS NOT HOW I LIKE TO SPEND MY FUCKING LEISURE TIME.
ZOMBIES. FEH!
JASON.
YOU AND I MUST SPEAK.

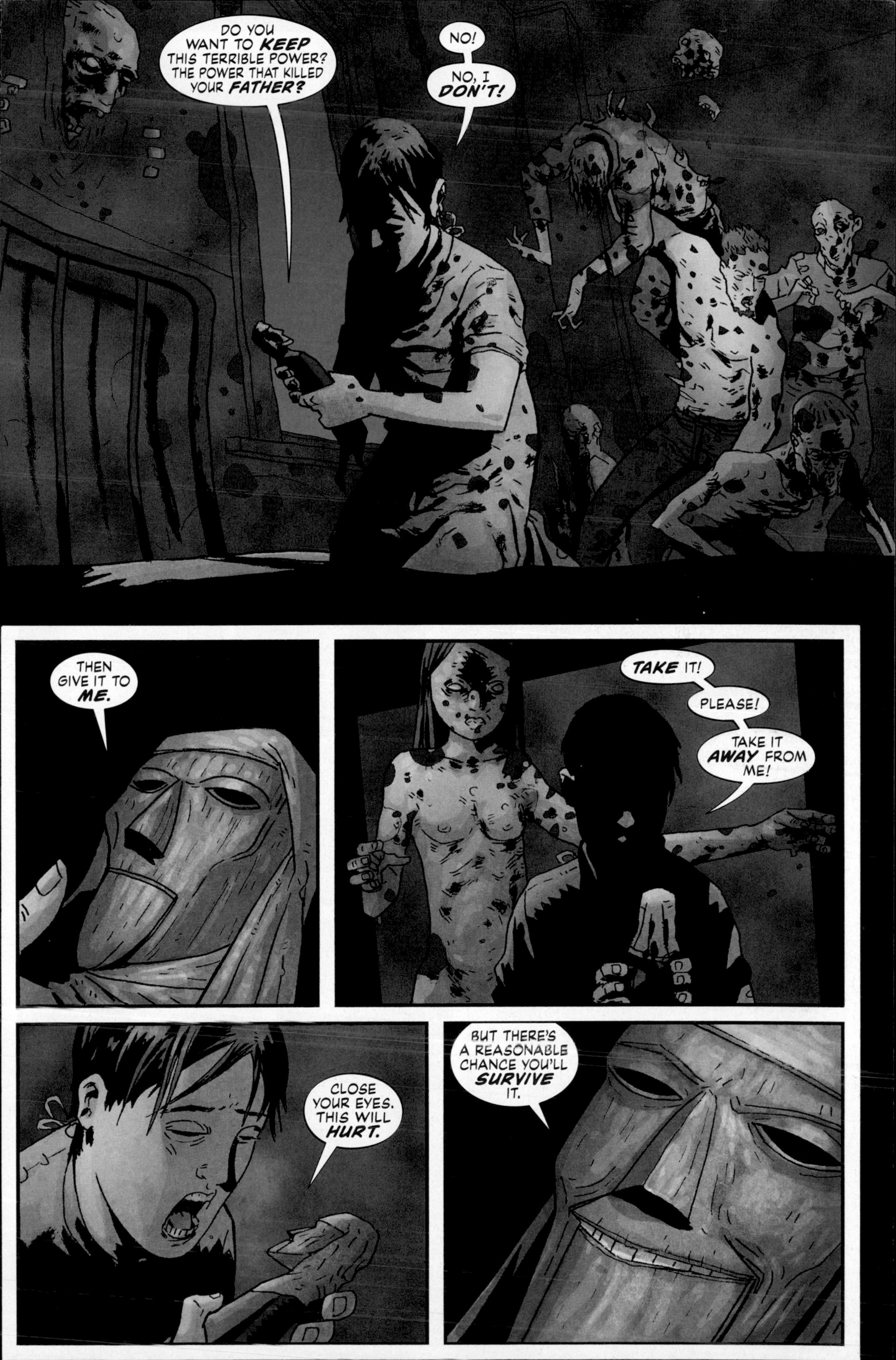
DO YOU WANT TO **KEEP** THIS TERRIBLE POWER? THE POWER THAT KILLED YOUR **FATHER?**
NO!
NO, I **DON'T!**
THEN GIVE IT TO **ME.**
**TAKE** IT!
PLEASE!
TAKE IT **AWAY** FROM ME!
CLOSE YOUR EYES. THIS WILL **HURT.**
BUT THERE'S A REASONABLE CHANCE YOU'LL **SURVIVE** IT.

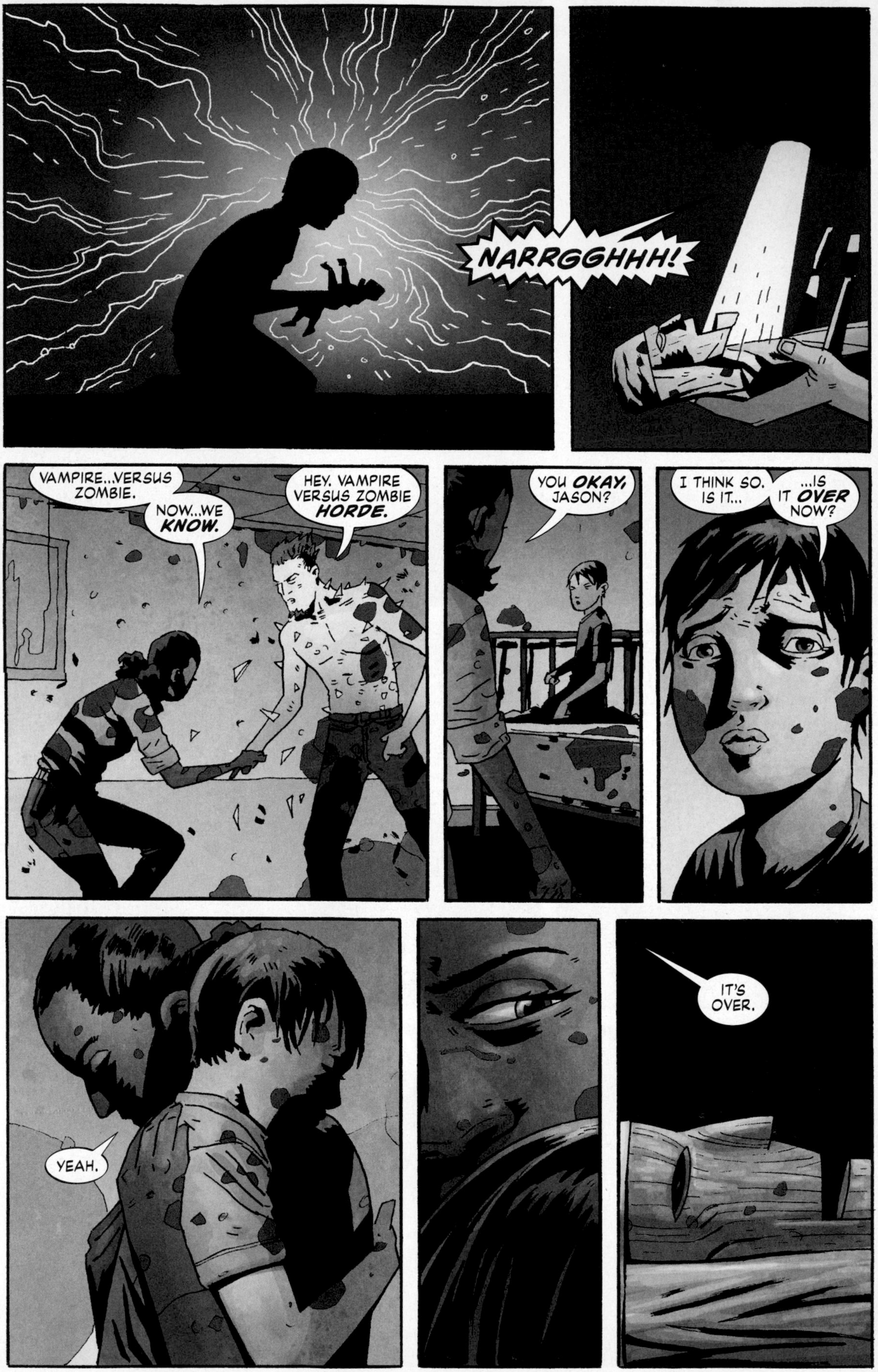
NARRGGHHH!
VAMPIRE...VERSUS ZOMBIE.
NOW...WE KNOW.
HEY. VAMPIRE VERSUS ZOMBIE HORDE.
YOU OKAY, JASON?
I THINK SO. IS IT...
...IS IT OVER NOW?
YEAH.
IT'S OVER.

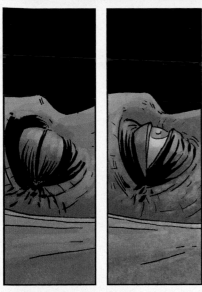

MADAME RAUSCH! YOU MUSTN'T TRY TO GET **UP.** YOU'RE FAR TOO **WEAK.**

NONSENSE. GET YOUR FOUL **BREATH** OUT OF MY FACE, KUSSLER!

CALL THE SISTERS. HAVE THEM BRING ME MY BOX--THE **TOY THEATER.**

YOU... YOU SEEM MUCH **RECOVERED,** MADAME.

I WOULD HAVE SWORN YOU WERE AT DEATH'S **DOOR,** BUT NOW...

NOW?

NOW I HAVE SOMETHING TO **WORK** WITH.

NOW I HAVE A **DOG** IN THIS FIGHT.

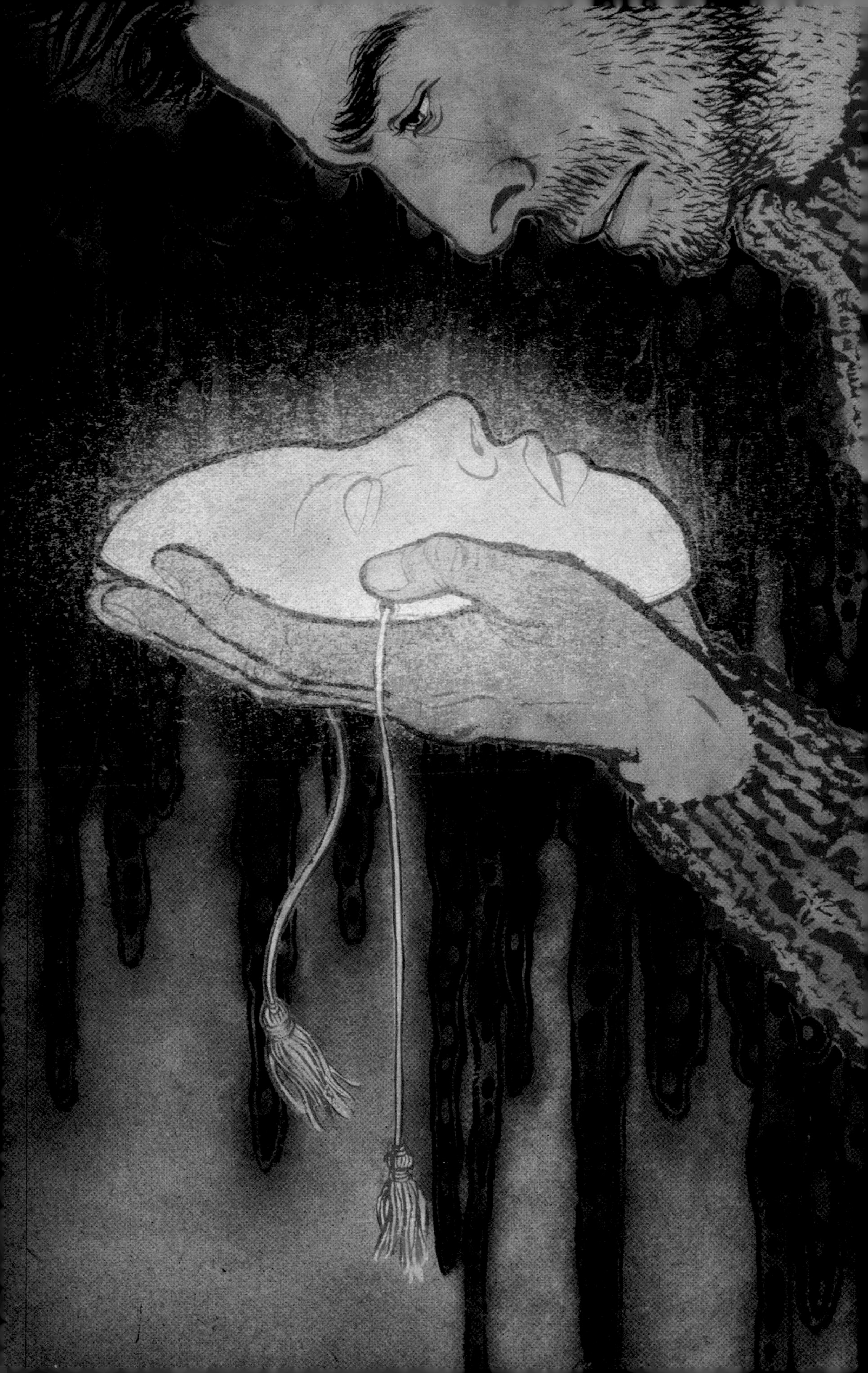

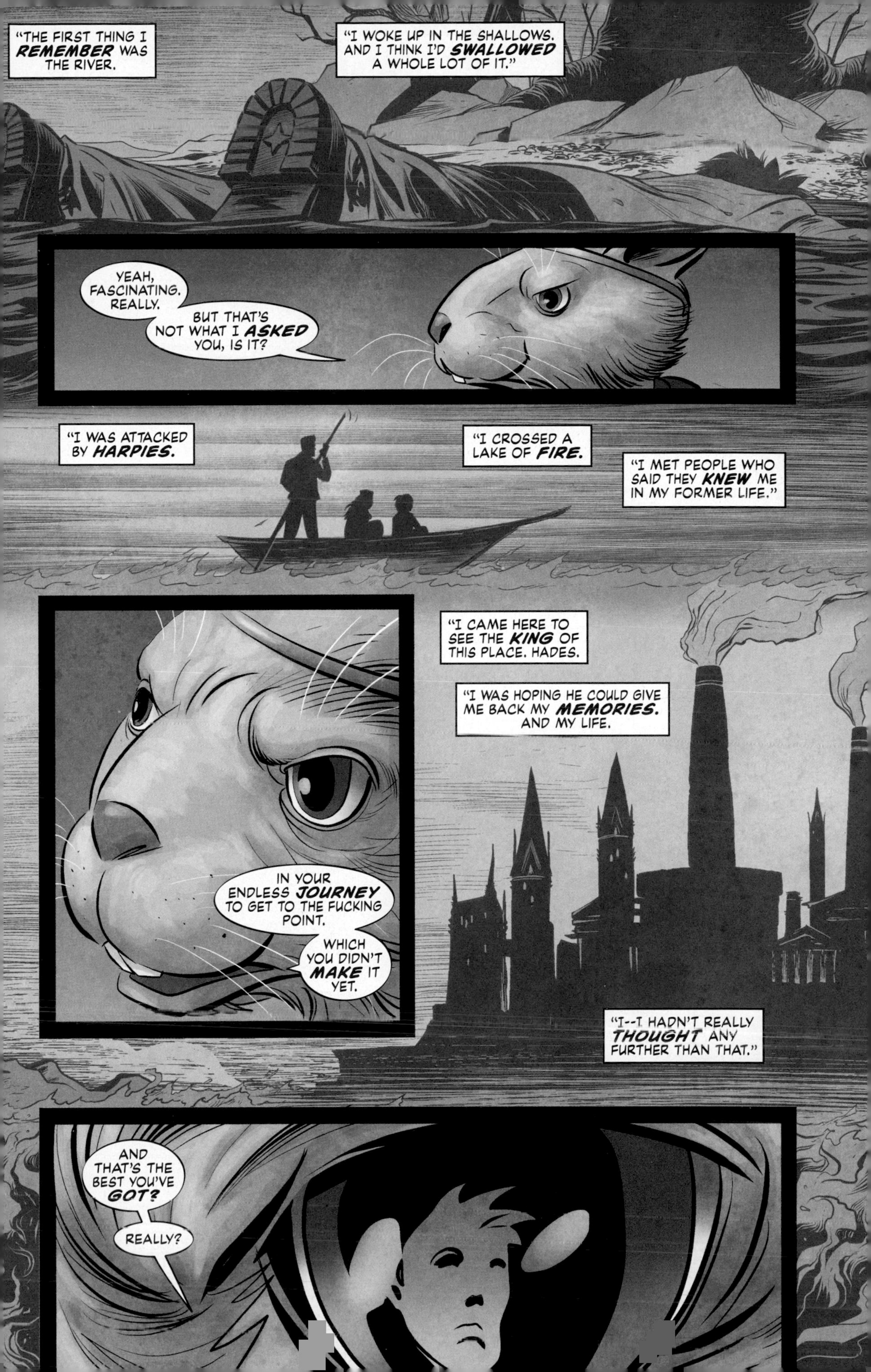
"THE FIRST THING I REMEMBER WAS THE RIVER.
"I WOKE UP IN THE SHALLOWS. AND I THINK I'D SWALLOWED A WHOLE LOT OF IT."
YEAH, FASCINATING. REALLY.
BUT THAT'S NOT WHAT I ASKED YOU, IS IT?
"I WAS ATTACKED BY HARPIES.
"I CROSSED A LAKE OF FIRE.
"I MET PEOPLE WHO SAID THEY KNEW ME IN MY FORMER LIFE."
"I CAME HERE TO SEE THE KING OF THIS PLACE. HADES.
"I WAS HOPING HE COULD GIVE ME BACK MY MEMORIES. AND MY LIFE.
IN YOUR ENDLESS JOURNEY TO GET TO THE FUCKING POINT.
WHICH YOU DIDN'T MAKE IT YET.
"I--I HADN'T REALLY THOUGHT ANY FURTHER THAN THAT."
AND THAT'S THE BEST YOU'VE GOT?
REALLY?

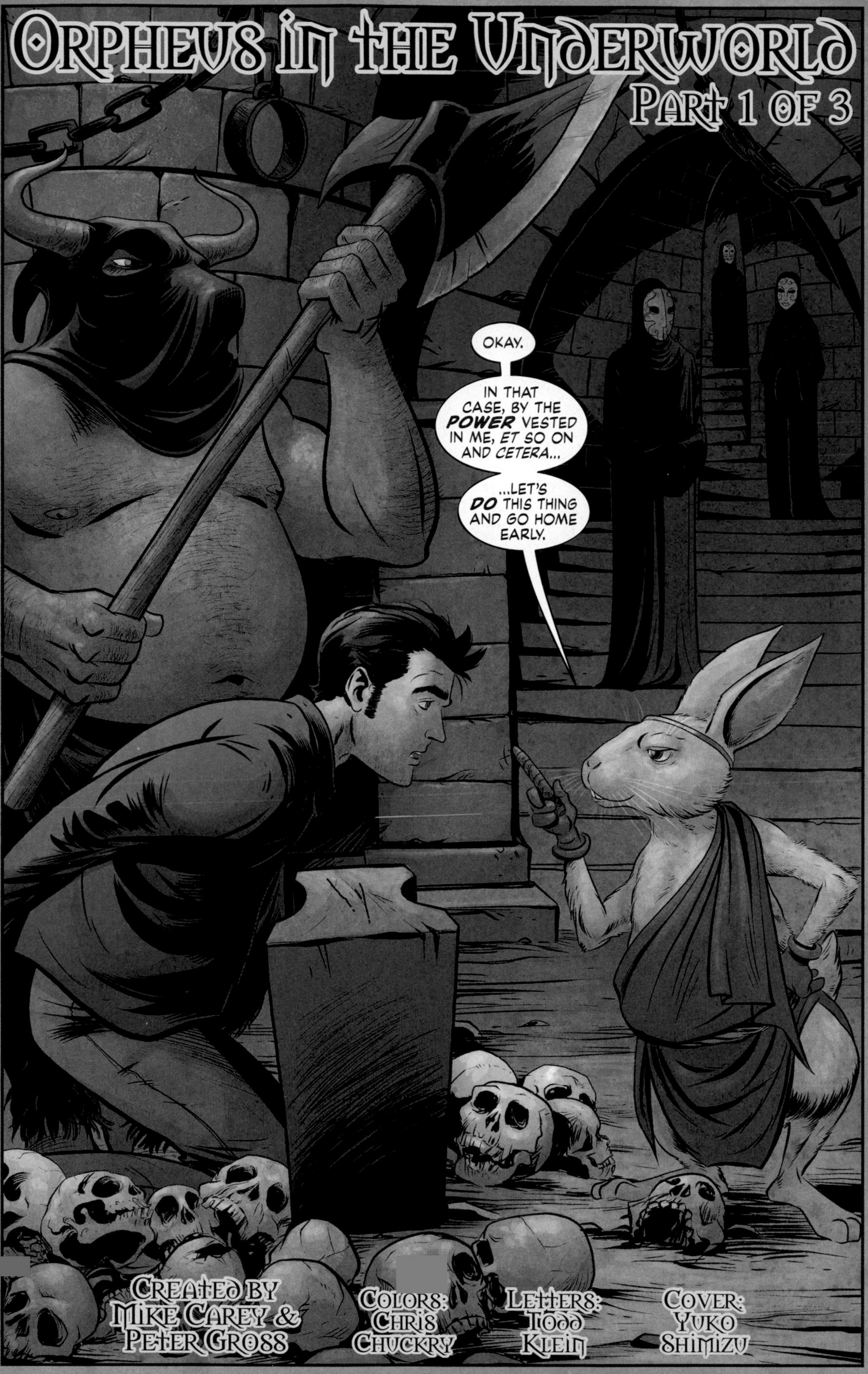
ORPHEUS IN THE UNDERWORLD
PART 1 OF 3
OKAY.
IN THAT CASE, BY THE POWER VESTED IN ME, ET SO ON AND CETERA...
...LET'S DO THIS THING AND GO HOME EARLY.
CREATED BY MIKE CAREY & PETER GROSS
COLORS: CHRIS CHUCKRY
LETTERS: TODD KLEIN
COVER: YUKO SHIMIZU

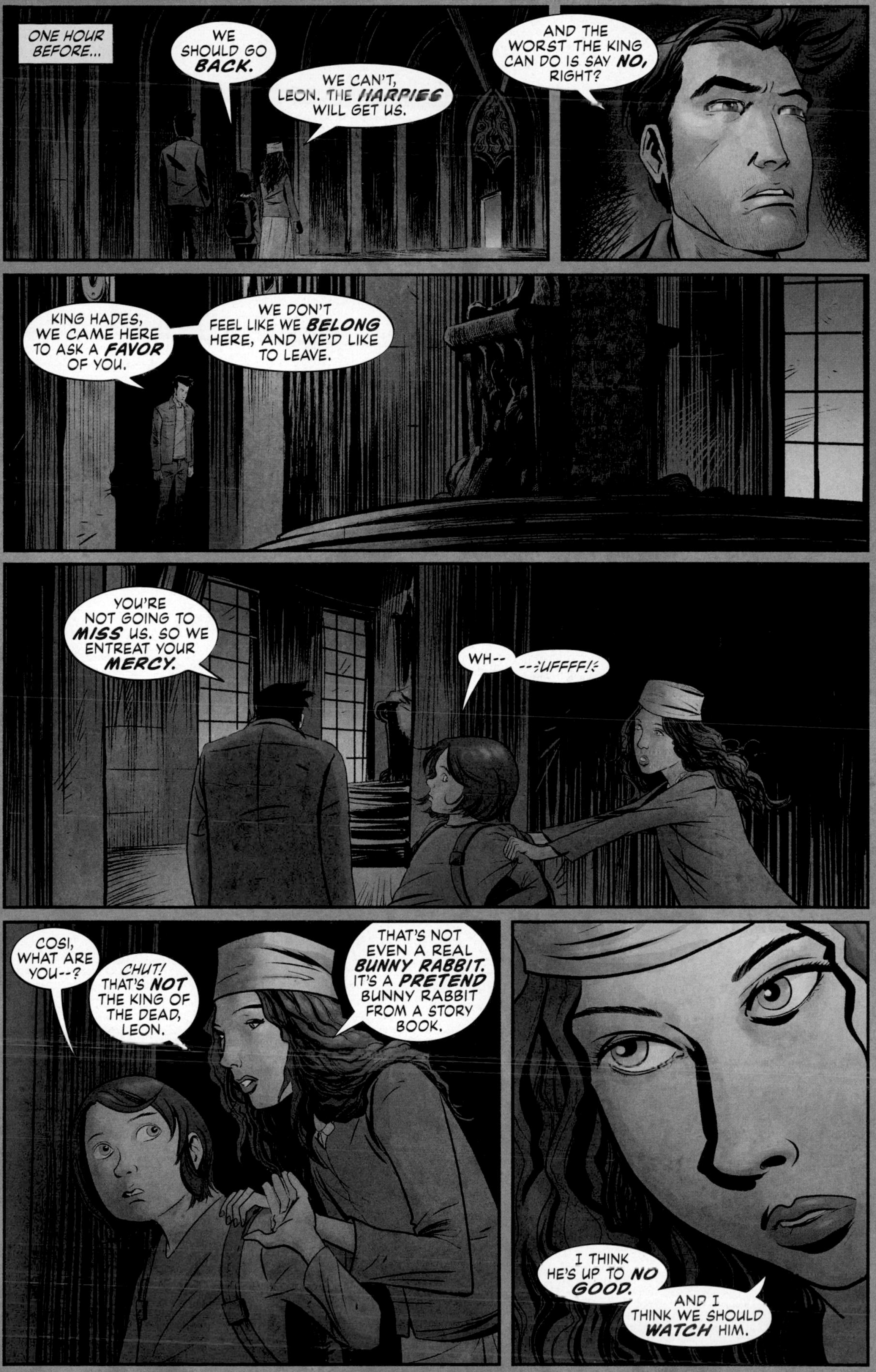
ONE HOUR BEFORE...
WE SHOULD GO BACK.
WE CAN'T, LEON. THE HARPIES WILL GET US.
AND THE WORST THE KING CAN DO IS SAY NO, RIGHT?
KING HADES, WE CAME HERE TO ASK A FAVOR OF YOU.
WE DON'T FEEL LIKE WE BELONG HERE, AND WE'D LIKE TO LEAVE.
YOU'RE NOT GOING TO MISS US. SO WE ENTREAT YOUR MERCY.
WH--
--UFFFF!
COSI, WHAT ARE YOU--?
CHUT! THAT'S NOT THE KING OF THE DEAD, LEON.
THAT'S NOT EVEN A REAL BUNNY RABBIT. IT'S A PRETEND BUNNY RABBIT FROM A STORY BOOK.
I THINK HE'S UP TO NO GOOD.
AND I THINK WE SHOULD WATCH HIM.

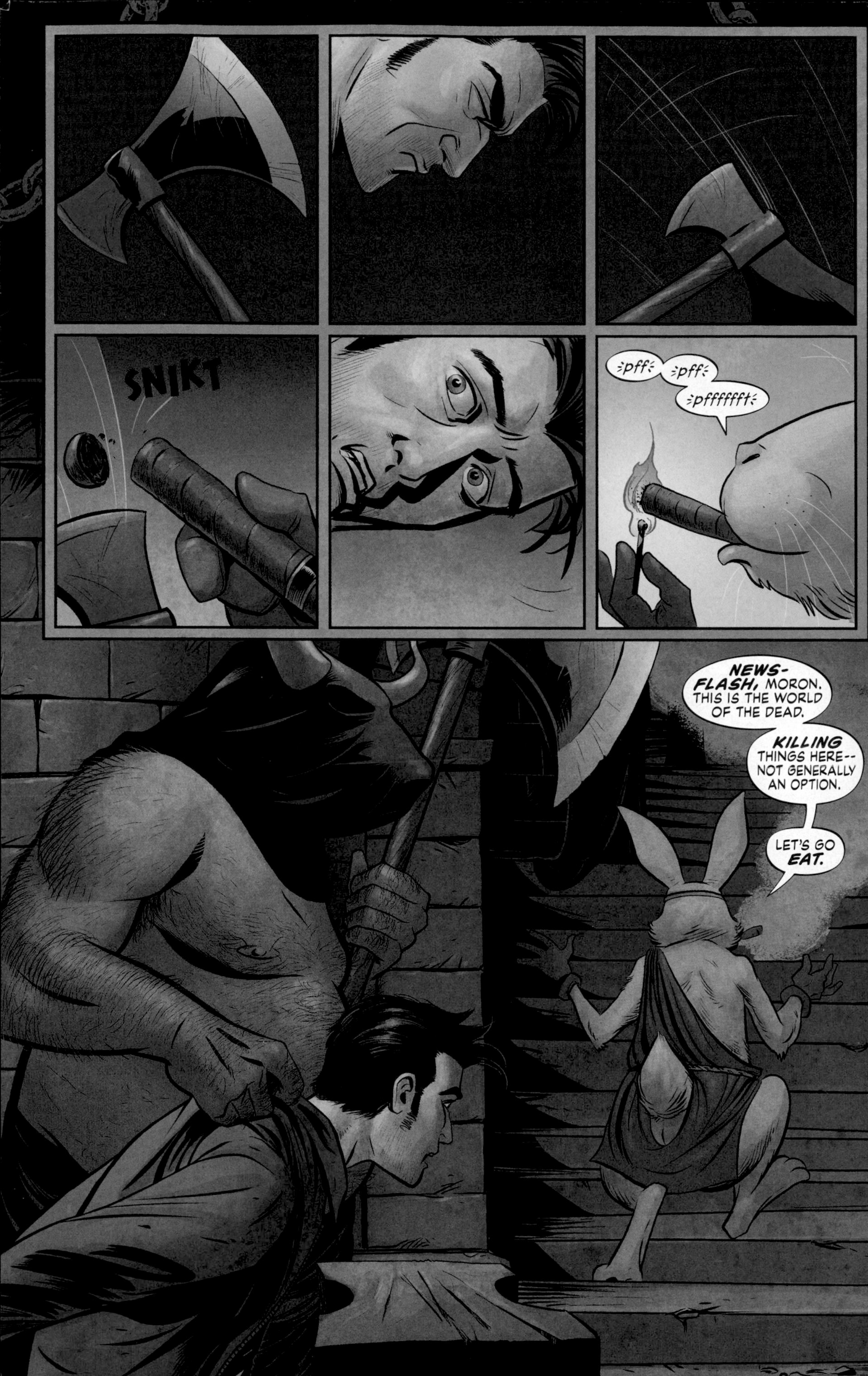
SNIKT
pff
pff
pfffffft
NEWS-FLASH, MORON. THIS IS THE WORLD OF THE DEAD.
KILLING THINGS HERE--NOT GENERALLY AN OPTION.
LET'S GO EAT.

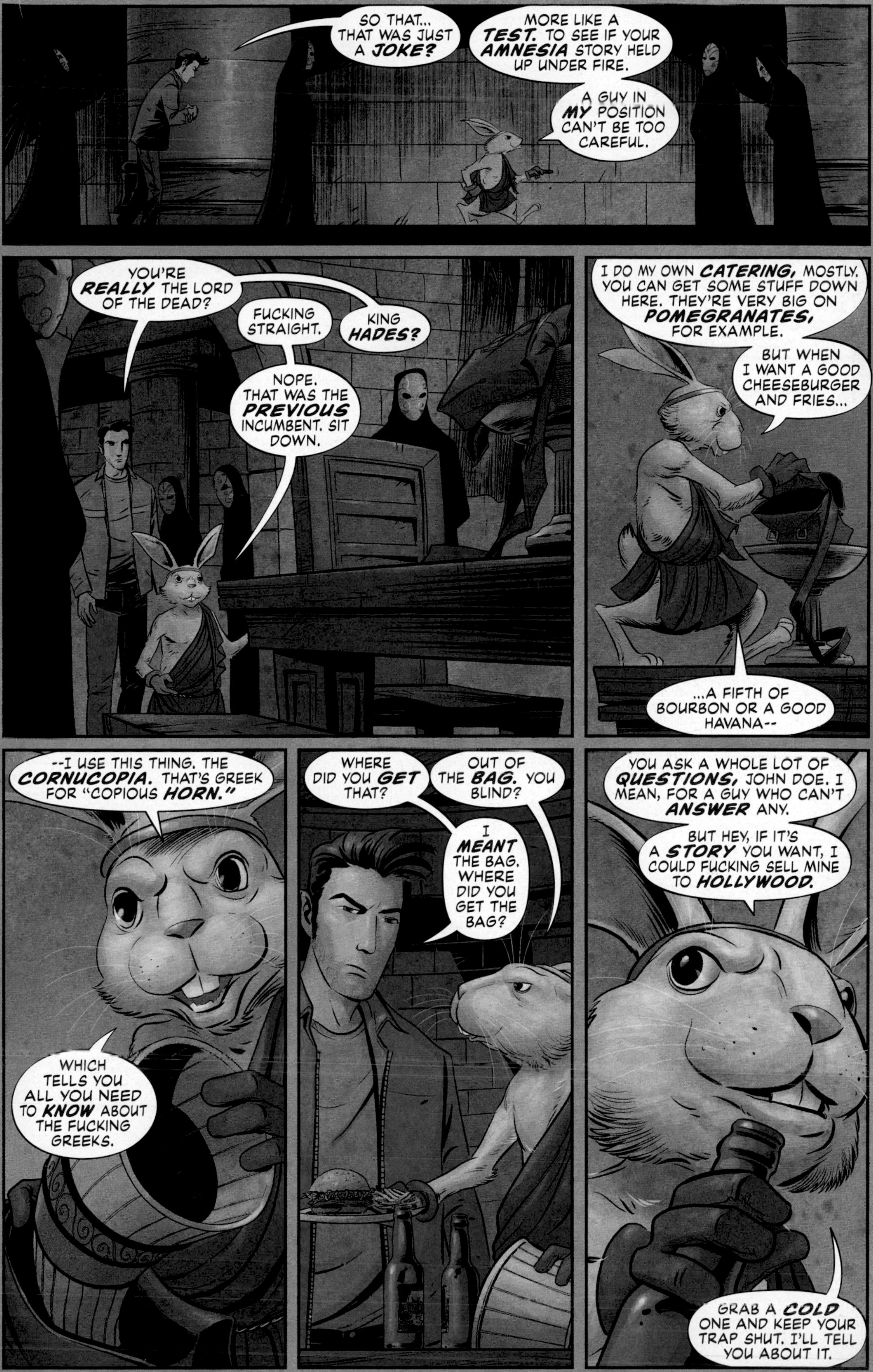
SO THAT... THAT WAS JUST A JOKE?
MORE LIKE A TEST. TO SEE IF YOUR AMNESIA STORY HELD UP UNDER FIRE.
A GUY IN MY POSITION CAN'T BE TOO CAREFUL.
YOU'RE REALLY THE LORD OF THE DEAD?
FUCKING STRAIGHT.
KING HADES?
NOPE. THAT WAS THE PREVIOUS INCUMBENT. SIT DOWN.
I DO MY OWN CATERING, MOSTLY. YOU CAN GET SOME STUFF DOWN HERE. THEY'RE VERY BIG ON POMEGRANATES, FOR EXAMPLE.
BUT WHEN I WANT A GOOD CHEESEBURGER AND FRIES...
...A FIFTH OF BOURBON OR A GOOD HAVANA--
--I USE THIS THING. THE CORNUCOPIA. THAT'S GREEK FOR "COPIOUS HORN."
WHICH TELLS YOU ALL YOU NEED TO KNOW ABOUT THE FUCKING GREEKS.
WHERE DID YOU GET THAT?
OUT OF THE BAG. YOU BLIND?
I MEANT THE BAG. WHERE DID YOU GET THE BAG?
YOU ASK A WHOLE LOT OF QUESTIONS, JOHN DOE. I MEAN, FOR A GUY WHO CAN'T ANSWER ANY.
BUT HEY, IF IT'S A STORY YOU WANT, I COULD FUCKING SELL MINE TO HOLLYWOOD.
GRAB A COLD ONE AND KEEP YOUR TRAP SHUT. I'LL TELL YOU ABOUT IT.

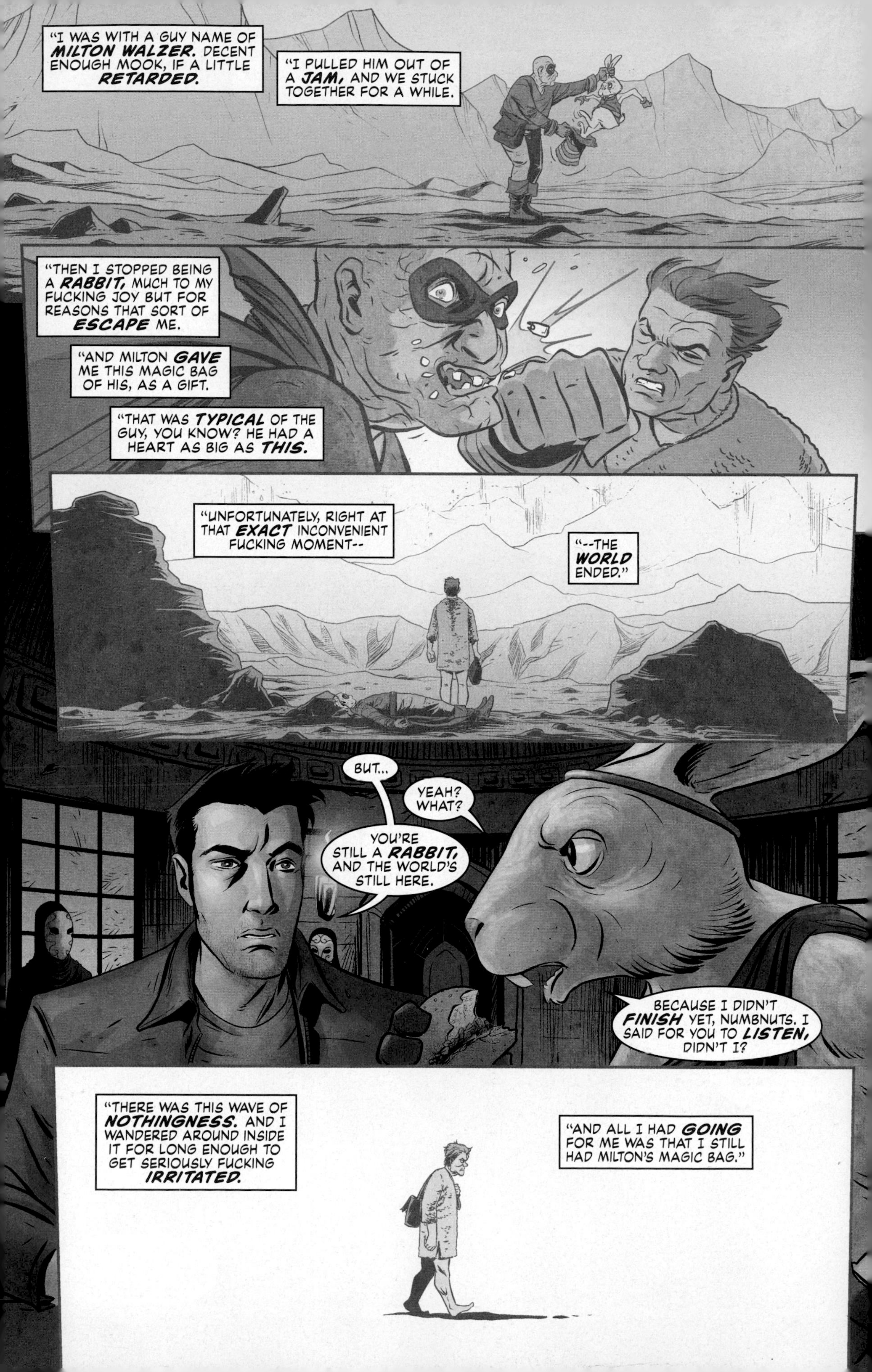
"I WAS WITH A GUY NAME OF MILTON WALZER. DECENT ENOUGH MOOK, IF A LITTLE RETARDED.
"I PULLED HIM OUT OF A JAM, AND WE STUCK TOGETHER FOR A WHILE.
"THEN I STOPPED BEING A RABBIT, MUCH TO MY FUCKING JOY BUT FOR REASONS THAT SORT OF ESCAPE ME.
"AND MILTON GAVE ME THIS MAGIC BAG OF HIS, AS A GIFT.
"THAT WAS TYPICAL OF THE GUY, YOU KNOW? HE HAD A HEART AS BIG AS THIS.
"UNFORTUNATELY, RIGHT AT THAT EXACT INCONVENIENT FUCKING MOMENT--
"--THE WORLD ENDED."
BUT...
YEAH? WHAT?
YOU'RE STILL A RABBIT, AND THE WORLD'S STILL HERE.
BECAUSE I DIDN'T FINISH YET, NUMBNUTS. I SAID FOR YOU TO LISTEN, DIDN'T I?
"THERE WAS THIS WAVE OF NOTHINGNESS. AND I WANDERED AROUND INSIDE IT FOR LONG ENOUGH TO GET SERIOUSLY FUCKING IRRITATED.
"AND ALL I HAD GOING FOR ME WAS THAT I STILL HAD MILTON'S MAGIC BAG."

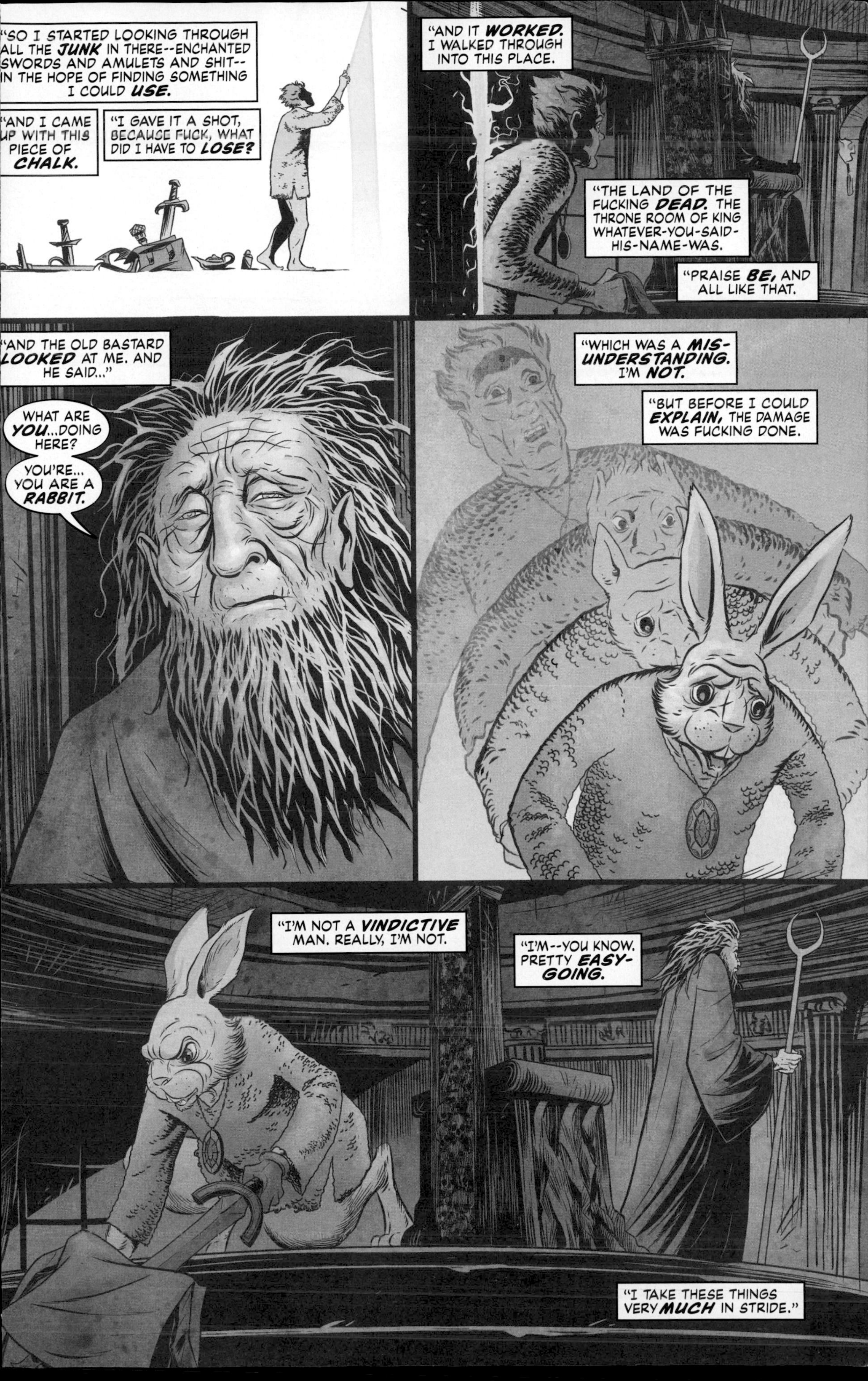
"SO I STARTED LOOKING THROUGH ALL THE JUNK IN THERE--ENCHANTED SWORDS AND AMULETS AND SHIT--IN THE HOPE OF FINDING SOMETHING I COULD USE.
"AND I CAME UP WITH THIS PIECE OF CHALK.
"I GAVE IT A SHOT, BECAUSE FUCK, WHAT DID I HAVE TO LOSE?
"AND IT WORKED. I WALKED THROUGH INTO THIS PLACE.
"THE LAND OF THE FUCKING DEAD. THE THRONE ROOM OF KING WHATEVER-YOU-SAID-HIS-NAME-WAS.
"PRAISE BE, AND ALL LIKE THAT.
"AND THE OLD BASTARD LOOKED AT ME. AND HE SAID..."
WHAT ARE YOU...DOING HERE?
YOU'RE... YOU ARE A RABBIT.
"WHICH WAS A MIS-UNDERSTANDING. I'M NOT.
"BUT BEFORE I COULD EXPLAIN, THE DAMAGE WAS FUCKING DONE.
"I'M NOT A VINDICTIVE MAN. REALLY, I'M NOT.
"I'M--YOU KNOW. PRETTY EASY-GOING.
"I TAKE THESE THINGS VERY MUCH IN STRIDE."

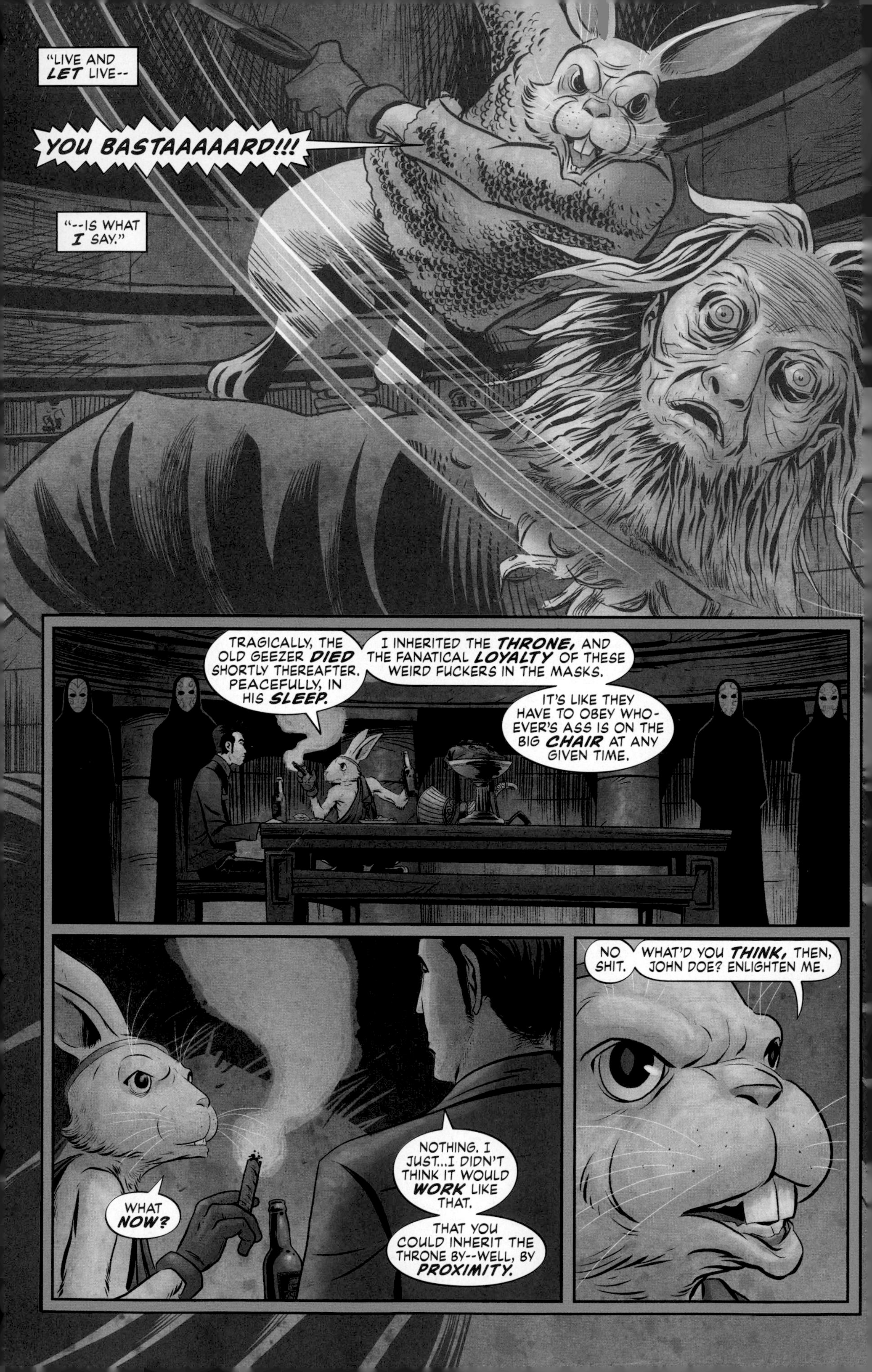
"LIVE AND LET LIVE--
YOU BASTAAAAARD!!!
"--IS WHAT I SAY."
TRAGICALLY, THE OLD GEEZER DIED SHORTLY THEREAFTER. PEACEFULLY, IN HIS SLEEP.
I INHERITED THE THRONE, AND THE FANATICAL LOYALTY OF THESE WEIRD FUCKERS IN THE MASKS.
IT'S LIKE THEY HAVE TO OBEY WHO-EVER'S ASS IS ON THE BIG CHAIR AT ANY GIVEN TIME.
WHAT NOW?
NOTHING. I JUST...I DIDN'T THINK IT WOULD WORK LIKE THAT.
THAT YOU COULD INHERIT THE THRONE BY--WELL, BY PROXIMITY.
NO SHIT.
WHAT'D YOU THINK, THEN, JOHN DOE? ENLIGHTEN ME.

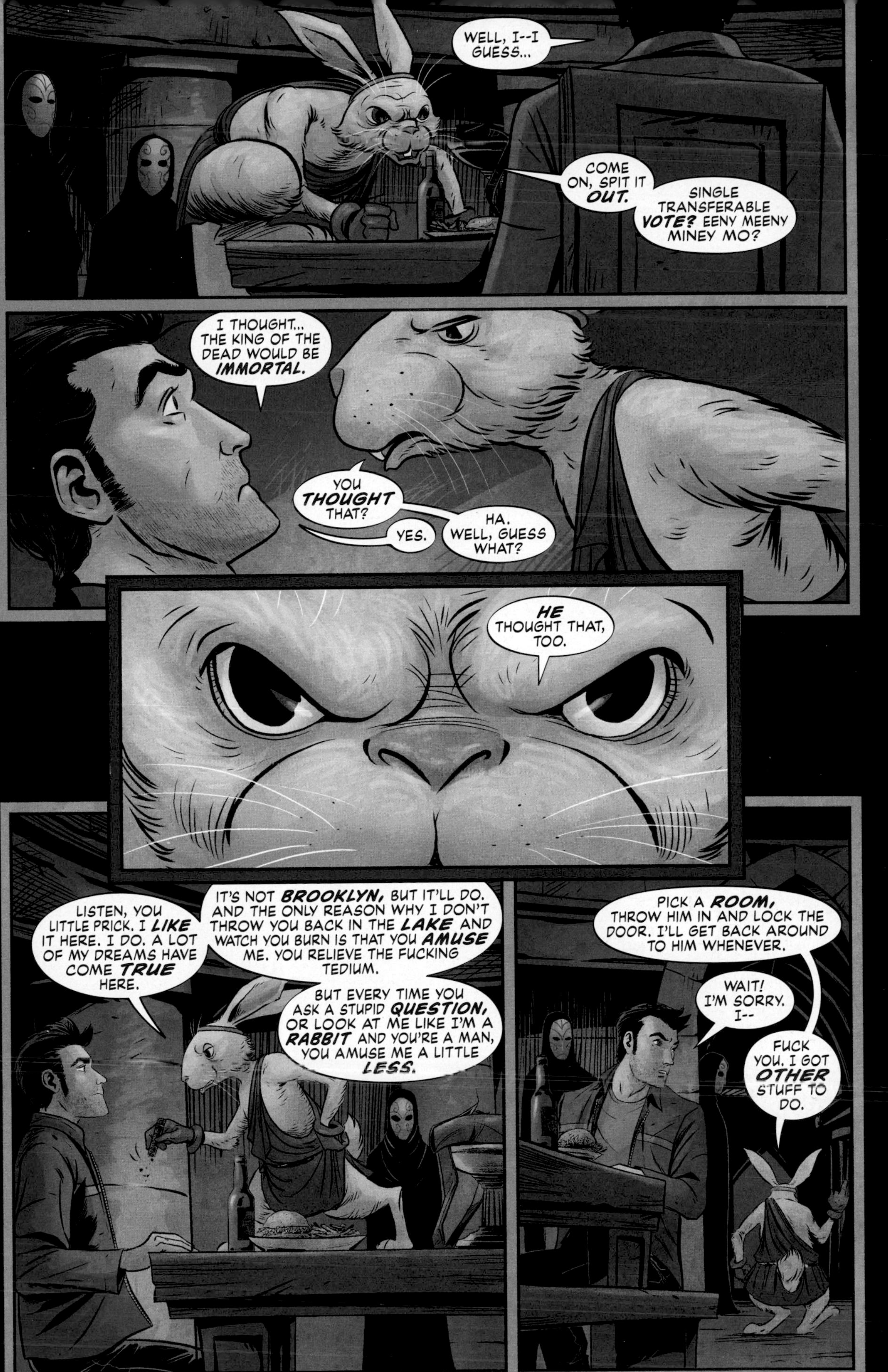
WELL, I--I GUESS...
COME ON, SPIT IT OUT.
SINGLE TRANSFERABLE VOTE? EENY MEENY MINEY MO?
I THOUGHT... THE KING OF THE DEAD WOULD BE IMMORTAL.
YOU THOUGHT THAT?
YES.
HA. WELL, GUESS WHAT?
HE THOUGHT THAT, TOO.
LISTEN, YOU LITTLE PRICK. I LIKE IT HERE. I DO. A LOT OF MY DREAMS HAVE COME TRUE HERE.
IT'S NOT BROOKLYN, BUT IT'LL DO. AND THE ONLY REASON WHY I DON'T THROW YOU BACK IN THE LAKE AND WATCH YOU BURN IS THAT YOU AMUSE ME. YOU RELIEVE THE FUCKING TEDIUM.
BUT EVERY TIME YOU ASK A STUPID QUESTION, OR LOOK AT ME LIKE I'M A RABBIT AND YOU'RE A MAN, YOU AMUSE ME A LITTLE LESS.
PICK A ROOM, THROW HIM IN AND LOCK THE DOOR. I'LL GET BACK AROUND TO HIM WHENEVER.
WAIT! I'M SORRY. I--
FUCK YOU. I GOT OTHER STUFF TO DO.

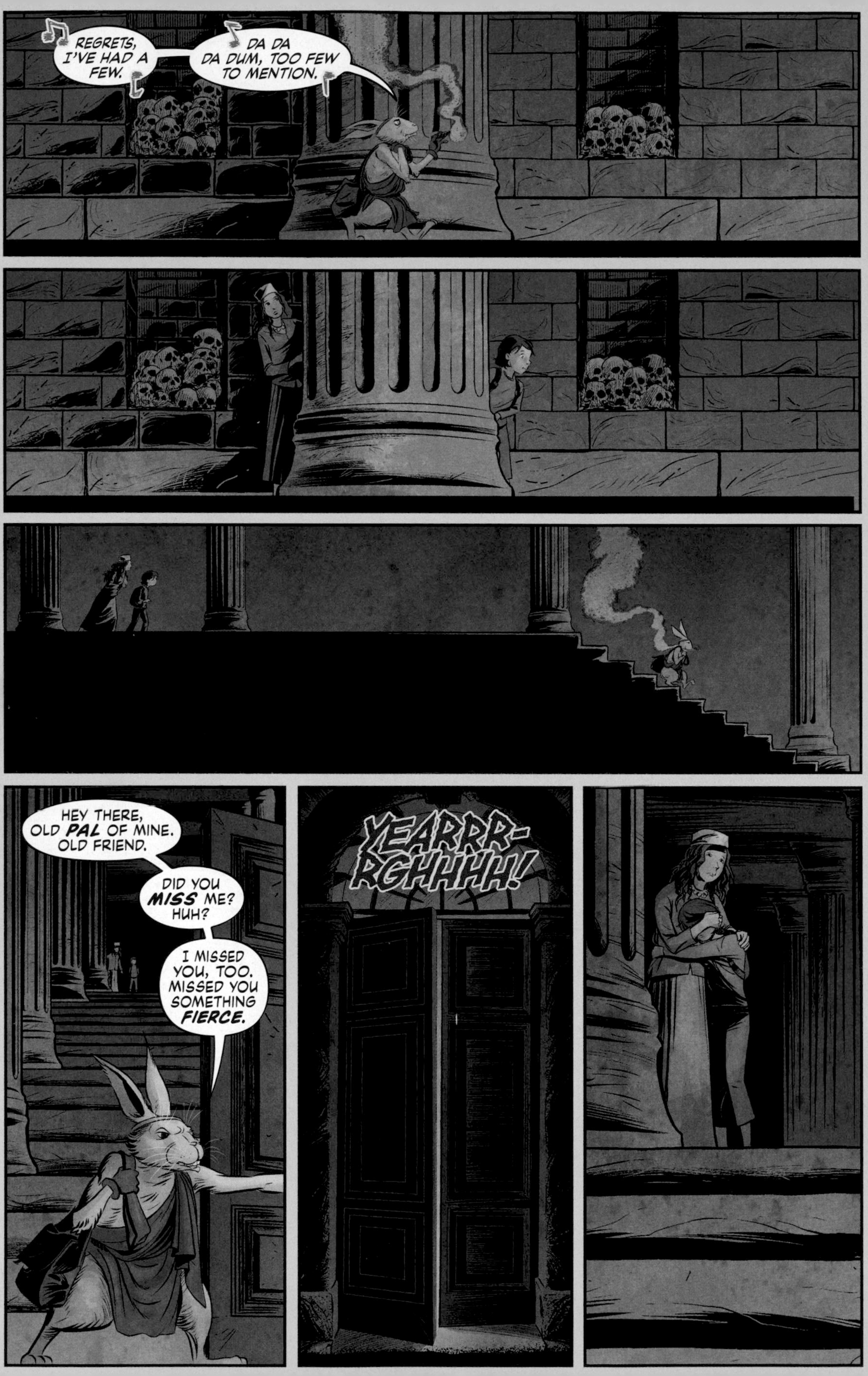
REGRETS, I'VE HAD A FEW.
DA DA DA DUM, TOO FEW TO MENTION.
HEY THERE, OLD PAL OF MINE. OLD FRIEND.
DID YOU MISS ME? HUH?
I MISSED YOU, TOO. MISSED YOU SOMETHING FIERCE.
YEARRR-RGHHHH!

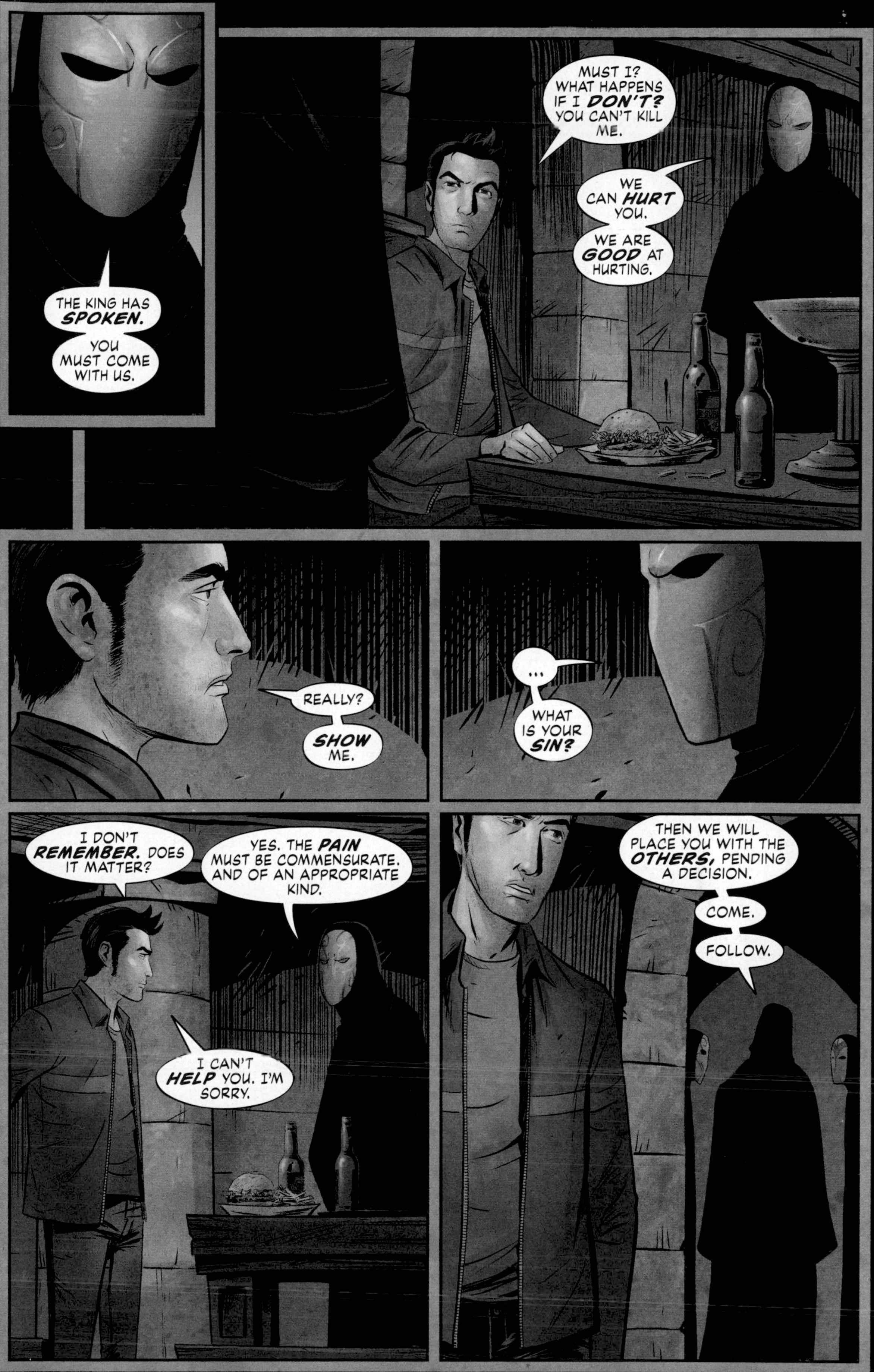
THE KING HAS SPOKEN.
YOU MUST COME WITH US.
MUST I? WHAT HAPPENS IF I DON'T? YOU CAN'T KILL ME.
WE CAN HURT YOU.
WE ARE GOOD AT HURTING.
REALLY?
SHOW ME.
...
WHAT IS YOUR SIN?
I DON'T REMEMBER. DOES IT MATTER?
YES. THE PAIN MUST BE COMMENSURATE. AND OF AN APPROPRIATE KIND.
I CAN'T HELP YOU. I'M SORRY.
THEN WE WILL PLACE YOU WITH THE OTHERS, PENDING A DECISION.
COME.
FOLLOW.

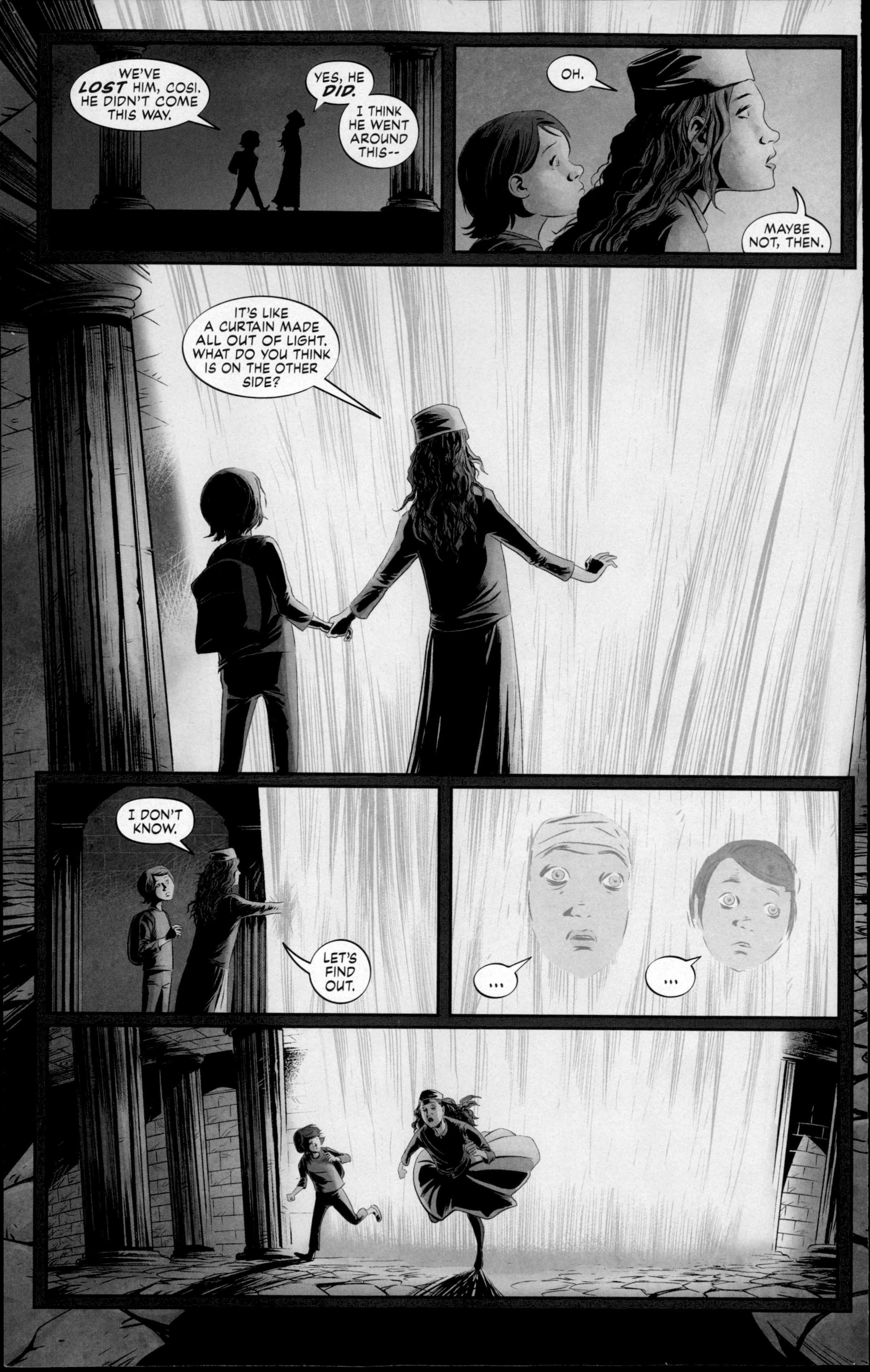
WE'VE LOST HIM, COSI. HE DIDN'T COME THIS WAY.
YES, HE DID.
I THINK HE WENT AROUND THIS--
OH.
MAYBE NOT, THEN.
IT'S LIKE A CURTAIN MADE ALL OUT OF LIGHT. WHAT DO YOU THINK IS ON THE OTHER SIDE?
I DON'T KNOW.
LET'S FIND OUT.
...
...

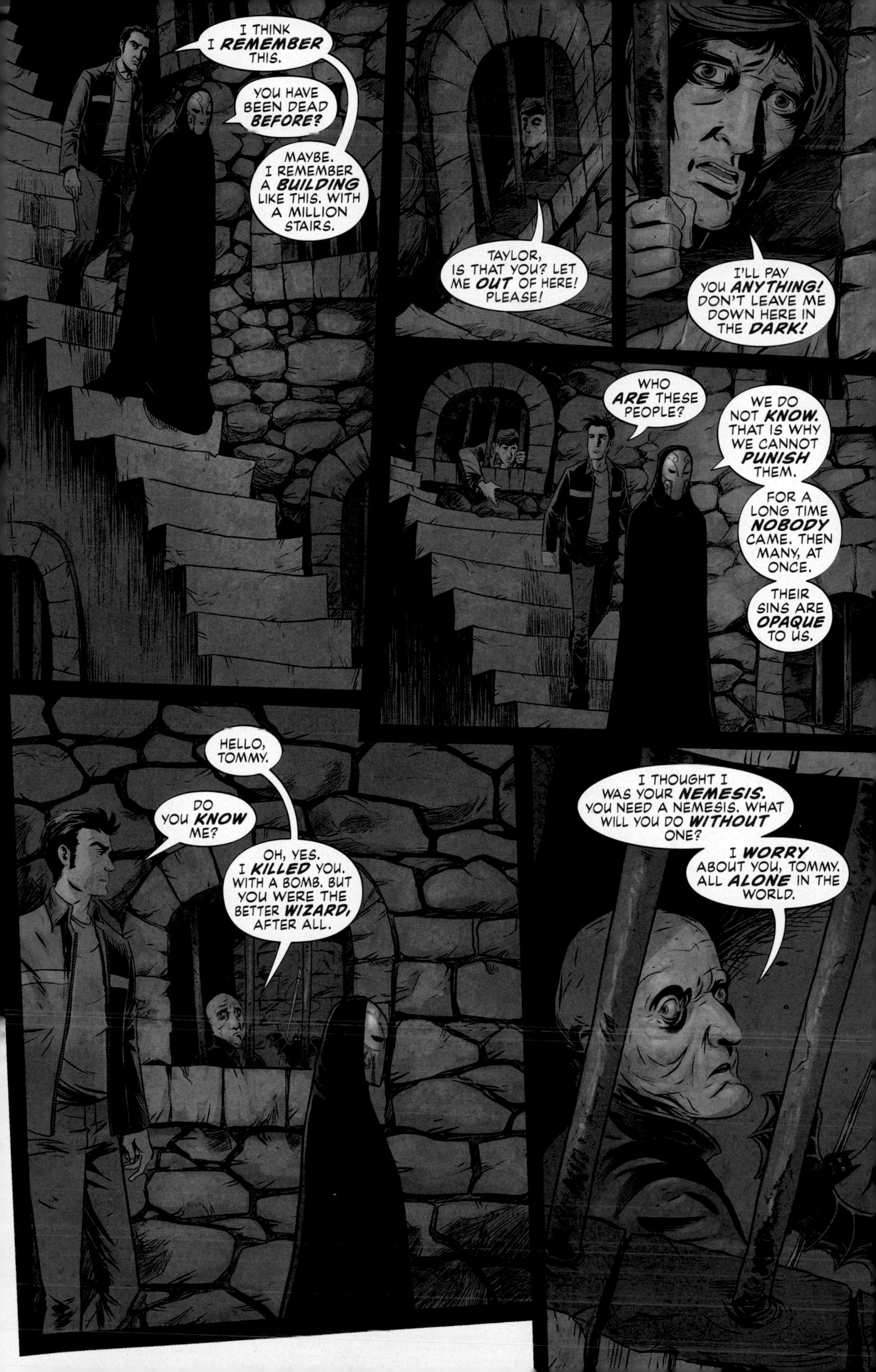
I THINK I REMEMBER THIS.
YOU HAVE BEEN DEAD BEFORE?
MAYBE. I REMEMBER A BUILDING LIKE THIS. WITH A MILLION STAIRS.
TAYLOR, IS THAT YOU? LET ME OUT OF HERE! PLEASE!
I'LL PAY YOU ANYTHING! DON'T LEAVE ME DOWN HERE IN THE DARK!
WHO ARE THESE PEOPLE?
WE DO NOT KNOW. THAT IS WHY WE CANNOT PUNISH THEM.
FOR A LONG TIME NOBODY CAME. THEN MANY, AT ONCE.
THEIR SINS ARE OPAQUE TO US.
HELLO, TOMMY.
DO YOU KNOW ME?
OH, YES. I KILLED YOU. WITH A BOMB. BUT YOU WERE THE BETTER WIZARD, AFTER ALL.
I THOUGHT I WAS YOUR NEMESIS. YOU NEED A NEMESIS. WHAT WILL YOU DO WITHOUT ONE?
I WORRY ABOUT YOU, TOMMY. ALL ALONE IN THE WORLD.

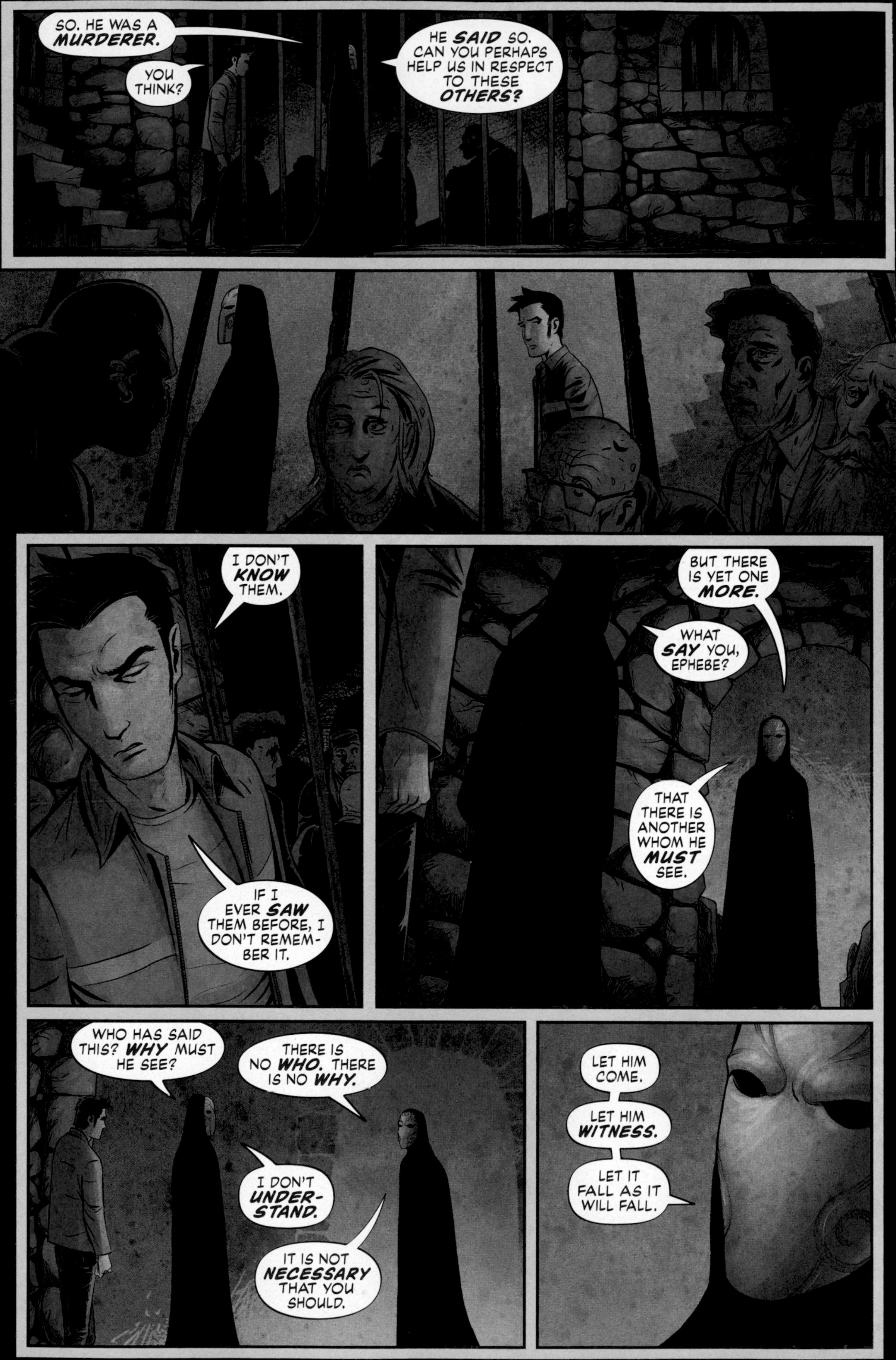
SO. HE WAS A MURDERER.
YOU THINK?
HE SAID SO. CAN YOU PERHAPS HELP US IN RESPECT TO THESE OTHERS?
I DON'T KNOW THEM.
IF I EVER SAW THEM BEFORE, I DON'T REMEMBER IT.
BUT THERE IS YET ONE MORE.
WHAT SAY YOU, EPHEBE?
THAT THERE IS ANOTHER WHOM HE MUST SEE.
WHO HAS SAID THIS? WHY MUST HE SEE?
THERE IS NO WHO. THERE IS NO WHY.
I DON'T UNDERSTAND.
IT IS NOT NECESSARY THAT YOU SHOULD.
LET HIM COME.
LET HIM WITNESS.
LET IT FALL AS IT WILL FALL.

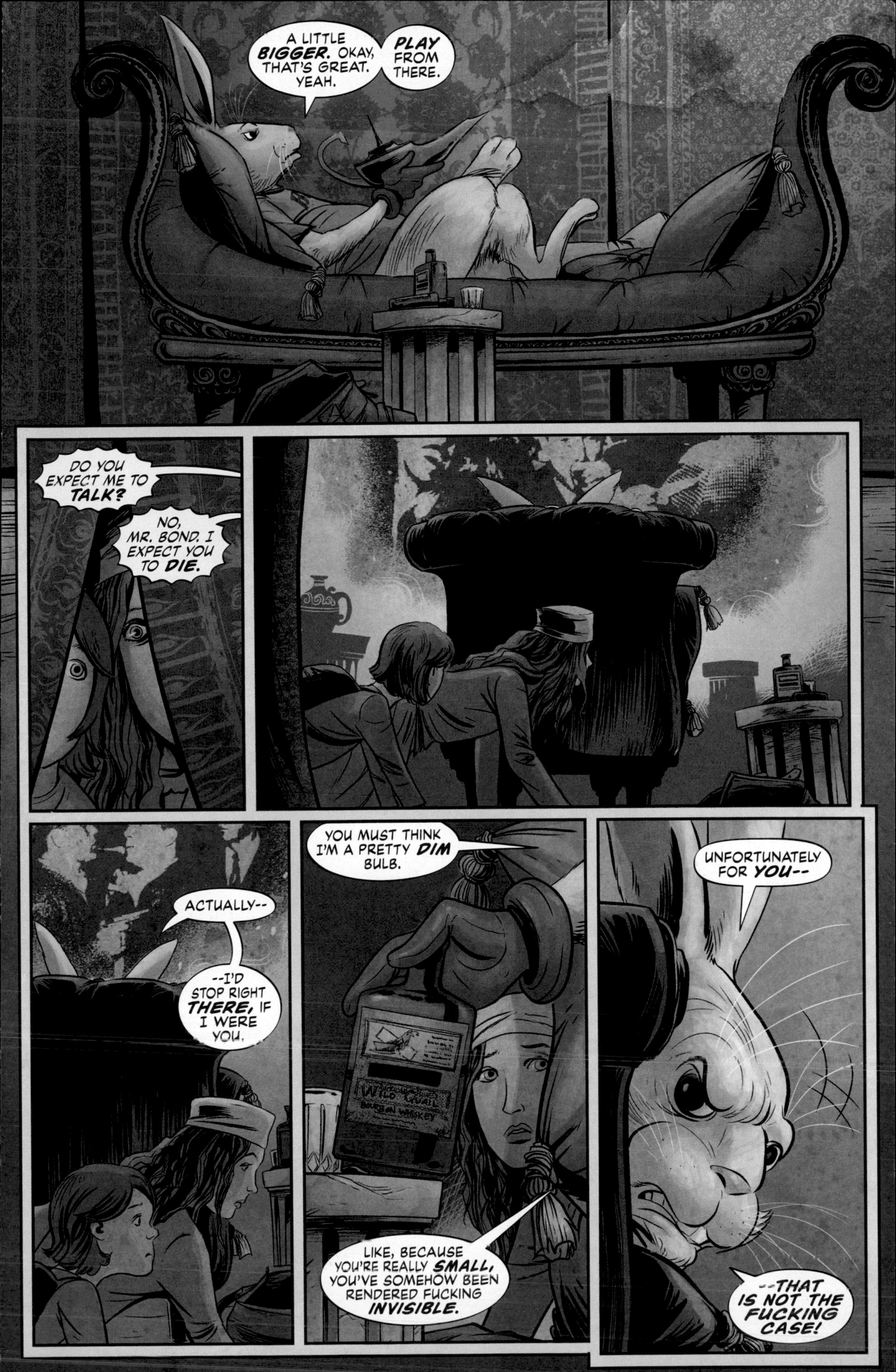
A LITTLE BIGGER. OKAY, THAT'S GREAT. YEAH.
PLAY FROM THERE.
DO YOU EXPECT ME TO TALK?
NO, MR. BOND. I EXPECT YOU TO DIE.
ACTUALLY--
--I'D STOP RIGHT THERE, IF I WERE YOU.
YOU MUST THINK I'M A PRETTY DIM BULB.
WILD QUAIL
BOURBON WHISKEY
LIKE, BECAUSE YOU'RE REALLY SMALL, YOU'VE SOMEHOW BEEN RENDERED FUCKING INVISIBLE.
UNFORTUNATELY FOR YOU--
--THAT IS NOT THE FUCKING CASE!

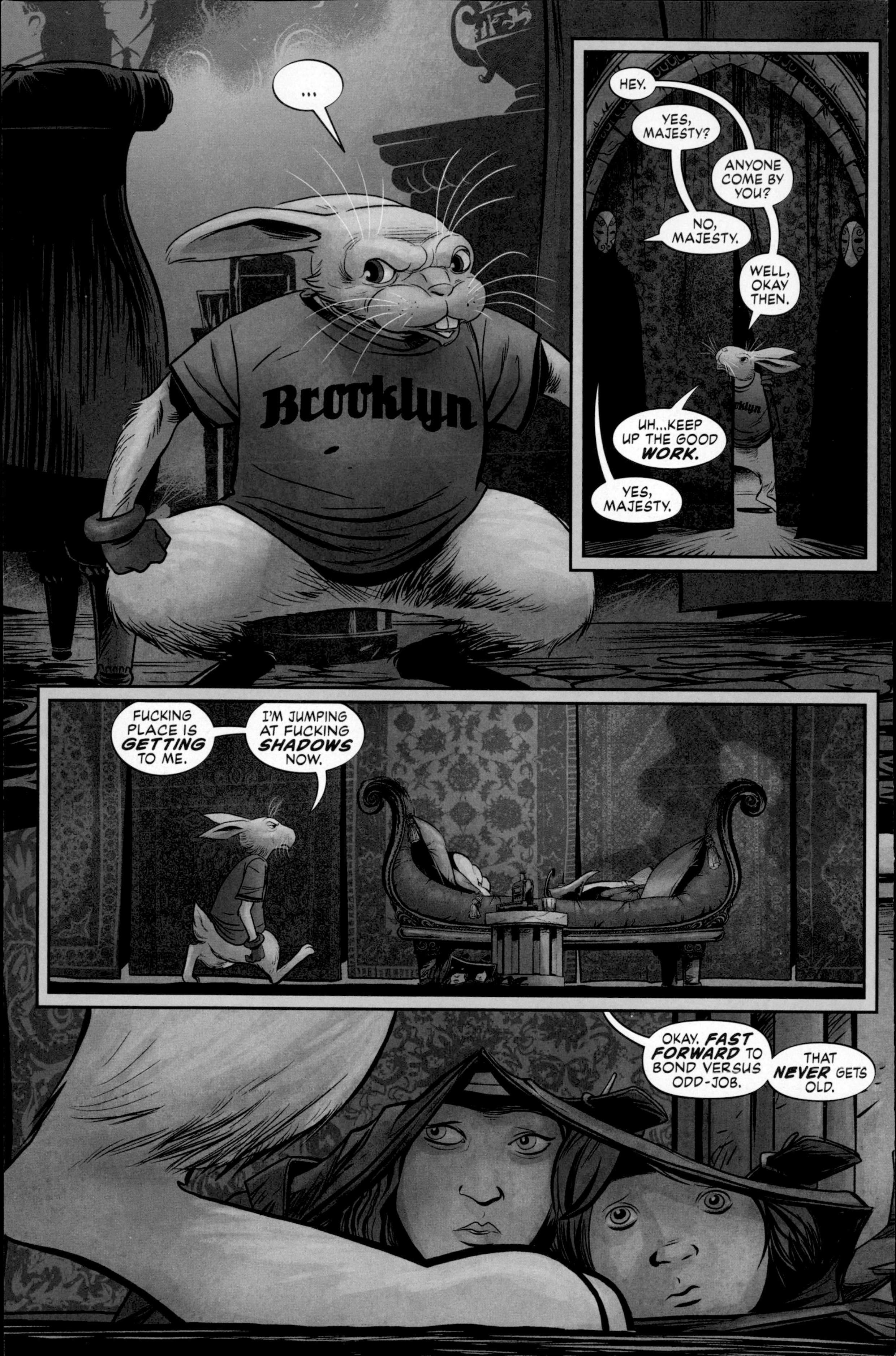
...
Brooklyn
HEY.
YES, MAJESTY?
ANYONE COME BY YOU?
NO, MAJESTY.
WELL, OKAY THEN.
UH...KEEP UP THE GOOD WORK.
YES, MAJESTY.
FUCKING PLACE IS GETTING TO ME.
I'M JUMPING AT FUCKING SHADOWS NOW.
OKAY. FAST FORWARD TO BOND VERSUS ODD-JOB.
THAT NEVER GETS OLD.

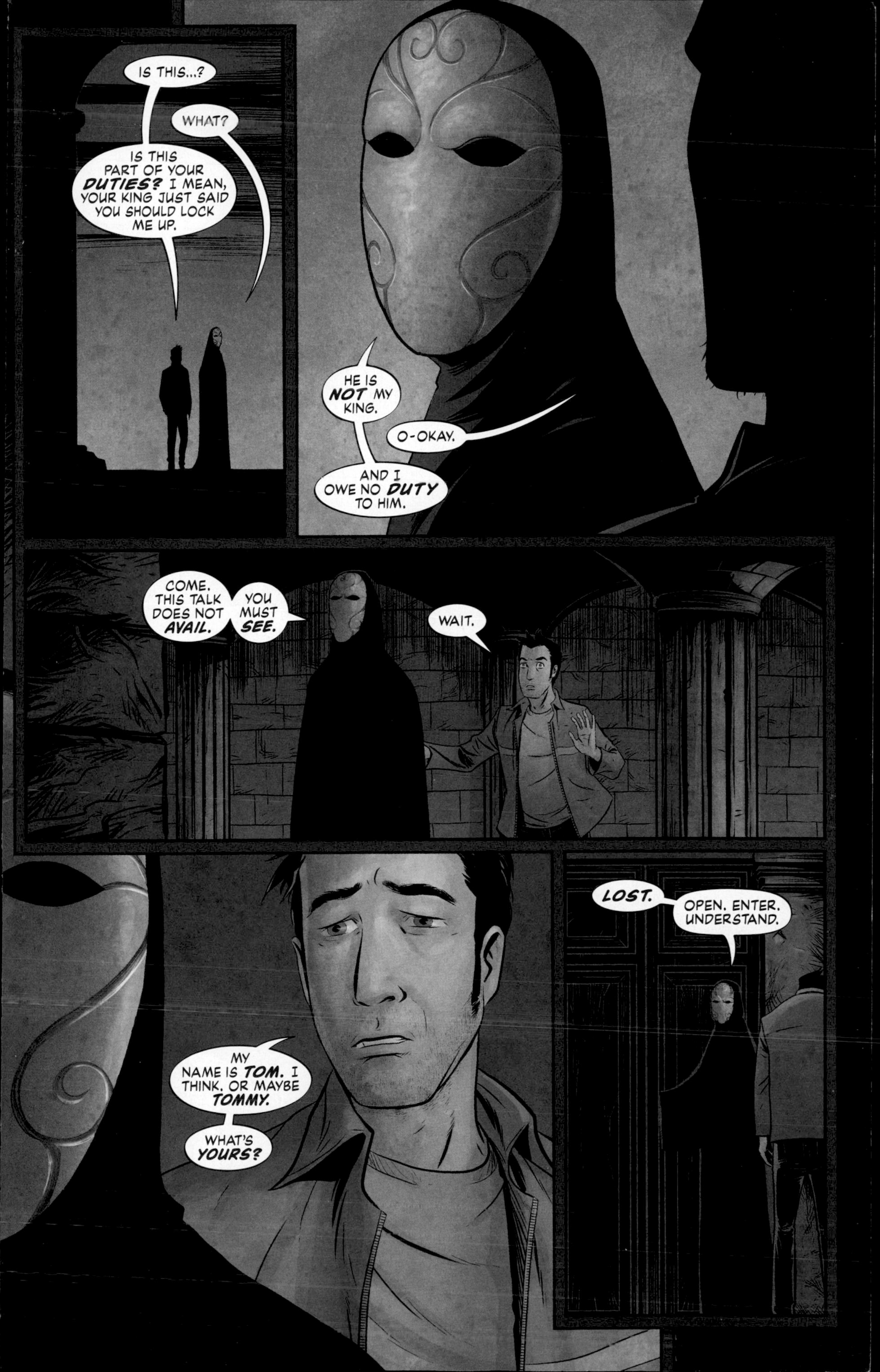
IS THIS...?
WHAT?
IS THIS PART OF YOUR DUTIES? I MEAN, YOUR KING JUST SAID YOU SHOULD LOCK ME UP.
HE IS NOT MY KING.
O-OKAY.
AND I OWE NO DUTY TO HIM.
COME. THIS TALK DOES NOT AVAIL.
YOU MUST SEE.
WAIT.
MY NAME IS TOM. I THINK. OR MAYBE TOMMY.
WHAT'S YOURS?
LOST.
OPEN. ENTER. UNDERSTAND.

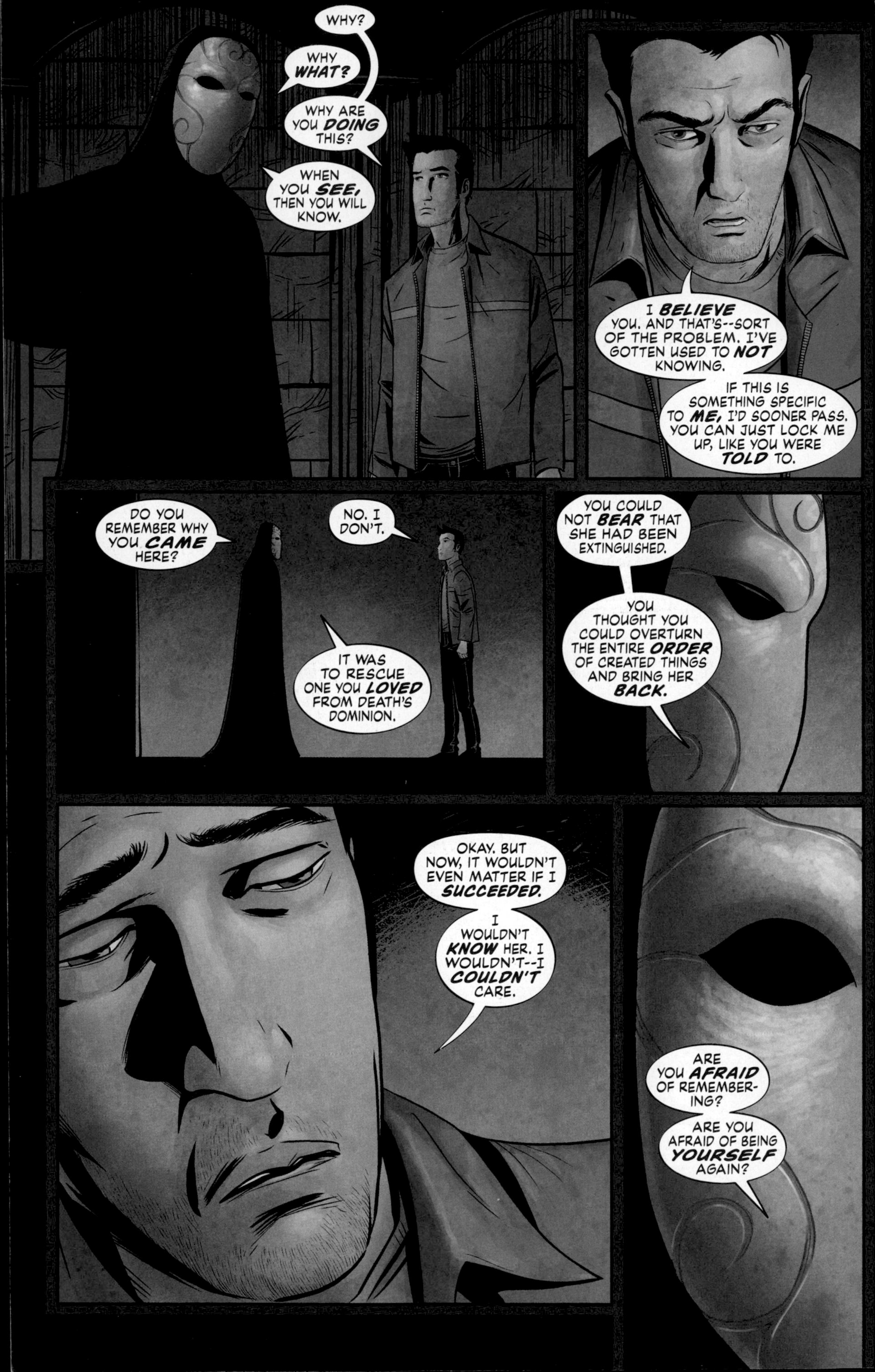
WHY?
WHY WHAT?
WHY ARE YOU DOING THIS?
WHEN YOU SEE, THEN YOU WILL KNOW.
I BELIEVE YOU. AND THAT'S--SORT OF THE PROBLEM. I'VE GOTTEN USED TO NOT KNOWING.
IF THIS IS SOMETHING SPECIFIC TO ME, I'D SOONER PASS. YOU CAN JUST LOCK ME UP, LIKE YOU WERE TOLD TO.
DO YOU REMEMBER WHY YOU CAME HERE?
NO. I DON'T.
IT WAS TO RESCUE ONE YOU LOVED FROM DEATH'S DOMINION.
YOU COULD NOT BEAR THAT SHE HAD BEEN EXTINGUISHED.
YOU THOUGHT YOU COULD OVERTURN THE ENTIRE ORDER OF CREATED THINGS AND BRING HER BACK.
OKAY. BUT NOW, IT WOULDN'T EVEN MATTER IF I SUCCEEDED.
I WOULDN'T KNOW HER. I WOULDN'T--I COULDN'T CARE.
ARE YOU AFRAID OF REMEMBERING?
ARE YOU AFRAID OF BEING YOURSELF AGAIN?

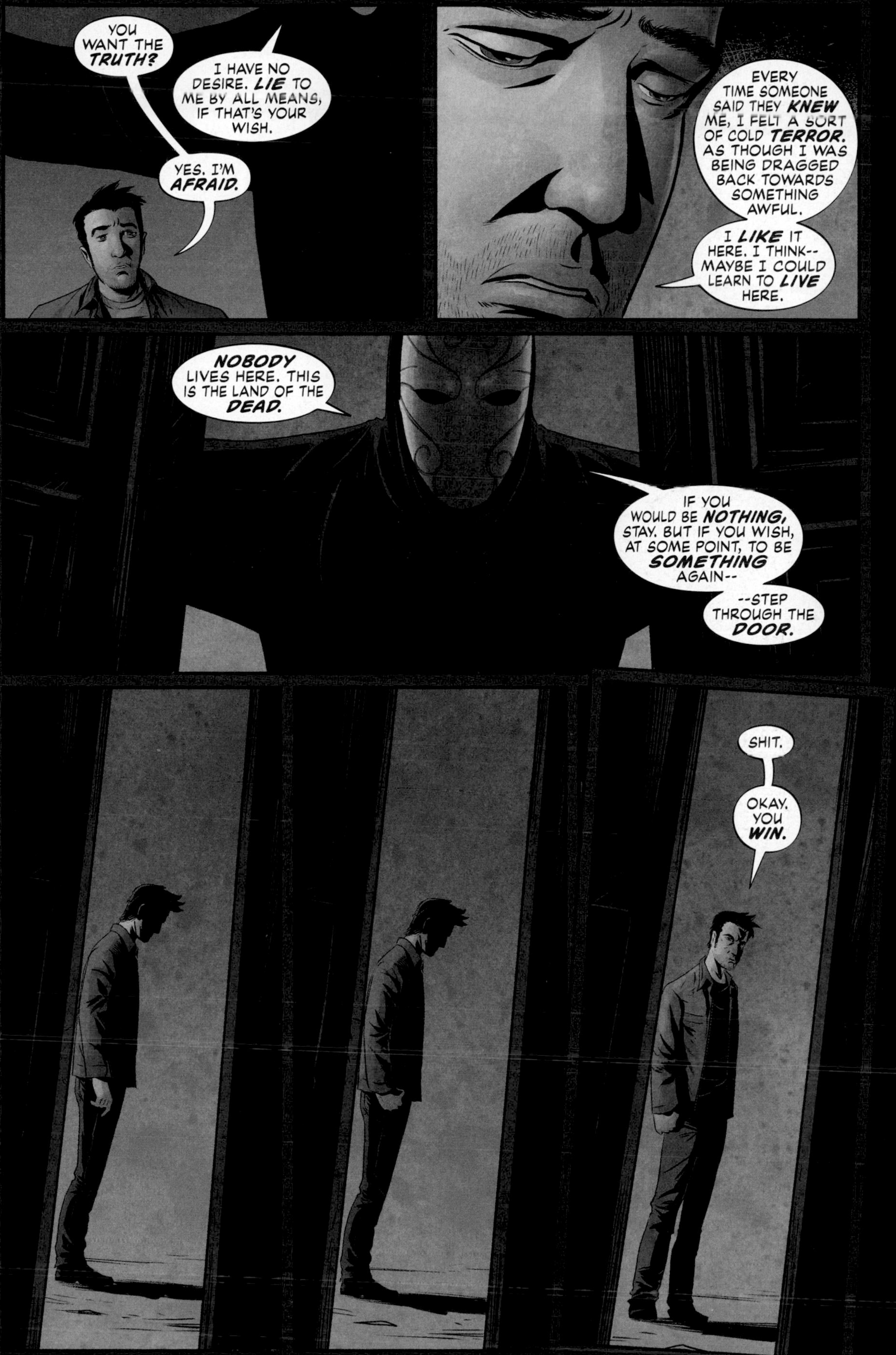
YOU WANT THE TRUTH?
I HAVE NO DESIRE. LIE TO ME BY ALL MEANS, IF THAT'S YOUR WISH.
YES. I'M AFRAID.
EVERY TIME SOMEONE SAID THEY KNEW ME, I FELT A SORT OF COLD TERROR. AS THOUGH I WAS BEING DRAGGED BACK TOWARDS SOMETHING AWFUL.
I LIKE IT HERE. I THINK-- MAYBE I COULD LEARN TO LIVE HERE.
NOBODY LIVES HERE. THIS IS THE LAND OF THE DEAD.
IF YOU WOULD BE NOTHING, STAY. BUT IF YOU WISH, AT SOME POINT, TO BE SOMETHING AGAIN--
--STEP THROUGH THE DOOR.
SHIT.
OKAY. YOU WIN.

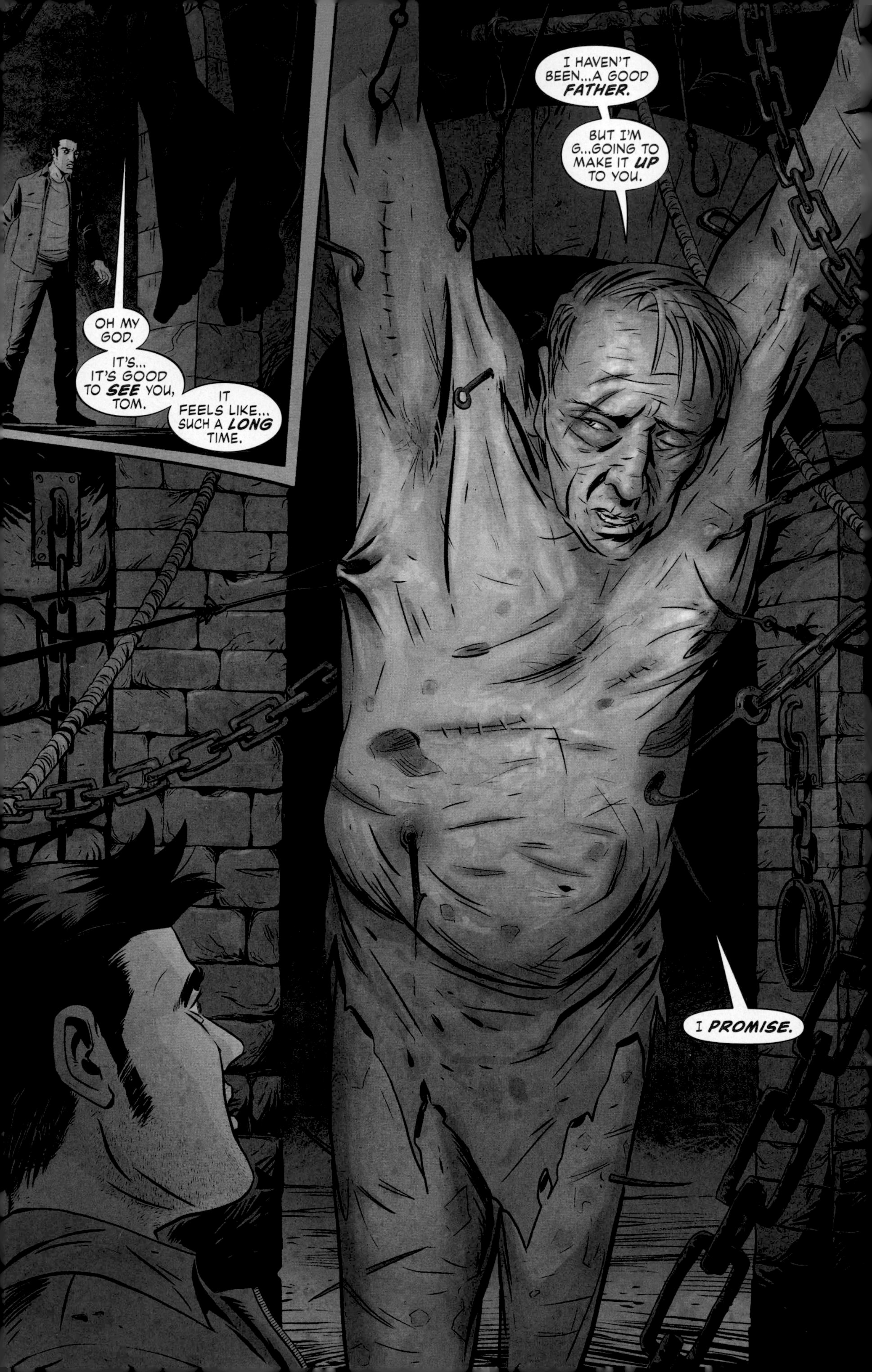
OH MY GOD.
IT'S... IT'S GOOD TO SEE YOU, TOM.
IT FEELS LIKE... SUCH A LONG TIME.
I HAVEN'T BEEN...A GOOD FATHER.
BUT I'M G...GOING TO MAKE IT UP TO YOU.
I PROMISE.

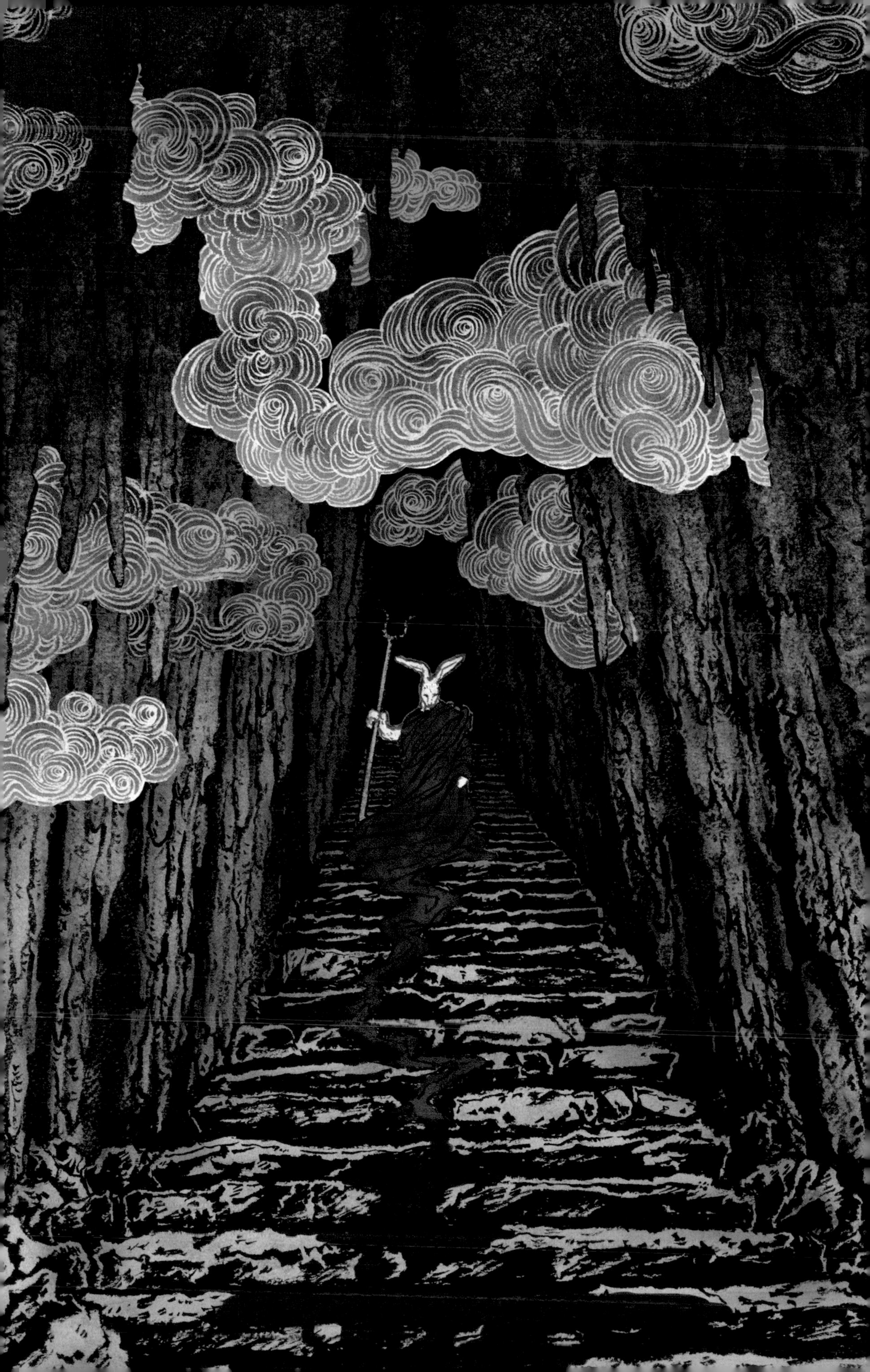

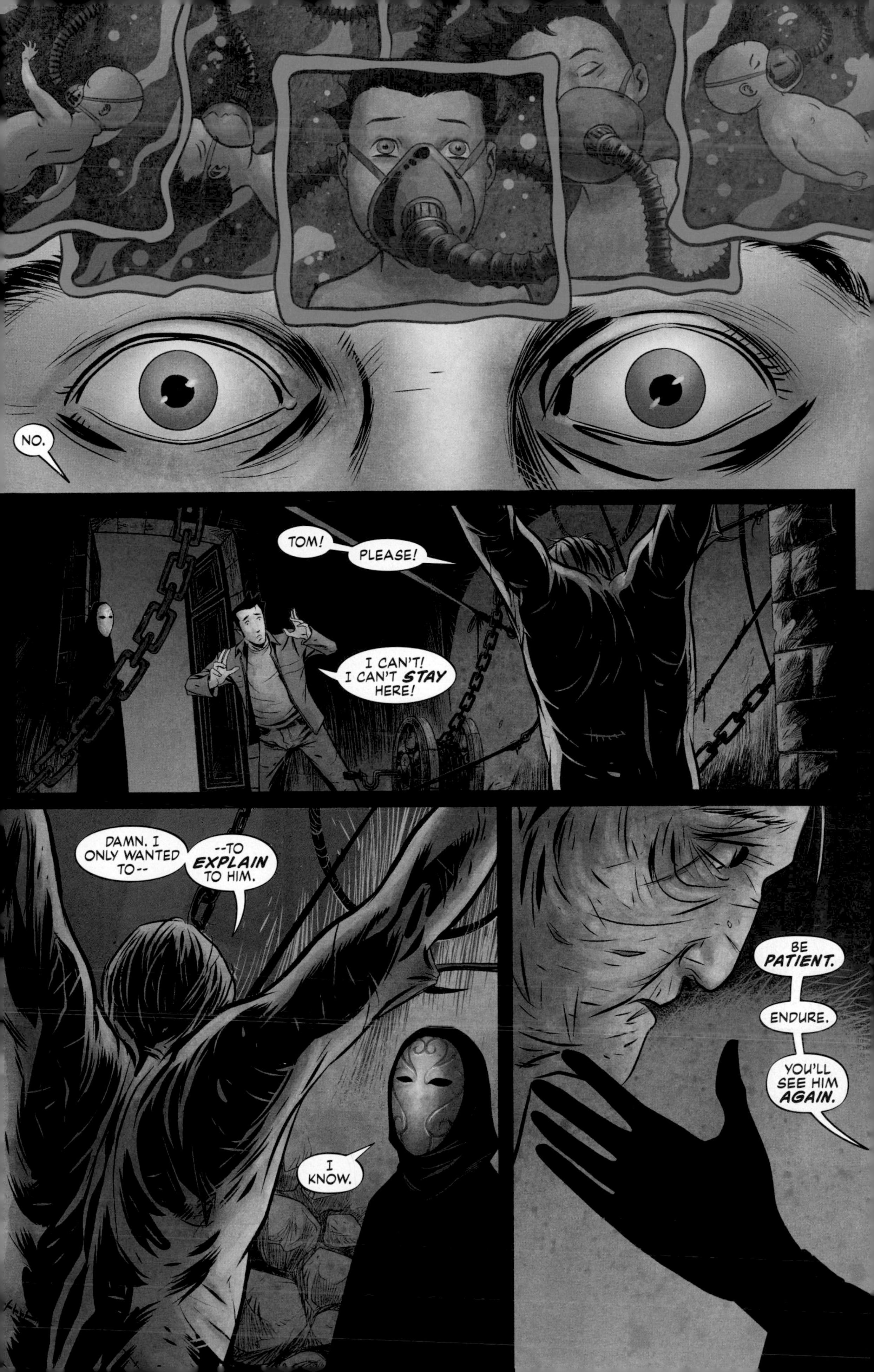
NO.
TOM!
PLEASE!
I CAN'T! I CAN'T STAY HERE!
DAMN. I ONLY WANTED TO--
--TO EXPLAIN TO HIM.
I KNOW.
BE PATIENT.
ENDURE.
YOU'LL SEE HIM AGAIN.

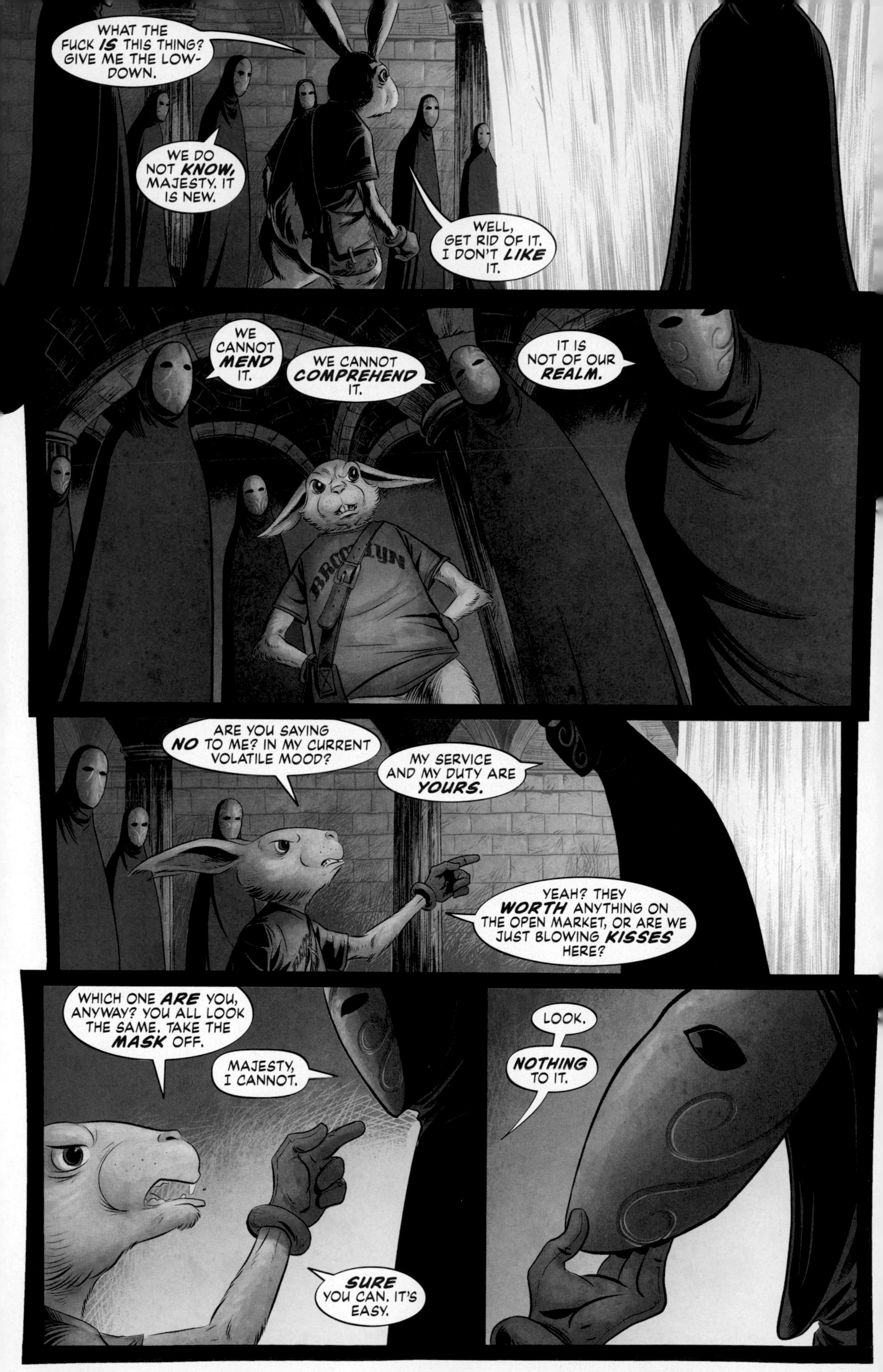
WHAT THE FUCK IS THIS THING? GIVE ME THE LOW-DOWN.
WE DO NOT KNOW, MAJESTY. IT IS NEW.
WELL, GET RID OF IT. I DON'T LIKE IT.
WE CANNOT MEND IT.
WE CANNOT COMPREHEND IT.
IT IS NOT OF OUR REALM.
ARE YOU SAYING NO TO ME? IN MY CURRENT VOLATILE MOOD?
MY SERVICE AND MY DUTY ARE YOURS.
YEAH? THEY WORTH ANYTHING ON THE OPEN MARKET, OR ARE WE JUST BLOWING KISSES HERE?
WHICH ONE ARE YOU, ANYWAY? YOU ALL LOOK THE SAME. TAKE THE MASK OFF.
MAJESTY, I CANNOT.
SURE YOU CAN. IT'S EASY.
LOOK.
NOTHING TO IT.

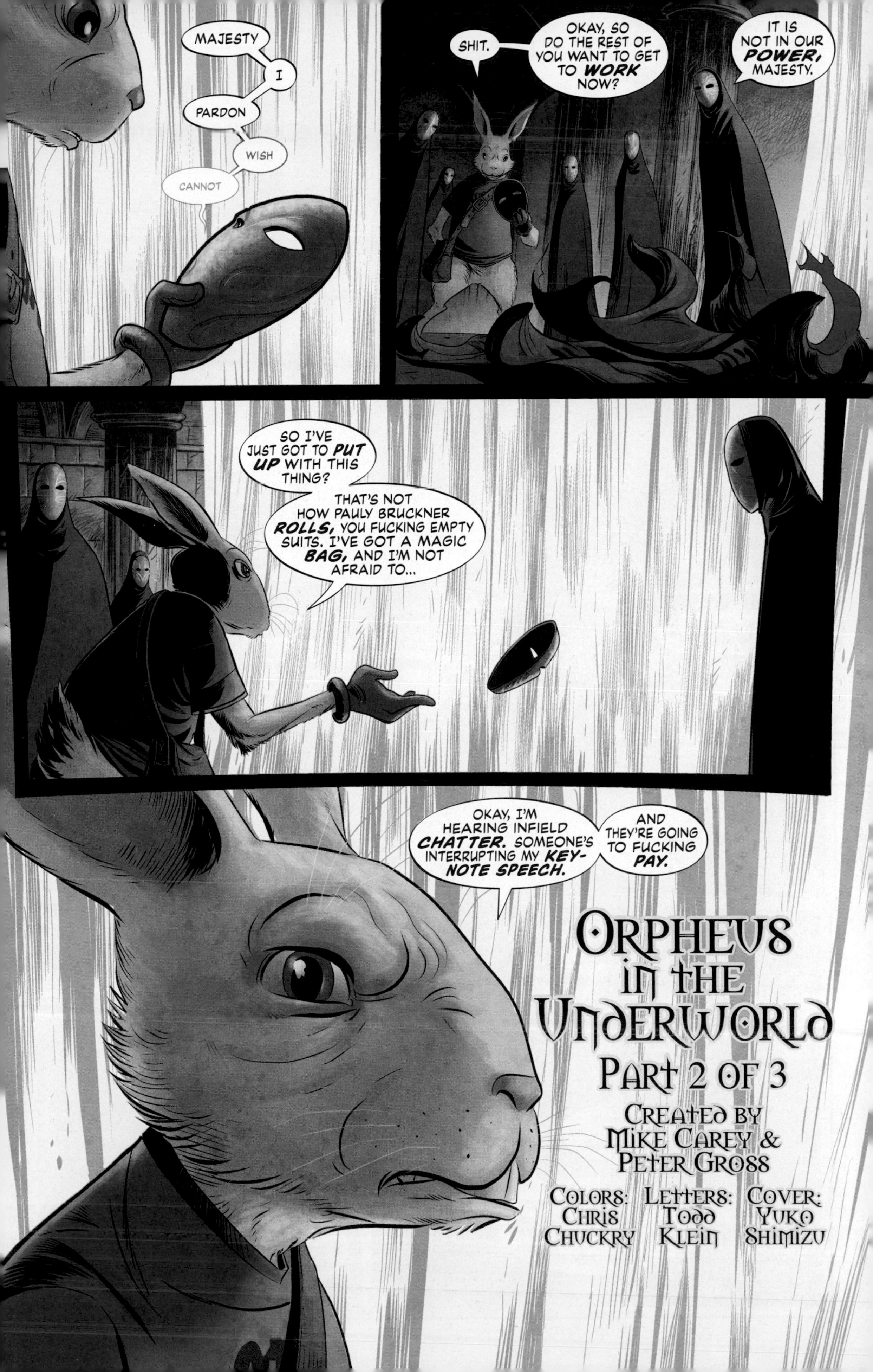
MAJESTY
I
PARDON
WISH
CANNOT
SHIT.
OKAY, SO DO THE REST OF YOU WANT TO GET TO WORK NOW?
IT IS NOT IN OUR POWER, MAJESTY.
SO I'VE JUST GOT TO PUT UP WITH THIS THING?
THAT'S NOT HOW PAULY BRUCKNER ROLLS, YOU FUCKING EMPTY SUITS. I'VE GOT A MAGIC BAG, AND I'M NOT AFRAID TO...
OKAY, I'M HEARING INFIELD CHATTER. SOMEONE'S INTERRUPTING MY KEY-NOTE SPEECH.
AND THEY'RE GOING TO FUCKING PAY.
ORPHEUS IN THE UNDERWORLD
PART 2 OF 3
CREATED BY MIKE CAREY & PETER GROSS
COLORS: CHRIS CHUCKRY
LETTERS: TODD KLEIN
COVER: YUKO SHIMIZU

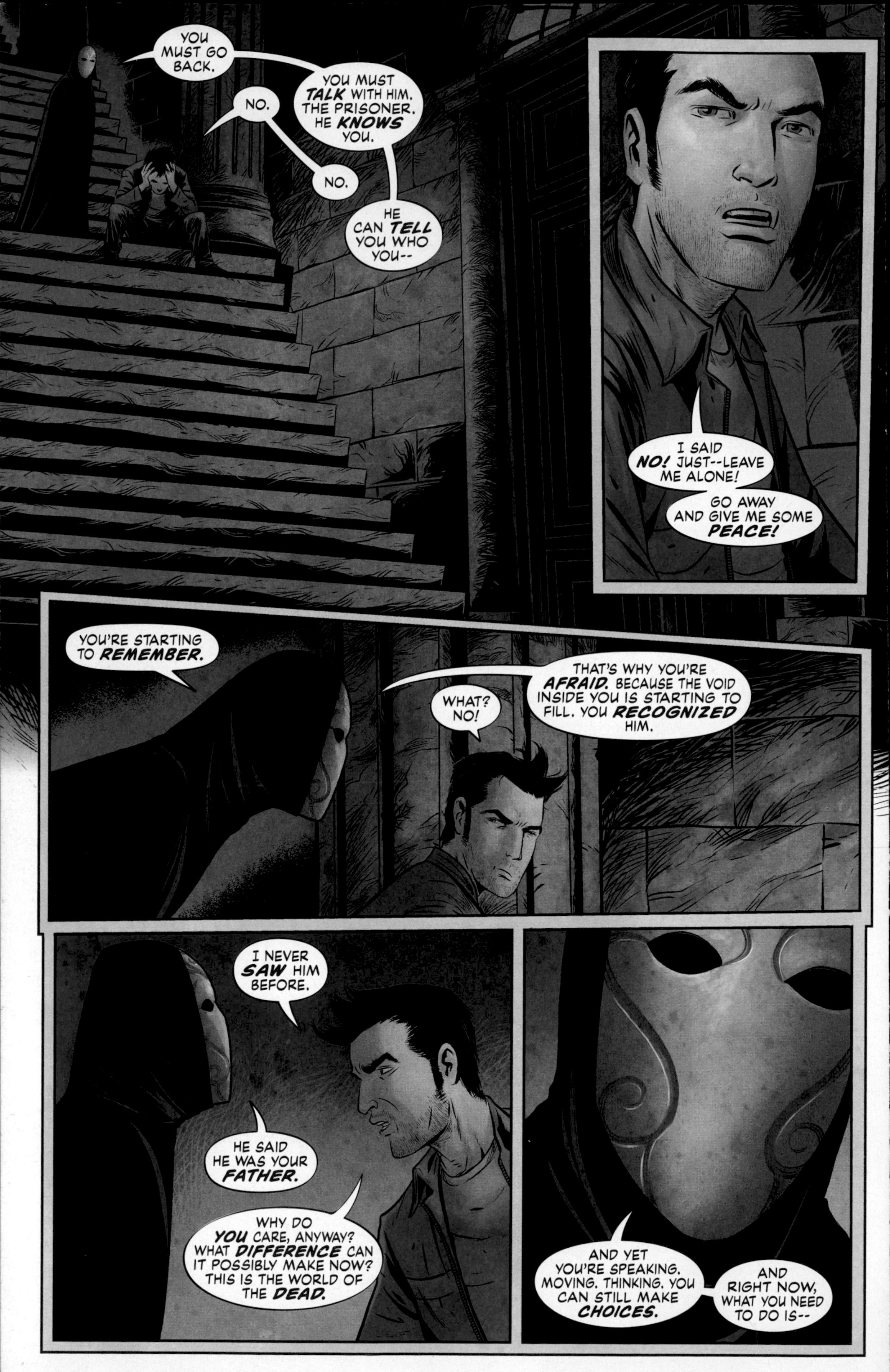
YOU MUST GO BACK.
YOU MUST TALK WITH HIM. THE PRISONER. HE KNOWS YOU.
NO.
NO.
HE CAN TELL YOU WHO YOU--
I SAID NO! JUST--LEAVE ME ALONE!
GO AWAY AND GIVE ME SOME PEACE!
YOU'RE STARTING TO REMEMBER.
WHAT? NO!
THAT'S WHY YOU'RE AFRAID. BECAUSE THE VOID INSIDE YOU IS STARTING TO FILL. YOU RECOGNIZED HIM.
I NEVER SAW HIM BEFORE.
HE SAID HE WAS YOUR FATHER.
WHY DO YOU CARE, ANYWAY? WHAT DIFFERENCE CAN IT POSSIBLY MAKE NOW? THIS IS THE WORLD OF THE DEAD.
AND YET YOU'RE SPEAKING. MOVING. THINKING. YOU CAN STILL MAKE CHOICES.
AND RIGHT NOW, WHAT YOU NEED TO DO IS--

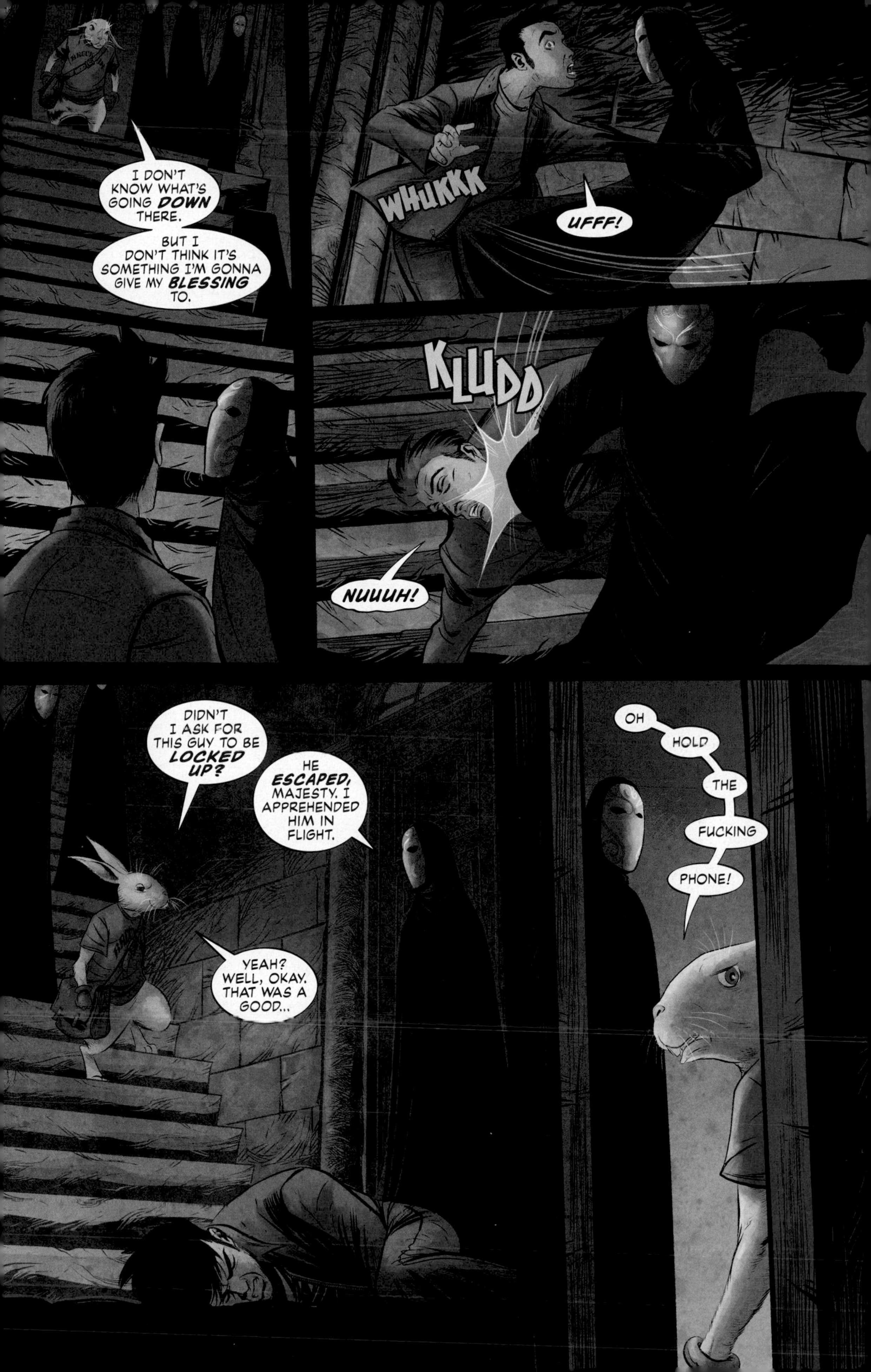
I DON'T KNOW WHAT'S GOING **DOWN** THERE.
BUT I DON'T THINK IT'S SOMETHING I'M GONNA GIVE MY **BLESSING** TO.
WHUKKK
UFFF!
KLUDD
NUUUH!
DIDN'T I ASK FOR THIS GUY TO BE **LOCKED UP?**
HE **ESCAPED,** MAJESTY. I APPREHENDED HIM IN FLIGHT.
YEAH? WELL, OKAY. THAT WAS A GOOD...
OH HOLD THE FUCKING PHONE!

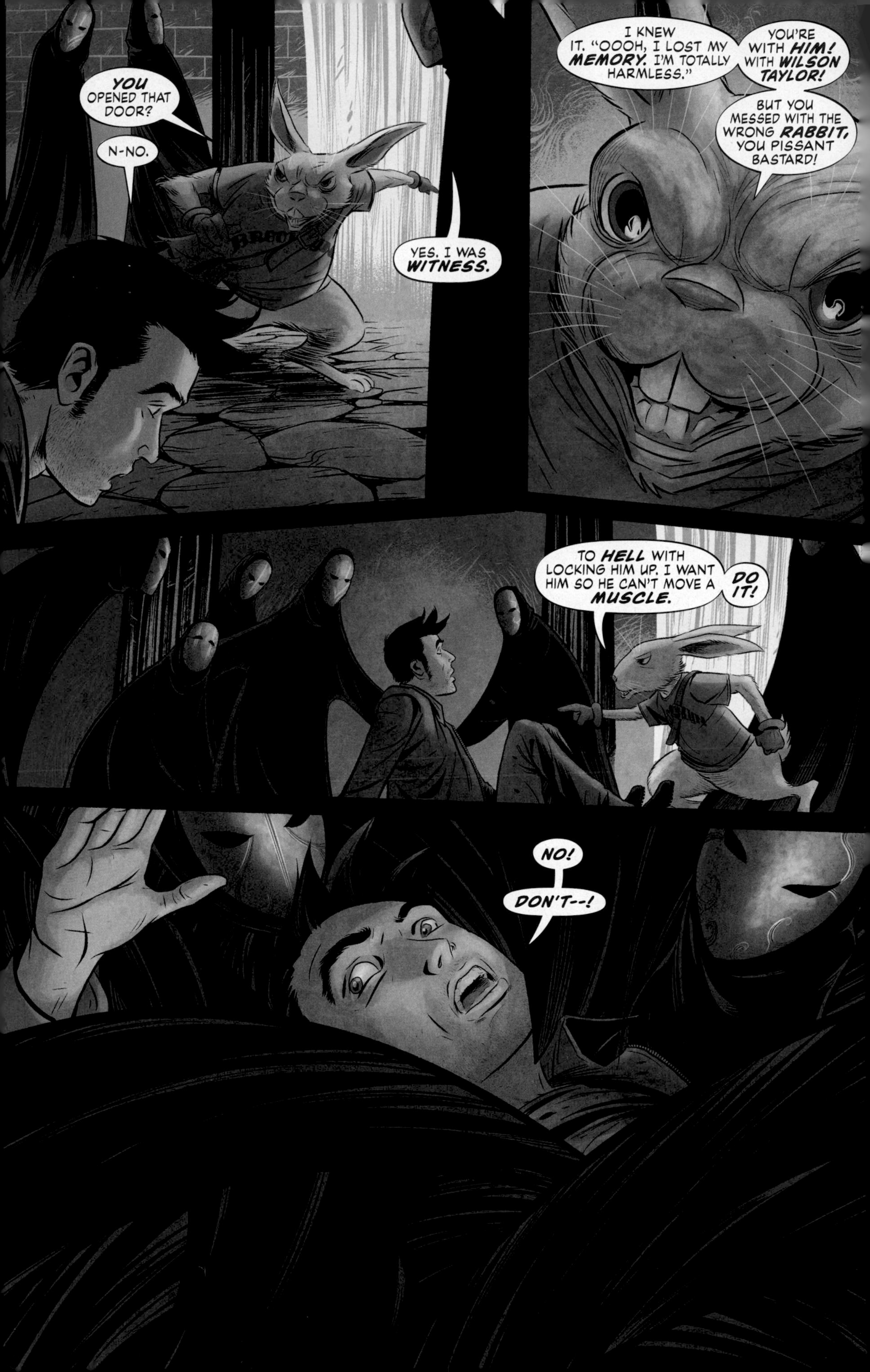
YOU OPENED THAT DOOR?
N-NO.
YES. I WAS WITNESS.
I KNEW IT. "OOOH, I LOST MY MEMORY. I'M TOTALLY HARMLESS."
YOU'RE WITH HIM! WITH WILSON TAYLOR!
BUT YOU MESSED WITH THE WRONG RABBIT, YOU PISSANT BASTARD!
TO HELL WITH LOCKING HIM UP. I WANT HIM SO HE CAN'T MOVE A MUSCLE.
DO IT!
NO!
DON'T--!

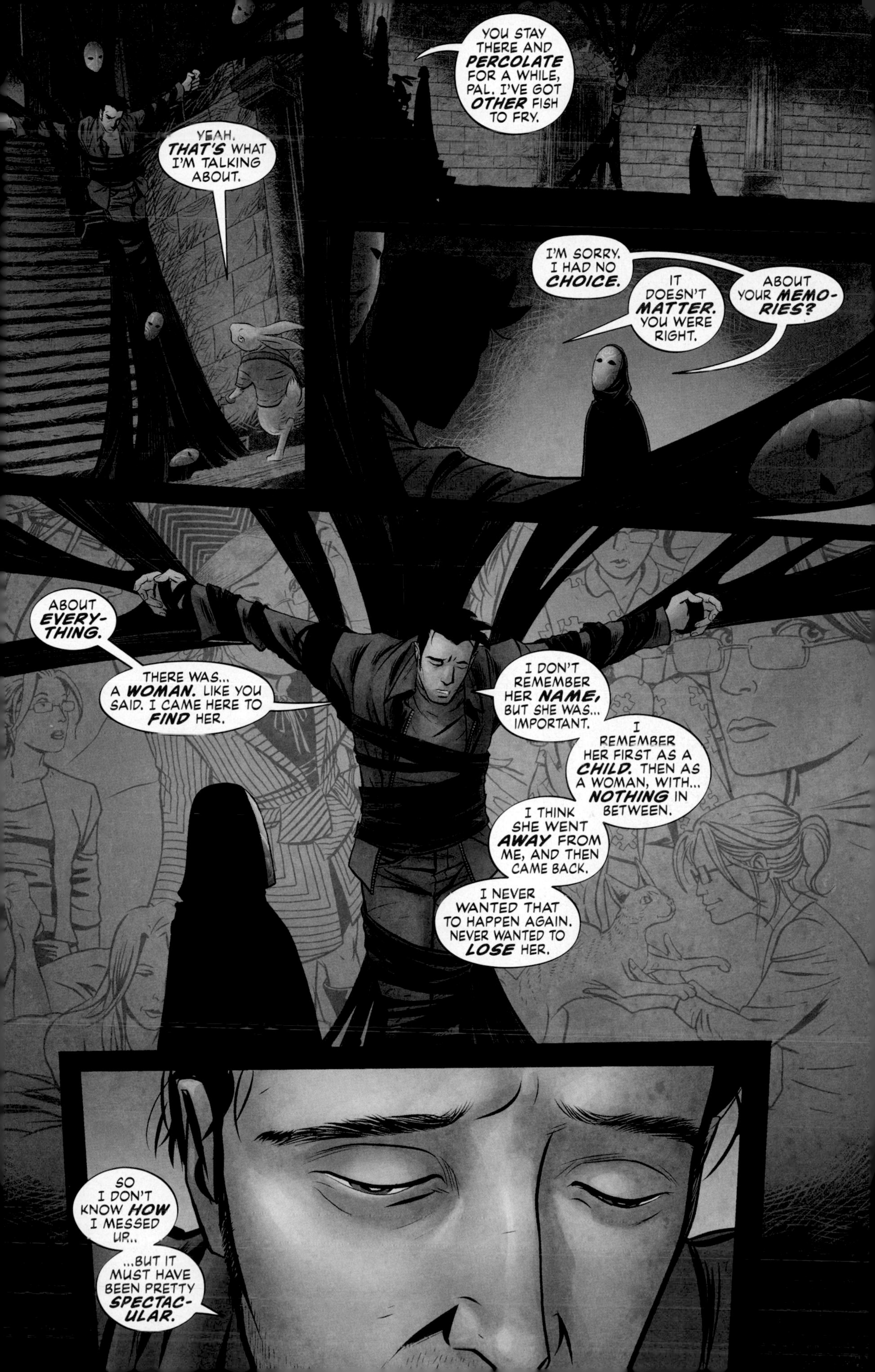
YEAH. THAT'S WHAT I'M TALKING ABOUT.
YOU STAY THERE AND PERCOLATE FOR A WHILE, PAL. I'VE GOT OTHER FISH TO FRY.
I'M SORRY. I HAD NO CHOICE.
IT DOESN'T MATTER. YOU WERE RIGHT.
ABOUT YOUR MEMORIES?
ABOUT EVERYTHING.
THERE WAS... A WOMAN. LIKE YOU SAID. I CAME HERE TO FIND HER.
I DON'T REMEMBER HER NAME, BUT SHE WAS... IMPORTANT.
I REMEMBER HER FIRST AS A CHILD. THEN AS A WOMAN, WITH... NOTHING IN BETWEEN.
I THINK SHE WENT AWAY FROM ME, AND THEN CAME BACK.
I NEVER WANTED THAT TO HAPPEN AGAIN. NEVER WANTED TO LOSE HER.
SO I DON'T KNOW HOW I MESSED UP..
...BUT IT MUST HAVE BEEN PRETTY SPECTACULAR.

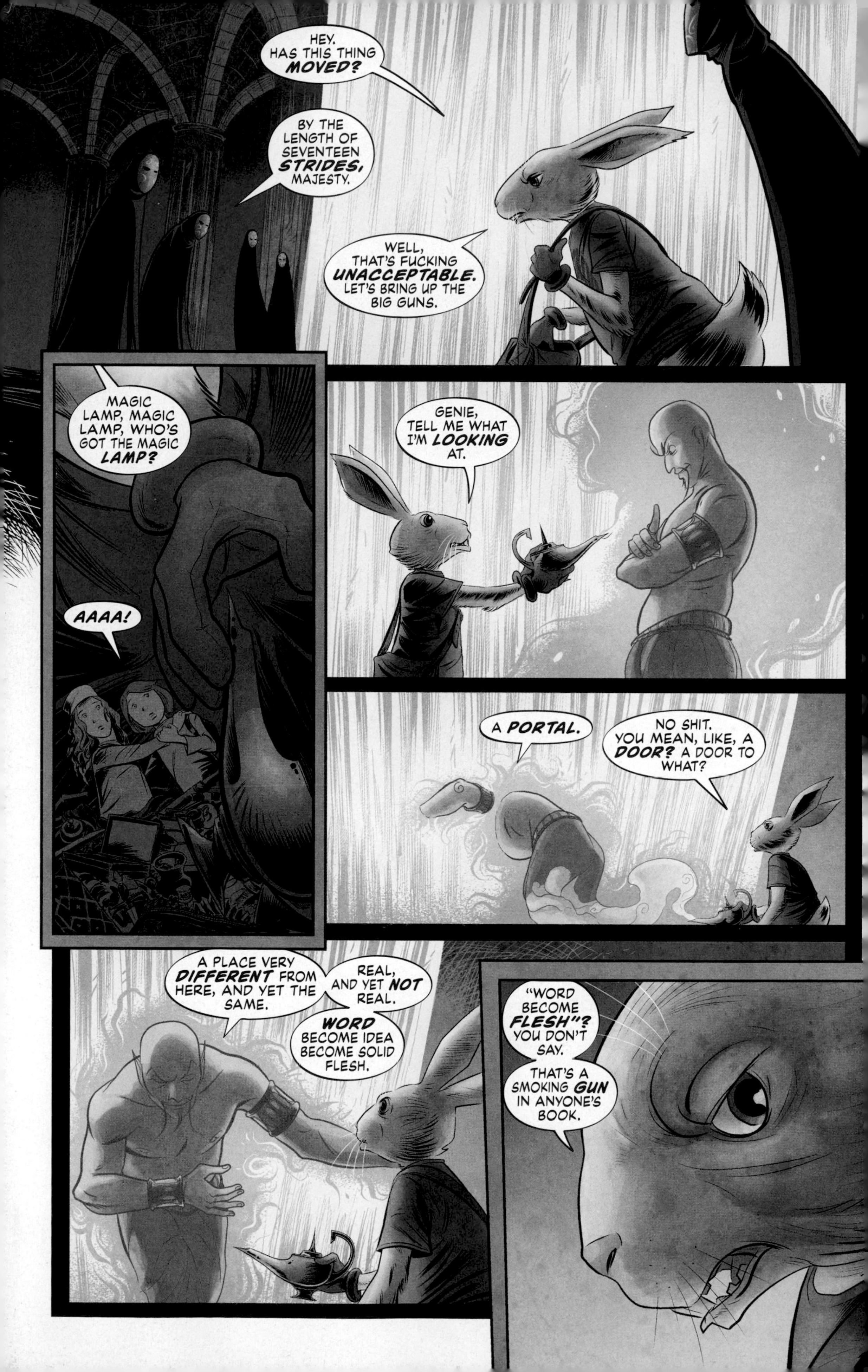
HEY. HAS THIS THING MOVED?
BY THE LENGTH OF SEVENTEEN STRIDES, MAJESTY.
WELL, THAT'S FUCKING UNACCEPTABLE. LET'S BRING UP THE BIG GUNS.
MAGIC LAMP, MAGIC LAMP, WHO'S GOT THE MAGIC LAMP?
AAAA!
GENIE, TELL ME WHAT I'M LOOKING AT.
A PORTAL.
NO SHIT. YOU MEAN, LIKE, A DOOR? A DOOR TO WHAT?
A PLACE VERY DIFFERENT FROM HERE, AND YET THE SAME.
REAL, AND YET NOT REAL.
WORD BECOME IDEA BECOME SOLID FLESH.
"WORD BECOME FLESH"? YOU DON'T SAY.
THAT'S A SMOKING GUN IN ANYONE'S BOOK.

YOU WANT TO TELL ME WHAT YOU'RE *UP* TO, YOU SACK OF SHIT?

OR DO I HAVE TO *PULL* IT OUT OF YOU WITH PLIERS?

I'M HANGING IN *CHAINS*, PAULY. WAITING FOR YOU TO RESUME *TORTURING* ME FOR IMAGINED CRIMES.

SCREW THAT! YOU SEE WHAT I'M HOLDING? THIS IS THE HAND OF FUCKING *GLORY*.

I *COMMAND* YOU TO GIVE ME A STRAIGHT ANSWER!

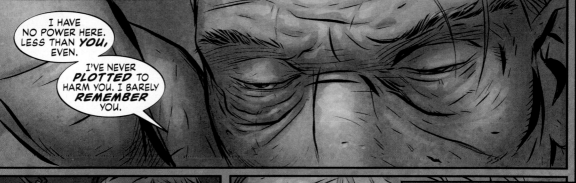

I HAVE NO POWER HERE. LESS THAN *YOU*, EVEN.

I'VE NEVER *PLOTTED* TO HARM YOU. I BARELY *REMEMBER* YOU.

SURE. YOU'RE MISTER FUCKING *INNO-CENT*.

I'M ONLY INNOCENT OF WHAT YOU'RE *ACCUSING* ME OF.

BULLSHIT. THIS ISN'T JUST HAPPENING. SOMEBODY'S *MAKING* IT HAPPEN.

OH YES.

SOME-BODY *IS*.

...

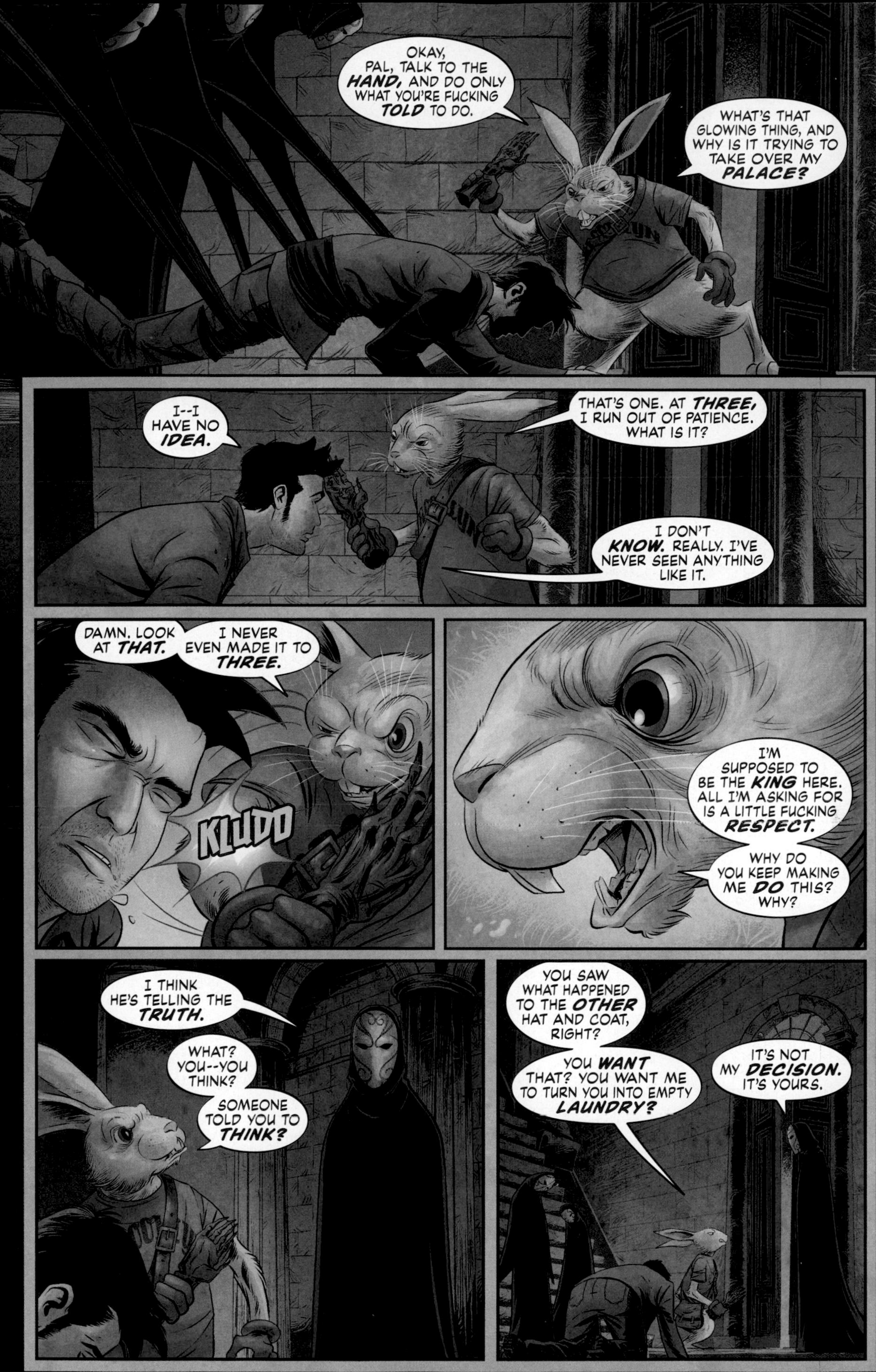
OKAY, PAL, TALK TO THE HAND, AND DO ONLY WHAT YOU'RE FUCKING TOLD TO DO.
WHAT'S THAT GLOWING THING, AND WHY IS IT TRYING TO TAKE OVER MY PALACE?
I--I HAVE NO IDEA.
THAT'S ONE. AT THREE, I RUN OUT OF PATIENCE. WHAT IS IT?
I DON'T KNOW. REALLY. I'VE NEVER SEEN ANYTHING LIKE IT.
DAMN. LOOK AT THAT.
I NEVER EVEN MADE IT TO THREE.
KLUDD
I'M SUPPOSED TO BE THE KING HERE. ALL I'M ASKING FOR IS A LITTLE FUCKING RESPECT.
WHY DO YOU KEEP MAKING ME DO THIS? WHY?
I THINK HE'S TELLING THE TRUTH.
WHAT? YOU--YOU THINK?
SOMEONE TOLD YOU TO THINK?
YOU SAW WHAT HAPPENED TO THE OTHER HAT AND COAT, RIGHT?
YOU WANT THAT? YOU WANT ME TO TURN YOU INTO EMPTY LAUNDRY?
IT'S NOT MY DECISION. IT'S YOURS.

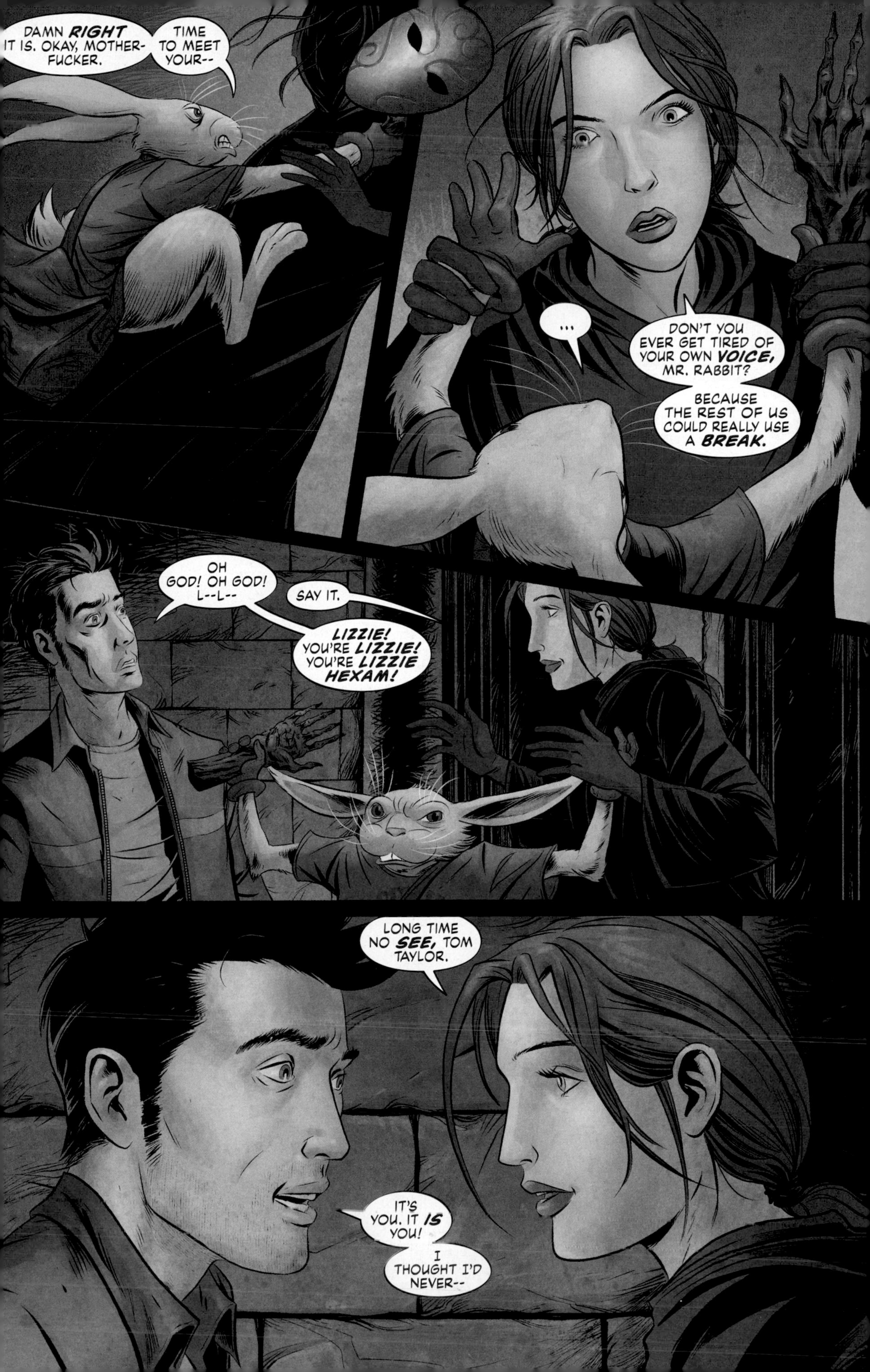
DAMN *RIGHT* IT IS. OKAY, MOTHER-FUCKER.
TIME TO MEET YOUR--
...
DON'T YOU EVER GET TIRED OF YOUR OWN *VOICE,* MR. RABBIT?
BECAUSE THE REST OF US COULD REALLY USE A *BREAK.*
OH GOD! OH GOD! L--L--
SAY IT.
*LIZZIE!* YOU'RE *LIZZIE!* YOU'RE *LIZZIE HEXAM!*
LONG TIME NO *SEE,* TOM TAYLOR.
IT'S YOU. IT *IS* YOU!
I THOUGHT I'D NEVER--

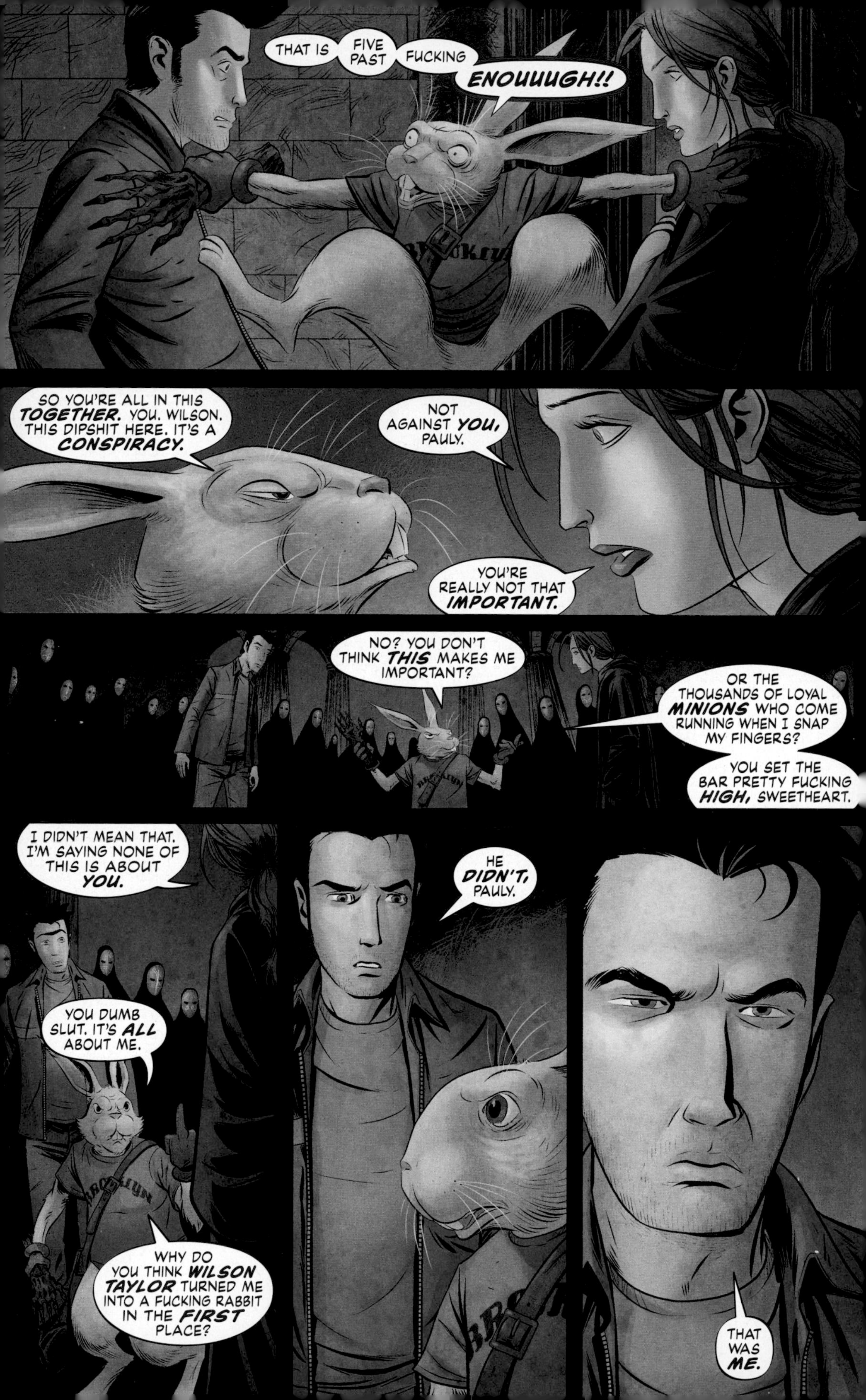
THAT IS
FIVE PAST
FUCKING
ENOUUUUGH!!
SO YOU'RE ALL IN THIS TOGETHER. YOU. WILSON. THIS DIPSHIT HERE. IT'S A CONSPIRACY.
NOT AGAINST YOU, PAULY.
YOU'RE REALLY NOT THAT IMPORTANT.
NO? YOU DON'T THINK THIS MAKES ME IMPORTANT?
OR THE THOUSANDS OF LOYAL MINIONS WHO COME RUNNING WHEN I SNAP MY FINGERS?
YOU SET THE BAR PRETTY FUCKING HIGH, SWEETHEART.
I DIDN'T MEAN THAT. I'M SAYING NONE OF THIS IS ABOUT YOU.
YOU DUMB SLUT. IT'S ALL ABOUT ME.
WHY DO YOU THINK WILSON TAYLOR TURNED ME INTO A FUCKING RABBIT IN THE FIRST PLACE?
HE DIDN'T, PAULY.
THAT WAS ME.

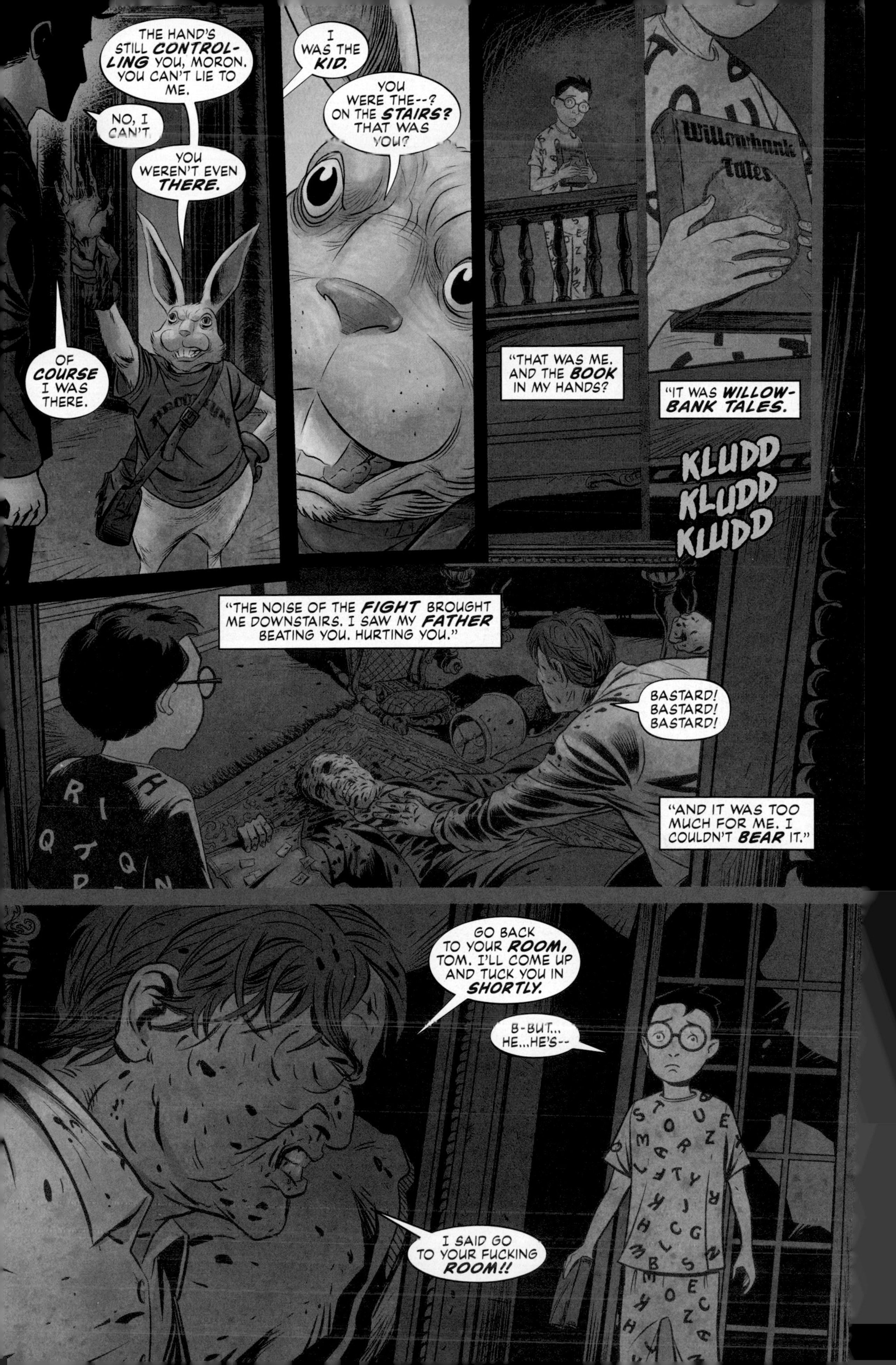
THE HAND'S STILL CONTROLLING YOU, MORON. YOU CAN'T LIE TO ME.
NO, I CAN'T.
YOU WEREN'T EVEN THERE.
OF COURSE I WAS THERE.
I WAS THE KID.
YOU WERE THE--? ON THE STAIRS? THAT WAS YOU?
"THAT WAS ME. AND THE BOOK IN MY HANDS?
Willowbank Tales
"IT WAS WILLOWBANK TALES.
KLUDD KLUDD KLUDD
"THE NOISE OF THE FIGHT BROUGHT ME DOWNSTAIRS. I SAW MY FATHER BEATING YOU. HURTING YOU."
BASTARD! BASTARD! BASTARD!
"AND IT WAS TOO MUCH FOR ME. I COULDN'T BEAR IT."
GO BACK TO YOUR ROOM, TOM. I'LL COME UP AND TUCK YOU IN SHORTLY.
B-BUT... HE...HE'S--
I SAID GO TO YOUR FUCKING ROOM!!

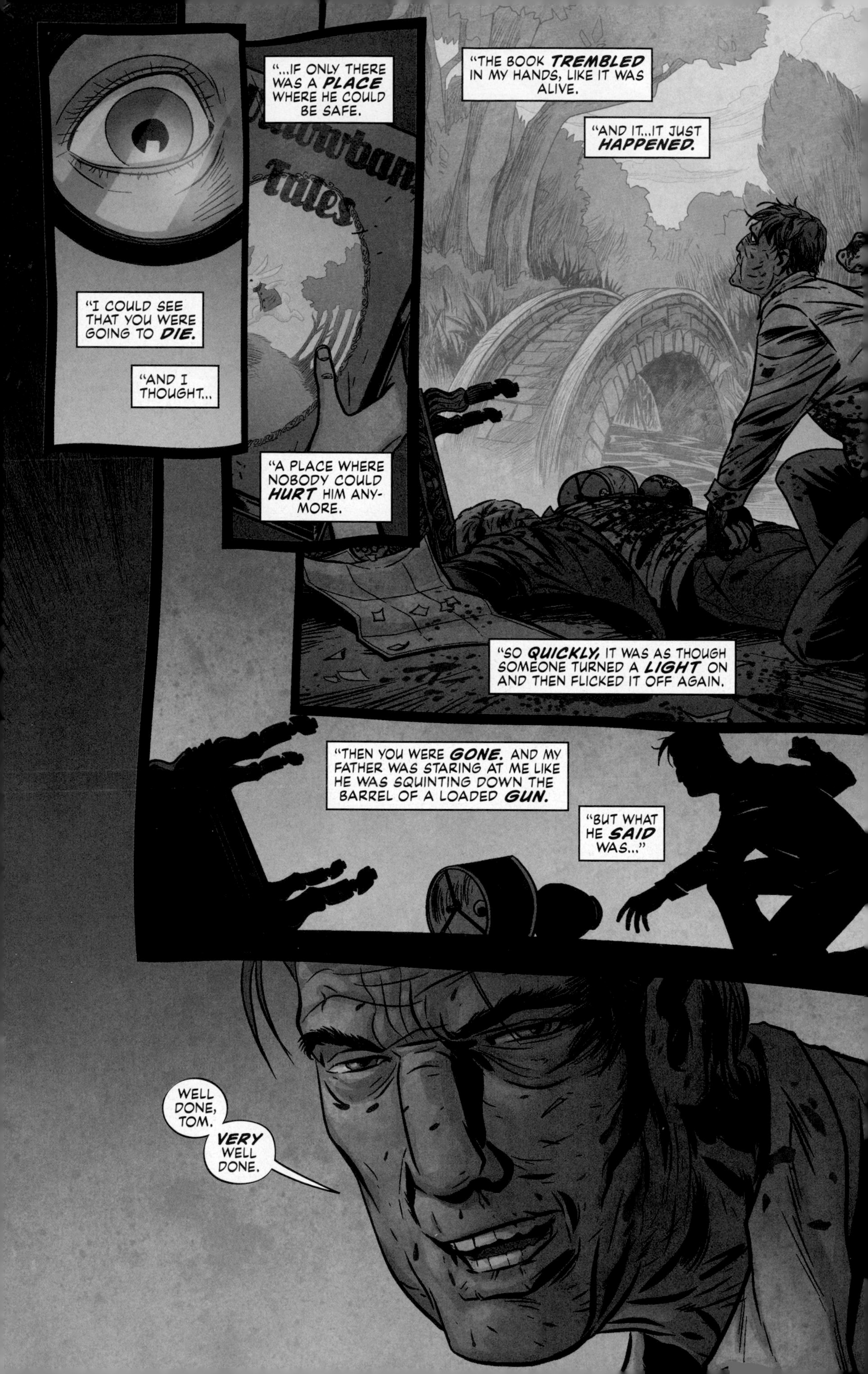

"...IF ONLY THERE WAS A PLACE WHERE HE COULD BE SAFE.
"THE BOOK TREMBLED IN MY HANDS, LIKE IT WAS ALIVE.
"AND IT...IT JUST HAPPENED.
"I COULD SEE THAT YOU WERE GOING TO DIE.
"AND I THOUGHT...
"A PLACE WHERE NOBODY COULD HURT HIM ANYMORE.
"SO QUICKLY, IT WAS AS THOUGH SOMEONE TURNED A LIGHT ON AND THEN FLICKED IT OFF AGAIN.
"THEN YOU WERE GONE. AND MY FATHER WAS STARING AT ME LIKE HE WAS SQUINTING DOWN THE BARREL OF A LOADED GUN.
"BUT WHAT HE SAID WAS..."
WELL DONE, TOM. VERY WELL DONE.

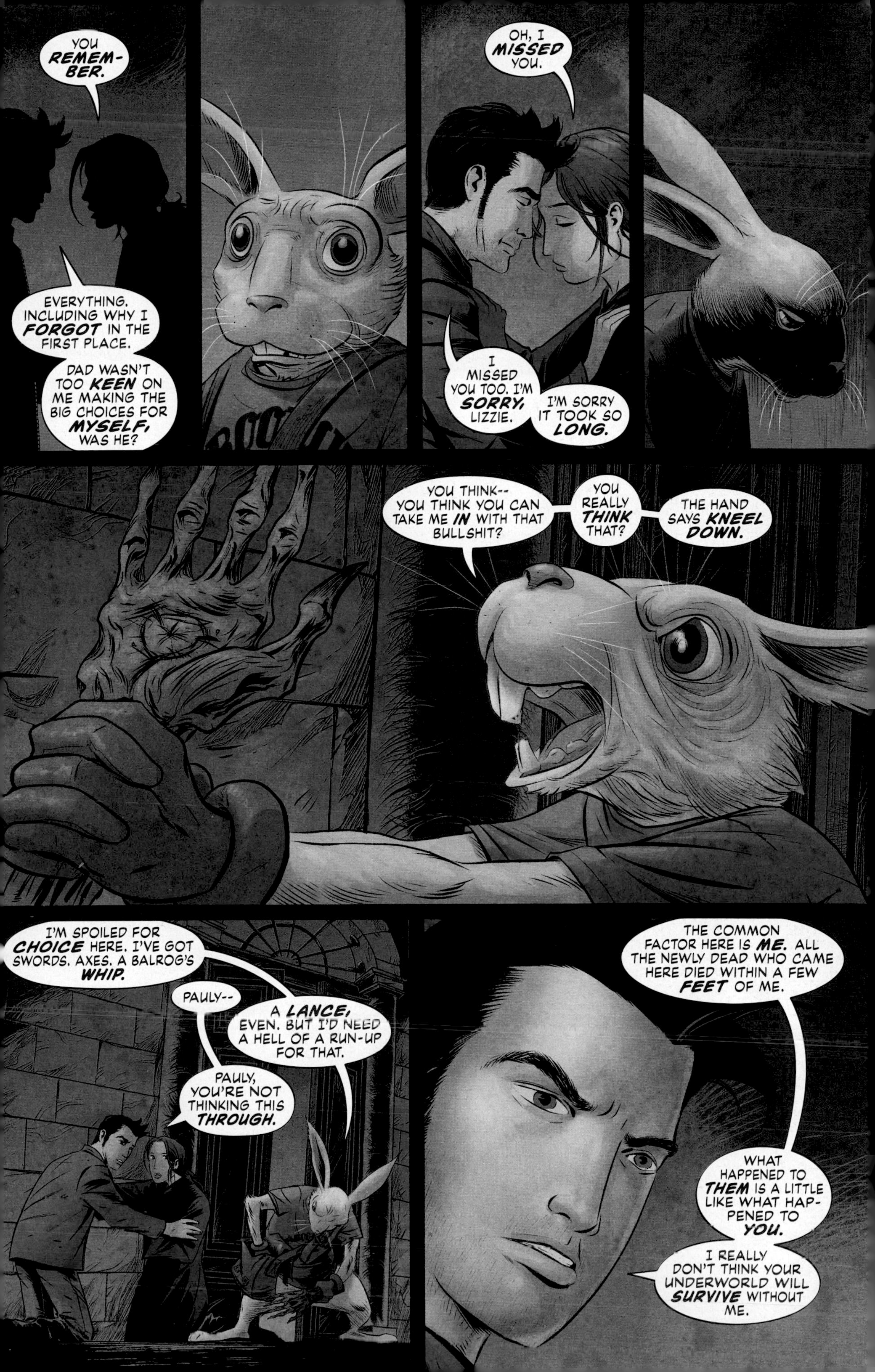
YOU REMEMBER.
EVERYTHING. INCLUDING WHY I FORGOT IN THE FIRST PLACE.
DAD WASN'T TOO KEEN ON ME MAKING THE BIG CHOICES FOR MYSELF, WAS HE?
OH, I MISSED YOU.
I MISSED YOU TOO. I'M SORRY, LIZZIE.
I'M SORRY IT TOOK SO LONG.
YOU THINK-- YOU THINK YOU CAN TAKE ME IN WITH THAT BULLSHIT?
YOU REALLY THINK THAT?
THE HAND SAYS KNEEL DOWN.
I'M SPOILED FOR CHOICE HERE. I'VE GOT SWORDS. AXES. A BALROG'S WHIP.
PAULY--
A LANCE, EVEN. BUT I'D NEED A HELL OF A RUN-UP FOR THAT.
PAULY, YOU'RE NOT THINKING THIS THROUGH.
THE COMMON FACTOR HERE IS ME. ALL THE NEWLY DEAD WHO CAME HERE DIED WITHIN A FEW FEET OF ME.
WHAT HAPPENED TO THEM IS A LITTLE LIKE WHAT HAPPENED TO YOU.
I REALLY DON'T THINK YOUR UNDERWORLD WILL SURVIVE WITHOUT ME.

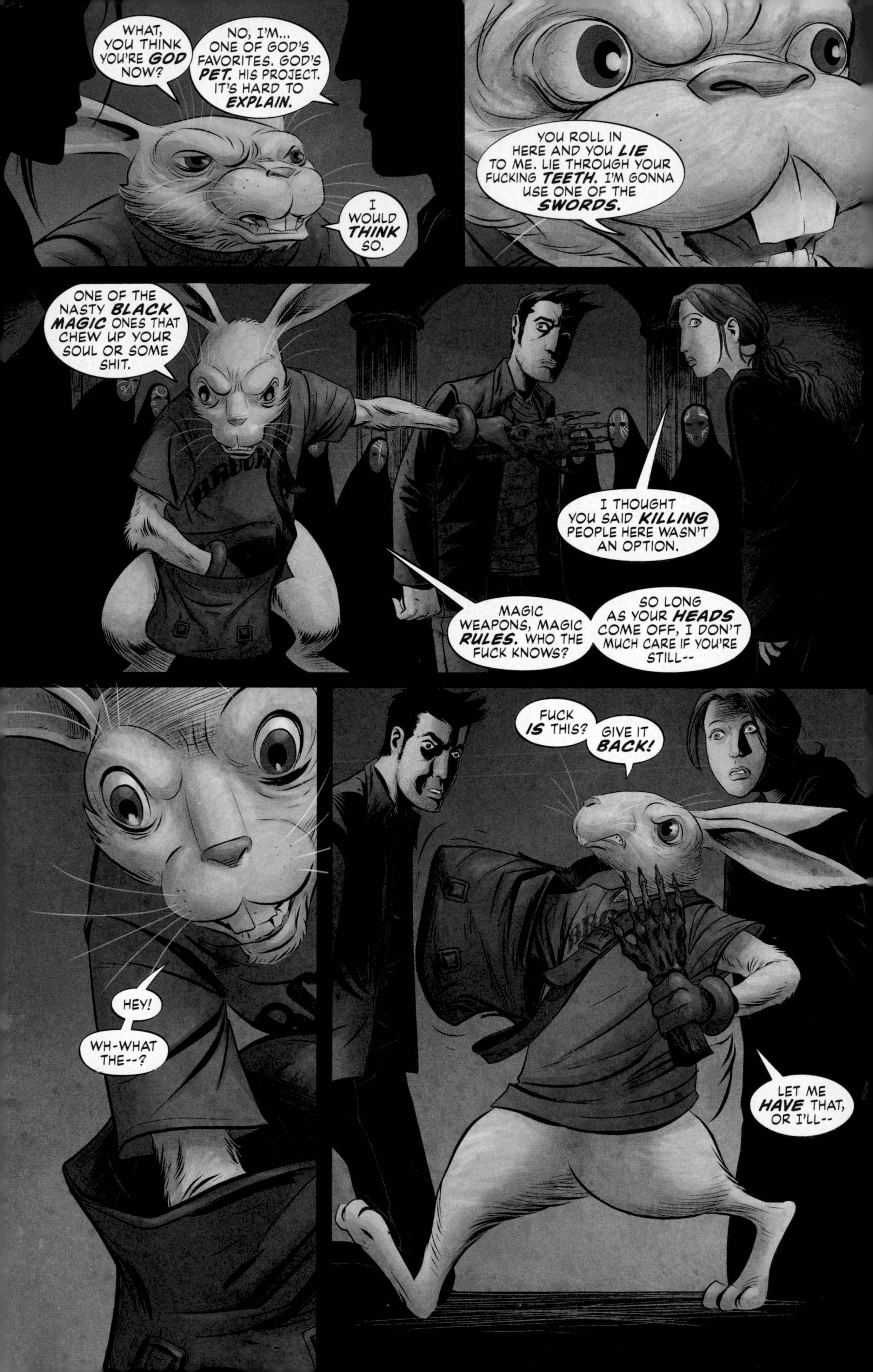
WHAT, YOU THINK YOU'RE GOD NOW?
NO, I'M... ONE OF GOD'S FAVORITES. GOD'S PET. HIS PROJECT. IT'S HARD TO EXPLAIN.
I WOULD THINK SO.
YOU ROLL IN HERE AND YOU LIE TO ME. LIE THROUGH YOUR FUCKING TEETH. I'M GONNA USE ONE OF THE SWORDS.
ONE OF THE NASTY BLACK MAGIC ONES THAT CHEW UP YOUR SOUL OR SOME SHIT.
I THOUGHT YOU SAID KILLING PEOPLE HERE WASN'T AN OPTION.
MAGIC WEAPONS, MAGIC RULES. WHO THE FUCK KNOWS?
SO LONG AS YOUR HEADS COME OFF, I DON'T MUCH CARE IF YOU'RE STILL--
HEY!
WH-WHAT THE--?
FUCK IS THIS?
GIVE IT BACK!
LET ME HAVE THAT, OR I'LL--

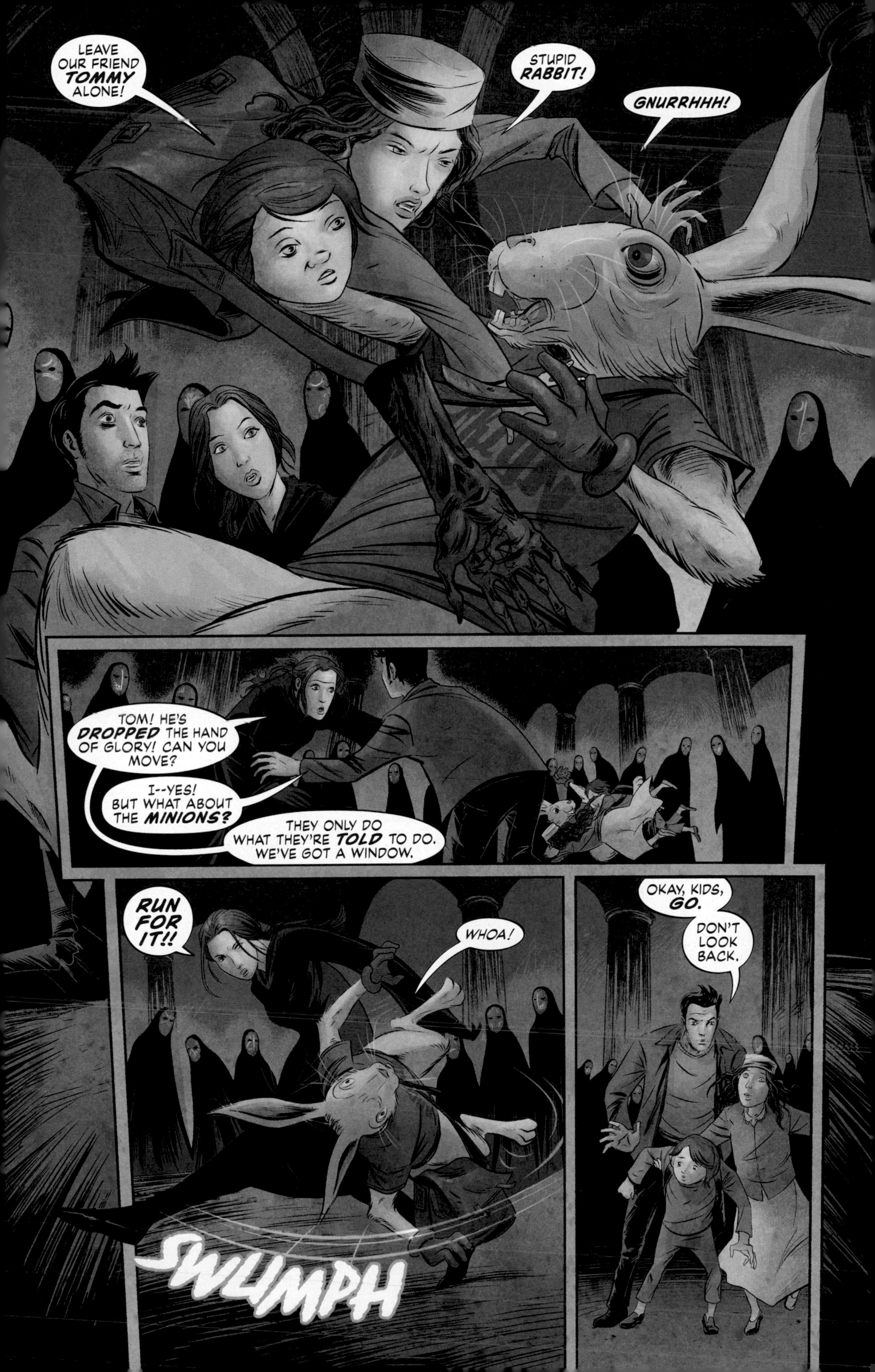
LEAVE OUR FRIEND TOMMY ALONE!
STUPID RABBIT!
GNURRHHH!
TOM! HE'S DROPPED THE HAND OF GLORY! CAN YOU MOVE?
I--YES! BUT WHAT ABOUT THE MINIONS?
THEY ONLY DO WHAT THEY'RE TOLD TO DO. WE'VE GOT A WINDOW.
RUN FOR IT!!
WHOA!
SWUMPH
OKAY, KIDS, GO.
DON'T LOOK BACK.

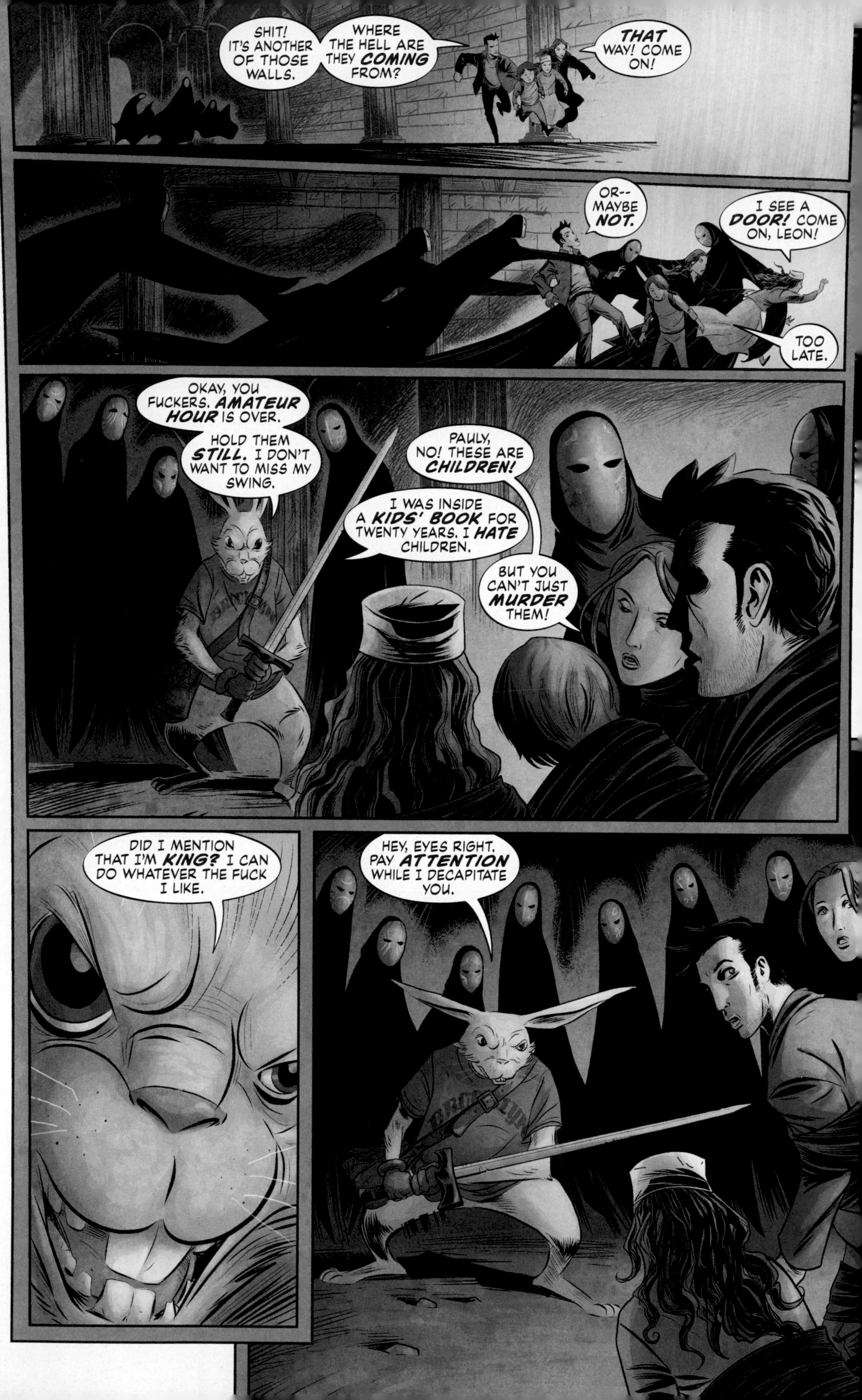

SHIT! IT'S ANOTHER OF THOSE WALLS.
WHERE THE HELL ARE THEY COMING FROM?
THAT WAY! COME ON!
OR-- MAYBE NOT.
I SEE A DOOR! COME ON, LEON!
TOO LATE.
OKAY, YOU FUCKERS. AMATEUR HOUR IS OVER.
HOLD THEM STILL. I DON'T WANT TO MISS MY SWING.
PAULY, NO! THESE ARE CHILDREN!
I WAS INSIDE A KIDS' BOOK FOR TWENTY YEARS. I HATE CHILDREN.
BUT YOU CAN'T JUST MURDER THEM!
DID I MENTION THAT I'M KING? I CAN DO WHATEVER THE FUCK I LIKE.
HEY, EYES RIGHT. PAY ATTENTION WHILE I DECAPITATE YOU.

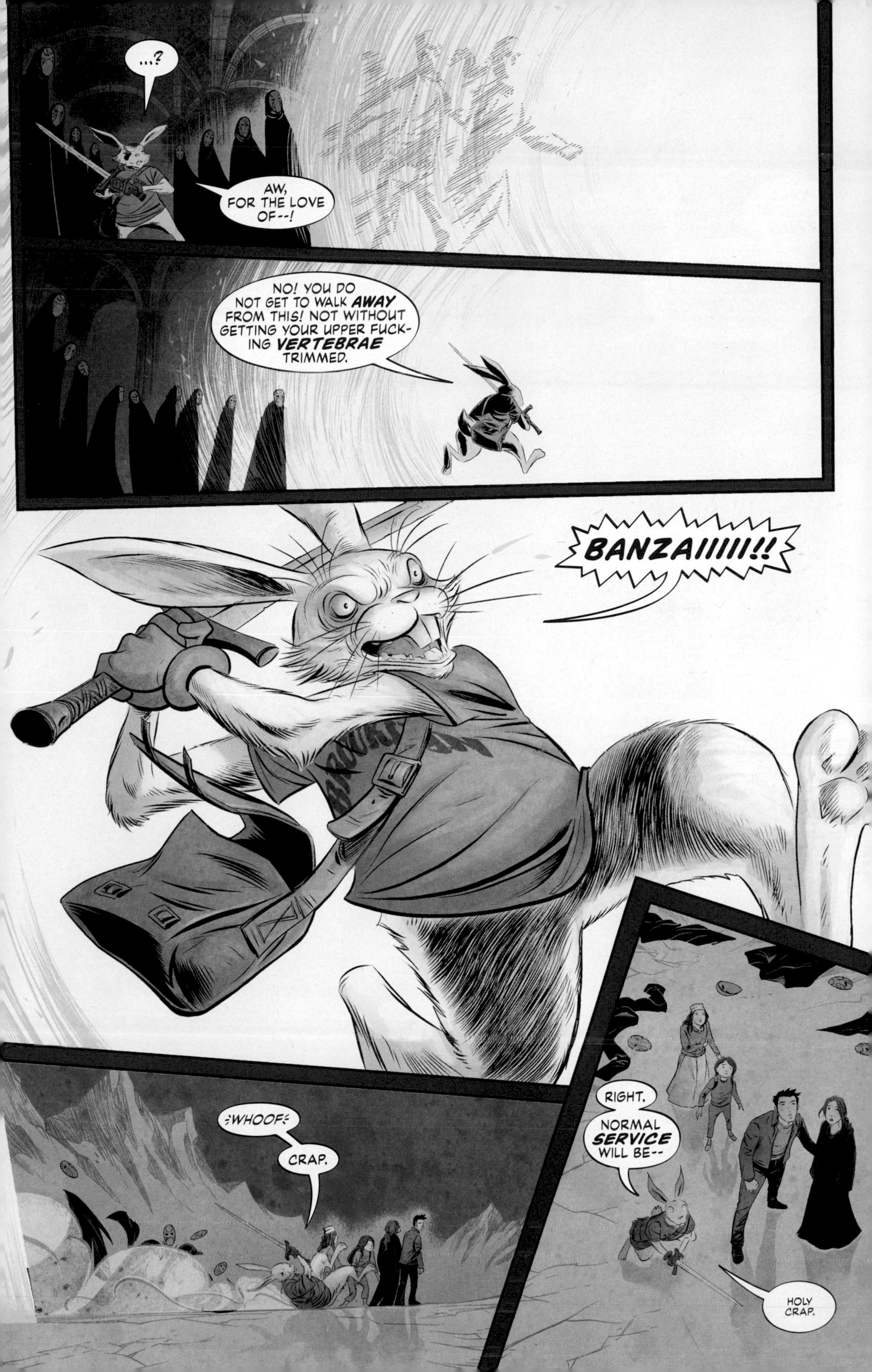
...?
AW, FOR THE LOVE OF--!
NO! YOU DO NOT GET TO WALK AWAY FROM THIS! NOT WITHOUT GETTING YOUR UPPER FUCK-ING VERTEBRAE TRIMMED.
BANZAIIIIII!!
WHOOF
CRAP.
RIGHT.
NORMAL SERVICE WILL BE--
HOLY CRAP.

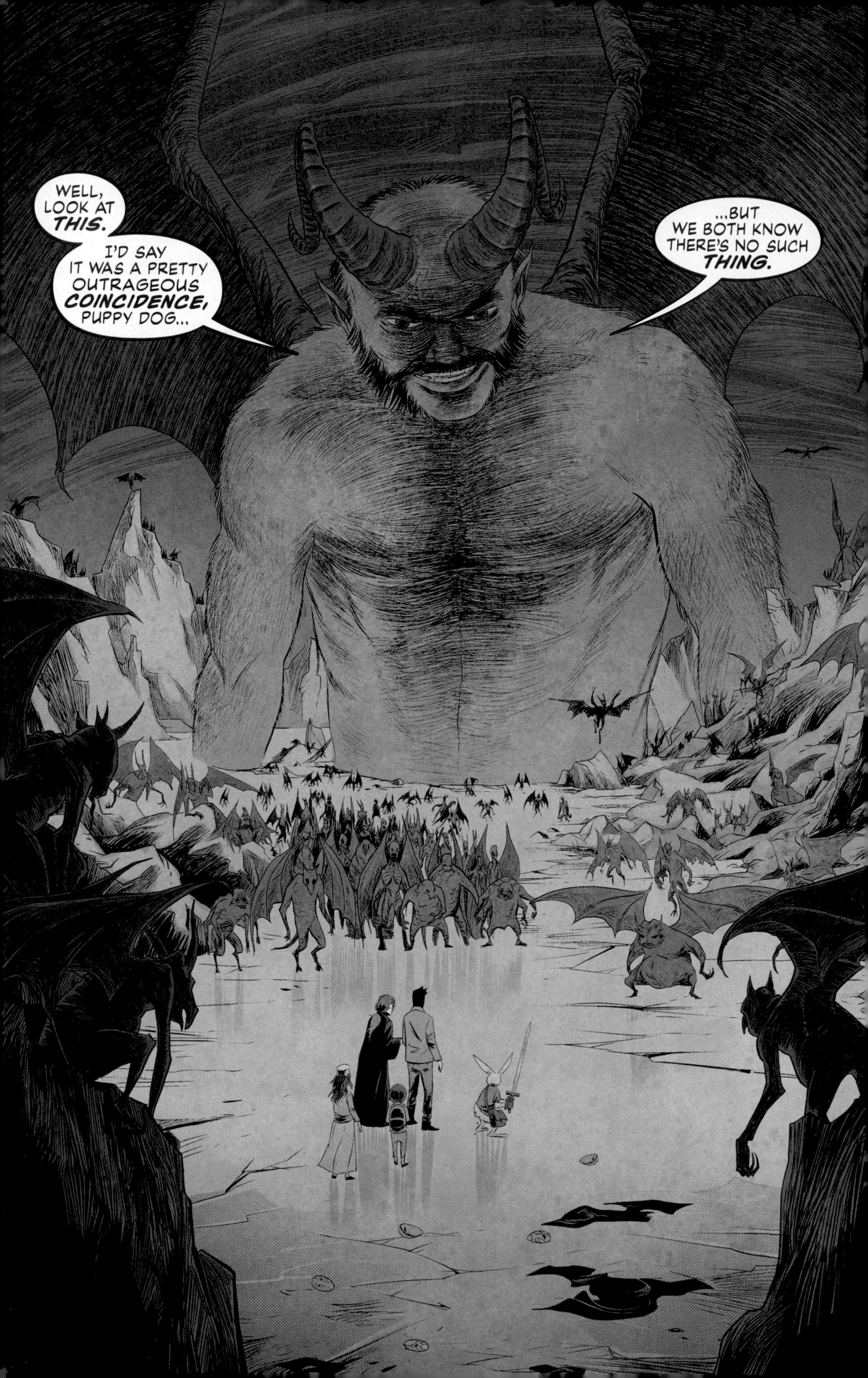
WELL, LOOK AT THIS.
I'D SAY IT WAS A PRETTY OUTRAGEOUS COINCIDENCE, PUPPY DOG...
...BUT WE BOTH KNOW THERE'S NO SUCH THING.

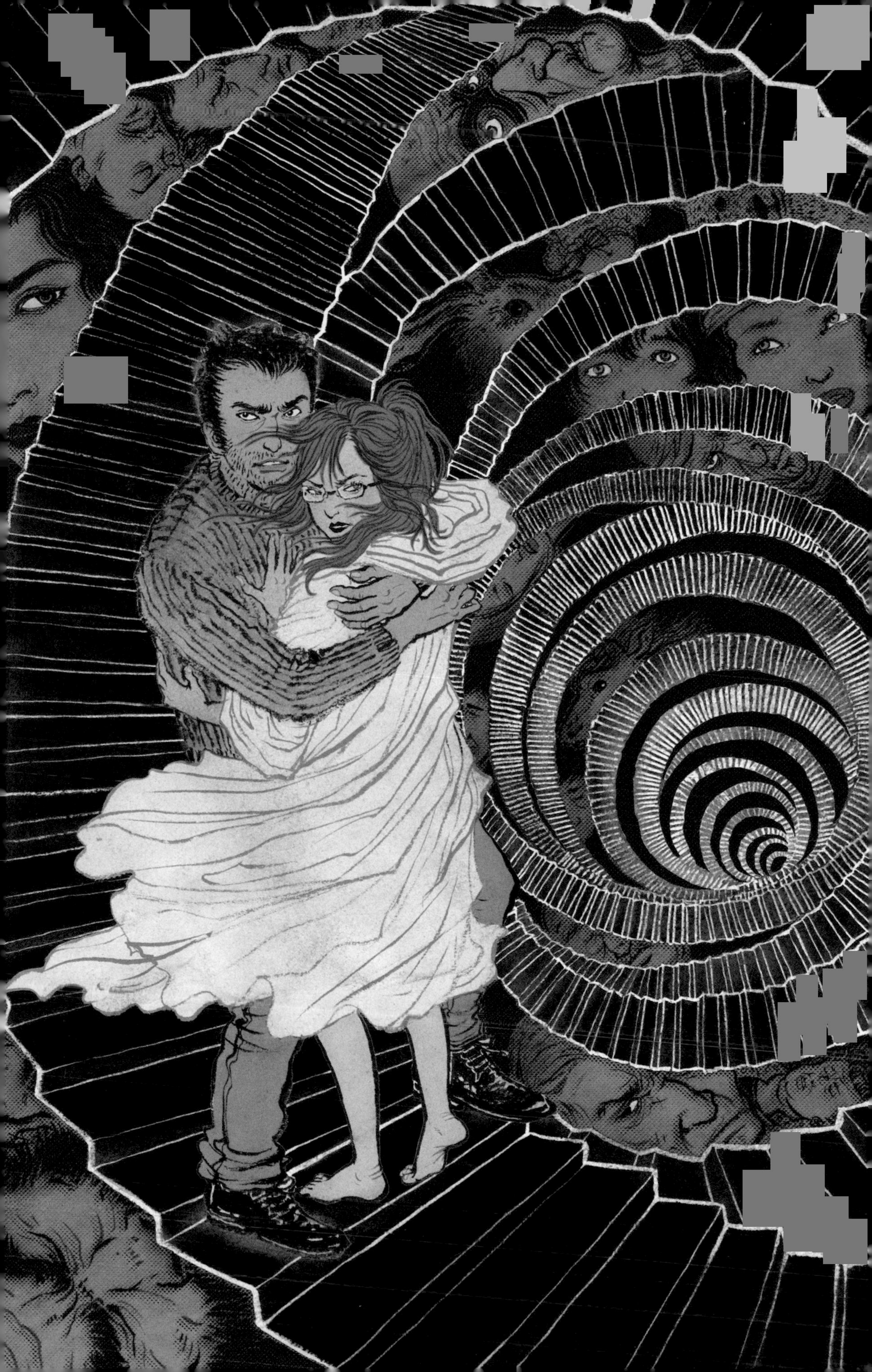

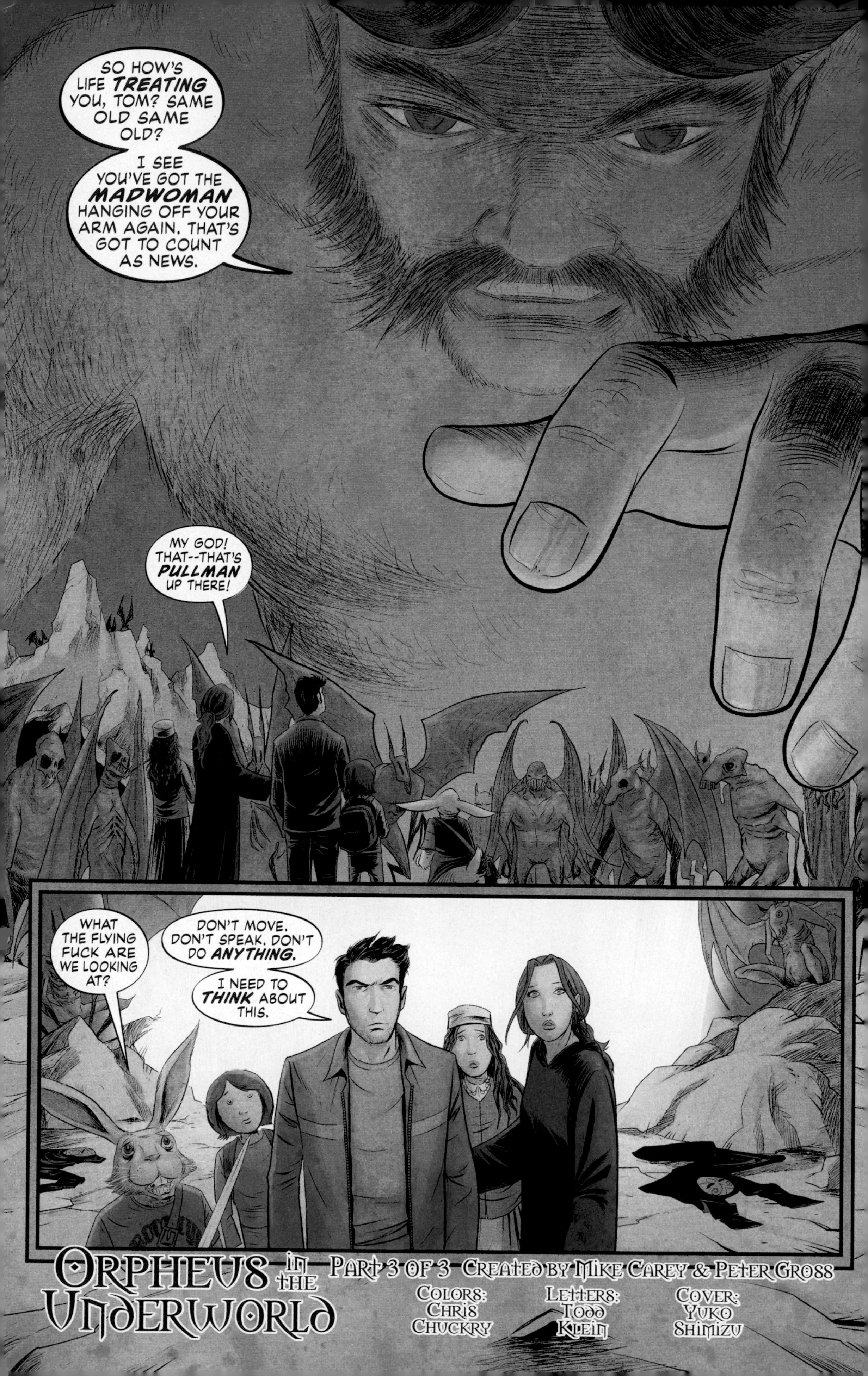
SO HOW'S LIFE TREATING YOU, TOM? SAME OLD SAME OLD?
I SEE YOU'VE GOT THE MADWOMAN HANGING OFF YOUR ARM AGAIN. THAT'S GOT TO COUNT AS NEWS.
MY GOD! THAT--THAT'S PULLMAN UP THERE!
WHAT THE FLYING FUCK ARE WE LOOKING AT?
DON'T MOVE. DON'T SPEAK. DON'T DO ANYTHING.
I NEED TO THINK ABOUT THIS.
ORPHEUS IN THE UNDERWORLD
PART 3 OF 3 CREATED BY MIKE CAREY & PETER GROSS
COLORS: CHRIS CHUCKRY
LETTERS: TODD KLEIN
COVER: YUKO SHIMIZU

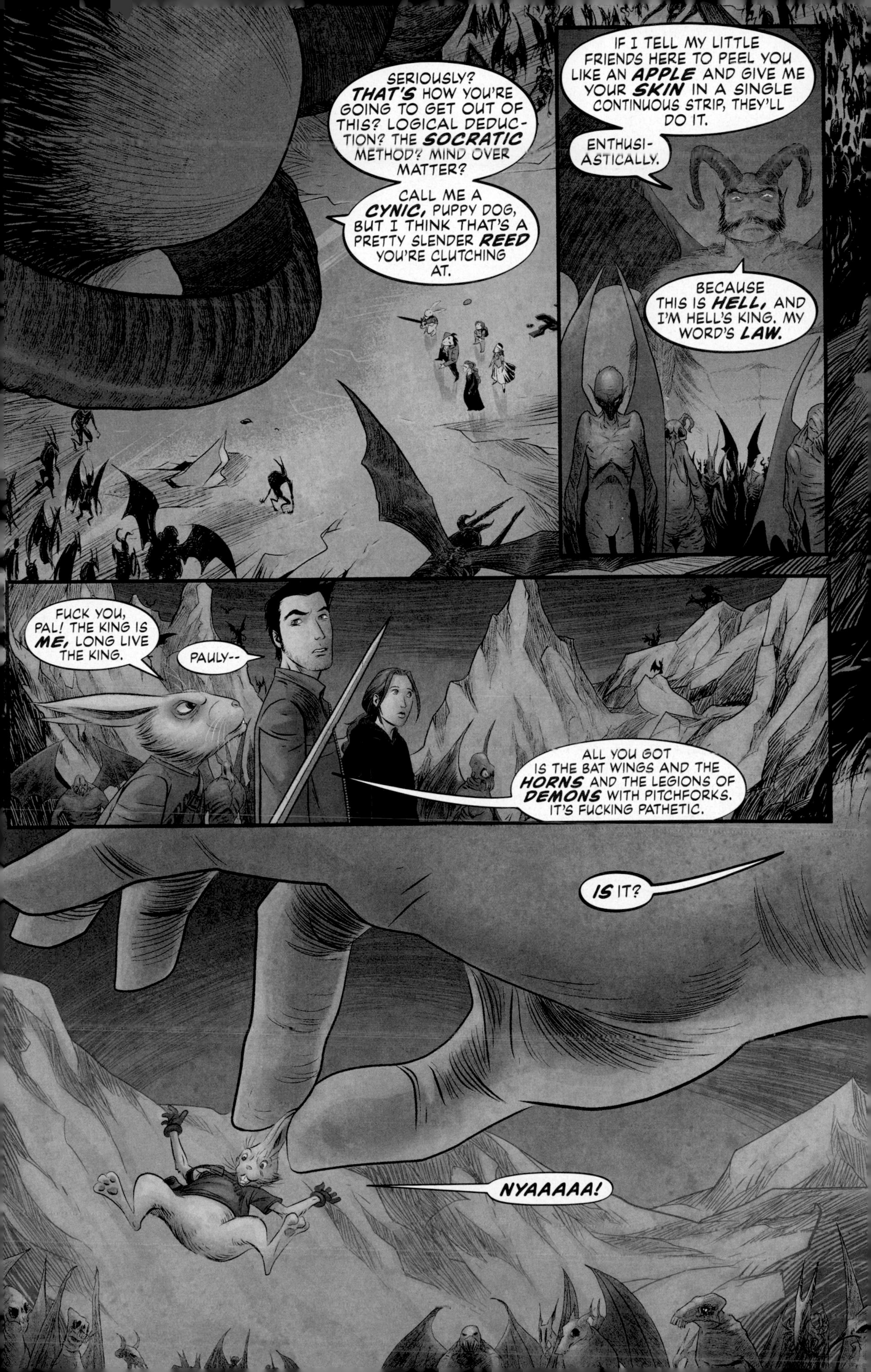
SERIOUSLY? THAT'S HOW YOU'RE GOING TO GET OUT OF THIS? LOGICAL DEDUCTION? THE SOCRATIC METHOD? MIND OVER MATTER?
CALL ME A CYNIC, PUPPY DOG, BUT I THINK THAT'S A PRETTY SLENDER REED YOU'RE CLUTCHING AT.
IF I TELL MY LITTLE FRIENDS HERE TO PEEL YOU LIKE AN APPLE AND GIVE ME YOUR SKIN IN A SINGLE CONTINUOUS STRIP, THEY'LL DO IT.
ENTHUSI-ASTICALLY.
BECAUSE THIS IS HELL, AND I'M HELL'S KING. MY WORD'S LAW.
FUCK YOU, PAL! THE KING IS ME, LONG LIVE THE KING.
PAULY--
ALL YOU GOT IS THE BAT WINGS AND THE HORNS AND THE LEGIONS OF DEMONS WITH PITCHFORKS. IT'S FUCKING PATHETIC.
IS IT?
NYAAAAA!

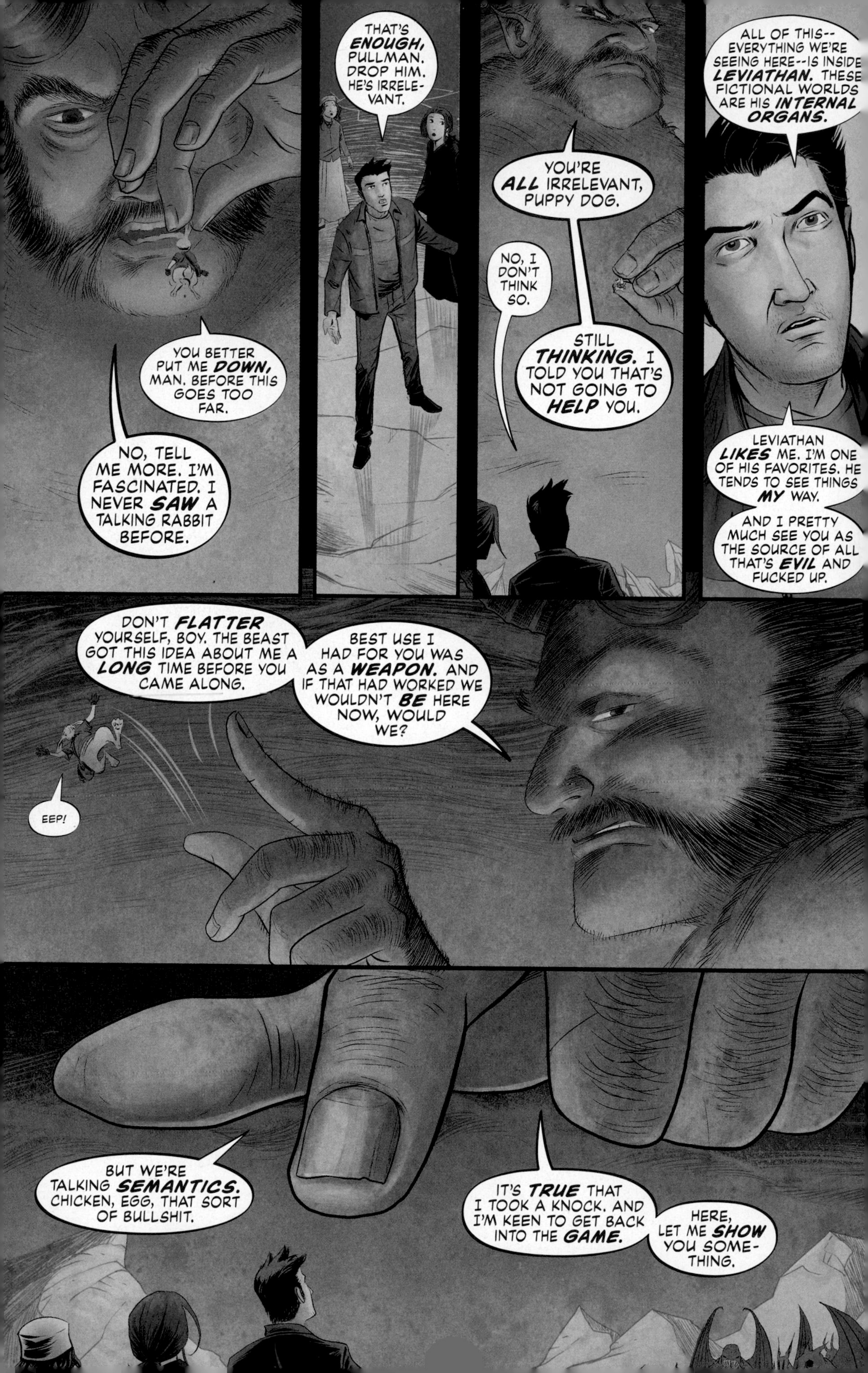
YOU BETTER PUT ME DOWN, MAN. BEFORE THIS GOES TOO FAR.
NO, TELL ME MORE. I'M FASCINATED. I NEVER SAW A TALKING RABBIT BEFORE.
THAT'S ENOUGH, PULLMAN. DROP HIM. HE'S IRRELE-VANT.
YOU'RE ALL IRRELEVANT, PUPPY DOG.
NO, I DON'T THINK SO.
STILL THINKING. I TOLD YOU THAT'S NOT GOING TO HELP YOU.
ALL OF THIS--EVERYTHING WE'RE SEEING HERE--IS INSIDE LEVIATHAN. THESE FICTIONAL WORLDS ARE HIS INTERNAL ORGANS.
LEVIATHAN LIKES ME. I'M ONE OF HIS FAVORITES. HE TENDS TO SEE THINGS MY WAY.
AND I PRETTY MUCH SEE YOU AS THE SOURCE OF ALL THAT'S EVIL AND FUCKED UP.
DON'T FLATTER YOURSELF, BOY. THE BEAST GOT THIS IDEA ABOUT ME A LONG TIME BEFORE YOU CAME ALONG.
BEST USE I HAD FOR YOU WAS AS A WEAPON. AND IF THAT HAD WORKED WE WOULDN'T BE HERE NOW, WOULD WE?
EEP!
BUT WE'RE TALKING SEMANTICS. CHICKEN, EGG, THAT SORT OF BULLSHIT.
IT'S TRUE THAT I TOOK A KNOCK. AND I'M KEEN TO GET BACK INTO THE GAME.
HERE, LET ME SHOW YOU SOME-THING.

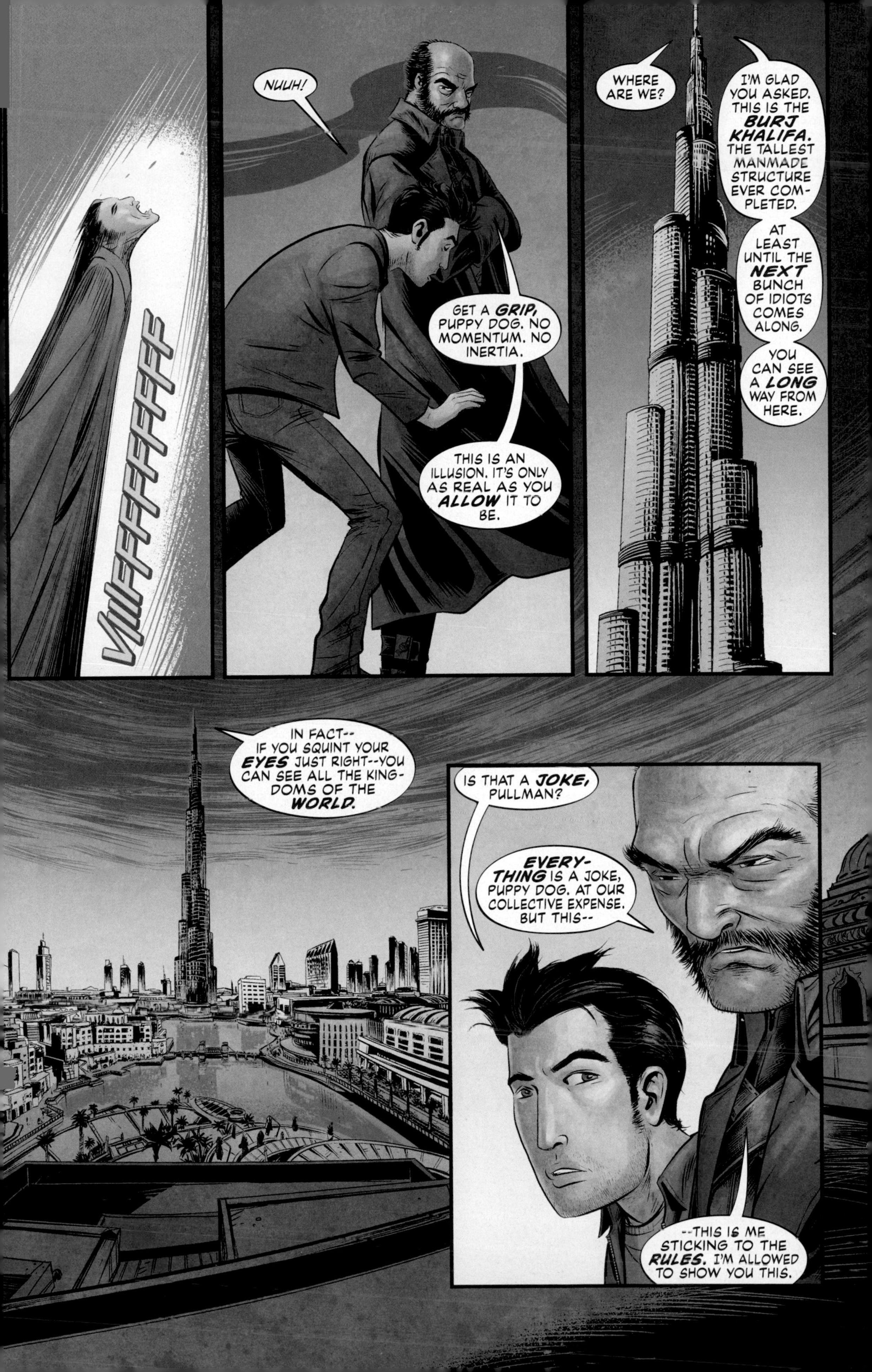
VWFFFFFFFFF
NUUH!
GET A GRIP, PUPPY DOG. NO MOMENTUM. NO INERTIA.
THIS IS AN ILLUSION. IT'S ONLY AS REAL AS YOU ALLOW IT TO BE.
WHERE ARE WE?
I'M GLAD YOU ASKED. THIS IS THE BURJ KHALIFA. THE TALLEST MANMADE STRUCTURE EVER COMPLETED.
AT LEAST UNTIL THE NEXT BUNCH OF IDIOTS COMES ALONG.
YOU CAN SEE A LONG WAY FROM HERE.
IN FACT-- IF YOU SQUINT YOUR EYES JUST RIGHT--YOU CAN SEE ALL THE KINGDOMS OF THE WORLD.
IS THAT A JOKE, PULLMAN?
EVERYTHING IS A JOKE, PUPPY DOG. AT OUR COLLECTIVE EXPENSE. BUT THIS--
--THIS IS ME STICKING TO THE RULES. I'M ALLOWED TO SHOW YOU THIS.

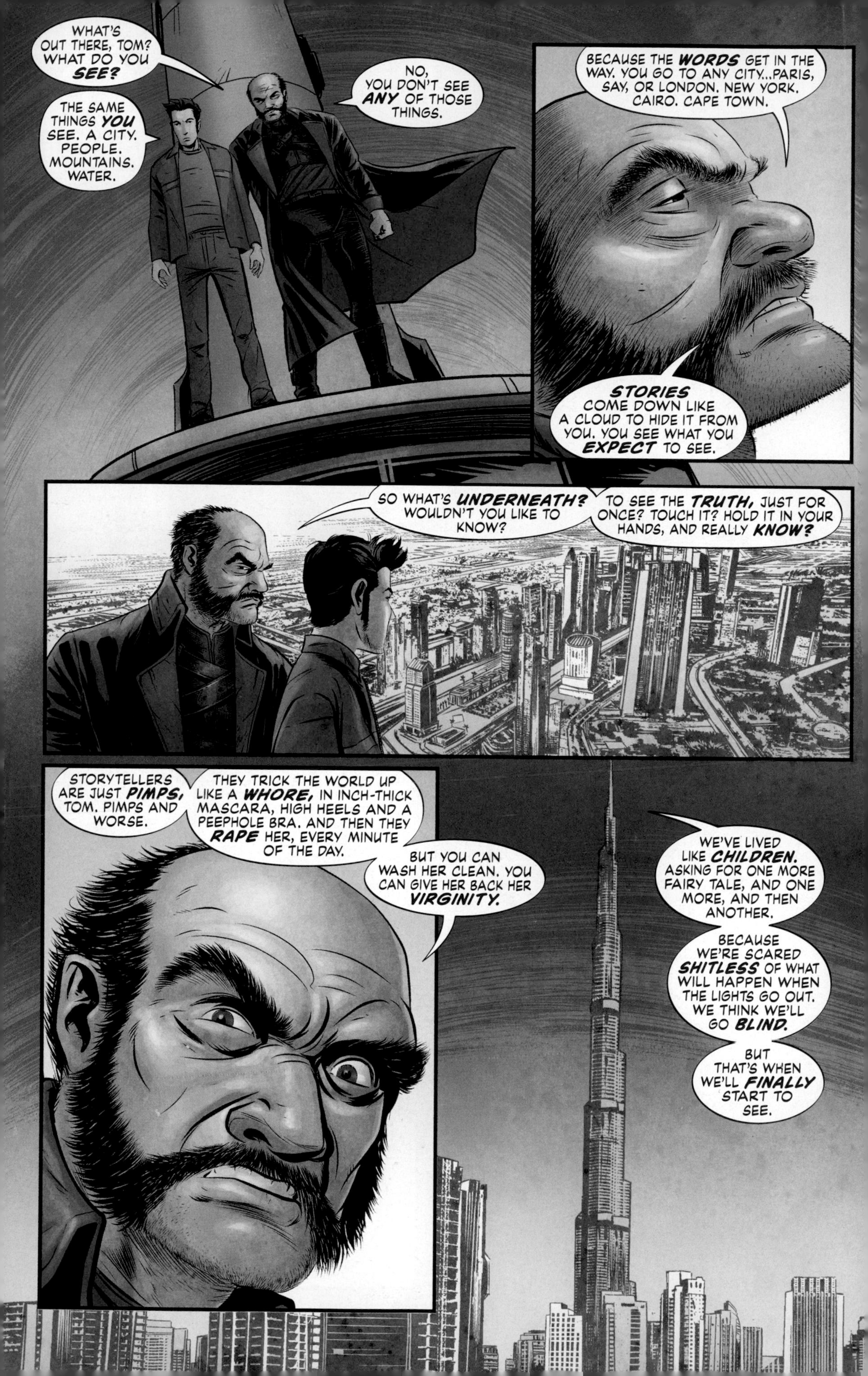
WHAT'S OUT THERE, TOM? WHAT DO YOU SEE?
THE SAME THINGS YOU SEE. A CITY. PEOPLE. MOUNTAINS. WATER.
NO, YOU DON'T SEE ANY OF THOSE THINGS.
BECAUSE THE WORDS GET IN THE WAY. YOU GO TO ANY CITY...PARIS, SAY, OR LONDON. NEW YORK. CAIRO. CAPE TOWN.
STORIES COME DOWN LIKE A CLOUD TO HIDE IT FROM YOU. YOU SEE WHAT YOU EXPECT TO SEE.
SO WHAT'S UNDERNEATH? WOULDN'T YOU LIKE TO KNOW?
TO SEE THE TRUTH, JUST FOR ONCE? TOUCH IT? HOLD IT IN YOUR HANDS, AND REALLY KNOW?
STORYTELLERS ARE JUST PIMPS, TOM. PIMPS AND WORSE.
THEY TRICK THE WORLD UP LIKE A WHORE, IN INCH-THICK MASCARA, HIGH HEELS AND A PEEPHOLE BRA. AND THEN THEY RAPE HER, EVERY MINUTE OF THE DAY.
BUT YOU CAN WASH HER CLEAN. YOU CAN GIVE HER BACK HER VIRGINITY.
WE'VE LIVED LIKE CHILDREN. ASKING FOR ONE MORE FAIRY TALE, AND ONE MORE, AND THEN ANOTHER.
BECAUSE WE'RE SCARED SHITLESS OF WHAT WILL HAPPEN WHEN THE LIGHTS GO OUT. WE THINK WE'LL GO BLIND.
BUT THAT'S WHEN WE'LL FINALLY START TO SEE.

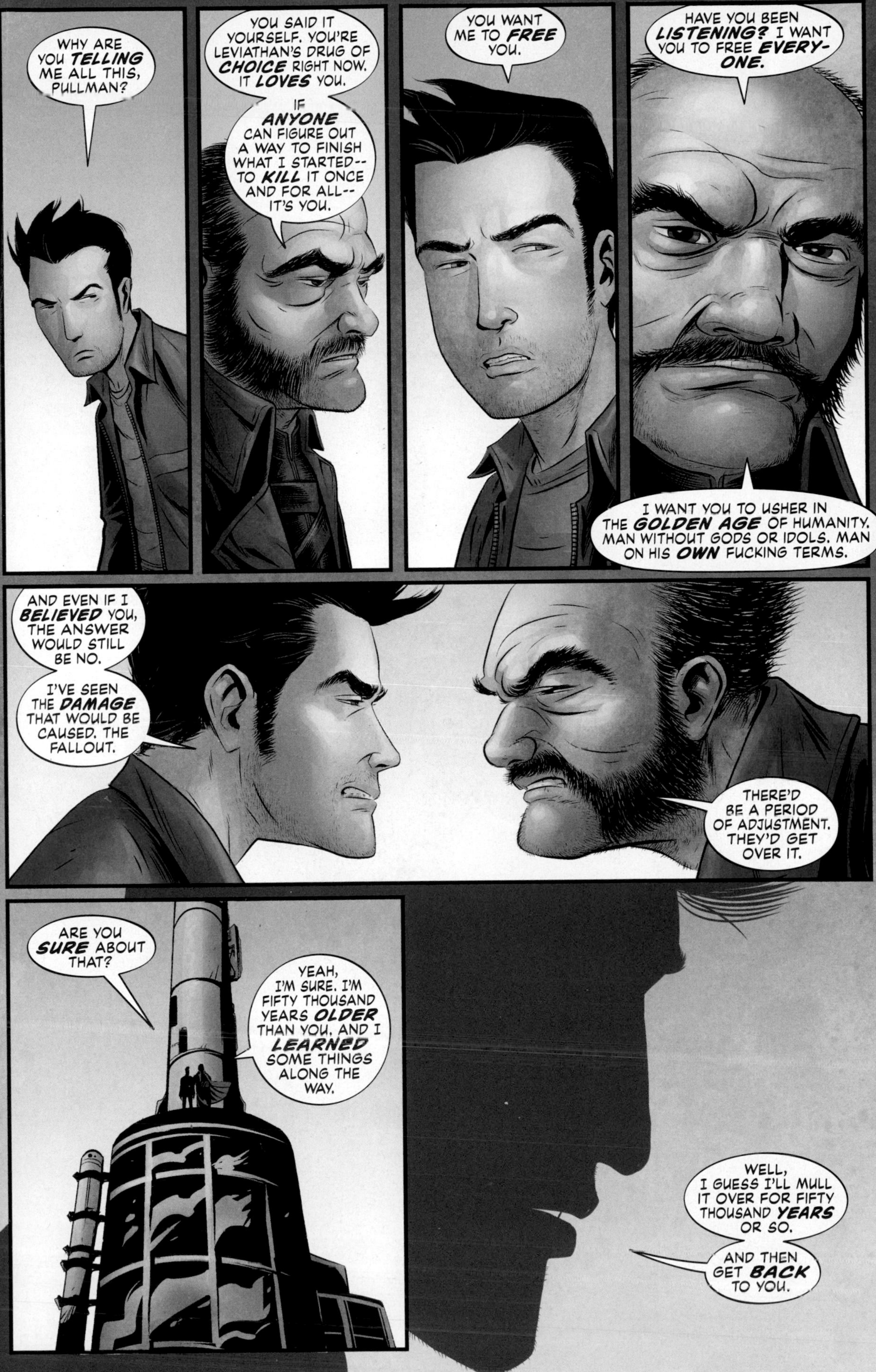
WHY ARE YOU TELLING ME ALL THIS, PULLMAN?
YOU SAID IT YOURSELF. YOU'RE LEVIATHAN'S DRUG OF CHOICE RIGHT NOW. IT LOVES YOU.
IF ANYONE CAN FIGURE OUT A WAY TO FINISH WHAT I STARTED-- TO KILL IT ONCE AND FOR ALL-- IT'S YOU.
YOU WANT ME TO FREE YOU.
HAVE YOU BEEN LISTENING? I WANT YOU TO FREE EVERY-ONE.
I WANT YOU TO USHER IN THE GOLDEN AGE OF HUMANITY. MAN WITHOUT GODS OR IDOLS. MAN ON HIS OWN FUCKING TERMS.
AND EVEN IF I BELIEVED YOU, THE ANSWER WOULD STILL BE NO.
I'VE SEEN THE DAMAGE THAT WOULD BE CAUSED. THE FALLOUT.
THERE'D BE A PERIOD OF ADJUSTMENT. THEY'D GET OVER IT.
ARE YOU SURE ABOUT THAT?
YEAH, I'M SURE. I'M FIFTY THOUSAND YEARS OLDER THAN YOU, AND I LEARNED SOME THINGS ALONG THE WAY.
WELL, I GUESS I'LL MULL IT OVER FOR FIFTY THOUSAND YEARS OR SO.
AND THEN GET BACK TO YOU.

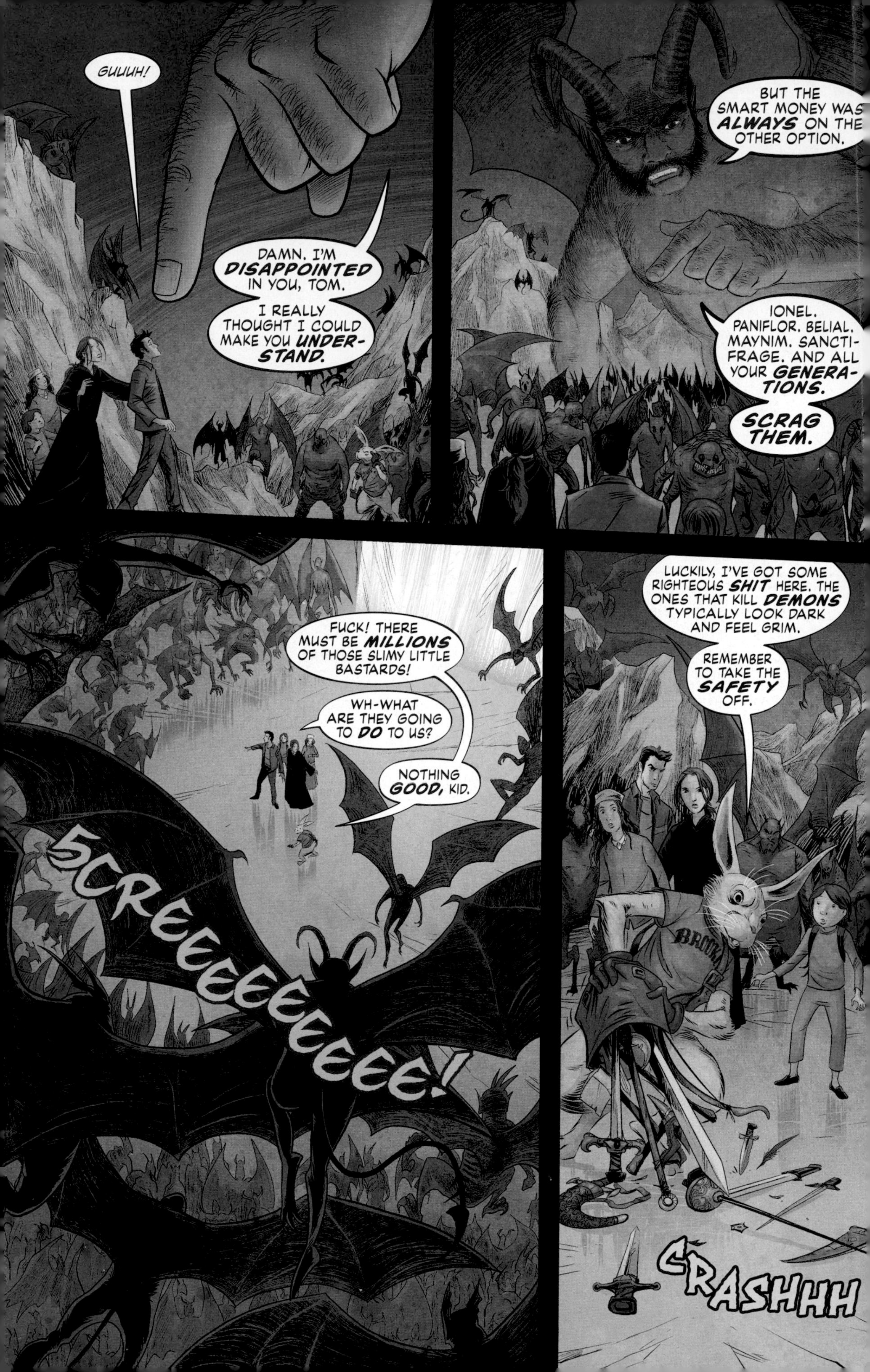
GUUUH!
DAMN. I'M **DISAPPOINTED** IN YOU, TOM.
I REALLY THOUGHT I COULD MAKE YOU **UNDER-STAND.**
BUT THE SMART MONEY WAS **ALWAYS** ON THE OTHER OPTION.
IONEL. PANIFLOR. BELIAL. MAYNIM. SANCTI-FRAGE. AND ALL YOUR **GENERA-TIONS.**
**SCRAG THEM.**
FUCK! THERE MUST BE **MILLIONS** OF THOSE SLIMY LITTLE BASTARDS!
WH-WHAT ARE THEY GOING TO **DO** TO US?
NOTHING **GOOD,** KID.
SCREEEEEEEEEE!
LUCKILY, I'VE GOT SOME RIGHTEOUS **SHIT** HERE. THE ONES THAT KILL **DEMONS** TYPICALLY LOOK DARK AND FEEL GRIM.
REMEMBER TO TAKE THE **SAFETY** OFF.
CRASHHH

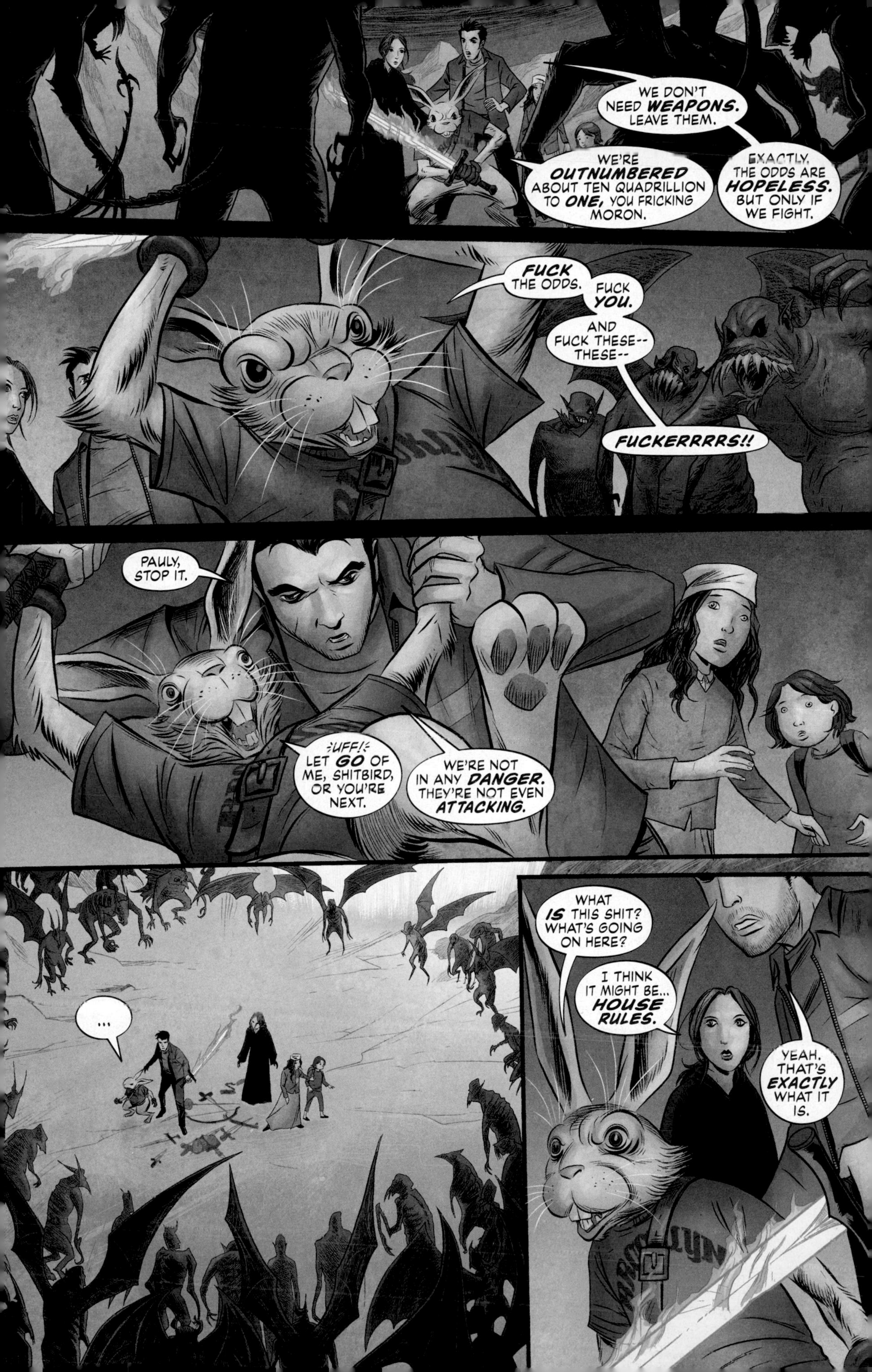
WE DON'T NEED WEAPONS. LEAVE THEM.
WE'RE OUTNUMBERED ABOUT TEN QUADRILLION TO ONE, YOU FRICKING MORON.
EXACTLY. THE ODDS ARE HOPELESS. BUT ONLY IF WE FIGHT.
FUCK THE ODDS.
FUCK YOU.
AND FUCK THESE-- THESE--
FUCKERRRRS!!
PAULY, STOP IT.
UFF! LET GO OF ME, SHITBIRD, OR YOU'RE NEXT.
WE'RE NOT IN ANY DANGER. THEY'RE NOT EVEN ATTACKING.
...
WHAT IS THIS SHIT? WHAT'S GOING ON HERE?
I THINK IT MIGHT BE... HOUSE RULES.
YEAH. THAT'S EXACTLY WHAT IT IS.

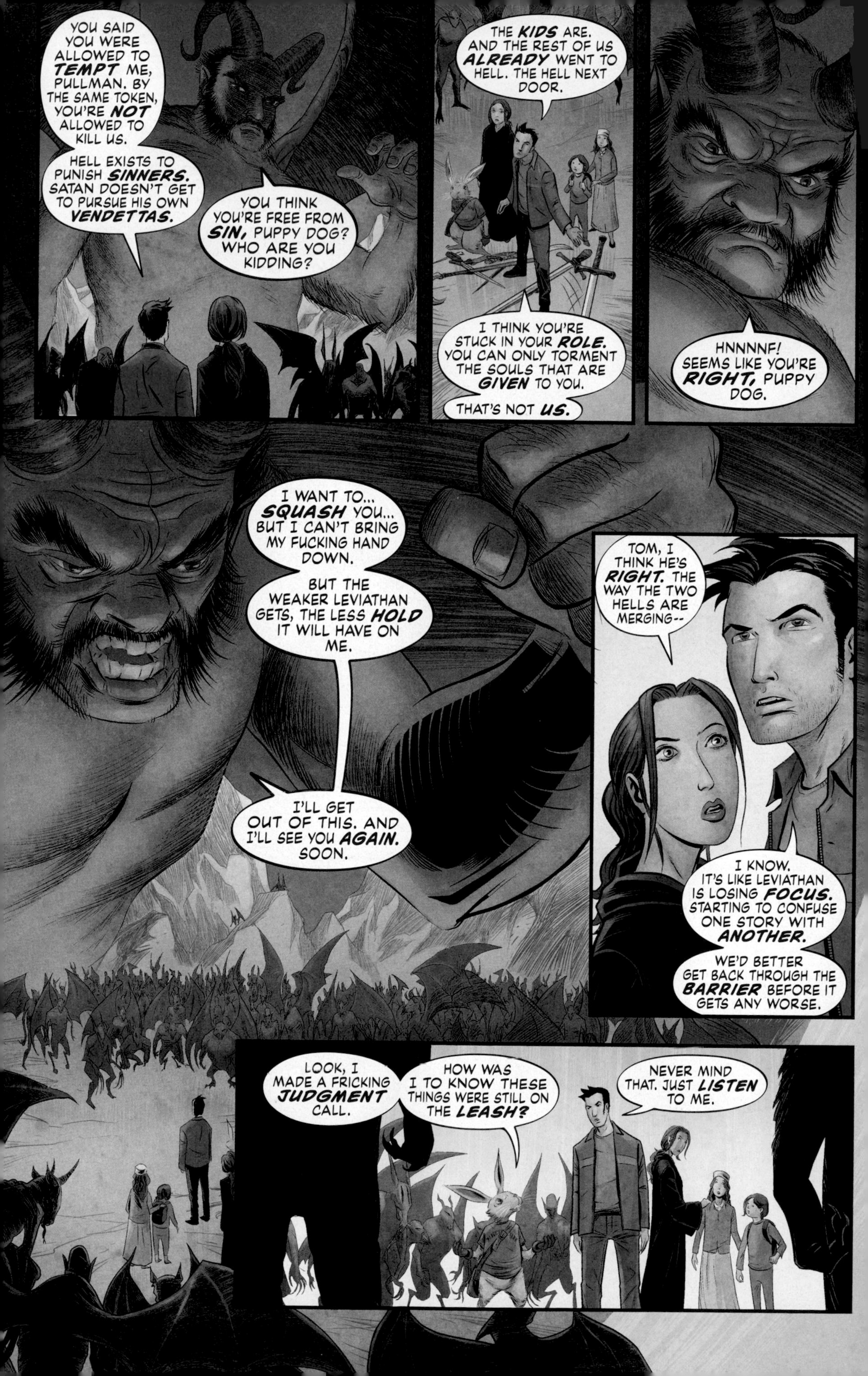

YOU SAID YOU WERE ALLOWED TO TEMPT ME, PULLMAN. BY THE SAME TOKEN, YOU'RE NOT ALLOWED TO KILL US.
HELL EXISTS TO PUNISH SINNERS. SATAN DOESN'T GET TO PURSUE HIS OWN VENDETTAS.
YOU THINK YOU'RE FREE FROM SIN, PUPPY DOG? WHO ARE YOU KIDDING?
THE KIDS ARE. AND THE REST OF US ALREADY WENT TO HELL. THE HELL NEXT DOOR.
I THINK YOU'RE STUCK IN YOUR ROLE. YOU CAN ONLY TORMENT THE SOULS THAT ARE GIVEN TO YOU.
THAT'S NOT US.
HNNNNF! SEEMS LIKE YOU'RE RIGHT, PUPPY DOG.
I WANT TO... SQUASH YOU... BUT I CAN'T BRING MY FUCKING HAND DOWN.
BUT THE WEAKER LEVIATHAN GETS, THE LESS HOLD IT WILL HAVE ON ME.
I'LL GET OUT OF THIS. AND I'LL SEE YOU AGAIN. SOON.
TOM, I THINK HE'S RIGHT. THE WAY THE TWO HELLS ARE MERGING--
I KNOW. IT'S LIKE LEVIATHAN IS LOSING FOCUS. STARTING TO CONFUSE ONE STORY WITH ANOTHER.
WE'D BETTER GET BACK THROUGH THE BARRIER BEFORE IT GETS ANY WORSE.
LOOK, I MADE A FRICKING JUDGMENT CALL.
HOW WAS I TO KNOW THESE THINGS WERE STILL ON THE LEASH?
NEVER MIND THAT. JUST LISTEN TO ME.

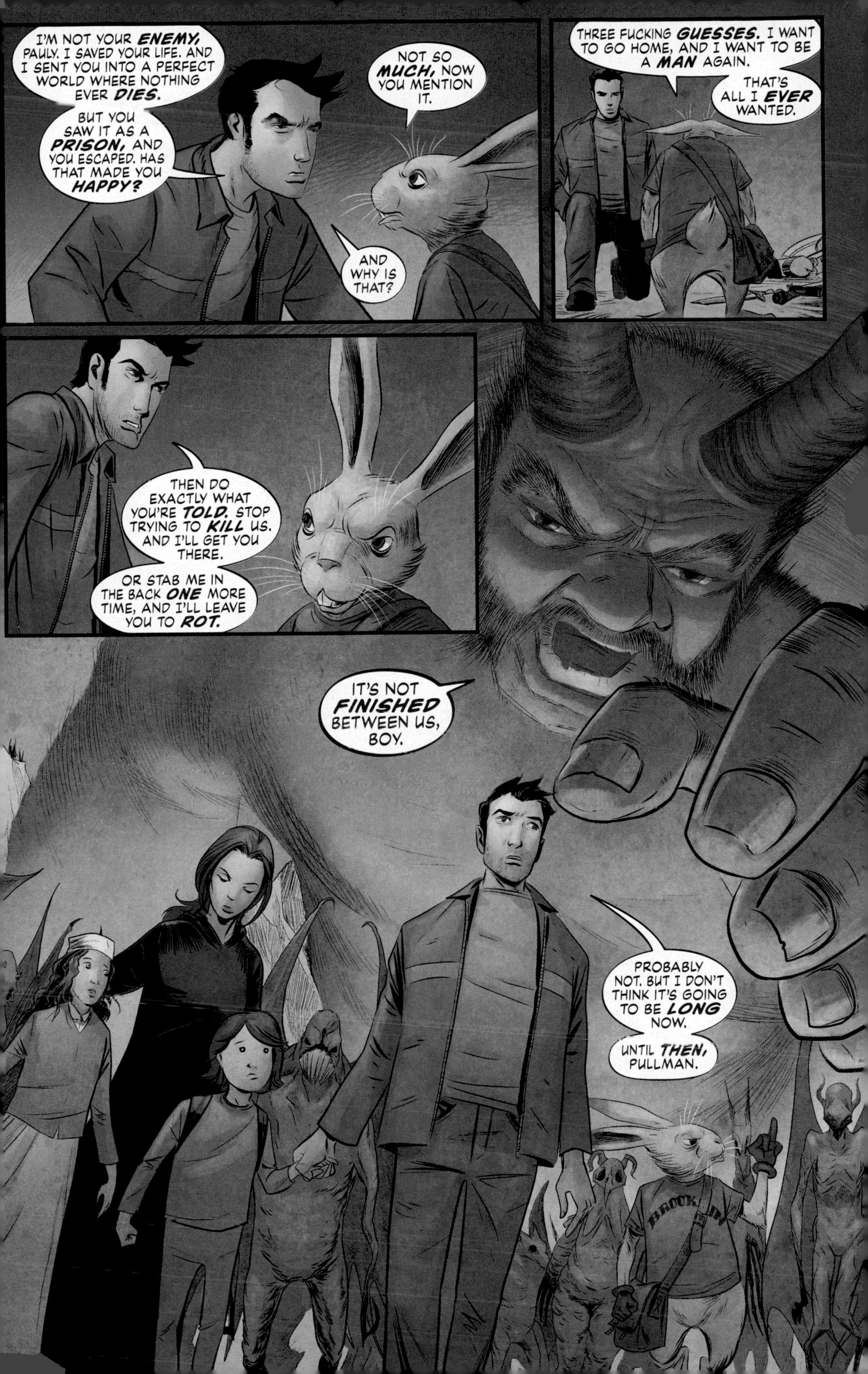
I'M NOT YOUR ENEMY, PAULY. I SAVED YOUR LIFE. AND I SENT YOU INTO A PERFECT WORLD WHERE NOTHING EVER DIES.
BUT YOU SAW IT AS A PRISON, AND YOU ESCAPED. HAS THAT MADE YOU HAPPY?
NOT SO MUCH, NOW YOU MENTION IT.
AND WHY IS THAT?
THREE FUCKING GUESSES. I WANT TO GO HOME, AND I WANT TO BE A MAN AGAIN.
THAT'S ALL I EVER WANTED.
THEN DO EXACTLY WHAT YOU'RE TOLD. STOP TRYING TO KILL US. AND I'LL GET YOU THERE.
OR STAB ME IN THE BACK ONE MORE TIME, AND I'LL LEAVE YOU TO ROT.
IT'S NOT FINISHED BETWEEN US, BOY.
PROBABLY NOT. BUT I DON'T THINK IT'S GOING TO BE LONG NOW.
UNTIL THEN, PULLMAN.
BROOKLYN

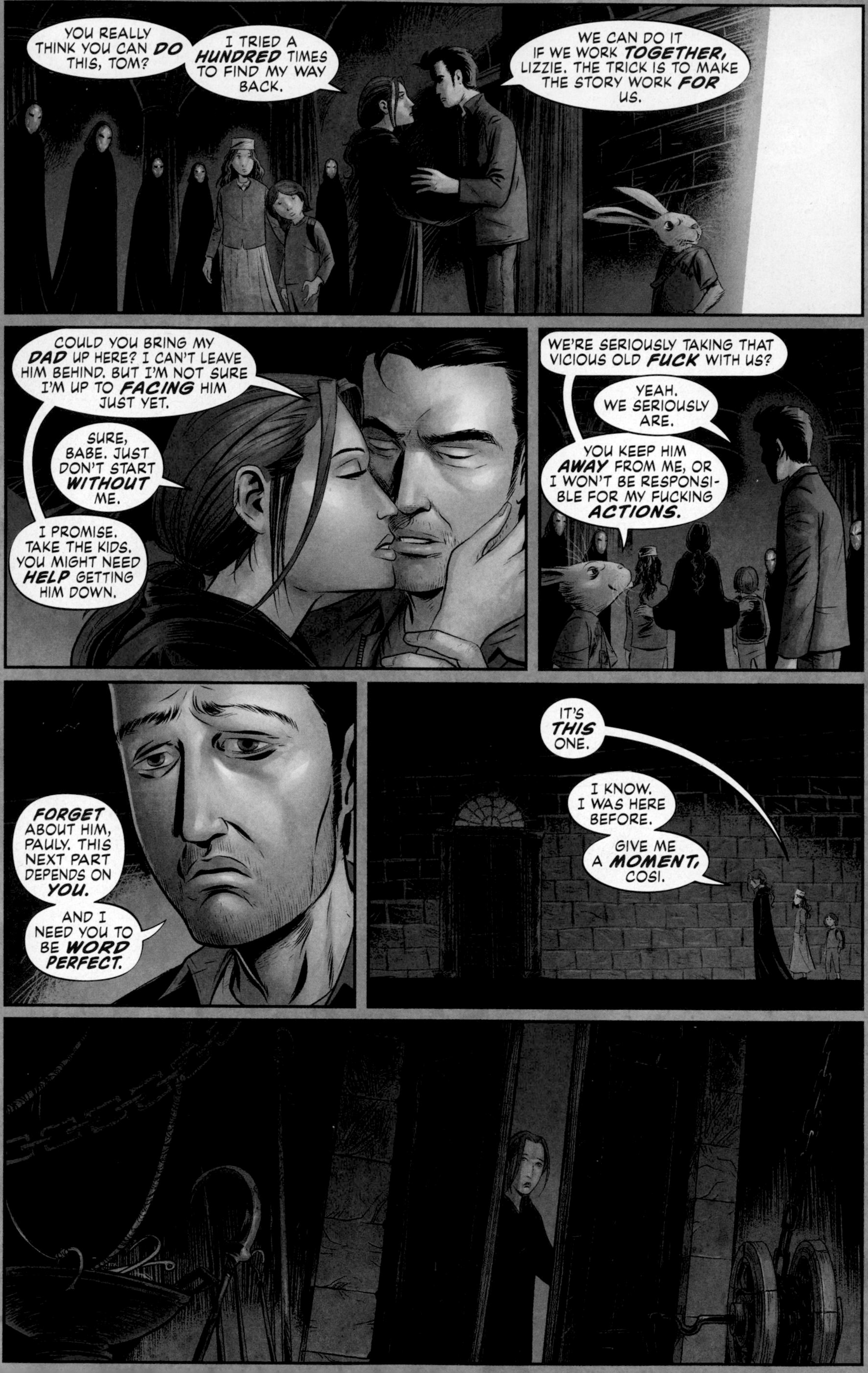
YOU REALLY THINK YOU CAN DO THIS, TOM?
I TRIED A HUNDRED TIMES TO FIND MY WAY BACK.
WE CAN DO IT IF WE WORK TOGETHER, LIZZIE. THE TRICK IS TO MAKE THE STORY WORK FOR US.
COULD YOU BRING MY DAD UP HERE? I CAN'T LEAVE HIM BEHIND. BUT I'M NOT SURE I'M UP TO FACING HIM JUST YET.
SURE, BABE. JUST DON'T START WITHOUT ME.
I PROMISE. TAKE THE KIDS. YOU MIGHT NEED HELP GETTING HIM DOWN.
WE'RE SERIOUSLY TAKING THAT VICIOUS OLD FUCK WITH US?
YEAH. WE SERIOUSLY ARE.
YOU KEEP HIM AWAY FROM ME, OR I WON'T BE RESPONSIBLE FOR MY FUCKING ACTIONS.
FORGET ABOUT HIM, PAULY. THIS NEXT PART DEPENDS ON YOU.
AND I NEED YOU TO BE WORD PERFECT.
IT'S THIS ONE.
I KNOW. I WAS HERE BEFORE.
GIVE ME A MOMENT, COSI.

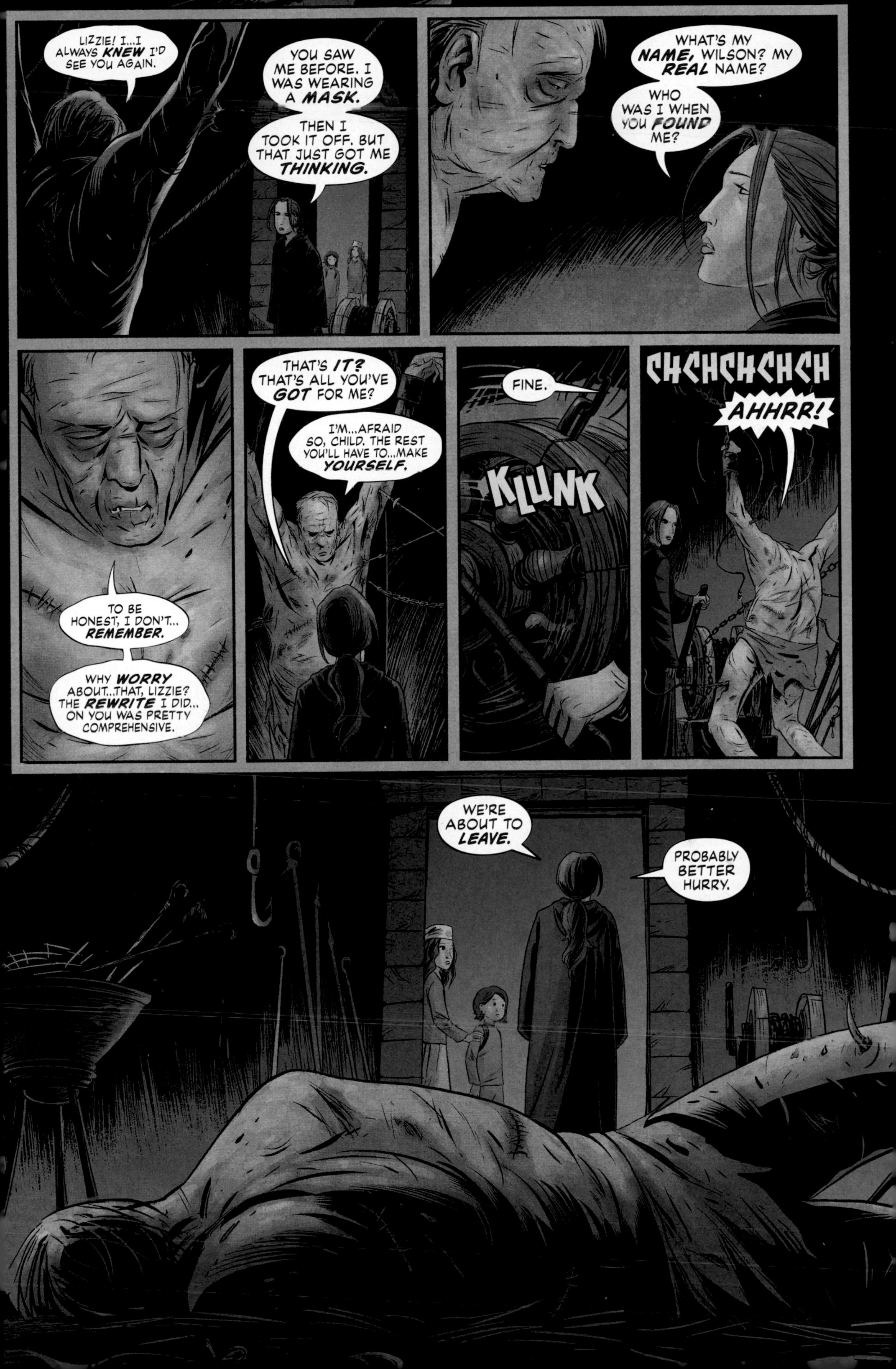
LIZZIE! I...I ALWAYS KNEW I'D SEE YOU AGAIN.
YOU SAW ME BEFORE. I WAS WEARING A MASK.
THEN I TOOK IT OFF. BUT THAT JUST GOT ME THINKING.
WHAT'S MY NAME, WILSON? MY REAL NAME?
WHO WAS I WHEN YOU FOUND ME?
TO BE HONEST, I DON'T... REMEMBER.
WHY WORRY ABOUT...THAT, LIZZIE? THE REWRITE I DID... ON YOU WAS PRETTY COMPREHENSIVE.
THAT'S IT? THAT'S ALL YOU'VE GOT FOR ME?
I'M...AFRAID SO, CHILD. THE REST YOU'LL HAVE TO...MAKE YOURSELF.
FINE.
KLUNK
CHCHCHCHCH
AHHRR!
WE'RE ABOUT TO LEAVE.
PROBABLY BETTER HURRY.

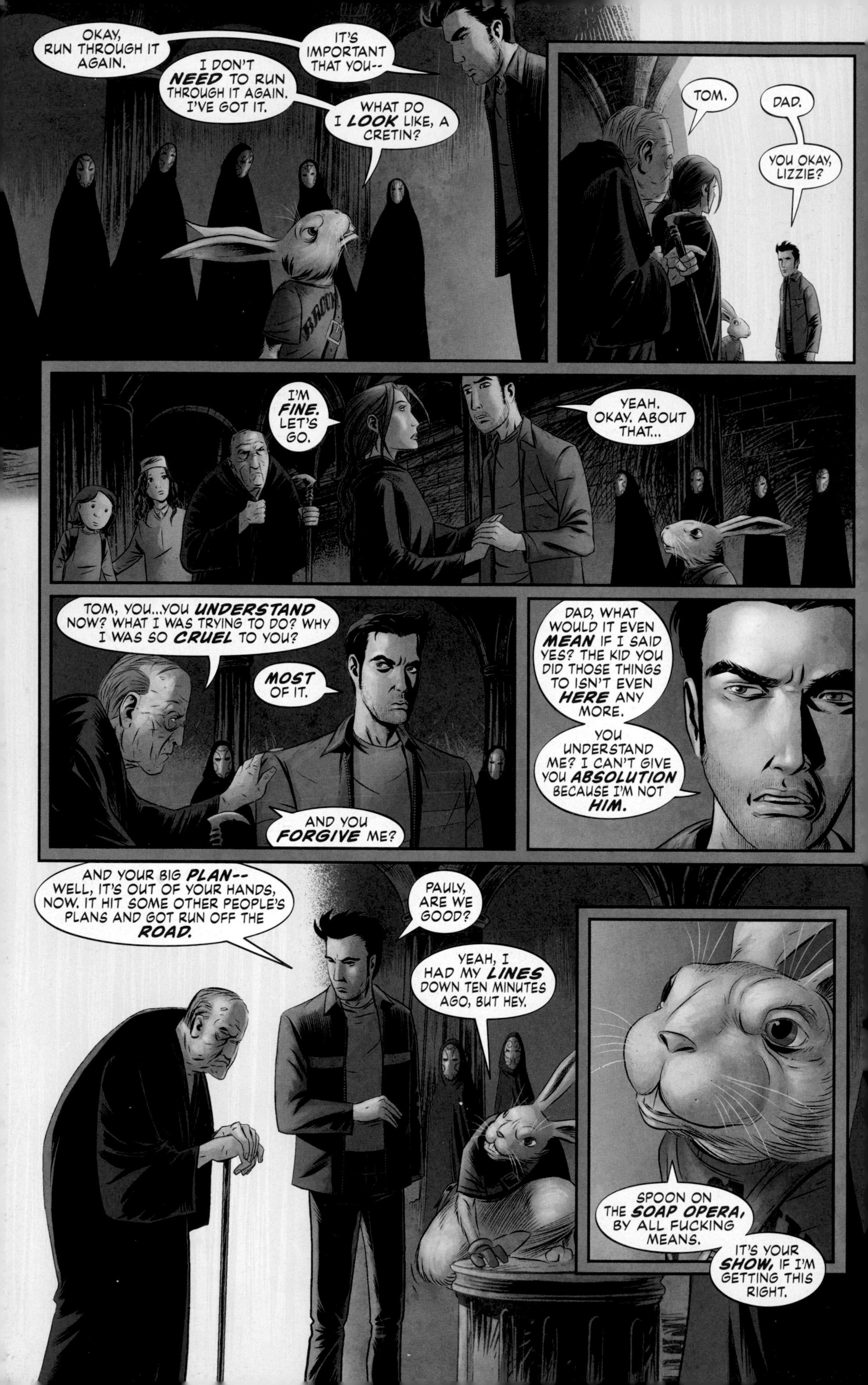
OKAY, RUN THROUGH IT AGAIN.
IT'S IMPORTANT THAT YOU--
I DON'T NEED TO RUN THROUGH IT AGAIN. I'VE GOT IT.
WHAT DO I LOOK LIKE, A CRETIN?
TOM.
DAD.
YOU OKAY, LIZZIE?
I'M FINE. LET'S GO.
YEAH. OKAY. ABOUT THAT...
TOM, YOU...YOU UNDERSTAND NOW? WHAT I WAS TRYING TO DO? WHY I WAS SO CRUEL TO YOU?
MOST OF IT.
AND YOU FORGIVE ME?
DAD, WHAT WOULD IT EVEN MEAN IF I SAID YES? THE KID YOU DID THOSE THINGS TO ISN'T EVEN HERE ANY MORE.
YOU UNDERSTAND ME? I CAN'T GIVE YOU ABSOLUTION BECAUSE I'M NOT HIM.
AND YOUR BIG PLAN-- WELL, IT'S OUT OF YOUR HANDS, NOW. IT HIT SOME OTHER PEOPLE'S PLANS AND GOT RUN OFF THE ROAD.
PAULY, ARE WE GOOD?
YEAH, I HAD MY LINES DOWN TEN MINUTES AGO, BUT HEY.
SPOON ON THE SOAP OPERA, BY ALL FUCKING MEANS.
IT'S YOUR SHOW, IF I'M GETTING THIS RIGHT.

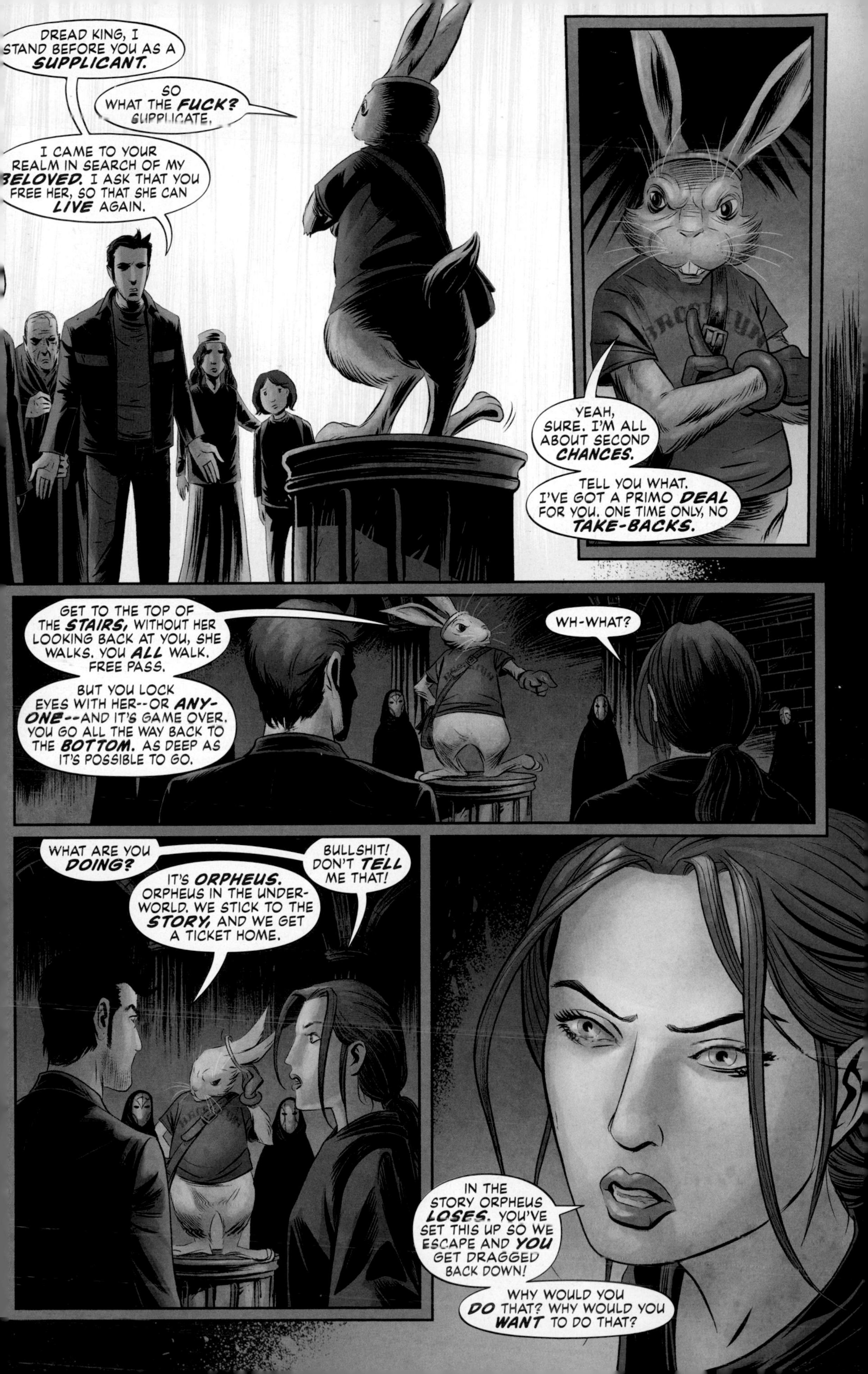
DREAD KING, I STAND BEFORE YOU AS A SUPPLICANT.
SO WHAT THE FUCK? SUPPLICATE.
I CAME TO YOUR REALM IN SEARCH OF MY BELOVED. I ASK THAT YOU FREE HER, SO THAT SHE CAN LIVE AGAIN.
YEAH, SURE. I'M ALL ABOUT SECOND CHANCES.
TELL YOU WHAT. I'VE GOT A PRIMO DEAL FOR YOU. ONE TIME ONLY, NO TAKE-BACKS.
GET TO THE TOP OF THE STAIRS, WITHOUT HER LOOKING BACK AT YOU, SHE WALKS. YOU ALL WALK. FREE PASS.
BUT YOU LOCK EYES WITH HER--OR ANYONE--AND IT'S GAME OVER. YOU GO ALL THE WAY BACK TO THE BOTTOM. AS DEEP AS IT'S POSSIBLE TO GO.
WH-WHAT?
WHAT ARE YOU DOING?
IT'S ORPHEUS. ORPHEUS IN THE UNDERWORLD. WE STICK TO THE STORY, AND WE GET A TICKET HOME.
BULLSHIT! DON'T TELL ME THAT!
IN THE STORY ORPHEUS LOSES. YOU'VE SET THIS UP SO WE ESCAPE AND YOU GET DRAGGED BACK DOWN!
WHY WOULD YOU DO THAT? WHY WOULD YOU WANT TO DO THAT?

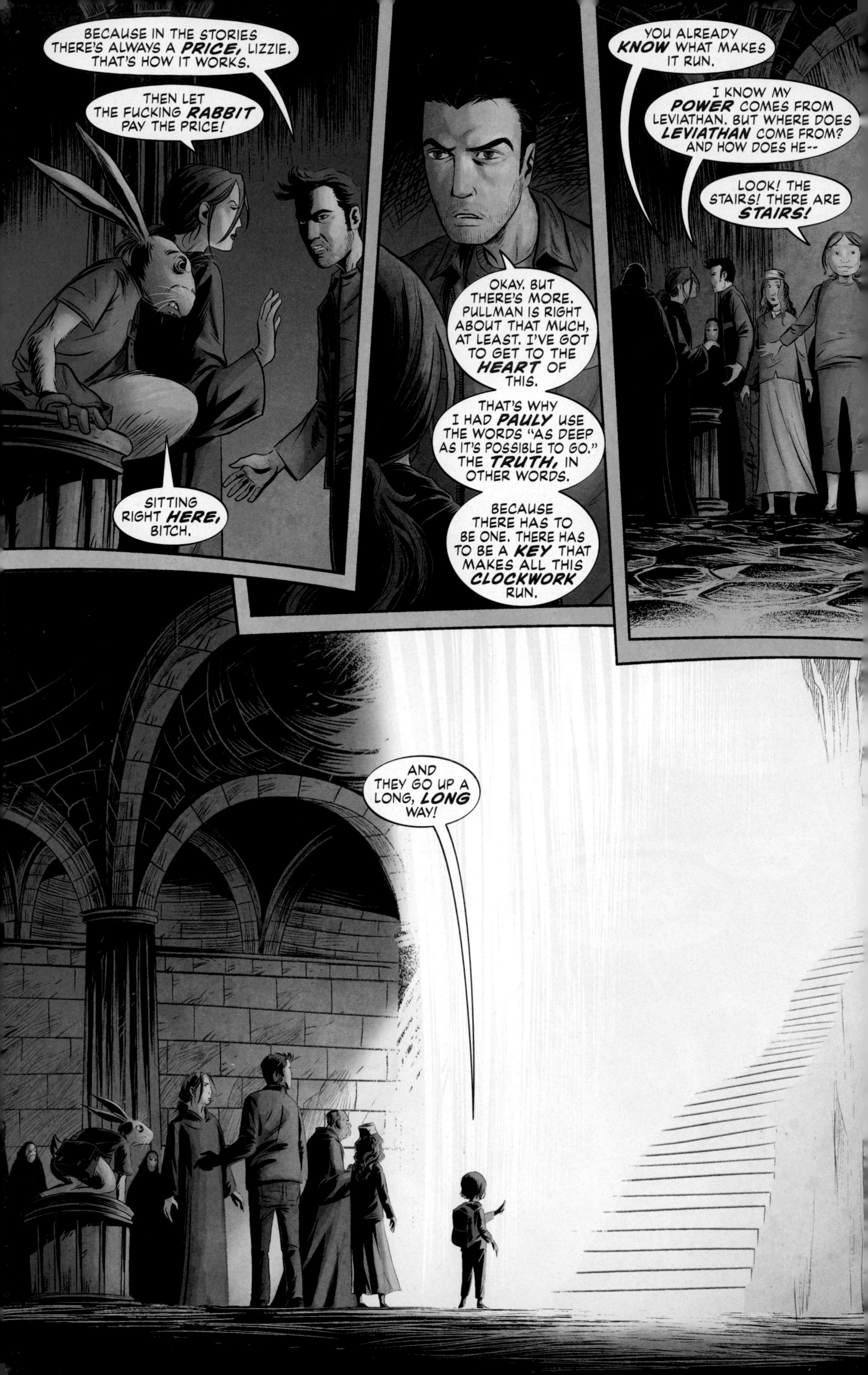
BECAUSE IN THE STORIES THERE'S ALWAYS A PRICE, LIZZIE. THAT'S HOW IT WORKS.
THEN LET THE FUCKING RABBIT PAY THE PRICE!
SITTING RIGHT HERE, BITCH.
OKAY. BUT THERE'S MORE. PULLMAN IS RIGHT ABOUT THAT MUCH, AT LEAST. I'VE GOT TO GET TO THE HEART OF THIS.
THAT'S WHY I HAD PAULY USE THE WORDS "AS DEEP AS IT'S POSSIBLE TO GO." THE TRUTH, IN OTHER WORDS.
BECAUSE THERE HAS TO BE ONE. THERE HAS TO BE A KEY THAT MAKES ALL THIS CLOCKWORK RUN.
YOU ALREADY KNOW WHAT MAKES IT RUN.
I KNOW MY POWER COMES FROM LEVIATHAN. BUT WHERE DOES LEVIATHAN COME FROM? AND HOW DOES HE--
LOOK! THE STAIRS! THERE ARE STAIRS!
AND THEY GO UP A LONG, LONG WAY!

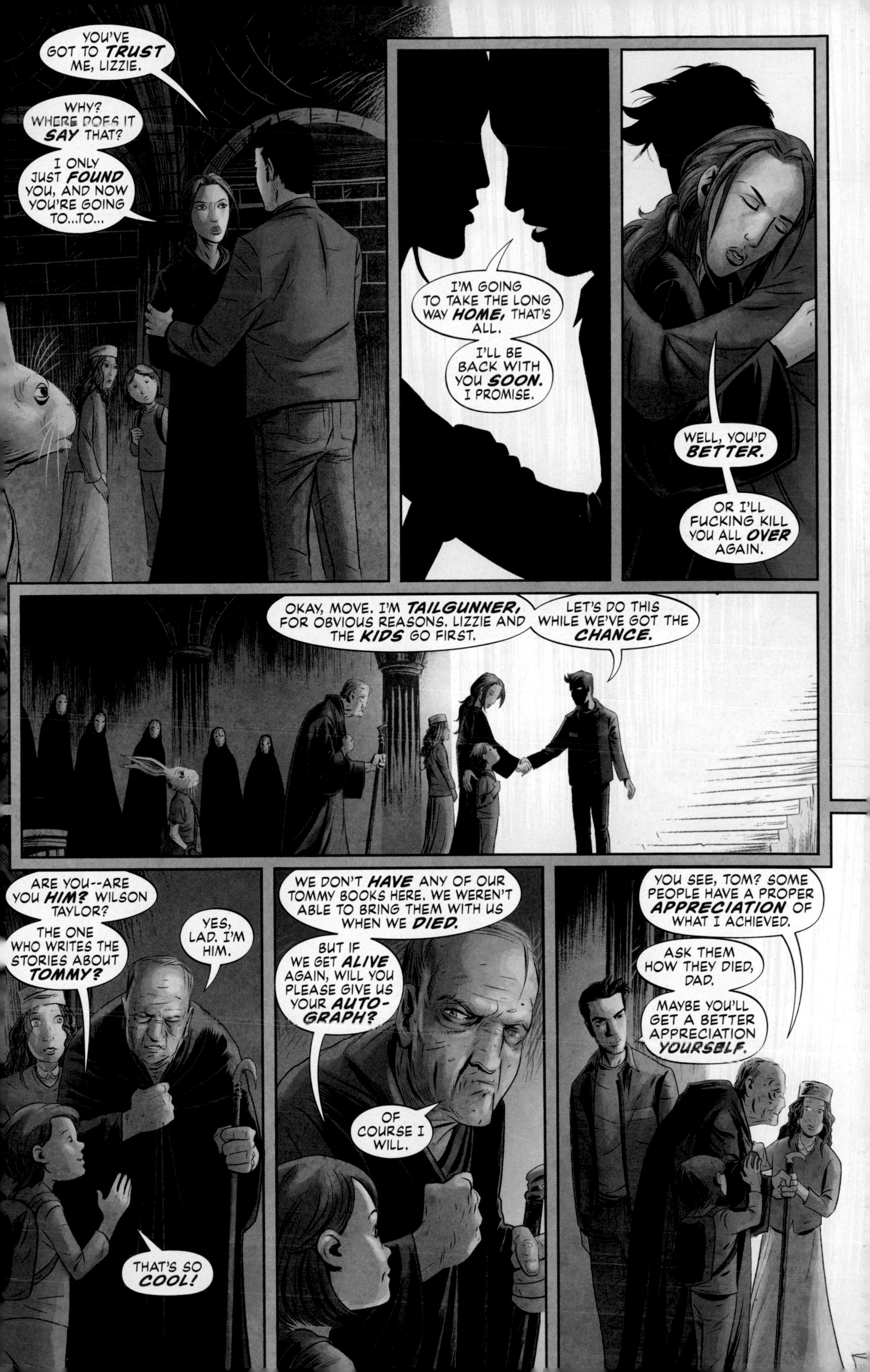
YOU'VE GOT TO TRUST ME, LIZZIE.
WHY? WHERE DOES IT SAY THAT?
I ONLY JUST FOUND YOU, AND NOW YOU'RE GOING TO...TO...
I'M GOING TO TAKE THE LONG WAY HOME, THAT'S ALL.
I'LL BE BACK WITH YOU SOON. I PROMISE.
WELL, YOU'D BETTER.
OR I'LL FUCKING KILL YOU ALL OVER AGAIN.
OKAY, MOVE. I'M TAILGUNNER, FOR OBVIOUS REASONS. LIZZIE AND THE KIDS GO FIRST.
LET'S DO THIS WHILE WE'VE GOT THE CHANCE.
ARE YOU--ARE YOU HIM? WILSON TAYLOR?
THE ONE WHO WRITES THE STORIES ABOUT TOMMY?
YES, LAD. I'M HIM.
THAT'S SO COOL!
WE DON'T HAVE ANY OF OUR TOMMY BOOKS HERE. WE WEREN'T ABLE TO BRING THEM WITH US WHEN WE DIED.
BUT IF WE GET ALIVE AGAIN, WILL YOU PLEASE GIVE US YOUR AUTO-GRAPH?
OF COURSE I WILL.
YOU SEE, TOM? SOME PEOPLE HAVE A PROPER APPRECIATION OF WHAT I ACHIEVED.
ASK THEM HOW THEY DIED, DAD.
MAYBE YOU'LL GET A BETTER APPRECIATION YOURSELF.

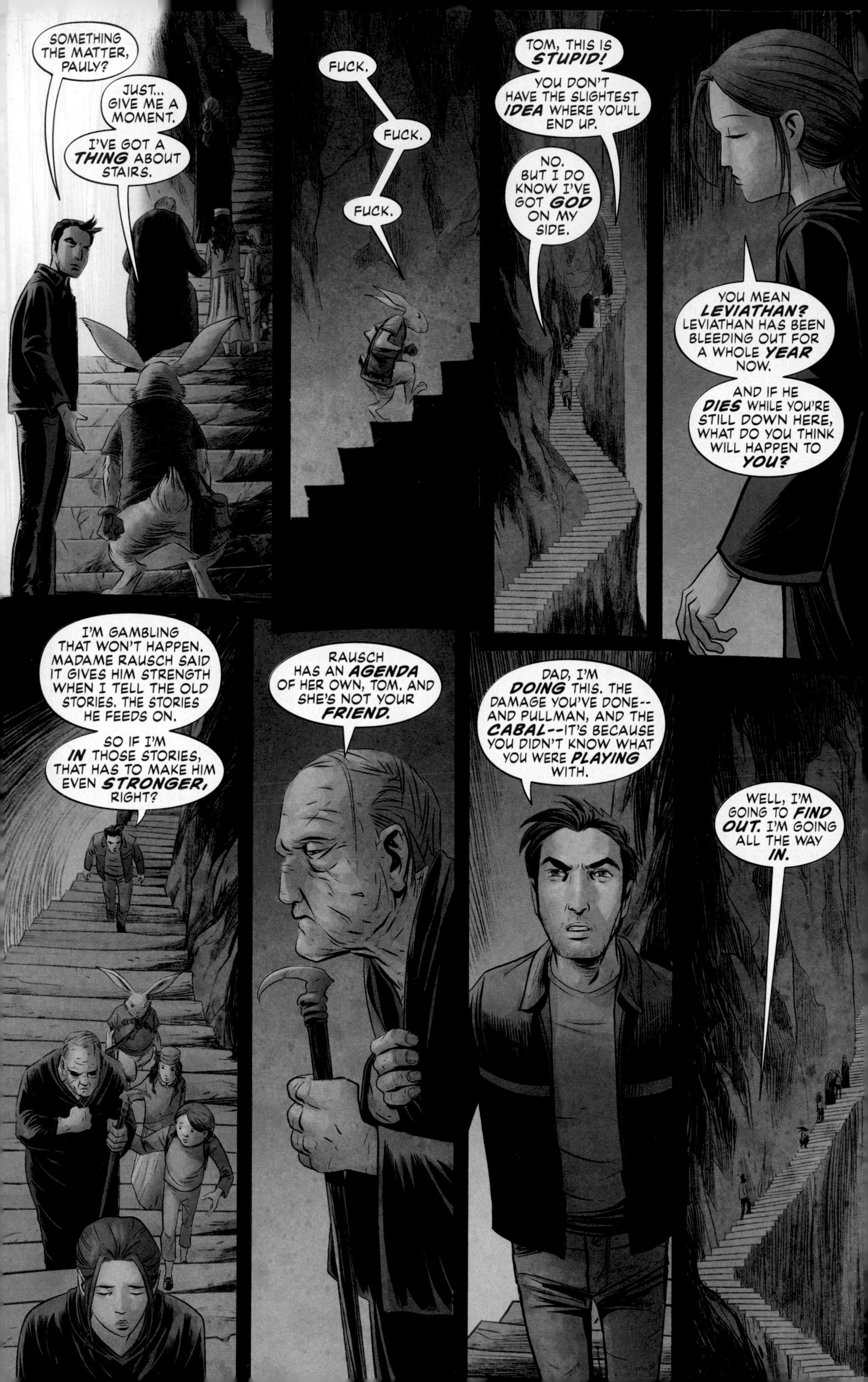
SOMETHING THE MATTER, PAULY?
JUST... GIVE ME A MOMENT.
I'VE GOT A THING ABOUT STAIRS.
FUCK.
FUCK.
FUCK.
TOM, THIS IS STUPID!
YOU DON'T HAVE THE SLIGHTEST IDEA WHERE YOU'LL END UP.
NO. BUT I DO KNOW I'VE GOT GOD ON MY SIDE.
YOU MEAN LEVIATHAN? LEVIATHAN HAS BEEN BLEEDING OUT FOR A WHOLE YEAR NOW.
AND IF HE DIES WHILE YOU'RE STILL DOWN HERE, WHAT DO YOU THINK WILL HAPPEN TO YOU?
I'M GAMBLING THAT WON'T HAPPEN. MADAME RAUSCH SAID IT GIVES HIM STRENGTH WHEN I TELL THE OLD STORIES. THE STORIES HE FEEDS ON.
SO IF I'M IN THOSE STORIES, THAT HAS TO MAKE HIM EVEN STRONGER, RIGHT?
RAUSCH HAS AN AGENDA OF HER OWN, TOM. AND SHE'S NOT YOUR FRIEND.
DAD, I'M DOING THIS. THE DAMAGE YOU'VE DONE--AND PULLMAN, AND THE CABAL--IT'S BECAUSE YOU DIDN'T KNOW WHAT YOU WERE PLAYING WITH.
WELL, I'M GOING TO FIND OUT. I'M GOING ALL THE WAY IN.

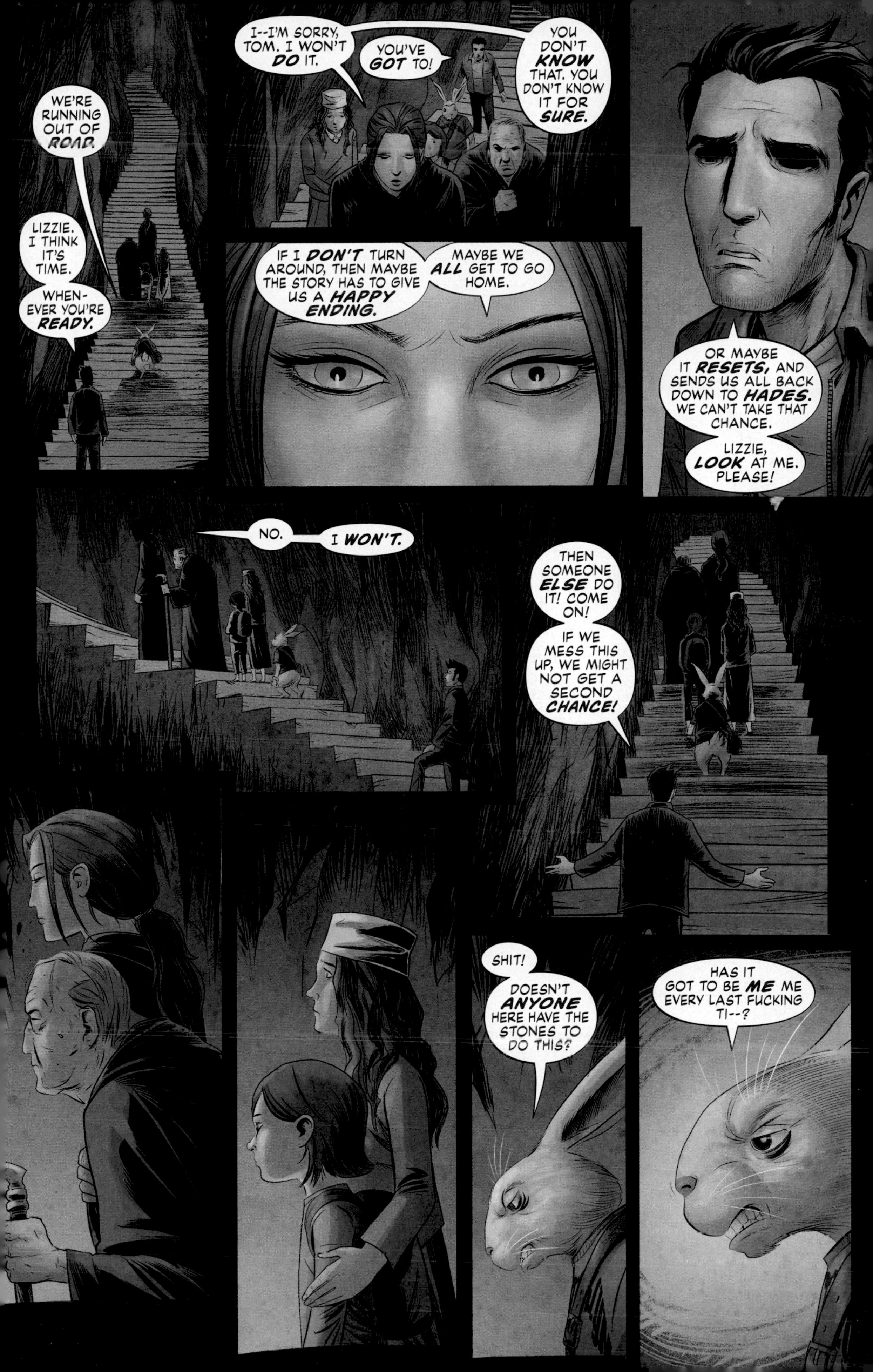

WE'RE RUNNING OUT OF ROAD.
LIZZIE. I THINK IT'S TIME.
WHEN-EVER YOU'RE READY.
I--I'M SORRY, TOM. I WON'T DO IT.
YOU'VE GOT TO!
YOU DON'T KNOW THAT. YOU DON'T KNOW IT FOR SURE.
IF I DON'T TURN AROUND, THEN MAYBE THE STORY HAS TO GIVE US A HAPPY ENDING.
MAYBE WE ALL GET TO GO HOME.
OR MAYBE IT RESETS, AND SENDS US ALL BACK DOWN TO HADES. WE CAN'T TAKE THAT CHANCE.
LIZZIE, LOOK AT ME. PLEASE!
NO.
I WON'T.
THEN SOMEONE ELSE DO IT! COME ON!
IF WE MESS THIS UP, WE MIGHT NOT GET A SECOND CHANCE!
SHIT!
DOESN'T ANYONE HERE HAVE THE STONES TO DO THIS?
HAS IT GOT TO BE ME ME EVERY LAST FUCKING TI--?

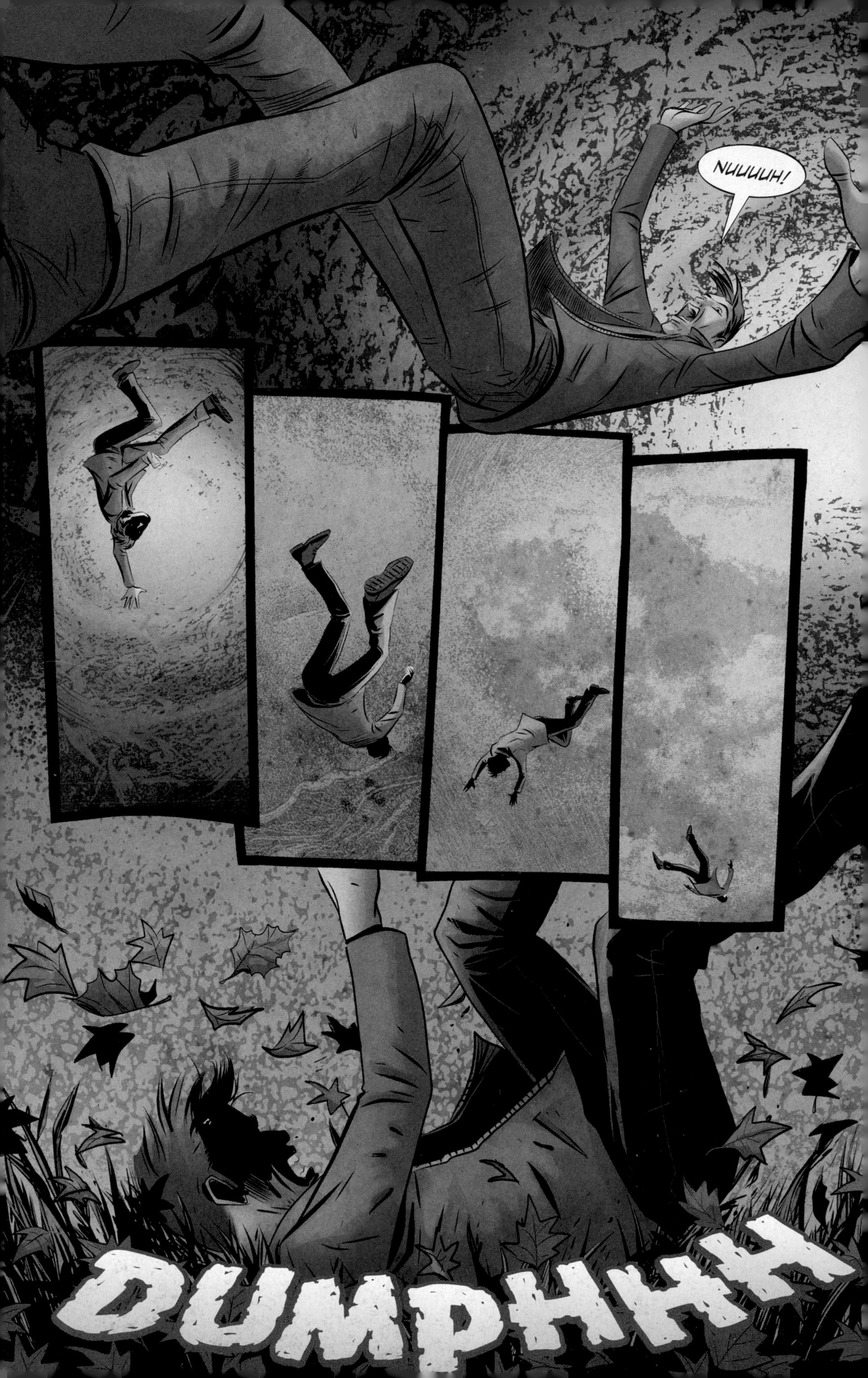
NUUUUH!
DUMPHHT

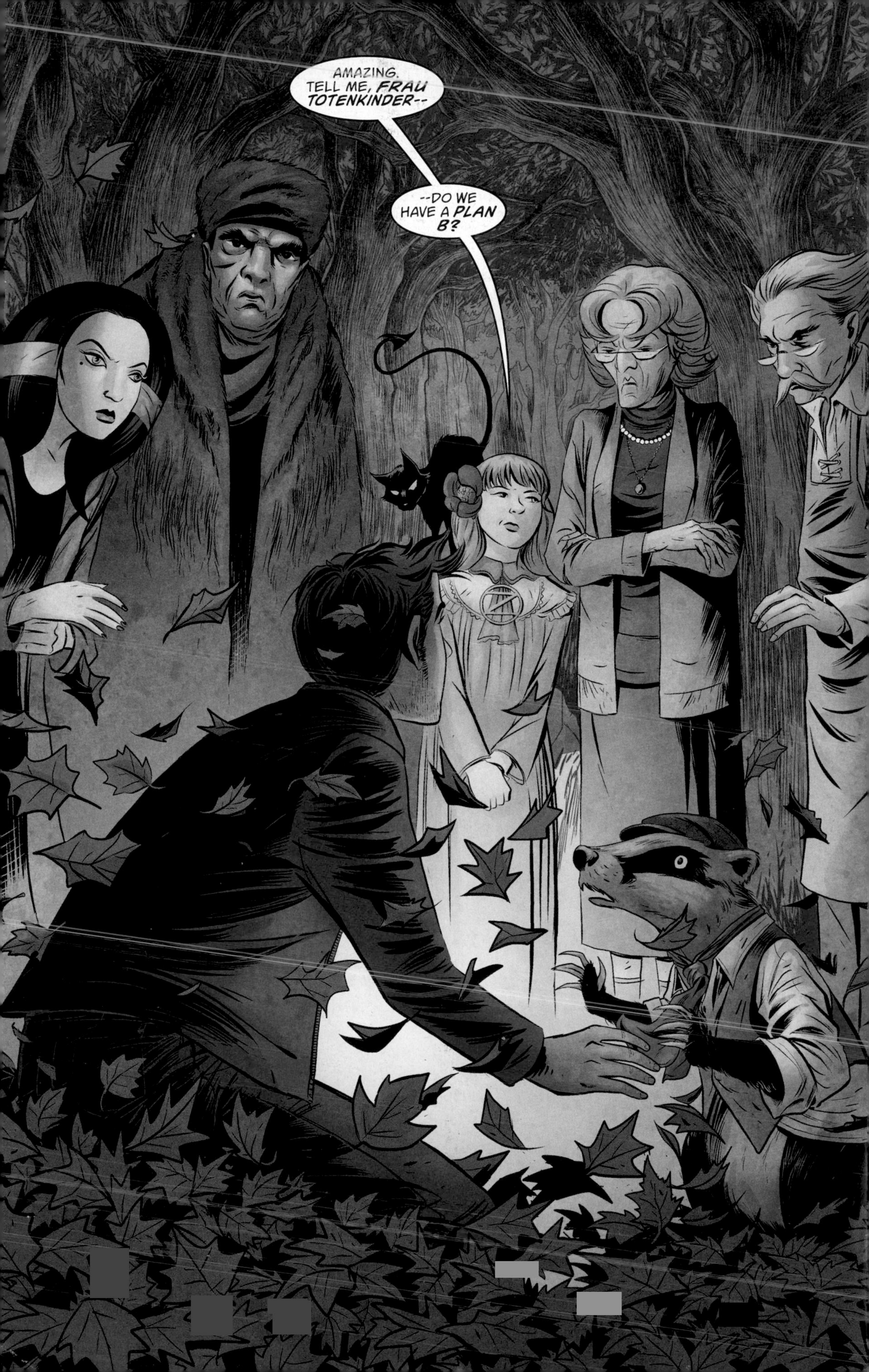
AMAZING. TELL ME, FRAU TOTENKINDER--
--DO WE HAVE A PLAN B?

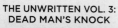

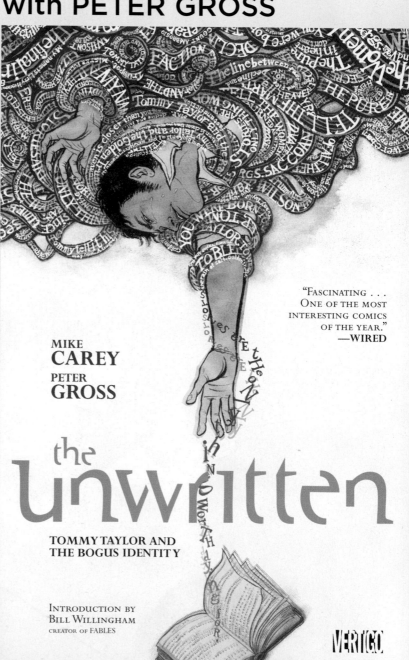